ACCLAIM FOR GERALD CLARKE'S

Too Brief a Treat:

THE LETTERS OF TRUMAN CAPOTE

"Capote's letters [are] as addictive as potato chips, often very funny and re-flect a gift for empathy." —*Los Angeles Times Book Review*

"[A] real pleasure for Capote fans. . . . Clarke, the author of the warm, sympathetic and insightful 1988 biography *Capote*, has served his subject well, gathering letters from all over the world, and providing thoughtful introductions to each section of Capote's life. . . . There is wicked fun in reading these letters. . . . Truman Capote was a breath of fresh air, rare and witty and urbane." —*The Times-Picayune*

"There are, as one would expect, lovely, delicate lines . . . along with the nervy charm of the writer's unabashed effeminacy. . . . There are also sharp sightings . . . and some feline boldface dispatches [and] a measure of scandalous fizz." —*The New Yorker*

"Charming. . . . Intriguing. . . . The letters will doubtless provide many tasty morsels for students of midcentury American social and publishing history." —*The New York Times Book Review*

"Offer[s] Capote acolytes a compendium of snappy remarks and several details of more serious interest." —*The Advocate*

"Among the most unexpectedly hilarious reads of the year." —*Genre Magazine*

"Poised, poignant, persuasive . . . full of affection and caring. . . . Reading his letters . . . is a singular experience. . . . They are newsy, capricious, full of endearments, a bit precious, funny, emphatic, occasionally duplicitous, and always signature Capote." —*Library Journal*

GERALD CLARKE

Too Brief a Treat

Gerald Clarke is the author of *Capote: A Biography* and *Get Happy: The Life of Judy Garland*. He has also written for many publications, including *Architectural Digest*, *Time*, where he was a senior writer, and *Esquire*. A graduate of Yale, he now lives in Bridgehampton, New York.

INTERNATIONAL

ALSO BY GERALD CLARKE

Get Happy: The Life of Judy Garland

Capote: A Biography

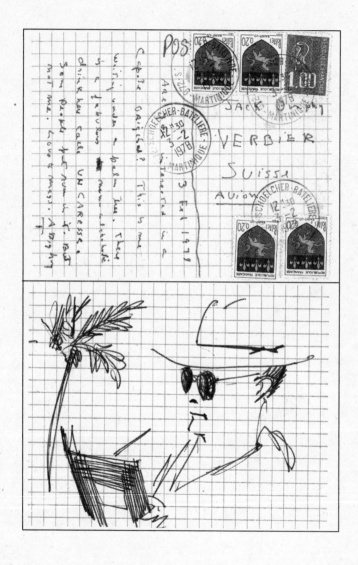

Too Brief a Treat

THE LETTERS OF TRUMAN CAPOTE

EDITED BY GERALD CLARKE

VINTAGE INTERNATIONAL

VINTAGE BOOKS

A DIVISION OF RANDOM HOUSE, INC.

NEW YORK

FIRST VINTAGE INTERNATIONAL EDITION, SEPTEMBER 2005

Copyright © 2004 by Gerald Clarke
Truman Capote material copyright © 2004 by The Truman Capote Literary Trust

All rights reserved. Published in the United States by Vintage Books, a division of
Random House, Inc., New York, and in Canada by Random House of Canada
Limited, Toronto. Originally published in hardcover in the United States
by Random House, an imprint of The Random House Publishing Group,
a division of Random House, Inc., New York, in 2004.

Vintage is a registered trademark and Vintage International
and colophon are trademarks of Random House, Inc.

Frontispiece: Postcard to Jack Dunphy, February 3, 1978, with self-portrait.

Photo credits: p. 3, courtesy Cecil Beaton's Studio Archive, Sotheby's London;
p. 61, courtesy Gerald Clarke collection; p. 271, courtesy Phil Stern/Cpi;
p. 427, courtesy Gerald Clarke collection.

The Library of Congress has cataloged the Random House edition as follows:
Capote, Truman.
Too brief a treat: the letters of Truman Capote; edited by Gerald Clarke.—1st ed.
p.   cm.
Includes index.
1. Capote, Truman, 1924—Correspondence.   2. Authors, American—
20th century—Correspondence.   I. Clarke, Gerald.   II. Title.
PS3505.A59Z495 2004
813'.54—dc22
2004050313

Vintage ISBN: 0-375-70241-5

www.vintagebooks.com

Printed in the United States of America
10 9 8 7 6 5 4 3 2 1

To Truman and Jack,

who remained true

in sunshine and in shadow

"Your letter was too brief a treat . . ."

TO ROBERT LINSCOTT, MAY 6, 1949

"Sir—Why have you not answered my letter? I only write letters so that I will get them; please put this on a paying basis."

TO JOHN MALCOLM BRINNIN, JULY 14, 1950

Contents

Introduction

Truman Capote wrote to his friends as he spoke to them, without constraints, inhibitions or polite verbal embroidery. Not for him was the starchy vow of Samuel Johnson, who complained that since it had become the fashion to publish letters, "I put as little into mine as I can." Capote did just the opposite: he put as much into his letters as he could—his hurts, his joys, his failures, his successes. The thought that his correspondence might someday be published apparently never occurred to him. "<u>Destroy</u>!!!" Capote, then only twenty-one, scrawled at the top of one gossipy letter. But how little he meant that command can be adduced from the sotto voce instruction that followed—"after showing Barbara."

Christened Truman Persons, he became Truman Capote (pronounced Capote-e) after his parents divorced and he was adopted by his stepfather, Joe Capote. The first letter in this volume, written to his real father, Arch Persons, in the fall of 1936, when Truman was eleven or twelve, was his assertion of his new identity over the old one. "I would appreciate it," he told Persons, "if in the future you would address me as Truman Capote, as everyone knows me by that name."

The many letters that follow constitute a kind of autobiography. There is the very young Capote, childlike in his exuberance and high spirits, who, in the months that followed the end of World War II, jumped feetfirst into the turbulent waters of the New York literary scene. There is the only slightly subdued Capote of the fifties. Living most of the time in Europe with Jack Dunphy, who had been his companion since 1948, he busied himself with plays and screenplays, fiction and journalistic experiments.

Then there is the Capote of the early sixties, deeply involved in the research and writing of the most daunting and traumatic book of his life. That book was *In Cold Blood*, the story of the murders of a family of four in rural Kansas and of the two men—Perry Smith and Dick Hickock—who murdered them. The publishing sensation of the decade, *In Cold Blood* combined the techniques of fiction with the factual reporting of nonfiction and it permanently transformed the writing of popular nonfiction. Thanks to the book's success, the hungry eye of television and his own flamboyant personality, for several years Capote was the most famous writer in America, and probably much of the rest of the world as well.

Finally there is the Capote of the seventies and early eighties—he died in 1984—who was disillusioned with both his life and his career and who became increasingly, and all too publicly, dependent on drugs and alcohol. The letters dwindled to almost nothing, mostly postcards and telegrams, and this book ends with a telegram from Capote in New York to Dunphy, who was, as always, spending the winter in Switzerland. All it said was: "miss you need you cable when can i expect you Love Truman." (A chronology of Capote's life may be found in the back of the book.)

BETWEEN THE FIRST LETTER and that last plaintive telegram there is, for the reader, a world of fascination, pleasure and fun. Capote did not work at "the great epistolick art"—to quote Dr. Johnson again. He came by it naturally. A man who rewrote and polished everything else that bore his name, sometimes pausing for hours to find the right word, wrote his letters at breakneck speed, rushing, as he sometimes said, to get them to the post office before the last pickup of the day. "Have 10 minutes before the post-office closes," he told one friend, "so this is in haste." As a result, his letters have a spontaneity that is often lacking in the correspondence of more cautious and deliberate writers. "Your letter was too brief a treat," he told one friend, but he was really describing his own letters, which really are too brief a treat—the title I have chosen for this book. As lively now as the day they were written, they possess so much energy that they all but leap off the page, demanding to be read.

Capote loved gossip, both the telling and the hearing. "Send me another of those lovely gossipy letters; it makes me feel we are having a drink together somewhere," he wrote one correspondent. "Write me! And answer all the above questions," he commanded another. Living in Europe for most of the fifties, Capote missed the excitement of Manhattan. "New York in the autumn—really, it is the only place to be," he said, and he prodded, cajoled and begged for news. "Hello! And why haven't you written me?" he inquired of one friend. "Write me, my precious heart, for your adoring friend has you always in his thoughts," he told another.

To liven the day, as well as to winkle out letters from tardy correspondents, he invented a new game that he called "IDC"—International Daisy Chain. "You make a chain of names," he wrote friends in New York, "each one connected by the fact that he or she has had an affair with the person previously mentioned; the point is to go as far and as incongruously as possible." The combinations were endless, but his favorite chain, the most incongruous of all, was the one that linked Cab Calloway to Adolf Hitler. The all-American jazzman and the model of all evil were separated, according to Capote's reckoning, by only three partners.

Capote addressed men as well as women with ever more inventive terms of endearment, starting with "honey," "dear" and "darling" and proceeding to "precious baby," "lover lamb," "Magnolia my sweet" and "Blessed Plum." Anyone not better informed would assume that he had carried on affairs with most of the people in this book. But the truth is more interesting, if less lurid. Like a child craving affection, he loved his friends without reservation—he told them so again and again—and he expected from them an equal affection. "I feel full of love for you today," he wrote Andrew Lyndon, a man with whom sex was never considered; "woke up thinking about you and wishing that it wasn't Sunday so there would be at least the hope of a letter." Who could resist such an embrace?

For his enemies Capote had a tongue as sharp and wounding as an assassin's dagger. But he did not write to his enemies. He wrote to his friends, and to them he was, from beginning to end, almost saintly in his generosity. He smothered even their thinnest achievements with praise, comforted them when they were down and offered help and money, even when he had very little himself. When one betrayed him, however, he never forgave. In the early fifties, for example, he extended his help and his hand to William Goyen, a Texas writer living in New York. A quarter of a century later, when Goyen's wife requested a favorable comment for the twenty-fifth anniversary edition of her husband's first novel, Capote suggested she look at Goyen's dismissive, indeed contemptuous, review of *Breakfast at Tiffany's* to realize "how really ludicrous" her request was. "I was helpful and kind to your friend at the beginning of his career—his response (as it was to K. A. Porter and his former lover Stephen Spender) was one of total treachery."

A LOVING FRIEND, a zestful gossip, a buoyant spirit—Capote was all of those. But he was also, almost to the end, a writer of vaulting ambition and spartan dedication. "To be an artist today is such an act of faith," he told one friend; "nothing can come back from it except the satisfaction of the art itself." He was only twenty-five when he wrote those words, and he was determined, even then, to join that holy gallery of Flaubert, Proust, James and Faulkner. "These last few pages!" he wrote Robert Linscott, his Random House editor, shortly before turning in his first novel, *Other Voices, Other Rooms.* "Every word takes blood." For his part, Linscott was the ideal editor for a sensitive young writer, warmly encouraging, yet critical when he felt criticism was necessary. "Wonderful wonderful wonderful," Capote wrote him after receiving praise for the first chapters of his second novel, *The Grass Harp.* But when Linscott expressed disappointment with the novel's ending, Capote was devastated. "I cannot endure it that all of you think my book a failure," he said.

In fact, Capote was his own best critic, as perceptive about his own writing as he was about other people's. Writing to William Shawn, the editor of *The New Yorker,* he said that he had finished a piece, "A Daughter of the Russian Revolution," but had belatedly realized that "it did not accelerate with the right rhythm" and would have to be reworked. Later he abandoned it entirely. "I seem to have lost faith in the piece, or at least in my ability to do it," he told Shawn. For any writer, novice or seasoned professional, his letters should be instructive, as well as inspirational. But nonwriters, I suspect, will find in them equal rewards.

"No good letter was ever written to convey information or to please the recipient," Lytton Strachey wrote. "It may achieve both these results incidentally; but its fundamental purpose is to express the personality of the writer." The letters that follow prove the justness of Strachey's observation. They convey information—and plenty of it—and they often aim to please. But, more than anything else, they express what otherwise would be inexpressible, a personality so buoyant and expansive that it defied the accepted laws of human gravity.

Gerald Clarke
Bridgehampton, N.Y.
April 1, 2004

An Editorial Note

These are Truman Capote's letters, not mine, and I have made only minor changes to make them readable. Capote wrote most of his letters by hand, but in the dozen or so he typed he followed the bad habit of many typists: he ignored the capitalization key and typed everything, including names, in lowercase. Since a letter without capitals is awkward to read, I have silently added the necessary capitals. In all his letters, including those written by hand, he also rarely bothered with apostrophes—he seemed to have an aversion to them. He usually rendered a contraction like "it's" as "its," as if it were a possessive pronoun. And he almost never bothered with apostrophes to indicate possession; "Jack's book," for instance, might be written "Jacks book." If I were to flag all such omissions, his letters would be a jungle of "[sic]" marks. To avoid that, I have placed the apostrophe where it is warranted.

I have also corrected mistakes obviously made in haste, which I regard as the equivalent of typographical errors. On several occasions, for instance, Capote wrote two words, such as "the the" or "be be," when he clearly meant to use one. I have left out one of them. Or he might have left out an "o" in "Phoebe," the name of one of his best friends and a word he had spelled correctly many times. In such a case I have added the obvious "o."

In no sense have I attempted to sanitize the letters, however, and when Capote made a mistake that really was a mistake, I have left it in and followed it with the obligatory "[sic]." For the most part, Capote was a good speller, but there were certain words, such as "receive," "genius" and "disappoint," he could never get right, and I have retained his misspellings—"recieve," "genuis" and "dissapoint." Nor could he remember how many "n's" and "s's" there are in "Tennessee"—Tennessee Williams's name occurs frequently. I have left in his misspelling, but put the correct spelling in adjoining brackets, as I have done with all other names he has misspelled. I have ignored occasional errors of grammar, such as "she has not written either Jack or I." Too many "[*sics*]" I find obnoxious.

With the minor exceptions I have noted, I have presented his letters just as Capote wrote them. I have not altered or shortened them—I believe a letter should be included in full or not at all—and the occasional ellipsis or parenthesis is his, not mine. Aside from footnotes, my editorial additions are always enclosed in brackets. Though I can make the small boast that I am an expert at reading Capote's handwriting, there are a few places where his penmanship baffled me or where I could not make out the word in a bad photocopy. Rather than guess what he meant, I have put "unclear" in brackets. He frequently neglected to write the date. When envelopes with postmarks are also missing, I have relied on internal evidence to determine, as best I could, when a letter was written.

At the bottom of each letter I have indicated where the original resides, whether with a person or a library. Several times, however, I have included a letter of whose whereabouts I am ignorant. Some I came across when I was researching my biography of Capote a decade and more ago. In the years since then the person who gave me the copy may have died or may have handed it on to someone else. In such cases I have had to write "Collection Unknown." I have also obtained copies of some letters that were later sold at auction. If I have no knowledge of the purchaser, I have also marked them "Collection Unknown."

Too Brief a Treat

The Exuberant Years:
A Merlin in Alabama
and a Puck in New York

TRUMAN CAPOTE BEGAN LIFE under a cloud. By the time he was born, in New Orleans on September 30, 1924, his parents' marriage was over in all but name. His mother, Lillie Mae, a small-town beauty, went her way, and his father, Arch Persons, a charming but irresponsible schemer, went his. For much of his childhood, Truman was thus raised by the same middle-aged cousins who had raised his orphaned mother: three old maid cousins and their bachelor brother in the little town of Monroeville, Alabama. Though he never lacked for care, that early abandonment by his parents left an emotional wound that remained open until the day he died.

Small—"I'm about as tall as a shotgun, and just as noisy," was how he later described himself—Truman was spirited and inventive enough to make himself the center of any gathering. "A pocket Merlin" was how Harper Lee, his best friend during those early years, later described him in her semiautobiographical novel, *To Kill a Mockingbird*. In 1932 his mother, who had dropped her back-country name, Lillie Mae, in favor of the more sophisticated Nina, brought him north to live with her and her new husband, a Cuban named Joe Capote, in New York. An indulgent stepfather with a good job on Wall Street, Joe Capote legally adopted him in 1935, and Truman Persons became Truman Capote.

In 1939 the Capotes left Manhattan for the upscale bedroom community of Greenwich, Connecticut. There they settled into a handsome enclave of Tudor houses and tree-shaded streets. When he was still in Alabama, Capote had announced his ambition to become a writer, and at Greenwich High School, he found what every aspiring writer needs, a sympathetic and encouraging teacher—Catherine Wood was her name. In Greenwich, Truman also found a soul mate in Phoebe Pierce, a pretty, sophisticated girl whose own ambition was to be a poet. Although there is only one letter to her—"Phoebe devil" was how he affectionately addressed her—her name often comes up in his correspondence with others.

Three years after leaving, the Capotes returned to New York, to an apartment at 1060 Park Avenue. After belatedly graduating from high school, a private school on Manhattan's West Side, Capote landed a job at *The New Yorker*—but only as a copyboy. That magazine thought his stories too unconventional for its staid, Scarsdale tastes. In those days the women's fashion magazines published the most innovative fiction in America, and the talent *The New Yorker* sneered at was quickly embraced by two remarkable fiction editors, Mary Louise Aswell at *Harper's Bazaar* and George Davis at *Mademoiselle*. They vied for his stories, and in the months after World War II, Capote, still in his early twenties, became a hot commodity in the literary marketplace.

All was not going well at home, however. Nina Capote had become an alcoholic, and when she was not raging at Joe for his infidelities, she was attacking Truman for his homosexuality. Finding it harder and harder to work on Park Avenue, in 1946 Truman sought temporary refuge at Yaddo, a writers' and artists' colony on a bucolic estate in upstate New York. One writer who was there that summer compared him to Shakespeare's Ariel; but he was also Puck, the one who set the agenda for fun and adventure. Yaddo was famous for its romances, and Capote engaged in two, the first with Howard Doughty, a handsome married historian, the second with Newton Arvin, one of Doughty's best friends and sometime lover. For Truman, Doughty, who remained a friend, was just a fling. But Arvin, a professor of literature at Smith, a women's college in Northampton, Massachusetts, was real love.

They were an unlikely couple. At twenty-two, Capote looked several years younger; at forty-six, Arvin looked several years older, in appearance a mousy man, bald and bespectacled. In temperament they were also opposites. Capote could scarcely restrain his high spirits; shy and reserved, Arvin felt uncomfortable whenever he left his Northampton sanctuary. Arvin was brave in his writing, however, and unlike many professors of literature, he was an excellent writer himself, a critic of unassailable judgment and a tower of erudition. In the two years they were a pair—Capote traveled to Northampton on weekends—Arvin provided his young partner with the college education he had never had. Arvin, Capote liked to say, was his Harvard.

During the week Capote enjoyed New York, where the circles of his friends widened with every month. One set centered on Leo Lerman, a good-natured literary gadfly whose Sunday-night parties were a Manhattan institution, attracting just about everybody of note—writers and editors, movie stars and playwrights. Other sets revolved around his magazine editors, *Harper's Bazaar*'s much-loved Mary Louise Aswell and *Mademoiselle*'s slightly sinister George Davis, whose epigrams rivaled Oscar Wilde's. After publication of his first novel, *Other Voices, Other Rooms,* Capote asked Davis his opinion. "Well," said Davis, "I suppose someone had to write the fairy *Huckleberry Finn.*"

Capote discovered the world of a more established society when he walked into the East Side town house of Bennett Cerf, his new publisher at Random House, and Cerf's wife, Phyllis. There, too, he became the center of the room, telling tales and retailing gossip. Others among the dramatis personae of those postwar years—and Capote's frequent correspondents— were Donald Windham and Andrew Lyndon, two aspiring writers from Georgia, and John Malcolm Brinnin, a poet, college teacher, and, later, the head of the Poetry Center at the 92nd Street YMHA in Manhattan.

The publication of *Other Voices, Other Rooms* in the winter of 1948 brought Capote national fame—Americans of that day took literature more seriously than they do now—and a few months later he traveled to Europe, where, to no one's surprise, he met some of the leading English and French writers. When he returned, he realized that he had outgrown Arvin and his almost hermit-like isolation. For his part, Arvin, who had engaged in a clandestine romance with Andrew Lyndon while Capote was away, was only too willing to release his rambunctious and often tiring lover. Though they remained devoted friends until Arvin's death in 1963, Capote began looking around for a new companion.

In October 1948, he found him. Ten years Capote's senior, Jack Dunphy was athletic—he had been a dancer in the original production of *Oklahoma!*—and good-looking, in a surly kind of way. He said what he thought, to Capote and everybody else. Dunphy, too, was a writer—and a good one—with one novel to his credit, another on the way, and several plays in his future. This time love lasted, and Dunphy remained Capote's constant star for the rest of his life.

TO ARCH PERSONS

[St. John's Military Academy]
[Ossining, N.Y.]
[Probably Autumn 1936]

As you know my name was changed from Person's [*sic*] to Capote, and I would appreciate it if in the future you would address me as Truman Capote, as everyone knows me by that name.

[Collection Gerald Clarke]

TO THOMAS FLANAGAN[1]

[Greenwich, Connecticut]
[1939–41]

I do hereby solemnly affirm that any statements I may have made about Thomas Flanagan, or said that he had made, were calumnies and lies on my part.
    Truman Capote

[Collection Edmond Miller]

---

[1] Thomas Flanagan was one year ahead of Capote at Greenwich High School. When Capote spread some rumor about him, Flanagan wrote out this retraction and had Capote sign it. Flanagan, who became a scholar and historical novelist (*The Year of the French*), then kept the slip of paper for nearly fifty years before affixing it inside his copy of Gerald Clarke's biography, *Capote* (1988).

TO CATHERINE WOOD[1]

[Monroeville, Ala.]
[26 July 1941]

Dear Miss Wood,

I have been in New Orleans three weeks and I just got back to Monroeville last night. I was very pleasantly surprised to find your sweet note. I was so sorry to hear about your father and I do hope he is improving.

I have been gathering material here and there and some of it is rather good, I have written little but I have taken many notes and tried to give accurate accounts of things that will later stand me in good stead, (that was meant to be a period, but my typewriter slipped.)

Are you going up to visit Miss Pierce, I hope you do because her place in Maine sounded so quiet and restful—charmingly woodsy.

I have been traveling all over the south since I came. I went to Natchez, Miss. last week and I went on a picnic at a very scenic spot over looking [*sic*] the Mississippi River.

Teddy's mother wrote me a long letter telling me all about his doings, you know Teddy—he would'nt [*sic*] write anyone if his very life depended upon it.[2] She told me that you had written him and asked me to tell you all the news about the dear raven haired child.

1. He has a job with the Greenich [*sic*] Cab company and he makes fifteen dollars week.
2. He won $130.00 dollars [*sic*] at the Maidstone club dinner dance. He is taking flying lessons with it.
3. His mother is desperate!
4. They have moved into their new house—the address is 179 Park Ave. Greenwich.
5. They are pleased and delighted with Teddy and he seems to be improving. BUNK!

P.S. He was 17 last Sat.

---

[1] Catherine Wood was one of Capote's English teachers at Greenwich High School and perhaps the first one to encourage his writing.
[2] Along with Phoebe Pierce, Ted Walworth was one of Capote's best friends in Greenwich.

I have gone Russian with a vengeance! I finally finished WAR and Peace. Also I have read Huxley's "Point Counter Point." It is very badly written, not so badly written as confusing. But it is educating as to the point of ultra-modern sophistication.

I went all the way through the heart of Pearl River swamp in La. It took three days and it was like being in a jungle only more dangerous. These swamps are inhabited by Cajons (I believe that I spelled that correctly) and it is so wild in there that some of the younger children have never seen white people! It was really quite an experience and I collected all kinds of material and wild flowers—also a baby alligator which I will ship to you C.O.D any time that you will have him. He's a regular little monster.

I am so sorry for my procrastination in answering your letter but it was truly unavoidable. Please write me and tell me all the news as I am at present sorta this side of civilization, where the people think if you don't say "ain't" you just ain't right in the head and the double negative is accepted grammar.

Write me,

all my very best

Love,

Truman

[Collection New York Public Library]

TO CATHERINE WOOD[1]

Hotel Frances
Monroe, La.
[August 1942]

Ouichita [Ouachita]—Pronounced Wa-che-Ta

I hope all this isn't too much for your + Miss Pierce's[2] stomach.

They have the most wonderful river life here (Ouichita river, it flows into the Miss.). It is the most beautiful river! I went down it on a house boat for 157 miles + back, it took a week and a half. I am going to write a

---

[1] This is the second page only of a longer letter—the first page was unobtainable—written during a visit to Capote's father, Arch Persons, in Monroe, Louisiana.
[2] Wood's friend Marjorie Pierce.

story about the people that live (I mean really live) on houseboats along the banks + eat what they get from the water!

I suppose you know that I will not be at G.H.S. [Greenwich High School] this fall as we have taken an apartment in the city. But of course I will be in Greenwich often to see you. Phoebe [Pierce] will be in the city this winter also. If you have a guest room in your new house you can invite me out for a weekend, (forward, aren't I?)

I do hope you can read my handwriting, because I cannot.

[Collection Unknown]

TO ARCH PERSONS

[Monroeville, Alabama]
Dec 2, '43

Dear Daddy Nid,[1]

Please excuse pad & pencil, but just a hasty note to let you know I got your telegram. Mother sent it to me airmail.

I came here, thinking that, after all, you certainly couldn't be bothered with me at the present time.[2] I'm really terribly sorry about Myrtle, because I liked her very much, as you know.[3]

Then, too, I have no money of my own and I'm afraid you didn't understand that when I talked with you. I used what I did have to finance myself down here, but, needless to say, this is certainly not the place. I was far better off in New York.

Naturally your telegram sounded exciting and nothing could thrill me more than to see you and finish my work in New Orleans. But I assuredly do not feel as though I should impose upon you—and what with the war etc. I'm afraid you're in no position to be imposed upon.

I have a cold and feel rotten, it's so damned uncomfortable here. I think I will be going back to New York soon as Alabama is definitely not a writer's haven. Please write me, c/o V.H. Faulk, Box 346, M, Ala.

---

[1] One of Arch Persons's nicknames was "Ned."
[2] His father was living at the Hotel Roosevelt in New Orleans.
[3] Myrtle was his father's second wife. It is unclear why he speaks of her in the past tense when later in the letter he asks his father to give her a kiss.

Much love to you and a kiss for Myrtle,
Truman

P.S. I hope you can read this "nigger" scrawl.

[Collection Gerald Clarke]

TO ELIZABETH AMES

> Truman Capote
> 1060 Park Ave.
> New York, N.Y.
> Jan. 23, '46

Mrs. Elizabeth Ames
Director: Yaddo
Saratoga Springs, N.Y.

Dear Mrs. Ames,
    I am interested to know the possibilities of spending some time at YADDO this summer, as I am working on a book, a first novel, which I hope to finish in the Fall; the book is to be published by Random House: Robert N. Linscott is my editor. My stories have appeared in Harper's Bazaar, Mademoiselle, Story, Prarie [*sic*] Schooner, and other small reviews. I am twenty-one, from the South, now living in New York. For a short period I worked at The New Yorker, then read manuscripts for a motion-picture office, finally put together a monthly collection of rather tired anecdotes for a digest magazine. Now, at last, with the assistance of a publisher, I am able to go ahead with my writing.
    Several friends who have been there tell me I would like YADDO very much. Thank you, Mrs. Ames, for the consideration you may give this letter.[1]
    Most sincerely,
    Truman Capote

[Collection New York Public Library]

---

[1] In the Yaddo notes attached to the letter, Ames wrote: "Truman Capote—Let's consider him seriously." Someone else, remembered only by initials, added: "I certainly think so." A third person concluded: "Great talent here."

TO ROBERT LINSCOTT

> Yaddo
> Saratoga Springs
> N.Y.
> May '46

Dear Bob;

Have come, am here, am slowly freezing to death; my fingers are pencils of ice. But really, all told, I think this is quite a place, at least so far. The company is fairly good. Here at the moment are: Agnes Smedley, Carson [McCullers], Howard Doughty (he is very pleasant), Leo Lerman (who is keeping himself in control), Ralph Bates, Marguerite Young, and arriving today St. Katharine [*sic*] Anne P.[1]

I have a bedroom in the mansion (there are bats circulating in some of the rooms, and Leo keeps his light on all night, for the wind blows eerily, doors creak, and the faint cheep cheep of the bats cry in the towers above: no kidding. My studio is quite a distance from the house, and is enormous. It is a remodeled barn, and sitting in the loft is an old-fashioned barouche: I keep thinking of Rudyard's phantom rickshaw, which is all very disconcerting.[2] That is where I am now, in the studio, and you cannot imagine how cold it is, though there is a fine potbellied stove. However, I can't seem to keep the damn thing going. It is only ten o'clock in the morning but I think I will have to warm my gizzard with a shot of whiskey. From the studio I can see the mountains, and there are buttercups blooming outside the door.

Barbarra [Barbara Lawrence][3] phoned before I left, and told me what a delightful luncheon she'd had with you. I am finishing up my story today and tomorrow, then I'm going to let it cool for maybe two weeks, and work on Other Voices, before typing it off to send.[4] Will mail you a carbon, of course.

---

[1] Smedley was a writer and radical thinker; Carson McCullers was Capote's close friend and sometime rival; Howard Doughty was Francis Parkman's biographer; Bates and Young were writers; and St. Katharine was Katherine Anne Porter, whose short stories had already made her famous.

[2] He is referring to an eerie tale by Rudyard Kipling, "The Phantom Rickshaw."

[3] Barbara Lawrence had been a second-level editor at *The New Yorker* when Capote was a copyboy, and she offered helpful critical advice on the short stories he was beginning to write; she later became features editor of *Junior Bazaar*, sister magazine of *Harper's Bazaar*.

[4] *Other Voices, Other Rooms* was to be his first novel; it was published on January 19, 1948.

Sorry to write such a damn dull letter, but haven't acclimated myself enough yet to give much of a report. Will try to do better next time . . .

Best

t

[Collection Columbia University Library]

TO MARY LOUISE ASWELL

[Yaddo]
[Saratoga Springs, N.Y.]
[May 1946]
<u>Destroy!!!</u> (after showing Barbara)

Marylou, my angel,

Well, I knew it was too good to last: I'm in trouble, and it's all Leo [Lerman]'s fault.

According to Mrs. Ames, Howard Doughty and I are "insistently persecuting" him.[1] See, Leo has a real aberration about snakes: he makes me escort him every day from the mansion to his studio; but he has dramatized the whole thing to such a ridiculous extent that everybody here thought he was half-way joking. So yesterday Howard came to my studio for lunch.[2] When he left he stepped on a snake in my yard, and picked it up. Leo, who was standing in his doorway across the road, saw it, and began to scream: "You're mean, you're cruel!" then slammed the door, pulled down all his shades, and curled up under his desk, and stayed there the whole afternoon, in a real fit of terror: no one, of course, had any intention of frightening him. But two workmen who were putting firewood in our studios saw the whole thing and reported it to Mrs. A., who promptly sent a little "blue note" (all communication is carried on through these blue notes) saying that Mr. Lerman had been made ill by our (Howards' [sic] and mine) insistent persecution. I suppose it will blow over but it's all too absurd for words. Leo, of course, feels very badly that he got us in so much trouble. Howard wrote a wonderful note explaining

---

[1] Elizabeth Ames was Yaddo's matriarchal director.
[2] Although some of the writers and artists lived in Yaddo's main house, others were given private studios on its spacious grounds. Capote had moved from the main house to a cottage. He subsequently returned to the house.

everything (we felt like little naughty schoolboys, which annoyed Howard, for he is a professor at Harvard, and 42 years old.) Otherwise everything is o.k.

How goes "the house?" It is Terry, not Perry. Terry Murray.[1] I have not finished my story YET. But will this week. I wrote you about M. [Marguerite] Young in my last letter.[2] Darling, the strangest thing is going on, I'm dying to tell you, but am so afraid of putting it in a letter. Maybe I will phone you some day soon. You will have hysterics. Have pidgy pie, and my sweet dunny been in lately? I must write Barbarra [Barbara Lawrence] again, but she has never answered my last letter. Show her this. Has she met Terry yet?

Carson [McCullers] has been sick in bed, that is the reason she hasn't written you. She is better now, though, and may be up today. We had breakfast together, and she seemed much better. I took a seconal last night and feel so damn dizzy I can hardly see the typewriter. Katharine [sic] [Katherine] Anne Porter and I danced together till all hours last night. She must be about sixty, but oh how she can do the hootchy-cootchy.[3] She tries to act like a southern belle of sixteen or so. She is so unserious it is hard to believe she can write at all. She is like a little New York debutante. She thinks I am a wonderful dancer, and makes me dance with her all the time: it is simply awful, because she hasn't the faintest notion of how to do the simplest steps. I love Agnes Smedley.[4] Marvelous person. But of all the people here I like Howard Doughty the best.[5]

Oh my precious Marylou, I love you, and I love Barbarra [Barbara], and hope you both love me: you are both so dear to me. And I miss you so much it is like a real pain.

t

Enclosed, please find violets: I know they will be dry by the time they reach you, but remember how beautiful they were, and that is the way I send them to you, my darling dearest Marylou

[Collection Aswell Family]

---

[1] Murray was a friend of Carson McCullers who manufactured men's toiletries.

[2] Marguerite Young was a poet, essayist and novelist, whose major work, *Miss MacIntosh, My Darling*, was published in 1965.

[3] Porter was, in fact, fifty-six.

[4] Smedley was a writer and radical thinker.

[5] He had good reason. He was having an affair with Doughty, a tall, lanky man with exquisite manners, as befitted a descendant of Cotton Mather.

TO MARY LOUISE ASWELL

[Yaddo]
[Saratoga Springs, N.Y.]
[May 18, 1946]

My precious beloved,

Another sweet letter from you, darling! It is raining here, cold and grey, but those sweet words from you made everything seem so damn cheery. This is a strange haunted place, all right. Leo is so frightened he keeps his light burning all night, and the other night he begged me to let him sit in my room: he stayed there huddled in an old wicker chair till dawn. I am not afraid except when bats get into my room. I simply can't stand that cheep cheep crying as they circle in the dark. I have given up my barn studio, and moved into the tower of the mansion: you have to get there by climbing wierd [*sic*] stone stairs, and it is supposed to be haunted by a Spanish woman who was Mrs. Trask's companion.[1] Leo will not come anywhere near it. Richard [Hunter][2] saw it when he was here but at that time I had not moved in. Get him to tell you about it. It nearly scared him out of his wits.

Oh dear, I guess we might as well forget about the house. Too bad.

I am finishing my story soon. "Miriam" is being translated into German for State Department use. Seems like an odd choice for rehabilitation literature![3]

When are you coming? Please please please! And what has happened to Barabrra [Barbara Lawrence]. She is the meanest human white woman ever to trod this earth. Not one word! I am worried about her, and, knowing how much I love her, it is very cruel of her to worry me this way. I know she is not much of a hand at writing letters, but this is carrying a thing too far.

Dearest, there is so much to write, but I think I will wait till we get together. Can you imagine how much I miss you? If so, you're a genuis [*sic*]! Tell Gladys to get well. I doubt whether I'll get down for the concert, but I know it will be beautiful, and will be thinking of her, and wishing her the greatest luck. Oh Marylou Marylou Marylou

---

[1] Yaddo was founded in 1900 by Katrina Trask, who wrote poetry, and her husband, Spencer, who was a financier.

[2] Hunter, an artist, had been Lerman's companion for approximately ten years.

[3] Published by *Mademoiselle* in June 1945, "Miriam" is the story of a sinister little girl who moves in with a middle-aged widow and gradually takes over her life. Left unanswered is the question: is she real, or a product of the widow's imagination? The story brought Capote attention in literary circles and prompted Mary Louise Aswell, the fiction editor of *Harper's Bazaar,* to ask to see more of his stories.

I love you love you love you
yes I do, yes yes, yes I do
t

[Collection Aswell Family]

TO LEO LERMAN[1]

[Yaddo]
[Saratoga Springs, N.Y.]
[June 1946]

Leo—call mother: Atwater 9-3319
 Tell [her] I am well—about my lovely tower—ask her should I buy a tennis racket—whether anyone has phoned—tell her to send me some cookies—tell her to send me some underwear, give her my love, and tell her to write.[2]
 Truman

[Collection Columbia University Library]

TO LEO LERMAN

[Yaddo]
[Saratoga Springs, N.Y.]
[28 June 1946]

Leo dearest
 You can't escape blue notes! And this is one just to say how much I miss you, and how lonesome it is. Margurite [Marguerite Young] drove away in

---

[1] Leo Lerman was a New York cultural maven. He was features editor of *Mademoiselle* and *Vogue* and also authored books on Leonardo da Vinci, Michelangelo and the Metropolitan Museum of Art. Lerman's Sunday-night parties in the 1940s and 1950s were legendary. He met Capote in 1945 and remained a lifelong friend; it was at his house that Capote met Jack Dunphy in 1948.
 [2] Lerman had accompanied Capote to Yaddo at the beginning of May. This note was probably written when Lerman returned to New York after his stay at Yaddo; he lived at 20 East 88th Street, just around the corner from Capote's mother's apartment at 1060 Park Avenue.

a marvelous maroon convertible: she was wearing those slacks and that crazy white hat with all the sparkling discs: she arrived in it, and she left in it: just shows what a sense of form that girl has. The man who came for her, Towner, is the most terrific Queen you ever laid eyes on. LIFE, too, has departed.[1] Phyllis showed me a note Townsend gave her. It began: "The dog in the Yaddo pictures is FRANKY'S BOY O' LONGLEIGH. He will be two years old this August." and it went on for pages and pages. Phyllis says she will write the caption to read: "The dog is Boy, and is owned by the son of Mrs. Ames's secretary." Takes a woman to bitch a woman every time. Newton is quite dead from all the doings, and is spending the day in bed reading. George [Cole] left a note asking if he could draw me, which struck me odd considering how many times he said he hates to do portraits. Anyway I posed for him and the result is one of the most arresting things I've ever seen. It is a wonderful likeness, but there is a strange pathological intensity about it that is absolutely flooring. Everyone here thinks it wonderful, but I cannot bear to look at it too long. He gave it to me, so I will bring it home and you can see. We (Newton and myself) may leave here the 20th and go to the Isle of Shoals, Appledore, for two weeks before I come home.[2] I have started back on my book and do not intend to have further truck with Yaddo social life. Newton sends his best, and I of course send love

t

And love to darling Richard [Hunter]: a bushel, a peck, a hug around the neck.

I got <u>this</u> envelope & stamp from Newton.

[Collection Columbia University Library]

---

[1] The article "*Life* Visits Yaddo" (*Life* magazine, July 15, 1946) showed Capote at work on *Other Voices, Other Rooms* and in conversation with Marguerite Young.

[2] Six miles off the coast and straddling the border of Maine and New Hampshire, the Isles of Shoals are nine small islands. Capote and Arvin did not, in the end, go there.

TO HOWARD DOUGHTY

[Yaddo]
[Saratoga Springs, N.Y.]
[June or July 1946]

Howard, dear,

Your letter! And it was wonderful, and I thank you. It's a good thing you got the haircut in Albany, not here, for I liked it the way it was.

There have been no eruptions around here to speak of. Yesterday EA [Elizabeth Ames] had a cocktail party, and everyone, including EA, got mighty high, and Esther [Rolick],[1] careening homeward, spotted George Vincent, and screamed: "I saw you last summer naked to the waist, and man that was something!" All of which gave our guests of honor (the Slades, the Willisons et al) quite a turn. Leo went to have lunch with EA, begging me to fetch him afterward (snakes, you know), so when I arrived I found him sitting in the grass with EA bending above him reading maledictions from the bible, and Leo protesting weakly, "But don't you believe in <u>ultimate</u> good." Those two, however, seem to be getting on better. Howard, I don't think you should feel so fiercely toward her; after all, she is only a rather ignorant woman, and God knows a thing like that can be taken in one's stride. She sent me a note today. "I have worked some magic: would you care to stay until July 30th?" I have not as yet written a reply, or made up my mind. NA [Newton Arvin] is wonderful, and I love him, but I will not write about it in this letter, for there is too much to say.

Talked with Carson on the phone yesterday. She called around five, and I was upstairs taking a bath, and went flying down in a state of fantastic disarray. She said she was going to Fire Island on Friday, and seemed fine, otherwise no news, except, of course "love to darling Howard." I send love, too: a bushel, a peck, a hug around the neck.

t

P.S. Think of me Thursday, and wish me luck. I <u>miss</u> you!

[Collection Unknown]

---

[1] Rolick was an artist.

TO LEO LERMAN

[Yaddo]
[Saratoga Springs, N.Y.]
[9 July 1946]

Leo dearest child,

At last . . . a letter, and just when I'd given up all hope . . . and such a sweet letter, too. I am so glad you liked Phoebe [Pierce], for she is a remarkable girl, and greatly gifted: at one time, you know, we were very much in love, and I still love her, though not in quite the same way, perhaps; still we have known each other so long, and been through so much together (as they say) that there will, I suppose, be always some deep connection between us no matter how hard I try to render it. And yes, George [Cole] and I are friends, good friends, I hope, and I am so ashamed not to have seen his really extraordinary qualities before; he is generous, and charming, loyal and intelligent: and heavens, what do you mean make judgements . . . me? No indeed, darling, anything that makes Richard [Hunter] happy, and you happy, is 100% wonderful by me, for I love and am devoted to you both, and to George, too: I know that you can give him an outlet to something he most desperately needs, and it is all so simple, and right, or at least it seems so to me.

Newton is fine, and I gave him your love, for which he thanks you, and returns the same. I love him, of course, and that too is simple and right and without complications. He is too good for me, too thoughtful, too kind: I am only glad that I am capable of appreciating him, and knowing his rarity, his delicate perfection: was there ever anyone more sensitive? In this day and age sensitivity like his is almost an anachronism. Did you ever, in that wonderland wilderness of adolesence [*sic*] ever, quite unexpectedly, see something, a dusk sky, a wild bird, a landscape, so exquisite terror touched you at the bone? And you are afraid, terribly afraid the smallest movement, a leaf, say, turning in the wind, will shatter all? That is, I think, the way love is, or should be: one lives in beautiful terror.

Marylou and B. [Barbara Lawrence] came, and we had an elegant time; EA [Elizabeth Ames] was marvelous to them, invited them to dinner, and gave a party at Pine Garde. Jerre [Mangione][1] had a small party for them, and I had one here in the tower, and I do think they had [a] happy refreshing time. Marylou is an angel; in her own way she is like Newton: too good

---

[1] Mangione was a writer.

to be true. George [Cole] did a marvelous new portrait of me, really miraculously good, for I am [a] hard person to draw, and Marylou is running it in the Bazaar, along with a little piece about George.

Howard [Doughty] came back yesterday. He is really a sweet wonderful person, VERY understanding, and he misses you badly: he said he just didn't know how he was going to be able to stand it here without you. You must write him a letter, for he is the sort that never writes first. Now you really must. And I am so pleased you're taking mother to lunch: did you? And how was it? Write all. I am working on my book, it was and is rather hard getting back into it, but everything will be allright [sic]. I miss you, darling Leo, and love you, and can't wait to see you. Newton and I are leaving here the 25th, and going someplace for a week before I come home. All love, sweet dearest Leo

t

[Collection Columbia University Library]

TO MARY LOUISE ASWELL

[45 Prospect Street]
[Northampton, Mass.]
[31 July 1946]

Darling,

Your letter reached me this morning, and I am sorry you did not know where I was; really, I should have phoned you when I reached N.Y., but there was only a ½ hour before catching the train here.

Sweetheart, you should not be upset about the money—I understand perfectly, and know it was in no way your fault, and I should not have requested it in the first place, but the trip was fantastically expensive, for reasons I will numerate later, and I'll bet I'm going to lose money on this deal, which is an irony for I never worked that arduous in my life—I nearly died of exhaustion, and had even to go to a doctor here—not complaining, though, not really, for it was curious + interesting: an experience, as they say, and I like [Henri] Cartier-Bresson extremely.[1]

---

[1] Capote is referring to a trip to New Orleans to research a travel article for *Harper's Bazaar*. Cartier-Bresson took the photographs.

About the change in the story.[1] For you, darling, yes. He can hold his hand over the boy's mouth. I will speak to Pearl [Kazin] about this.[2]

I am having a wonderful time here with Newton. He is going to give a full-sized lecture on contemporary American literature here in the fall, and that will be your article: isn't that grand? He sends you his very best love, and I, of course, send all of mine to darling precious Mary Lou, my sweetheart. Love, too, to Pidgy pie & Dunny, and have a good time, darling, for I love all three of you so very very much.

T.

P.S. Write if you get a chance: I will be back at 1060 [Park Avenue] on Friday.

[Collection Aswell Family]

TO MARY LOUISE ASWELL

[1060 Park Avenue]
[New York]
[4 August 1946]

Dearest,

Are you having a wonderful time? And Dunny, and my best girlfriend, are they? Really, darling, I envy you mightily, for you must be near the sea, or on it, maybe, and how I long for the ocean: it has been years since I tasted salt water, or got knocked down by a wave.[3]

Something awful is the matter with the spacer on this damned machine! Bear with me.

I had a really terrible time in N.O.; I've never worked so hard in my life, and hope never to again, and I can see right now that I'm going to lose money on this little deal, for it was fabulously expensive . . . for reasons I will not go into here. The Bazaar is behaving badly, but please don't let this trouble you, for it is outside your province, and perhaps it will all work out when I go and talk to them which I haven't done as yet . . . however, they

---

[1] "The Headless Hawk," published in *Harper's Bazaar,* November 1946.
[2] Pearl Kazin was an editor at *Harper's Bazaar.*
[3] Aswell and her two children were vacationing on Maine's Bear Island.

sent me a bill for my fare down there . . . can you beat that?[1] The only thing is Pearl tells me they now want to run the piece on N.O. in October and keep my story till God knows when.[2] Well, of course that makes me frantic, for one of the reasons I stopped working on my book to write it, in fact the main one, was because [I] have not published a story in almost a year, and it is very important that I should, and really, they just must must must run that story in October. Anyway I have not given them the N.O. piece yet, and I think I will just hang on to it until it is too late for them etc., and I'm not going to give it to them at all unless they give me my money. But as I said do not worry your sweet precious head about any of this trivia, for it is no affair of yours. Pearl is a darling. You are certainly lucky to have her, and she absolutely worships you. Dear Marylou, everyone loves you so much! I am really jealous, because I love you more than anybody, but everyone keeps saying how much they love you without seeming to realize that you belong to me, and that I love you more than anyone . . . oh dear I'm not making very good sense . . . the result of too much to drink, and trying to think about too many things simultaneously.

I had a wonderful time in Northampton with Newton. I love him most tenderly, more really than I can tell you, for he is the sweetest, gentlest person, next to yourself, that I ever met. I had dinner with Marguerite [Young], another of your oh so ardent fans, and breakfast with Leo [Lerman] the other day. You know, no matter what his faults, Leo is a good person, and kind. I haven't seen B. [Barbara Lawrence], except for a quick glance, but I shall this coming week. Carson [McCullers] is on Nantucket visiting Tennessee Williams, and having a wonderful time. She has postponed her European jaunt indefinitely. I knew she wouldn't go.

Marylou, my dearest, I can never tell you what you really mean to me, I don't know how . . . but you are one of the awfully few people in this world I love to the very core of my heart, and, though I want you to have as marvelous and as long a vacation as possible, hurry home to me darling, hurry . . . because I don't want ever to be without you.

T.

[Collection Aswell Family]

---

[1] *Harper's Bazaar* was owned by the Hearst Corporation, which was notoriously stingy with its writers.

[2] The story was "The Headless Hawk."

TO JOHN MALCOLM BRINNIN

[1060 Park Avenue]
[New York]
[Early August 1946]

Thank you, dearest Malcolm, for the wonderfully amusing letter, and excuse me for not answering sooner, but things as you may imagine, have
been rather chaotic, excruciatingly so: my New Orleans trip was doubly
productive: blisters and fallen arches, that's what I got; oh it had its amusing side, indeed it did, for we photographed everything from the incum-
bents of aristocratic Louisiana homes, to the inmates of a nut house;
beautiful photographs, really, I can only hope my piece will be mildly worthy of them. However, a week in Northampton with Newton, and Newto-
nian wit has healed most of my wounds. He likes you enormously, for
which I am grateful, for I would like you to be friends, and you will not
meet anyone, Malcolm, who will appreciate your qualities more.

I had dinner last night with Marguerite [Young], and a curious thing
happened; the people next door were having a party, and the host (whose
name I forget) very kindly invited us over for a drink; Marguerite seemed
dubious, but we went, and who was there but your friends Howard Moss
and Anky Larrabee.[1] They were awfully nice to me, and I liked them very
much; she is most certainly not the monster someone informed me she
was, but, I thought, a very entertaining, slightly crazy but awfully sweet
girl, and Howard is charming. The party, though! M. rushed me out so fast
I did not get a chance really to talk with Howard, but I should like to sometime.

I'm sorry you did not get my room, but if no one is there then you can
use the terrace, can't you?[2] I miss you, Malcolm, and write me, please, and
let's see each other soon . . . please, also.

Love
T

[Collection University of Delaware Library]

---

[1] A poet and critic, Howard Moss was later poetry editor of *The New Yorker*, a position he held
for almost forty years; Anky Larrabee was a young woman about town whom Capote used as one
of his models for Holly Golightly in *Breakfast at Tiffany's*.
[2] Capote is referring to his old room at Yaddo.

TO MARY LOUISE ASWELL

[1060 Park Avenue]
[New York]
[10 August 1946]

You darling,

Your sweet letter came this morning, my darling Marylou, and I hope mine reaches you before departure for Clinton;[1] it must be very beautiful there on Bear Island; I have always loved the idea of islands, and I would like some day to go to Maine . . . the coast, preferably, where there would be gigantic cold waves dashing, as in mystery novels, on old dark cliffs.

Of course the seperation [*sic*] agreement seems to you an emblem of failure, though that, I think, is a very distorted conception; it was a step in the right direction, that's what I'd say dearest, for after all don't you associate with that period of your life mostly unhappy things?[2] You have two exquisite children, and you will always have them, and no one can take them away from you; they have the security of love, my dear, and that is the kind of security a child most needs.[3] I know. And they will always have a great deal more security of every kind than I did. I understand this feeling of failure you have, though: it is a tricky thing, based on all kinds of self-falsifications. Newton knows all about such things, too; he lived eight years with a woman who every day of her life tried to impress him with his own unimportance and ended by driving him out of his mind.[4] How can people be so insensitive, Marylou? Both you and Newton are as human beings the most successful people I know, for you are both very strong, and tender, and beautiful. Newton, of course, went through absolute hell, and thought he could never get his life straightened out, was, for the longest time, without any hope whatever . . . yet he <u>has</u>, and is living now the most satisfactory part of his life . . . he feels complete in every way, and happy. I do not think, my darling, you could ever reach quite the rockbottom he did . . . and you have so much of everything to live for. Those are marvelous chil-

---

[1] Clinton County is in the northeast corner of New York State, bordering on Lake Champlain.
[2] She was in the process of divorcing her husband, Edward Aswell, an editor at Harper & Brothers who was best known for bringing order to the sprawling manuscripts of Thomas Wolfe's three posthumous novels, *The Web and the Rock, You Can't Go Home Again,* and *The Hills Beyond.*
[3] Aswell's children were Duncan and Mary.
[4] Arvin had married one of his students, Mary Garrison, in 1932; they divorced in 1940. Capote is unfair in his characterization, however, and only when she was well into her marriage did Garrison discover that her husband's interests were concentrated on his own sex, not hers.

dren, Marylou, and they are yours, and you are going to have them . . . and everything of a practical nature will solve itself, too: it is curious, but do you know I've never worried about this at all, because I have feelings about things (I am almost a completely intuitive person) and I knew that it would come out far better and in a far simpler manner than you suspect.

I had a drink with Pearl Kazin the other day, and she is a dear person, and fantastically bright, much brighter, I think, than her brother, whose work I find very aggravating.[1] Had dinner with Marguerite last night, and we talked about you, and how much we both loved you (who doesn't?). B. [Barbara Lawrence] seems awfully busy, but in good spirits, and Leo has gone away for a couple of weeks. I went with Cartier [Henri Cartier-Bresson] to [Frances] McFadden with the N.O. pictures, and they were all crazy about them; they are really very wonderful, and I hope they like my piece only half so well; I'm turning it in early next week. McFadden is very nice.[2] I understand why you like her so much.

Newton is doing wonderfully at Wesleyan, laying them in the aisles, or so George Cole writes me.[3] I am going to see N. next weekend; I would like so much for you both to become GREAT friends, for you are the two people in the world who mean most to me . . . and that includes EVERYONE. Mille tenderesse [sic].

T

[Collection Aswell Family]

TO JOHN MALCOLM BRINNIN

[New York]
[Mid-August 1946]

Malcolm dear,

What an agreeable, though not, I must say, particularly prompt correspondent you do make: such an evocative letter, cherie [sic], always skimming on the verge of a major exposé (what IS the matter with Henrietta?),

---

[1] Her brother was Alfred Kazin, who had won instant recognition as a critic with his first book, *On Native Grounds* (1942).

[2] McFadden was the managing editor of *Harper's Bazaar,* Carmel Snow's deputy.

[3] Arvin was teaching summer classes at Wesleyan College in Middletown, Connecticut, then an all-male institution.

and managing to suggest direr situations than could possibly be. You are quite right, though, I do seem to give not much thought to Yaddo, which is odd, considering my GREAT interest in all the little intrigues, cabals etc. . . . but there is no time for that now: I'm merely drowning in the chaos of my personal life. You are a wise boy, Malcolm, to stay out of NY; it is no place for you, and it is certainly no place for me; I'm afraid I haven't the sneering façade necessary for this giant snake pit; everything one says here seems to be repeated, or rather everything one hasn't said; who are one's friends and who aren't?; nothing is never nothing and something is never something and everything is quite different from what it seems to be: Kafka, I feel, would've loved NY.

I ran into Ankey [Anky Larrabee] and Howard again at, of all places, B. Lawrence's, and I have been worried since for fear they might have thought me rude that night, but the truth of the matter is I was feeling nightmarish, strange, indeed, and with good reason, for the next day I woke up to find myself with a 102 fever and a left foot that resembled a ballon [sic]: infected, very, and for no reason the doctor can fathom: just happened. So here I am stretched out on my bed of pain with the typewriter propped over my knees. I have to take sulpher [sic] drugs, which make me dizzy from time to time, but I am working . . . on my N.O. [New Orleans] notes, book, and an article I'm writing for a very chichi French magazine called ART ET STYLE. The article is supposed to be a kind of refutation of the French theory that the only American writers are Faulkner, Steinbeck, Dashiell Hamett [Hammett] and Hemingway. I am mentioning you in it, do you mind? You are a "distinguished young American poet whose work deserves international attention." Hotcha! That will be $25, please.

Malcolm, this is something I've been meaning to write you about . . . solo, but I may as well put it in this letter. Now in November Cartier-Bresson's sister, Nicole, is coming to NY; she is an extremely gifted poet: her book, Le Double Depart, won the Paul Valery prize last year; I have the book here, and it is marvelous; she is twenty-two, very presentable (from photographs that I have seen), and she wants to lecture to college groups on young French poets; she has lectured in Vienna, Switzerland, and, I think, Spain. I thought perhaps Vassar might be interested, and that you could arrange something: Cartier would like to have her lectures lined up before she arrives, for she will not be here too long; both Lionel Trilling, to whom I have spoken about her, and Newton, are receptive, and I just thought perhaps you might be interested, too.[1] Let me know.

---

[1] Brinnin was teaching at Vassar College.

Yes, Cartier has done some portraits (they are very strange, I must say, but the photography is, of course, beautiful) and I will send you one if ever he gives me any prints, but he has been selling them all, and that means I cannot have them till after they appear.

G. [George] Davis, so I understand, is grievously annoyed with me (soenso said that I said etc. Oh God!); fond as I am of George, I don't think I will make the effort to clear it up, for I'm afraid it would only become more involved. Too bad, though.

Provided my foot is all better I will be seeing Newton this weekend: I wrote him today, relaying all your gossip, which will amuse him no end.

I am beginning to feel a trifle dizzy, dear Malcolm, so excuse me please if I leave the room; write me, and know that I miss you.   Love from

    T

p.s. The Bazaar informs me they are in receipt of a beautiful poem. That's our Malcolm!

[Collection University of Delaware Library]

TO MARY LOUISE ASWELL

[1060 Park Avenue]
[New York]
[Week beginning 12 August 1946]

My darling,

I hope this reaches you at Clinton, and that you are having a fine time with your old friends; Mrs Saunders was so charming the night I met her (at the Russian Tea Room, remember?) and I know that she will take good care of you, precious.

Newton writes that he mailed you a note a few days ago; have you recieved [sic] it? We are spending the weekend together in Northampton . . . and no doubt will talk of you a good deal, for we both love you very much. I love you more than anyone, though: keep that in mind, young lady, and do not go throwing your affections around lightly.

I took my N.O. piece into the Bazaar today, and they seemed to like it very much, and I have got my finances more or less straightened out, so all is quiet on the western front. What is more, McFadden seems to think they will run my story in October after all.[1] I saw dear little Peral [Pearl Kazin] for a few minutes, and B. [Barbara Lawrence], and both appeared to be fine, though busy busy busy.

Carson, as I may have written you, has been in Nantucket adapting The Member into a play with Tennessee Williams.[2] She is looking better than I've ever seen her. She said to send you her love, and that she would see you as soon as you returned.

Marguerite [Young] tells me Eudora [Welty] is coming to live in New York . . . in September. Newton has been urging me to call Helen Eustis and make a date for lunch, but I am shy about such things, so when you come back will you arrange for the three of us to dine?[3]

Leo is out of town at the moment, but returns next week. I love him dearly; and I am ashamed that I did not see, really see what a sweet beautiful person he was from the beginning. I rode up to Conn. with the Trillings last Saturday (how this came about is very amusing; Leo had shown me some photographs of them, and while I was buying my train ticket who should be standing in line behind me but etc. . . . so I introduced myself, wasn't that bold? and we had a very pleasant time) and liked them ever so much.[4]

Marylou, my precious, I miss you terribly, and I love you: a bushel, a peck, a hug around the neck

　　T

[Collection Aswell Family]

TO LEO LERMAN

　　[Northampton, Mass.]
　　[16 August 1946]

Dearest Leo—

　　And how was the vacation? Wonderful, I hope.

　　I'm sitting here waiting for N. to arrive from Wesleyan, so thought I'd drop you a 'welcome home' note—mainly to say how very good I thought

---

[1] "Notes on N.O." was published in the October 1946 issue of *Harper's Bazaar*. Frances Mc-Fadden was the magazine's managing editor, second only to the top editor, Carmel Snow.
[2] Carson McCullers's novel *The Member of the Wedding* was published in 1946.
[3] Helen Eustis was yet another editor at *Harper's Bazaar*.
[4] Lionel and Diana Trilling were both eminent literary critics.

your Kavan review was.[1] It is a wonderful piece of work, Leo, and I am proud of you.

The Bazaar has my N.O. piece now, and they seemed to like it. I will probably be back in N.Y. before you are—call me when you get home—and we will have a good talk & I will show you the "article."

A curious thing happened—I went to Conn. [Connecticut] that Saturday you left, and who should be standing in the ticket line alongside but the Trillings: I recognized them because of the photographs you showed me.[2] So I introduced myself, and I am glad I did, for they were very sweet, and we had a pleasant ride on the train together. They were going to Westport. I liked them enormously—but, because of various things, I'm afraid I was in rather a jittery state, and made a bad impression. Anyway, they <u>love</u> you dearly—and so do I.

T

[Collection Columbia University Library]

TO MARY LOUISE ASWELL

[Northampton, Mass.]
[17 September 1946]

Darling

A quick note, just to say I got your precious letter; isn't it funny, I wrote you that same day, so you must've recvd. my missive on Monday, too. Or did it come? I could not remember Mrs Saunder's [Saunders's] initials.

The weather is superb, so autumn like, and I can only pray that this continues. The reviews of the O.Henry have been very nice to me, more than nice, and a little foolish, too: the Times, for instance, said my story was as "unforgettable as anything that has appeared since Henry James," and the Post said it was "a masterpiece," and lots more. Hooray for our team! And the O.Henry introduction said that A Tree Of Night was a better story than Miriam, which of course it is, and raved on and on about it. Wait until they read The Headless Hawk: they ain't seen nothin yet.

---

[1] Lerman had reviewed *Asylum Piece*, a collection of short stories by the British author Anna Kavan, in *The Saturday Review of Literature*, August 10, 1946.

[2] Critics Diana and Lionel Trilling.

Newton came last weekend, and oh what a wonderful time we had, and how we longed for you. Biddy came for dinner, and B. too, and Newton and I saw Henry V, and had lunch with Leo and Marguerite . . . all that was missing, darling, was you. And Newton is coming back Friday . . . why oh why aren't you here?!! We are going to spend Saturday with Carson. Dearest precious Marylou, I love you with all of me

T

[Collection Aswell Family]

TO JOHN MALCOLM BRINNIN

[1060 Park Avenue]
[New York]
[September 1946]

Faithful friend,

Your letter and I arrived in New York at approximately the same time, but in rather different conditions: the letter was bright and witty and sweet, everything a letter should be, while I, on the other hand, am ill, unkempt, achy: I have contracted a touch of flu, not much, to be sure, just enough to put me in bed. But I had a wonderful time in Northampton. As always. Newton is very well, but very tired: those six weeks at Wesleyan were quite a strain . . . and he has so much to do, getting his Smith classes rolling, starting Melville, preparing a November lecture . . .[1] Newton takes it all very seriously, which of course he should. Anyway, I know that he intends writing you, has spoken of it several times.

How miserable to have missed you! And I certainly plan on seeing you Oct. 5. You may stay here in this apartment if you like (please, Mr. Brinnin, lower that eyebrow), where, I assure you, you will be perfectly safe, for I am very moral these days.[2] I had a letter from Henri while I was in Northampton, and he was disappointed about the Detroit project; Barbarra

---

[1] Arvin was beginning a biography of Herman Melville.
[2] Capote was staying in his mother's and stepfather's apartment at 1060 Park Avenue.

[Barbara Lawrence], on the other hand, was, in a note, tres excited about the poetry-painting piece.

Could your Cuban friend be the gentleman who came to call on me last Sunday? I was not here unfortunately, but Joe enjoyed him enormously.[1]

Really, I ought to send you that photograph . . . but where am I going to get a print? Perhaps Marylou [Aswell] will have some made for me, inasmuch as she is having one made for herself. It is going to be in their November issue: would that be any help? And speaking of pictures, you promised me one . . . which I have never received.

So that g.d.g.d. (god damn George Davis) thinks I've let him down. Ha ha, I'm laughing yet.

My book of stories has come to rather a halt. All terribly complicated, with cons outweighing pros at this point, even in my own mind. Still, the decision is still my own; I can if I want to, or so Random [House] says. But anyway I'd like to talk with you about it.

Maya Deren paid me a little call just before I left.[2] Did you know she was an ex-student of Newton's? He does not remember her with any pleasure. I kind of liked her though . . . that day. She is perfectly serious about these films, isn't she? And some of her ideas are interesting. I wonder, however, if she has the talent to make anything of it. I have been reading some of Garrigue's verse: Oh Malcolm, it's so awful![3] What merit can you possibly find? Have you ever read Miss Lonelyhearts.[4] I think you would like it.

Write me, dear Malcolm, and know that I miss you. Send me a card September 30th (or a little Duesenberg runaround, should you feel in the mood), for that is my birthday: I will be 22. Much love to you

    T

[Collection University of Delaware Library]

---

[1] Joe Capote, Capote's stepfather, was also Cuban.
[2] Maya Deren was an avant-garde filmmaker and film critic.
[3] Despite her French name, Jean Garrigue was born in Evansville, Indiana.
[4] Nathanael West's novel Miss Lonelyhearts, published in 1933.

TO HOWARD DOUGHTY

[New York]
[30 September 1946]

Howard dear,

I would have written before, but have been in bed all week with the flu; I should really rest a while longer, but today is my birthday, and I really cannot bare [sic] foregoing the festivities planned; a luncheon at the Ritz, no less, a cocktail party at the St. Regis, no less, and an evening soiree at Mrs. Aswell's. Then I will go back to bed for a week of recuperating.

A letter from Malcolm informed me he was on his way to Yaddo. Did you have a good time? I hope so.

Esther Rolick came huffing and puffing up here the other day, and brought me an enormous piece of sculpture; she said she was leaving for New Orleans over the weekend. A long chapter from Marguerite's novel is in the September Bazaar, but I don't suppose you have seen it. And Newton has a wonderful review of Orwell in the newest Partisan. Carson has, or so I understand, abandoned her play, which is a shame, because what she read of it to me was really very good. Leo is in the midst of wild activities; at least he dashes around like that headless chicken, and comes to visit at strange hours: two in morning, and such.

Tell me, Howard, are you angry with me, or peeved? Your letters are nothing more than rather cold wig wags, and your signatures have declined from "love," to affectionately, to affect., to Best. If you have some grievance, I wish you would let me know. In the meantime, much love from

T

[Collection Unknown]

TO MARY LOUISE ASWELL

[Northampton, Mass.]
[October 1946]

Darling Sister,

It was so sweet and so like you!, to send the telegram that eerie day. I am glad you liked the N.O. notes—nothing could please me more.

It is beautiful here, the weather; crystal. The mountains rimming the town are burning green, and blue, and there is the cold brown touch of Autumn everywhere; An enormous apple tree, very heavy with fruit, grows under the window; aside from burning leaves, is there anything more nostalgic than the odor of ripening October apples?

I am working hard, and <u>thinking clearly</u>, and am so very happy here with Newton: he is so good to me, and for me. He is at his office now, otherwise he would send a little love note as you did (which touched him deeply)—but he sends love and love, darling sister, and so, of course, do I.

Your little brother
T

P.S. Give love to my other sister, and say hello to sweet Pearl.

[Collection Aswell Family]

TO HOWARD DOUGHTY

[1060 Park Avenue]
[New York]
[17–19 October 1946]

Howard dear,
You were sweet to write, and thank you; and I am so disappointed that I did not get to see you; it must've been fun with Leo, and isn't his apartment fantastic?: Vogue magazine is photographing me there Monday amid all the books and music boxes: after that appears, I suppose I might as well leave NY.

I am going to the hospital on Wednesday; I do not know how long I will be there, not more than a few days, I expect.[1] Anyway, aside from all the pain of this, I am appalled by the expense; it is unbelievable! And my bank account is slipping out from under me, but fast. I think I will be all right, though, and fairly soon.

It was wonderful with Newton this last weekend. I love October so much I wish it could always be, and we went out into the country for a

---

[1] He was to have his tonsils removed.

day . . . to Deerfield, to Amherst, all around . . . and it was so very beautiful.

The bad part about my ailment is it makes me so infernally and constantly tired and, though I want to go on writing and writing to you, I've just got to lie down now. I think of you Howard, dear, and miss you.

love,
T

[Collection Unknown]

TO JOHN MALCOLM BRINNIN

[1060 Park Avenue]
[New York]
[October or November 1946]

Malcolm, my pet

You do write wonderful letters, and the one this morning has cheered me up no end; inasmuch as I am going to the death-house tomorrow I could not have asked for a prettier farewell. The reason for this journey is as follows: my red corpucles [sic] are destroying my white ones rather like leukemia but not, I assure you, so fatal. One of the roots of this ailment is my tonsils, so out they come; aside from that there is nothing to be done but take a variety of tiresome and tiring drugs. However, I shall be in the hospital only a few days, for my other treatments can be taken anywhere . . . and there is no real pain involved in this, other than a constant state of fatigue. Anyway, it should not be much longer now. And a happy lad I'll be, for I have not been able to work (which makes me _really_ sick), and such goings on do limit one's activities.

Newton is not to my knowledge giving a lecture in New York now after all . . . too busy: he works terribly hard you know, being, as he is, so concientious [sic] . . . but he will be here Saturday Nov. 23rd. Perhaps, if you are here, we could have dinner together. As to Elizabeth [Ames]: no, I don't think there was anything to that hint; she is just a very lax person. She is in New York now, and dropped me a card asking if I would call her . . . but, with all my troubles, I have not been able to yet. Ely told me about your Sunday together, and how much she enjoyed it, even with a high fever. Speaking [of] fevers, I've had one of a 102 for two weeks: little T, who never allows anything to go to waste has, of course, made endless notes on the marvellous distortion of things.

No, the New Orleans notes haven't appeared, but should by Saturday. That poor Bazzar [*sic*], they had trouble with the printers, and here comes their Oct. issue in November.

Funny about McCarthy and Bowden.[1] You are different from them, Malcolm. Very. They represent everything I most dislike. If only such people could allow themselves a little honesty. They belong to that ever-increasing tribe, the cold-hearted ones. If you exclude emotion, as they have, then you die a little inside, and everyday [*sic*]. She, of course, has certain gifts, unhealthy though they be, but as for Bowden, how do you suppose he manages to justify himself to himself? And yet you know inside that boy I'm sure there must be a touch of tenderness left: as a child I'm sure he must've suffered very much. Strange then, isn't it, that all his values should be negative, distorted? Excuse this ranting, please.

When you write Howard [Doughty] please, after extracting a goodly share for yourself, send him my love.

T

[Collection University of Delaware Library]

TO JOHN MALCOLM BRINNIN

[1060 Park Avenue]
[New York]
[Late November 1946]

Malcolm dear,

Hello! And why haven't you written me? Surely you must realize, my dear, that in my precarious state I need all the encouragement my friends can give me. Or don't you know about my precarious state? Precarious enough, at least, to put me in the hospital . . . Wednesday.[2] Do send orchids, and a little love.

---

[1] Mary McCarthy, the novelist and acerbic social critic, and her third husband, Bowden Broadwater, who was on the staff of *The New Yorker*.

[2] He was recovering from the removal of his tonsils.

Ankey [Anky Larrabee] came here to see me yesterday, and we spent a pleasant afternoon together, me propped up in bed, and her at the foot leaning against a blue water-silk pillow, drinking, and eating fried chicken. A wonderful girl, Ankey, and I love her; in fact, I do not know when I have felt so warmly toward anyone.

As you probably know, Howard [Doughty] was in town last weekend, but I did not see him as I was in Northampton; however, he called Newton, and I talked to him, and he sounded tres cheerful. Also, I've heard the good news about the Men of Letters series wanting his Parkman.[1] This should be the pick-me-up he needs.

Have you seen the reviews of Anais's book?[2] The Times labelled it a Surrealist Soap Opera. Of course I think it deserves a little better than that, but not much. [Edmund] Wilson goes on trial here Tuesday and he asked NA to come and testify in his behalf, but he couldn't.

Did I remember to tell you how sweet I thought Bill Reed [Read] was?[3]

Leo Lerman is having an elegant soiree this aft. for Carson and, despite my inner collapse, I'm going to put in a brief appearance. I will give your love to all.

George Davis and I have patched up, and he is being very kind, even sent me an album of Gieseking records.[4] Bob Lowry (you know him, don't you?) has moved in with George, and they have been having little 'at homes' which are very pleasant.

I am beginning to think you are right . . . about the ballet. Went last week, and it was dreadful, a mixture of Minsky and music by Muzak. I hope never to return.

My love to the Vassarites, my love to you.

T

P.S. When you get the time, please write NA a good long letter, as he is and has been over-working, and one of your inimitable relaxations would do worlds for him. But do not mention my Ill-nez. Thank you, M.

[Collection University of Delaware Library]

---

[1] Howard Doughty was writing a biography of Francis Parkman, the nineteenth-century American historian.

[2] Anaïs Nin's book was *Ladders to Fire*.

[3] Read was or soon became Brinnin's lifelong companion.

[4] Walter Gieseking was a German pianist, renowned for his interpretations of Debussy and Ravel.

TO JOHN MALCOLM BRINNIN

17 Clifton Place
Brooklyn 5, N.Y.
[Late November 1946]

Malcolm dear,

It was so sweet, so wonderful to have your letter; forgive me for not having answered sooner, but I have been in the hospital again (the Northampton hospital), this time with various infections. I saw Howard, as you may
know: he was driving through N. [Northampton] with Granville [Hicks].[1]
And was delighted to find him in such gay good spirits.

As you can see, I have changed addresses, have moved to a little lost
mews in darkest Brooklyn . . . for various reasons: I wanted most to get
away from hectic, nerve-wracking influences, to escape and get on with my
work.[2] I had reached a point where I was so nervous I could hardly hold a
cigarette, and my work was not going too well. So here I am living in quiet
Victorian splendor in a private house belonging to two elderly, rather mad
ladies; I have a charming (moderately) parlor, and a rather cheerful bedroom: I can't wait for you to see it. There is a telephone: Main 2-7070 . . .
but under no circumstances are you to tell it to anyone, neither family (not
even my mom knows it) or friends. I want to get in touch with Ankey [Anky
Larrabee]. Please send me her address. What other news? Newton is well.
He gave a wonderful evening lecture at Smith, and the Bazaar has bought
it. He will be in New York next weekend.

Dearest Malcolm, I hope you are well. I miss seeing you, and want to
so much. When you come to town next do try and save a goodly share of
your time for me. And write me at once. Much love to you, darling

T

[Collection University of Delaware Library]

---

[1] Granville Hicks was a critic—he examined American literature from a Marxist point of
view—and a friend of Arvin's.

[2] The "nerve-wracking influences" were his mother's alcoholic rages.

TO JOHN MALCOLM BRINNIN

> [1060 Park Avenue]
> [New York]
> [December 1946]

Malcolm dear,

Thank you for the letter; it cheered me enormously—indeed, took the chill off an otherwise icy day. And I was glad to hear of your pleasant weekend with Howard [Doughty]. But, my dear boy, however did you manage five heavyweights over such a protracted period?

And thank you, too, for being so kind about the Hawk.[1] If you really liked it, then nothing would please me more. There is a story coming out in the Atlantic with which I feel a little more satisfied.[2]

I had dinner last night with Aaron Copland. He wants me to do the libretto for an opera. However, I do not think myself at all qualified. Would you be interested?

Yes, I certainly wish I could clear away a few of the obstructions, and "get on" with my work. Alas, there are so many. Dramatic as it may sound, I wonder really whether I shall be able to live through the winter: everything I do seems to turn against me. It is very hard now for me to be alone: there are so many things I cannot do for myself. Yet there is no one for me to turn to, really no one. Newton, poor darling, never could cope with it, try as he does, and try as he will. Of course, all my friends are wonderful to me, and I know, would do most anything for me. Unfortunately, there is no stability in this. Oh Malcolm, dear Malcolm, do please excuse such running on: I am very ashamed to so indulge myself. And anyway, I expect the new year will bring me better luck.

I am going to Northampton on Friday, and will be back the following Tuesday. If you're coming to town, drop me a line, please. My very best love to you

T

P.S. I have read The Wound and the Weather.[3] It is not a particularly exciting talent, but certainly a most pleasing one. And three or four of the poems approach a kind of perfection. I think I should be more interested in his second book.

[Collection University of Delaware Library]

---

[1] "The Headless Hawk."
[2] "Shut a Final Door," *The Atlantic Monthly* (August 1947).
[3] Howard Moss's volume of poetry, *The Wound and the Weather,* had just been published.

TO HOWARD DOUGHTY

17 Clifton Place
Brooklyn 5, N.Y.
December 18, 1946

Howard dear,

It has been so long since I've seen or heard from you; of course I've probably owed you a letter all along, but I'm not sure: in any case, I never write under that theory, but only when I most genuinely want to.

As you may know, I've moved over here to Brooklyn to an old Victorian house furnished, I should say, after the owners read one of Mrs. Belloc-Lowndes's penny-shockers. It is pleasant, though, quiet and warm and such a relief after what I once rather absurdly referred to as my 'proper setting.' Malcolm has been here to visit, so he probably has given you a description. I shall probably stay here until May . . . unless, that is, I can find something more convenient.

Since seeing you in Northampton, I have been in still another hospital. I am getting quite bored with whatever my mysterious ailment might be.

I had cocktails with Elizabeth [Ames] the other day; it was really very pleasant, and I enjoyed it; away from Yaddo, she is a much more agreeable person. She told me you were working hard, which was of course good news. Speaking of work, Newton has really out-done himself, and is, I'm afraid, in a very high-strung state. I am going up there on Saturday, and will be there for Christmas. Every day this last week I've devoted to buying his presents, and I think I've done quite well: a Mark Cross brief case with his initials and a departmented [*sic*] interior of blue morroco [*sic*], a pair of antique mercury-glass candlesticks which are very beautiful, the new Daumier book, an album of Maggie Teyte,[1] and an album of records all selected seperately [*sic*]. God knows how I am going to get all this to Northampton.

I had dinner with Cyril Connolly last week.[2] He is a fat, remote but pleasant guy, and is going to use a story in Horizon.

The picture of Malcolm in Junior Bazaar is awfully good. Did you see it?

---

[1] Maggie Teyte was a renowned English soprano.
[2] Cyril Connolly was a well-known English literary critic, as well as the co-founder, along with Stephen Spender, of *Horizon,* a small but influential English literary magazine.

Lionel Trilling has finished his novel; I haven't read it, but someone who has said it was not too good.[1] A letter from Carson says she has been sick, but in love with Paris; she is going to live in Edita Morris's house which is about twenty miles outside Paris.[2] What other news? I may do the libretto for Aaron Copland's potential opera; at least he has asked me. I just can't make up my mind. I have written one new story and it is going to be in The Atlantic, of all places.[3] The lecture Newton gave last November is going to be [in] the March issue of Harper's Bazaar. It is beautiful.

Dear Howard, aside from love, there comes with this letter a very real wish for a happy new year.

T

[Collection Unknown]

TO JOHN MALCOLM BRINNIN

[17 Clifton Place]
[Brooklyn]
Sunday
[2 February 1947]

Malcolm dear—

It is <u>so</u> long since I've heard from you; I hope this doesn't mean you haven't been well. As for me, my various ailments seem pretty much at a standstill, for which, needless to say, I am thankful.

I am still in Brooklyn—off and on—not very often, really. My family are leaving for Cuba this week, and so I'm taking over Park Avenue for a few weeks: therefore, if you are in town, please call me there: ATwater 9-3319. Indeed, that brings up a point: why don't you make a special trip? It has been so very long since we chewed our friends to pieces, and you could use the other bed-room (in <u>perfect</u> safety, I assure you.) Newton is coming next weekend; we are going to see <u>Androcles</u>, and am having a small party for him: Henri & Eli, Marylou and Barbara, Aaron Copland and his friend Victor: would you like to make it nine? A very brief party, to be sure: 5:30 to 7,

---

[1] Trilling's novel was *The Middle of the Journey* (1947).
[2] Edita Morris was a writer.
[3] "Shut a Final Door" appeared in *The Atlantic*, August 1947.

Sunday, the ninth. In any case, perhaps you will be at Henri's opening Tuesday night.

Your under-the-umbrella picture in <u>Mlle.</u> was awfully good.[1] There is a morbid photograph of me in the new Feb. 1 <u>Vogue</u>; I'm so weary of those dopefiend pictures, which are interesting, I suppose, but which, after all, don't really look like me. Or do they? In the same issue is a picture of your friend Valerie Bettis.[2]

A letter from Howard says you are going up to Yaddo soon. Well, best of luck. Do you think you will be spending any time there this summer?

Knowing your predilection for the movies, let me warn you not to miss, "Les Enfants du Paradis," which is opening here next week. And avoid at all cost "The Best Years of Our Lives," what a maudlin, false, dull piece of hokum!

Of course there are any number of things to write you, but it is getting late, and I have an appointment to keep. Let me hear from you. Meanwhile, much love from

T

[Collection University of Delaware Library]

TO MARY LOUISE ASWELL

[Northampton, Mass.]
[16 April 1947]

Marylou, divinely beloved

This must be <u>love</u>! For you are the only one I ever write: yes, it is love, but then of course who would not love one so beautiful and enchanting as M.L. Indeed, darling, I do not know that I have changed the <u>course of your life</u> (as Mr. Broaden Bowater[3] suggests), but <u>you</u>, fair creature, have altered the course of mine: you have done me more good, darling, than a hundred thousand dollars worth of Dr. Moultar, Selven, and Max whats-his-name. There now, you can use that as a testimonial when finally you leave 572 Madison and start giving your own method of psycho-exercise.[4]

---

[1] *Mlle.* was *Mademoiselle* magazine
[2] Valerie Bettis was an actress and choreographer.
[3] A takeoff on "Bowden Broadwater."
[4] The *Harper's Bazaar* offices were at 572 Madison Avenue.

I can just see you, pet! Oh yes, the Aswell method—ie: "Girls, if you want to keep a shapely mind and a [unclear] figure, then I tell you this: forget about men, sex, food, clothes, whiskey, friends (especially if their name is Lawrence or Barbara: those 2 names always accompany a <u>dangerous</u> type), furniture, music, books, politics—in other words, girls, just stretch out on a summery beach and forget: that is the Aswell road to happiness." Honey, with that formula I'll bet you could pick up a fast buck. Shall we write a brochure?

I have been reading the Chas. Olson book, and am rather surprised at you and Pearl for liking it so much.[1] It has a certain power, I will admit, but on the whole it seems to me a somewhat fraudulent performance: a pretty sweeping statement, I know, and one perhaps not easy to defend—however, tell Pearl that, after I've had a few <u>poker</u> lessons, I'll battle it out with her—and give her a huge kiss, because she is a precious girl and I am terribly, terribly fond of her.

Did you <u>see</u> the Guggenheim list?! Ralph Bates![2] Don't you know Marguerite [Young] is tearing down the joint? I think we all ought to chip in and buy her a stick of dynamite to shove up Mr. Moe's _____ (never say I'm not a gentleman). Some gossip for you, dear: Iris Barry is having an affair with a child who hasn't even begun to shave yet.[3]

Newton is fine, but awfully busy, of course: somebody in France wants to translate The New American Writers piece, and an Italian magazine wants to publish it, too. As for me, I am working away, and getting a little sunshine, too. The weather is beautiful.

I love our sister B.—but for God's sake don't tell her! The slightest little compliment, and that girl is <u>insufferable</u>.

Your ever-loving monster-child

T

[Collection Aswell Family]

---

[1] Charles Olson was an avant-garde critic and poet. The book, *Call Me Ishmael,* was a study of the literary influences on Melville's *Moby-Dick.* Capote's opinion may have been influenced by Arvin, who was writing a biography of Melville.

[2] A writer, Bates was at Yaddo with Capote and Young.

[3] Iris Barry was the first curator of the Museum of Modern Art's film collection.

TO ROBERT LINSCOTT

[Probably May 1947]

Dear Bob,

Thanks for the letter, thanks ever so much, and I am glad you like the story: I am aware, of course, that there are faults in it, but as far as I am concerned I accomplished at least eighty percent of what I set out to do, and that is the most I can ask of so elusive a thing.[1] It is not, for one thing, as concentrated as I should like it to have been, but [the] more or less poetic nature of the material defied that kind of diamond focus: I had to use a soft lens, a suggestive approach. I do hope it will have some success; that is, I hope that a few reader's [*sic*] will know and feel a little of what I put into it, for I want never to perpetrate a fraud, and by fraud I mean anything that wastes a reader's time. The reason it was turned down by Mlle. (for which I thank God!) is very complex, and very personal: I had a terrible argument with George Davis, in which he said, among other things, that I was a "prima donna" and etc.: all this merely because I would not consent to having the story cut, and refused to revise the more, as Mrs. Blackwell called them, "shocking parts."[2] Also, he had learned in some curious way that Marylou had read the story, and he thought this "shocking," too. The whole thing was reduced to the most disgusting and amateurish level, the sort of thing I should never allow myself to be mixed up in. I was really very afraid, as you know, that they would print it, which would've been a tragedy from my point of view, so all in all I am satisfied with the results. I hope Marylou does not have any trouble, I mean I hope her business dept. lets her buy it. I haven't heard from her as yet. And I also hope Rita [Smith] has learned a lesson, for all of this is her fault: her intentions were of course the very best, and I love her for her loyalty, but she does seem to have strange Ideas sometimes of what loyalty constitutes.[3] I think she realizes now that she made a mistake. Also I wish you had read the story with a clearer mind.

I am working on the book and it is really my love and today I wrote two pages and oh Bob I do want it to be a beautiful book because it seems important to me that people try to write beautifully, now more than ever be-

---

[1] It is not clear which story he is referring to.
[2] George Davis was the fiction editor of *Mademoiselle*; Betsy Talbot Blackwell was his boss, the magazine's editor.
[3] Rita Smith was George Davis's assistant at *Mademoiselle*, and she was the first to bring Capote to Davis's attention; she was also Carson McCullers's sister.

cause the world is so crazy and only art is sane and it has been proven time after time that after the ruins of a civilization are cleared away all that remains are the poems, the paintings, the sculpture, the books.[1]

LIFE was here all last week, and they took a great many pictures of me, and I hope some [of] them turn out well, though I don't suppose they will use more than one, if that. Dear Bob, I do not suppose you will feel much like writing me a letter there on your vacation, but if you do, please do. I miss you.

always

t

[Collection Washington University Libraries]

TO JOHN MALCOLM BRINNIN

[1060 Park Avenue]
[New York]
[May 1947]

Malcolm, sweetmeat,
What a lot of weight I'll bet you've lost; it took me months to get back the poundage discarded in N.O. [New Orleans] last summer; but really, isn't it fascinating? And God knows you are seeing America First . . . though it may turn out to be the last thing you ever see. And speaking of seeing things have you gazed upon my shocking photo in the current Life?[2] Believe me, never again! Quel travesty.

Did you ever get the other letter I sent you?

Well, as you probably know, Howard [Doughty] is now stationed in Milton, Mass. He came by to see N. and I (me?) in Northampton on his way there; I thought he was looking just finely, and seemed to be in cheerful spirit. Newton took me to Boston last week; it was my first trip there,

---

[1] The book was *Other Voices, Other Rooms*.
[2] *Life* magazine (June 2, 1947) featured a long article entitled "Young U.S. Writers." Several were mentioned, but it was "esoteric, New Orleans–born Truman Capote" who was pictured alone, somber and unsmiling, on the opening page. He was dressed in coat, tie, and vest, and, despite his disclaimer, he was almost certainly delighted with *Life*'s presentation.

and I had a wonderful time: we did such diverse things as having dinner with Matthiesen [F. O. Matthiessen] and go to the Old Howard: I'm an old burlesque fan, you know.[1] F. O. I did not especially like, but it would take a Proustian analysis to explain my reason, so I will save it for later. Did like Harry Levin, though.[2] Marguerite [Young] is at Yaddo now, and she writes that the place is filling up with an interesting, amusing crowd: Robert Lowell, Irwin Edman, [Malcolm] Cowley, Austin Warren, J. F. Powers. When are you going? Or are you? I'm leaving for Sconset[3] Tuesday the tenth, but, inasmuch as I'm not sure of the address, why don't you write me here and it will be forwarded; and Malcolm, do please come for a visit.

Marylou and B. [Barbara Lawrence] are very well; we speak of you often. There are no new people in my life, except [Christopher] Isherwood, whom I see now and like very much, though he baffles me somewhat. Now that classes are over, Newton is reviving; in fact, he is looking the best I've ever seen him. You ought to drop him at least a card; he is so very fond of you.

Tell Henri I have tried endless times to call Ely, but without marked success; she has been out of town over the weekend, but is suppose [sic] to be back this afternoon, so I will try then. Give him my best. Are they going to Yaddo, too?

I am really nearing the end of my book; the strain is terrific, and I'm scared to death it is a failure. Jesus, after all this work, and all this time. It does seem to me, though, that I have been put in an unfair position, and I do not take to this brand of pressure. Oh well.

I've missed you awfully, Malcolm. Write me.

much love

T

[Collection University of Delaware Library]

---

[1] The Old Howard, a famous theater in Boston's Scollay Square; formerly a grand opera house but by this time a tawdry burlesque establishment.

[2] Friends of Arvin, F. O. Matthiessen and Harry Levin were esteemed professors of literature at Harvard.

[3] Sconset is a familiar name for Siasconset.

TO ROBERT LINSCOTT

[Nantucket Island, Mass.]
[Late July 1947]

Dear Bob—

Oh thank you for the letter! Here in island isolation, arrival of mail is the sole event.

Of course, I feel like less than 2 cents for not having sent the ms. before now.[1] But these last few pages! Every word takes blood, I don't know why this should be, especially since I know exactly what I'm doing. Except for the last five or six pages I have had the book finished for the last 2 weeks. Of course I am making little revisions here and there, of the whole book, I mean.

Anyway, I am pretty sure I will finish it over the weekend. Then I am sending it to Marian and she will get it to you immediately.[2] Maybe you will be back in N.Y.

Isherwood was here for a week, and we had an extremely pleasant time.[3] I know you would like him. He may be going to visit Minna Curtis [Mina Curtiss] some time in August, so you will probably see him then.[4] Which reminds me, I haven't sent back that book I borrowed from Elaine Shaplen; it is so hard to mail anything from here, but tell her not to worry.

John Lane, the English publisher, offered me a 150 pound advance on my book. Should I take it? Probably it would be better to wait, because I've had seven offers, especially a very good one from Cyril Conolly [Connolly], who is going to publish books now.

I miss you Bob. Have faith! Love

T

[Collection Columbia University Library]

---

[1] *Other Voices, Other Rooms.*

[2] Marian Ives was his literary agent.

[3] Christopher Isherwood and his companion, Bill Caskey, arrived on July 13.

[4] Mina Curtiss—Capote misspelled both her first and last name—was at that time editing a book of Proust's letters.

TO LEO LERMAN ET AL.

Sunset Towers
8358 Sunset Blvd
Hollywood, Calif.
December 8, 1947

Dearest Cousinage[1]
My darlings, I am <u>mad</u> with horror: when I get back, if, indeed, I ever do, then I am taking all of you by your dear little paws and make you swear to me you will never, never set foot in Los Angeles County. Quel hole! I am living in a very posh establishment, the Sunset Towers, which, or so the local gentry tell me, is where every scandal that ever happened happened; for the most part, it is a hotel of kept-women—and, my dears, you should live to see what they take the trouble to <u>keep</u> in California. However, in the company of Hoynigen-Huene [Hoyningen-Huene],[2] I am going Wednesday to Death Valley, and when I come back I am moving elsewhere.

Better Death in Venice than life in Hollywood. Speaking of which, K.A. [Katherine Anne] Porter is leaving here to live in Venice.[3] At the next meeting of the Cats Head Club, will President Lerman please present a motion to change our Formal Attitude toward Miss Porter? She has been an absolute darling to me; really she has, and what is more, during my recent illness, which took place Saturday, she brought me calves-foot jelly and a bouquet of camellias. So far, things have gone well enough. Flo Homolka,[4] Operator Aswell's friend, gave a dinner party for me yesterday, and it was altogether charming, except for the fact that I sat next to a raté (as F McF [Frances McFadden] would say) little man who kept staring at me as though he were planning something unspeakably diabolic; he turned out to be Lion Feutchwanger [Feuchtwanger];[5] only I thought he was Franz Werfel;[6] that is to say, I said to <u>him</u>, where ever did he get the <u>ideas</u> for such <u>lovely</u> works as The Forty Days Of Musa Dagh and The Song of Bernadette.

---

[1] The "Cousinage" was a humorous reference to the friends who gathered around Lerman.

[2] Photographer George Hoyningen-Huene.

[3] Porter was in Hollywood to write screenplays.

[4] Photographer Florence Homolka, wife of actor Oscar Homolka. Her mother, Agnes Meyer, was a friend and translator of Thomas Mann.

[5] Lion Feuchtwanger, German-Jewish historical novelist whose *The Oppermanns* (1933) was the first anti-Nazi novel written by a German writer in exile. He fled Europe in 1940 and spent the rest of his life in the United States.

[6] Franz Werfel, Czech-born Austrian-Jewish playwright and novelist whose works included *The Forty Days of Musa Dagh* (1933) and *The Song of Bernadette* (1941). Werfel fled Europe in 1940 and settled in Southern California, where he died in 1945.

I had dinner at the Chaplins'—Friday, I guess it was—a rather viperish experience—and I spent a really beautiful afternoon with Walter Conrad Arensberg,[1] who is altogether charming: Cousins Lerman and Lyndon would lose their minds over him, his house, his paintings. But all this business about Persons & Places I will save for a meeting of the Cat's Heads.

I have had one terrible woe: getting out of the bath tub, I set my foot down on an electrical heating apparatus and burned it to a cinder. No joke. I had to have a doctor and am walking with a crutch.

When I leave here, I am going to San Francisco for a spell. Even so, I shall more than likely be back by Christmas. Meanwhile, keep a lamp burning in the windows, you cat's heads, and know that I love each of you, all of you. A million kisses, mille tenderesse [sic] from your faraway
T

[Small drawing of a tuxedoed cat with a cane in one hand and a cigarette in the other, with stars overhead]

Aside to Cousin B—I am seeing Miss Parsons and Miss Hepburn—both next Tuesday.

[Collection Columbia University Library]

TO CAROL AND WILLIAM SAROYAN

1060 Park Avenue
New York, N.Y.
Dec. 26, 1947

Hello Carol and Bill; look, here I am back east of the Rockies, with, my dear, a real 1883 blizzard swirling at the windows.[2] Indeed, it has been snowing for 2 days, and from time to time I've entertained the notion of tying a keg of brandy about my neck and trudging out to aid the helpless.

It was wonderful, the evening with you in San Francisco. I do wish I kept a diary; how pleasant it would have been to reread it on some such

---

[1] Poet and art collector.

[2] He was referring to the devastating blizzard of March 1888, not 1883. The blizzard of December 1947 set a record that was not to be surpassed for nearly half a century, until a similar snowstorm in January 1996.

page. At any rate, it will always have a permanent place among the pleasant occasions memory manages to retain.

I am happy that <u>Don't Go Away Mad</u> (a delightful title, by the way) is finished: a relief to you <u>both</u>, I'm sure.[1] Here's hoping the new year brings it to <u>us</u>, an ever eager audience.

By this time, my book is on its way to you.[2] Do let me know what you think, negative or otherwise, meanwhile, know that I am thinking of you, and looking forward to your N.Y. visit.

Always,
Truman

[Collection Unknown]

TO LEO LERMAN

[Hotel La Citadelle]
[Port-au-Prince, Haiti]
[February 1948]

Darling Leo,

I did not write before today because it was only last night that I really saw Richard [Hunter]: he came here for cocktails and supper; very pleasant; afterwards, we sat on this beautiful hotel's most beautiful terrace and talked in the moonlight; about twelve Richard went out into the night and made his way down the mountain to that curious, bougainvillea-covered hotel, the Excelsior. It is somehow difficult to report on our conversation.[3] First of all, he seems rather different; he is much better looking, for one thing: lean, tan, quite hard; and he appears to have more identity. I think for the first time in his life he has been really lonely, and that he has been trying desperately to establish a sense of values. But he is obsessed by the situation. Indeed, we discussed practically nothing else. He talked of you with a heartbreaking tenderness, and altogether I am convinced that he loves you more than anything, anyone in the world. And he "knows" about

---

[1] Saroyan's play *Don't Go Away Mad* was produced in 1949.
[2] *Other Voices, Other Rooms*, whose publication date was January 19, 1948.
[3] Richard Hunter and Leo Lerman had amicably ended their partnership of over a decade, and Hunter had taken up with Howard Rothschild, a fellow artist. Though he had a modest income from his family, Rothschild was not a member of the famous banking family.

Howard [Rothschild] absolutely, knows and says that he can expect nothing from Howard but destruction. When he comes back, which will be around the first of March, he wants to go away with you, perhaps to Europe, at least someplace where you can write your book, and he can look after you. Meanwhile H. remains something of a sexual idée-fixe, and this is what has happened: he bombards R. with cablegrams, letters, long-distance calls, all of which has sufficed to queer him with R's mother, and, to a great extent, with Richard as well. Actually, I think R. despises him . . . in the way the fox must despise the red-coated herd. But his ego, still a feeble thing, draws from it some poisonous nourishment. Which is not to say that I question the wisdom of your reticence: it was the wisest thing you could have done because, all in all, it has thrown H.'s stupidity into a kind of bas-relief. Now yesterday H. telephoned and said that he had booked a reservation and was arriving here on the 16th. However, I would not let this upset me; in a way, it seems to me that H. is bending his head for the côup-de-grace [sic]. R. excuses it on the grounds that H. is preparing to depart for Europe and that he will not see him again. Frankly, if I were you, I should hold judgement in limbo until R. returns; then, if he does as he says he wants to, you should be quite satisfied, and able to forget the whole thing.

Haiti is the first place in a great many years that has excited me; definitely you must come here; but I will spare you the details for a session at the Cafe Flore.

Dearest baby, have I ever told you that I loved You? I do, you know, very, very much. Mille tenderesse [sic], Myrt, and a million kisses.

Marge[1]

P.S. write me. R. loved the thin-mint valentine. Write me giving instructions

Your Haitian operative

[Collection Columbia University Library]

---

[1] Capote often addressed Lerman as "Myrt" and signed himself "Marge" since both were fans of an old radio serial, *Myrt and Marge* (1931–1942), about a struggling chorus girl (Myrt) and her daughter (Marge) who were in competition for the same vaudeville parts and the same men. "It was really marvelous," Capote said. "It was one of the all-time strange, peculiar, surrealist things. I had never met anybody who had ever heard of this program until one day I was talking to Leo Lerman about it. '*Myrt and Marge?* It was one of my favorite programs!' he said. After that we used to make up old Myrt and Marge things. It made us both feel good."

TO ELIZABETH AMES

1060 Park Avenue
New York, N.Y.
March 2, 1948

Dear Elizabeth,

Your letter made me very happy: it relieved me so much that you liked the book, for, being as it were one of my original sponsors, I felt I owed you, all of you, a great debt. You have been so good to me Elizabeth; and Newton, I don't know what I should have done without him. So you see, I owe Yaddo a great deal.

I wish I could send good news of myself. And in a way I can, for I feel encouraged and hopeful. But you know I have not really been well the last year or so. I continue to have these physical collapses at every turn. But perhaps I shall be all right now for a while.

Elizabeth, a young writer I know wants and needs very much an invitation to Yaddo. Her name is Patricia Highsmith, 353 East 56th St. New York. She is really enormously gifted, one story of hers shows a talent as fine as any I know. Moreover, she is a charming, thoroughly civilized person, someone I'm quite certain you would like. She is working on a novel now, and needs the sort of thing only Yaddo can provide. I have asked her to write you; if you feel that you can take an interest, then that would be wonderful.[1]

I want terribly to see you; you are so restful and sympathetic, and there is such a lot I have to tell. Perhaps when you are here next you will let me know.

Meanwhile, know that I think of you, Elizabeth, and accept all happiness from me. Fondly

Truman

[Collection New York Public Library]

---

[1] Highsmith was accepted at Yaddo, where she worked on her first novel, *Strangers on a Train*, which was published in 1950. Capote's high opinion of her work never wavered.

TO LEO LERMAN

[Paris]
[8 June 1948]

Myrt, my dearest mother,

C'est marvelleuse [*sic*], still I wake up every morning a little homesick, and wondering what the other half of this soapsuds drama is up to . . . and why hasn't she written me? Though I don't suppose I have quite the right to point a finger, but one way or another my life has been a riot or Riot, and the thought of detailing such vast activities depresses me no end. One thing that would interest you is that I saw a lot of David Cecil[1] in England: isn't he the one you like so much? He is an absolute darling, and he wants to come to the U.S. if some university will invite him, preferably Columbia. Chicago did, but he doesn't want to go there. Why don't you suggest it to [Lionel] Trilling.[2] I had a terribly good time in London, but oh dear it is a dreary place. But Paris is madly beautiful, it is the only time in my life I have felt really relaxed; I sleep a good deal, and am eating like a hog, and I think probably it is all going to be very good for me. Also, I am starting to work again. To leave America was the best thing I could have done, provided that now I manage wisely, I cannot describe the relief, temporary though it may be, to be here at such a distance from all the pressures that have made me miserable for so many years. If it were not for N. and you and my friends I would never come home. Not that I think it is so much better here, it is merely that I am better. Or maybe that is only because so far I don't understand the meanings of things too well, and am therefore not disturbed, as I would be at home, by the look of a child's face, a tone of voice, an accent, the quality of light in a street: nothing connects with memory, reverberates: do you see what I mean, how nice it is not to be pursued by desperate knowledge?

There are all kinds of funny stories, darling, but it is late now, and I have to meet someone for dinner. I am leaving here the first of July for Rome and Capri; but write me at once, care of American Express, Paris . . . meanwhile, I will try to send a more entertaining missive. I love you very

---

[1] Lord David Cecil, author and Oxford University professor.
[2] Trilling was a professor of literature at Columbia.

much; it is so sweet to say that, there are so few people about whom one really means it. Kisses from Paris

t

[Collection Columbia University Library]

TO MARY LOUISE ASWELL

Paris
June 15 1948

Darling Marylou,
 Merci buttercups cherie pour la lettre; I was worried not to have heard from you, but you sound most finely, which answers all my hopes for you. Nothing has happened in particular since I wrote the other day . . . except that I had dinner with Gide . . . about which I have just finished writing the gentleman in Northampton,[1] and it is all far too involved to go into <u>again</u>: leave us wait for a quiet afternoon and a good stiff drink. Paris seems more beautiful everyday, and I keep my room filled with flowers. Even so, I shall be leaving here in the next few weeks. I'm going to Denmark. No particular reason, simply I think I might like it. I suppose I ought to do some shopping before I leave; I haven't bought anything except an enormous bottle of Le Tabac Blonde . . . which stops people dead in their tracks.
 Darling, will you save a place in your January issue for The Man Who Bought Dreams?[2] I'm working on the other story[3] right now, and so The Man probably won't be ready until late August . . . that is to say I will most likely bring it home with me in September.
 Another thing. Please call Loren and Lloyd[4] and tell them that I have got them a reservation here at the Pont-Royal for July 10th. It is a wonderful place to stay, and I'm sure they will like it.
 I'm glad about B. [Barbara Lawrence], glad, that is, that she is taking advantage of her clinical talents. It is sad that she has broken with you, but

---

[1] Newton Arvin.
[2] Published as "Master Misery" in *Horizon,* January 1949, and in *Harper's Magazine,* February 1949.
[3] "Children on Their Birthdays."
[4] Poet Lloyd Frankenberg and his wife, artist Loren MacIver.

really, under the circumstances, it is the best thing, the best for you at any rate, though I know it must be very hard for her: she worshipped you. Poor darling, I do love her, in spite of her last dramatic performance . . . but that was the end in a way: these assumptions of hers had become far too extreme.

So Pearlie [Kazin] is an Aunt; give her a kiss of congratulations. And how is my angel Phoebe [Pierce]? Tell them both that I love them dearly. I talked with Newton on the telephone yesterday. It was tres exciting. I do hope you will see him. He says he never hears from any of you, you mean things!

It is getting twilight here, and Jesus how gorgeous Paris is at this hour. There is an iris-blue light all over the street, and those delicate pink lights are blooming in the Etoile, and there is a group of children going up and down the Quai singing La Vie En Rose. It would be so delirious if we could all be here together.

Do you love me? And can you imagine how much I

love

you?

t

[Collection Columbia University Library]

TO ANDREW LYNDON

Paris
June 29 1948

Darling little A.

How heartbroken I've been: you, of all people, never to have written me a single line! Really, my dear, it is too loathesome of you. N. says you and H. [Harold Halma] are trying to sublet 339.[1] By this, I take it you have found another apt. If so, hurray! And are you working? Please, angel, I hope so— though heaven knows I'm not one to talk—however, I seem to be getting a grip on myself, at last, at last. But Paris is an exceedingly distracting place. What a divine city, I could be <u>madly</u> happy if only N. and you and Phoebe [Pierce] were here. I have learned to ride a motorcycle, and so go scooting all over the place; the fact is, I'm going to go on it to Venice, presumably leaving

---

[1] Harold Halma, Lyndon's companion, was the photographer who took the famous photograph of Capote lying seductively on a chaise longue that was used on the dust jacket of *Other Voices, Other Rooms.*

Thursday: rather like crossing the Atlantic on a houseboat, yes? But I don't know, I feel not too well this week, and so may postpone departure. Yesterday I bought you a present: a huge folder of Braque reproductions from the Skara [Skira] Press. They have such beautiful art-books here. Is there something you want? Now let me know. If I could think of some way to get it home, I know an exquisite little table for Harold. Tenn [Tennessee Williams] was here about 2 weeks ago (scared out of his wits because Pancho[1] had cabled him that he was on his way over), but all his time was taken up with Gore [Vidal]: monsterous [*sic*] as it may seem, T. is really devoted to him. I had dinner with Sandy Campbell who was here, and thought him very likeable.[2] I suppose by this time you have heard about l'affaire Gide, and how I was arrested for transporting heroin: it gave me some uneasy moments, I'm here to tell you.[3]

Unlike Wendy Hiller, I don't know where I'm going—at least not exactly.[4] I shall leave a forwarding address with American Express, and I will be back here later on anyway. However, come what may, I will be home in time to go to Wellfleet with N. Write me to Paris. Love to you, precious angel, and love to H. A million kisses

T

P.S. Tell Phoebe to write me and give her another 1,000,000 kisses.

[Collection New York Public Library]

TO DONALD WINDHAM[5]

[Pont Royal Hotel]
[7, rue Montalembert]
[Paris]
[3 August 1948]

Peaches precious

Just the briefest of notes . . . because I'm in the midst of everything . . . namely, arrangements for departure; honey, we shoulda stood in

[1] Tennessee Williams's lover was Pancho Rodriguez y Gonzalez.
[2] A young actor, Campbell was the companion of Capote's friend Donald Windham.
[3] Unfortunately, l'affaire Gide has been lost to history.
[4] Wendy Hiller, British screen actress who starred in *I Know Where I'm Going* (1945).
[5] Donald Windham, American novelist and short-story writer, perhaps best known for his collaboration with Tennessee Williams on the 1945 play *You Touched Me!*, an adaptation of D. H. Lawrence's story.

Sirmione! It is frightful hot here, and a ghost town to boot, except for hundreds of millions of Americans: the worst variety, natch. And I can't begin to tell you what my trip here was like: not only did I fail to have a wagon-lit,[1] but I didn't even have a seat until we were in Switzerland . . . yep, stood all the way in the worst heat ever. Anyway, Tenn is here, having failed to show up in London for his opening, and we went out dancing last night. The play[2] got rather bad reviews, and he seems to be upset about it, though I can't imagine why: good god, who cares what anyone in England thinks? Well, his mother and brother showed up unexpectedly this morning, apparently in a great fury, so I haven't seen him. Oh yes . . . he sent for that boy in Rome and is importing him to New York. Real folly I should think. We may be on the same boat as I am trying to get passage on the Queen Mary, sailing the 7th . . . which is the boat he goes on, too.[3] I hope you are having great luck, peaches . . . and working hard, It is such a beautiful book, an important one really.[4] Finish it and come on home. Meanwhile, oodles of passion

t

p.s. My address in New York is 1060 Park Avenue

[Collection Beinecke Library, Yale University]

TO DONALD WINDHAM

[New York]
[19 October 1948]

Donny lamb,
    Thank you for the card, sweetie; and I feel a wretch not to have written you sooner, but ah! I'm just beginning to get on my feet, following a few rude experiences; however, I suppose everything is going to work out now. I have started to work again on that story I was doing in Sirmione, and hope to finish it this week.[5] Nothing could have pleased me more than to hear

---

[1] A European sleeping car.
[2] *The Glass Menagerie.*
[3] Capote did get passage, and he and Williams returned to America together.
[4] Windham was writing his first novel, *The Dog Star.*
[5] Probably either "Master Misery" or "Children on Their Birthdays."

you have sent off your book: it is so very beautiful and moving, I think of it constantly. But this business about a publisher is very important, my dear; I have no intention whatever of allowing you to let that book get lost in a shuffle. It <u>must</u> be published by a first-rate house . . . in which category I do not, for a variety of reasons, include Harcourt. I am mad for Random to do it, especially if [Albert] Erskine or [Robert] Linscott will take it over. They have asked [Audrey] Wood for it, but I do not think as yet she has recieved [*sic*] the mss.[1]

Congratulate me, sweetie, I won the O.Henry Memorial award, 300 bucks, so trotted right out and had myself a suit made at Knize for 400 bucks . . . which is merely to show you how close I am to the edge of madness.[2] Also, as Sandy [Campbell] may have written you, I was arrested for illegally entering Tenn's apt., a circumstance which Mr Winchell and others have very much enjoyed. It is too involved a tale for telling here, but some day, over a relaxing martini, I guarantee an amusing half hour.[3]

Tenn had a party last night for the departing company of S and S . . . awfully pleasant, with Marlon [Brando] appearing in what might as well have been a jock-strap union suit.[4] Sandy was there with his new dyed hair, which I don't especially like.[5] What a sweet boy he is though. I have seen him two or three times since I came back. He is missing you very much, most certainly. But then, so am I . . . which is to say, when are you coming back? Soon, soon, dearheart; meanwhile, much love

t

P.S. Please send me your list of titles.

[Collection Beinecke Library, Yale University]

---

[1] Audrey Wood was a literary agent.

[2] Capote won first prize in the annual O. Henry Awards for his story "Shut a Final Door," which had been published in *The Atlantic Monthly*, August 1947.

[3] It was, indeed, an amusing story. One night Capote and Andrew Lyndon decided to visit Tennessee Williams unannounced. Hearing no answer to their knock, Capote suggested they wait for him inside, and he had Lyndon push him through the transom. This feat of athleticism attracted the attention of three passing guardians of the law—two plainclothesmen and a policewoman—who entered the house after them and kept them in custody until Williams, accompanied by Gore Vidal, finally returned. "They broke into your house—do you want to press charges?" Williams was asked. Enjoying himself immensely, Williams appeared undecided. "Listen, Tennessee," said Capote, "don't you do anything of the sort!" Williams didn't, and the housebreakers were released.

[4] Williams's play *Summer and Smoke* was to close January 1, 1949. Brando was the star of *A Streetcar Named Desire,* another Williams play then on Broadway.

[5] Campbell also had a part in *Streetcar.*

The Years of Adventure: Off to See the World

FOR TEN YEARS, FROM 1949 TO 1959, Truman Capote lived outside the United States, returning only for relatively brief periods. A few months after they met, at the end of February 1949, he and Jack Dunphy sailed for Europe on the *Queen Mary.* They traveled through France, where Dunphy had fought during World War II, to Italy, where they spent several weeks on the island of Ischia, near Naples. From Ischia they went to Tangier for another prolonged stay. Returning to New York at the end of the year, they sailed for Europe again in April 1950, ending up in Taormina, an ancient resort town in Sicily, where they rented the same house D. H. Lawrence had occupied twenty-five years earlier.

After *Other Voices, Other Rooms,* Capote had begun a second novel, a social comedy set in New York that he titled *Summer Crossing.* Finally concluding that it was, in his words, "thin, clever, unfelt," he chose a subject closer to his heart, his Alabama boyhood. That book, *The Grass Harp,* whose characters he borrowed from the elderly cousins who had raised him in Monroeville, was published in 1951. At the urging of Arnold Saint-Subber, a producer with a record of hits, Capote then adapted it for Broadway. *The Grass Harp* was not one of Saint Subber's successes, however, and Capote and Dunphy returned to Italy, where Capote was soon recruited to help salvage two ailing screenplays—one for Vittorio De Sica's *Stazione Termini* (it was called *Indiscretion of an American Wife* in the United States), the other for John Huston's *Beat the Devil.* The first film, which starred Jennifer Jones and Montgomery Clift, even Capote disliked. But he retained an affection for *Beat the Devil,* for which he bears much more responsibility—the screenplay was almost entirely his. Featuring Humphrey Bogart, Jennifer Jones, Gina Lollobrigida, and Robert Morley, the movie is, indeed, a small comic gem, as delightfully offbeat and surprising today as it was in 1953.

At the beginning of 1954 Capote was forced to make a hurried trip home. Beset by financial troubles—Joe Capote had been fired from his job on Wall Street and faced criminal charges for misappropriating funds—his mother, Nina, had swallowed a bottle of Seconals and had fallen into a coma. She died on January 4, before Capote could reach her bedside and just a few weeks shy of her forty-ninth birthday. Though their differences had been profound, her only child, who had been the principal support for her and Joe Capote for many months, was nonetheless deeply affected. "She didn't have to do it," he told Andrew Lyndon. "She didn't have to die. I've got money."

Not long after his mother's funeral Capote resumed work on another play Saint Subber had convinced him to write: a musical adaptation of his short story "House of Flowers." Set in Port-au-Prince, Haiti, the musical version centered around the rivalry of the city's two reigning madams and the innocent young lovers who were caught in between. Capote wrote the book, Harold Arlen composed the music, and they collaborated on the lyrics. Once again, Saint Subber provided a first-class production, but once again Capote's play was doomed to a relatively short run, 165 performances. Within hours after it closed in May 1955, Capote and Dunphy returned to Europe.

For several years Capote had been intrigued by the possibilities of non-fiction. He had written many short factual articles, mostly about the places he had visited, but at the end of 1955 he had an opportunity to do something longer. Breaking through the ice of the Cold War, an all-black troupe was going to the Soviet Union to present George Gershwin's opera *Porgy and Bess* in Moscow and Leningrad (now St. Petersburg). Capote went along, and the result was *The Muses Are Heard,* a short book one reviewer aptly described as "wicked, witty and utterly devastating."

Toward the end of the decade Capote finally wrote a social comedy set in New York. He called it *Breakfast at Tiffany's,* modeling his scatty central character, Holly Golightly, on half a dozen of the charming young beauties he had squired around Manhattan during and after World War II. The list started with Phoebe Pierce, his old Greenwich chum, but it also included Gloria Vanderbilt, Carol Marcus, Doris Lilly, Anky Larrabee, and Oona O'Neill, Eugene O'Neill's daughter. "The most perfect writer of my generation" was how Norman Mailer described Capote after reading *Breakfast at Tiffany's*. "He writes the best sentences word for word, rhythm upon rhythm. I would not have changed two words in *Breakfast at Tiffany's,* which will become a small classic."

The letters Capote wrote during the fifties include the same cast of characters he had known in the forties. Among them were Leo Lerman, Donald Windham, John Malcolm Brinnin and Andrew Lyndon. But there were additions. Newton Arvin was one (if there were earlier letters, as seems likely, they cannot be found). William Goyen, a writer from Texas whose career he encouraged, was another. Bennett Cerf, his Random House publisher, and his wife, Phyllis, were two more, as were David O. Selznick, the producer of *Gone with the Wind,* and his wife, Jennifer Jones.

There are a few, more businesslike letters to William Shawn, the editor of *The New Yorker.* That magazine finally ran one of Capote's articles, "A Ride Through Spain," in 1950 and then went on, over the next fifteen years, to publish several more. The letters to his revered Random House editor, Robert Linscott, gradually taper off as Capote spent more of his time on plays and screenplays and less on books. They end altogether with Linscott's retirement in 1958. Perhaps his best new friend, as well as one of his most interesting correspondents, was Cecil Beaton. A product of both Harrow and Cambridge, the favorite photographer of the British royal family and a top theatrical designer in both London and New York, Beaton adored Capote as much as Capote adored him—though as brothers rather than lovers, despite Capote's many "Cecil Dearests."

Readers today might be puzzled by the frequent mentions of war and fears of war in Capote's letters. "No one here seems to feel there is going to be a big war," he wrote from Sicily in July 1950, just days after North Korea invaded South Korea and the United States sent in troops to prevent a Communist takeover. But many outside sleepy Sicily thought there might be a big war, and for most of the decade a conflict between East and West was, in fact, a distinct possibility.

TO ANDREW LYNDON

[Hotel d'Angleterre, Rome]
[18 March 1949]
New address: Bel Soggiorno
Taormina
Sicily[1]

Lovely you—

Both your sweet letters reached me here today—I just arrived myself from Florence: Tenn [Tennessee Williams] drove us down; quel journey, mon cher, what with Tenn losing the mss. of his new play, the police arresting Frankie [Merlo][2] (for traffic violations) and all of us in hysterias of fatigue: when we finally reached Rome it developed some piece of Roman trade had looted T.W.'s apt and all of us [were] afraid to go to the jail and identify him. We were in Rome last week before setting off on this unfortunate junket to Florence. In Venice some boy tried to kill himself in Peggy Guggenheim's palazzo where we were visiting. I can't tell you! But it is beautiful here now, really breathtaking. Marian [Ives] sent me a batch of reviews,[3] mostly very good, though some from small-town papers are absolutely screaming: my dear, do you know you are consorting with a "sick and terrified child"? If the New Yorker ever reviews it, do send it.

I am very upset about Random House and Phoebe. That is all too stupid for anything. They must be out of their minds. I am going to write Linscott to that effect. That is silly about the Atlantic, too.[4] Why don't you send it to Mademoiselle? I wish I could see your new one.

---

[1] He did not actually go to Sicily at this time.
[2] Merlo was Williams's new lover.
[3] The reviews were of his second book, *A Tree of Night and Other Stories*, published by Random House on February 28, 1949.
[4] *The Atlantic* had apparently turned down one of Lyndon's short stories.

Baby, could you send me a batch of magazines, like the Partisan, New Yorker, etc. We have nothing to read. I know it will cost a lot (air mail) but if it does not exceed $10 please do and I will send you a check. Has <u>Life</u> ever run the pictures of your sister and your Grandmother Grover Whelen?

That's funny about M.L.A. [Mary Louise Aswell]. Do you suppose her old man browns her? She ought to kick that dickey-Licker in the balls (?) and throw him in the street.[1]

Jack is fine, and sends his best. Give Harold a great big kiss and tell him I'm getting <u>everything</u> he always wanted for me—daily, nightly and after lunch.

I love you; I love your big brown eyes and your long long lashes. Oh dear, I do miss you

T

[Collection New York Public Library]

TO DONALD WINDHAM AND SANDY CAMPBELL

[Hotel d'Angleterre]
[Rome]
[ca. 25 March 1949]

Donny dear, Sandy Lamb—

Have lost track of time, but <u>think</u> I arrived in Rome a week ago: however we were no sooner here (literally) than T.W + F. [Tennessee Williams and Frank Merlo] had us in their car skidding (literally) over the hills to Florence, where all was almond blossoms and spring green—though we <u>did</u> have one little adventure, oh yes oh yes: first off, 10 [Tennessee] lost his typewriter and the mss. of his new play (still unrecovered, though expected momentarily); secondly, F. and the cabaneri (sp?) of Firenzi disagreed over certain traffic laws (less said about this etc.); and lastly, we slunk back into Rome to discover thieves had paid a call chez Williams for purposes of loot—said parties are now in the clink but 10 refuses to go there and iden-

---

[1] After her divorce from Edward Aswell, Mary Louise had married Fritz Peters, a writer who had spent much of his boyhood with Gurdjieff, the Greco-Armenian mystic who led a quasi-religious movement. Claiming, almost certainly accurately, that Peters had tried to seduce him, Capote tried to prevent the marriage, an attempt that caused a temporary rift in his relations with a woman he so obviously adored.

tify them: some little something makes him suspect they are trade of fond remembrance. 10, by the way, seems very well, a little restless perhaps; he is very devoted to F.—who is most certainly a kind, sweet boy. They are leaving Rome soon, either for Sicily or Paris: word has reached here that Maria B. [Britneva] is on her way.[1] She writes 10 almost every day. Tell her please that I delivered the folder—but that if she sees me to stay clear as I will slap her in the tits and kick her down the Spanish steps: you should see the things she has written 10 about me! Quel bitch. I mean this, you tell her. She is a dreadful liar. Everyone here asks after Donny and wonders when he is coming back: they say he "fits in," whatever that means. Are you coming, pet? We are leaving the first of the week for Sicily; heavens [sic] knows for how long, so do write me soon. The address: Bel Soggiorno, Taormina, Sicily. Love to you both

    T

P.S. Donny, what happened at Knopf?

[Collection Beinecke Library, Yale University]

TO LEO LERMAN

    March 25 1949
    Pensione De Lustro
    Forio D'ischia,
    Naples, Italy

Leo Love—
    Am settled at last my dear—on this strange, rather fantastic island off the coast from Naples: but Lord, what a series of journeys we had before reaching here—Paris, Venice, Florence, Perugia, Rome, Naples—some of it beautifully happy, but all of it cold. But this is a wonderful place; we have a charming apartment high-up overlooking the Meditternean [sic]; it is perhaps a little primitive (after dark we live by candle-light, a la 1453)[2] and more than a little isolated, but I think it is a fine place to be: Paris and

---

[1] Maria Britneva, later Maria St. Just, was one of Tennessee Williams's closest friends, his literary executor, and the model for Maggie in *Cat on a Hot Tin Roof* (1955).
[2] Lerman's address was 1453 Lexington Avenue.

Rome are filled with more monsters than Huysmans[1] ever concieved [*sic*] of. We decided against Sicily: all the reports were unvaryingly dismal and, aside from Forio being quite as beautiful, it has the added advantage of being a great deal cheaper—we live together for $2 a day including the apt, a maid, and all food (delicious). If Richard [Hunter] is taking a boat which lands in Naples tell him to come & visit us—tell him to come by in any event. Of course they will like the cities more. Rome and Paris are very expensive, though. The exchange for the Lira is dropping steadily. Tell them not to change their money until they reach Rome. I miss you Leo darling and hope always that you will be coming here. Write me all your news and send me all your love—as I send you mine

    T.

[Collection Columbia University Library]

TO CECIL BEATON

Cecil dearest—

    Pensione De Listro
    Forio D'ischia
    Prov. Di Napoli, Italy
    March 25 1949

After a voyage that was not so bon but certainly voyage, we arrived in Paris with raw tempers and even rawer colds—and looking for all the world like the Gish girls at their most pitiable moment. I tried twice calling Broadchalke 211: the first time with no success and on the second experiment I had quite a fuzzy conversation with some English dame who at length confirmed that this was not the residence of Mr Cecil Beaton. Alas, we went our way—to a snowy Venice, a rainy Florence, an expensive Rome, a crooked Naples—where we took the boat to this island—which is I must say another matter altogether: it is really very beautiful and strange: we have about a whole floor on the water-front overlooking the sea, the sun is diamond-hard and everywhere there is the pleasant Southern smell of wisteria and lemon leaves. I do so wish, dear heart, that you could fly here for a week or so: we could bathe all day (there are hot springs running into the

---

[1] Belgian naturalistic novelist J.-K. Huysmans.

sea) and laugh all night: think how charming you would look with a dark Italian tan. Or a dark Italian: there are many beauties of nature here. You were so delightfully starry-eyed that night you sailed: do you still twinkle? Please, I hope so. I am writing a book, and, silly goose that I am, I seem to think myself very happy—so perhaps I am. But happy or not, I miss you, sweet Cecil, and long so to see you. Write me—meanwhile,

mille tendresse [sic]

Truman

[Collection St. John's College, Cambridge University]

TO ANDREW LYNDON

Pensione Di Lustro
Forio D'Ischia
Naples
March 28 1949

Darling—

Your letter, the one forwarded from Rome, came this morning—and was a joy, even though it contained that item from the magazine which once advertised itself as "not for the Old Lady from Dubuque"; on the contrary, she must now surely be the audience they are aiming at. Am much amused by the Mme's McCarthy & Trilling.[1] If Diana wants really to know why this "alarming" increase in dickey-lickers, all she has to do is sit down and take a square look at herself in the mirror.[2] As for Fritz, do you mean to say he is writing a <u>third</u> novel? Or is this the second one? Oh dear, the Short Happy Life of Fritz Peters. I hope he does get five figures from Hollywood—then he can retire to New Mexico and pick fleas off the cattle. Where did you hear all the divine Yaddo gossip? I'm glad that Newton's resignation was not accepted; if there is going to be a Yaddo, he ought to have something to do with it.[3] Has he been in New York? I have not heard from him in several weeks.

---

[1] Critics Mary McCarthy and Diana Trilling.
[2] Diana Trilling had written an article in which she complained about homosexuality in postwar writing.
[3] Arvin was on Yaddo's board.

Ischia is the strangest, most haunting and beautiful place; nothing short of a hundred pages could describe it. We have a vast apartment high-up overlooking the sea; already I have the best tan I ever had—the sun is dazzling but the nights are very cold. The boat to Naples takes 3 hours and only goes 3 times a week, so when we go in for a round of city pleasure we have to stay over night. Naples is a mad place.

Tenn & Frankie drove us from Rome to Naples; there is no use going into all the details (and it would look like the London telephone directory if I did) but they got on my nerves so much I was ready for murder. They were coming on to Ischia, but in Naples we all had a terrific falling out and Jack and I proceeded alone.[1] However, we had only been here two days when who comes paddling to shore but those two. I could've screamed! But they had decided to be forgiving & forgetting (God help me!) and so here they are. We pray every minute they will go away. Taken in tiny doses I'm really very fond of them both, but darling I can't tell you what it's been like. They have simply latched onto us like barnacles. Frankie nags T.W. all day and night, and T.W., I have discovered, is a genuine paranoid. Please don't say anything about this to anyone. I wrote Phoebe, but it is better that no one else hears about it.

But other than that, baby, I am fine—knock on wood. We will stay here until we go back to Paris, which will probably be in June.

I miss you and miss you. Jack says hello. A big kiss for Harold and oo-dles of love from your

T

P.S. Darling, would you look by the Perroquet and see if it is really closed? I pd. those crooks in advance, and so naturally etc.

[Collection New York Public Library]

---

[1] The altercation came after Capote repeated a story that he had heard from friends in New York: that Margo Jones, the producer of *Summer and Smoke,* had gathered the cast together and said, "This is a play by a dying man." Williams, a famous hypochondriac, took deep offense. He picked up a table in Naples's Grand Hotel, where they were staying, turned it over on Capote and disappeared. "Tell me!" Williams wrote to Donald Windham on March 23. "What do you think Truman is, a bitch or not? I can never quite make up my mind about it."

TO ROBERT LINSCOTT

Pensione Di Lustro
Forio D'ischia
Naples, Italy
April 1st, 1949

Dear Bob—

What a strange, and strangely enchanted, place this is: an encantada in the Meditteranean [sic]. It is an island off the coast from Naples, very primitive, populated mostly by winegrowers, goatherders, W.H. Auden and the Mussolini family. I have a vast room overlooking the sea: it is wonderful to work in and I am doing quite a lot. Tennesee [Tennessee] W. has been here with us the last week but is leaving today. There is nothing to do but write and read and, thank God, I am reasonably content. The main batch of my reviews have gone astray, but those that have reached me are not too bad all in all and anyway not of that particular milieu where such things are made so much to matter I couldn't care less. But how does it go? The book, I mean: are you satisfied or is it a disappointment? You can tell me truthfully. I have fine hopes for <u>Summer Crossing</u>, and I feel alive and justified in doing it, but it makes me nervous all the time, which is probably a good sign, and I do not feel like talking about it, which is another.[1]

I suppose soon now you will have started going to your farm—I hope it will be a lovely spring, Bob, and that all your weekends there will be as good as you are.

I miss you; write me—and best love
Truman

[Collection Columbia University Library]

---

[1] *Summer Crossing*, his first novel after *Other Voices*, was soon abandoned.

TO DONALD WINDHAM

> Pensione di Lustro
> Forio D'ischia
> Naples
> April 12 1949

Donny dear—

Unlike you, I'm surprised you didn't get the Guggenheim: who are they for if not for you? You had such a very good list of sponsors I thought you probably would get it. And what of Random. I wrote Linscott a letter, but he has not answered yet. Thank you, dear, for the review. As it was the only even literate one the book got I enjoyed seeing it. Tenn & Frankie have returned to Rome. They have their troubles, and I feel vaguely that we aggravated them; left to themselves I think they get along fine: in the company of others the gestures of lovers become perhaps too meaningful, are thrown too much into relief—especially with two people like T + F, neither of whom is sure of the other.

You ask about [William] Aalto and [James] Schuyler.[1] Well, that is a story. They have divorced and in the most dramatic of fashions. According to Jimmy, Aalto is insane, has been insane for a very long time, all of which bothered him not one whit until one night about two months [ago] when Aalto tried to kill him.[2] My private suspicion is that there is a great deal to be said on both sides. Jimmy, who is still here, is carrying on an affair with a tiresome little party named Charles Heilleman, Aalto is living in Rome, and sends Jimmy three letters a day, which may be a sign of insanity, but I, the hopeless romantic, think it very sweet, for all the letters say is I love you, come back! come back!

Salvatori is here. He arrived, accompanied by his new keeper, namely Boo [Robert] Faulkner, only a few hours after Tenn left—dear Tenn, lucky to the last. Though I've scarcely spoken to him, he seems to be a sweet quiet boy. What a pity, though, that he has to trail around with that broken-down <u>wastrel</u>. He has a picture of you which he carries in his wallet—he

---

[1] Aalto was a Communist who had fought in the Spanish Civil War in the late thirties. Not long after the United States entered World War II he was recruited by the OSS (Office of Strategic Services), the precursor of the CIA. When they learned he was homosexual, both the OSS and the Communist Party expelled him from their ranks, proving that prejudice has no ideology. The younger Schuyler had had a less dramatic past; he was considered a member of the New York School of poets, along with John Ashbery, Frank O'Hara, Kenneth Koch and Barbara Guest.

[2] According to Donald Windham in his memoir, *Lost Friendships*, Aalto had broken a bottle of grappa over Schuyler's head.

likes to show it to people: "My good friend, Donald Windham? You know him?"

So Sandy is staying in the show.[1] Does that mean you will be in New York all summer? Would you like to go to Yaddo for a month or two. If so, write to Elizabeth Ames at once, and I will write her, too. You might like it there. I did.

What did you think of The Christmas Tree?[2] I thought it good—with about two million reservations.

Give my love to Sandy. I miss you 25 hours of the day. Best love

T

[Collection Beinecke Library, Yale University]

TO JOHN MALCOLM BRINNIN

Pensione di Lustro
Forio d'Ischia
Naples
April 19, 1949

Malcolm dear,

No doubt you've had my other letter by now, and your second arrived yesterday. Congratulations on being the new director of the Poetry Center.[3] As for your proposal, it seems to me a very nice one, and I should be delighted to comply—though I suppose this depends a little on <u>when</u> such an event would take place: do let me know what date you have in mind.[4]

Yes, I sent M.L. [Aswell] a proper if rather hypocritical, expression of sentiment.[5] What does B. Lawrence have to say about it? M.L. writes me they are coming here in September.

Too bad about Lowell.[6] I had a long letter from Newton detailing the whole thing. He sees quite a lot of Burford: innocently, or so he says, and

---

[1] A Streetcar Named Desire.
[2] The Christmas Tree (1949), the second novel by Isabel Bolton (pseudonym of Mary Britton Miller).
[3] From 1949 to 1956 Brinnin was the director of the Young Men's and Young Women's Hebrew Association Poetry Center, or the "92nd Street Y," as it was informally called.
[4] Brinnin had apparently asked Capote to give a reading at the Poetry Center.
[5] A note of congratulations on her marriage to Fritz Peters.
[6] Robert Lowell had several nervous breakdowns.

doubtless it is. What sort of person is Burford? I get no picture of him at all. And I wish you would stop teasing and tell me about Bill. For that matter, what has happened to the Boston Bill? You are very lax.

Have you heard anything about my book? It is so very strange—nobody mentions it, not even, in his letters to me, Linscott. I have the feeling that it has evaporated, or, indeed, was never printed at all.

Jack is fine: the most beautiful color. And he is learning how to sail a boat. We sailed all around the island this past weekend. Do you know anything about this boy William Goyen? His story in the March Horizon was, while a very bad story indeed, certainly well written. You ought to try and get him for D.M.[1] Best love, [unclear]

T

[Collection University of Delaware Library]

TO ANDREW LYNDON

Forio D'Ischia
April 20 1949

Darling Baby—

Why am I a monster child? My love is with you every minute, watching over you brighter than an Easter star. You and Phoebe [Pierce] are all that I miss. Thank you, precious, for the Guggenheim list. Who are those people? It does quite turn my stomach. What a shame that George did not get it.[2] I really hoped he might; but as usual, sister, your prophecies bore fruit.

This is my new letter style—it all looks like blank verse: very blank. Or chicken-shit, as dear Biddy [Helen Eustis] would say.

That's quite tiresome about Arthur Miller; the only tragedy involved is that, good in some ways as his play is, we should be in a position where there is nothing very much better to applaud.[3]

I envy you Lee Wiley.[4] The phonograph, alas, is broken, so I do not have even that solace. I am terribly bored with the Auden set here. They are

[1] Dodd, Mead, the publisher.
[2] It is unclear who the George was who was refused a Guggenheim fellowship.
[3] Arthur Miller's play *Death of a Salesman* (1949) won the Pulitzer Prize for drama.
[4] Lee Wiley was a singer who recorded songs with such jazz giants as Eddie Condon and Bobby Hackett.

really quite impossible. A good many dreary people have shown up in the last week, but we are going to stay on through May, for really it is a lovely place.

We are going tomorrow for a few days to a little fishing village near here called San Angelo. There are two German queens over there who run a delightful pensione.

Darling it is getting late and I do want to get this off to you. Love to Harold, and 57 varieties of love and kisses for my sweet sister

T

[Collection New York Public Library]

TO CECIL BEATON

Pensione Di Lustro
Forio D'ischia
Prov. Di Napoli
Italy
May 1st 1949

Cecil, love—
Or Beaton, baby
What a joy your letter was; though that was stupid about your cold; but you are all well now, I'm sure, and up to great things, while here still am I languishing on this primitive outpost. I want to stay another month, however, then go to Paris for at least the better part of June: maybe somehow we will see you around that time.

Personally, I prefer imagining you among your roses and cows[1] than in either the Plaza or amid the plumbing facilities of Mr Maughm [W. Somerset Maugham]: also, it is a better place to complete your second-act surgery:[2] as for the absence of loved ones, that, dear-heart, can sometimes be a blessing. Especially if you are trying to work.

It looks as if I am going to be evicted by long-distance from my New

---

[1] Beaton had recently moved into a new country house in Wiltshire, a county west of London.
[2] Beaton had spent part of the winter at Maugham's house, the Villa Mauresque, in the south of France. An enormously successful playwright as well as a novelist, Maugham had suggested changes to Beaton's play *The Gainsborough Girls*. All for naught. The critics were merciless, and the play was a flop.

York apartment. The owners want it for themselves. Nothing could be more trying.

Dear Juliet Duff is quite right: what did Theatre Arts do to me?[1] Little [Richard] Avedon has proved himself quite untrustworthy.[2] But do give the ogod boy my fondest.

Has Peter Watson arrived back in London? With or without Waldemar?[3] That poor tyke.

Wystan Auden has arrived here in Forio accompanied by an entourage of rather dismal youngsters—some of them not so young. And, except for Wystan, they are not very matey, but remain grandly aloof. I understand, too, that the horror's horror, and I do mean Brian Howard, is on his way here.[4]

So I daresay that by the end of May we shall leave without regret.

I am attending to my work with a fair degree of concentration; that makes me content; and so does Jack, who has proved to be a really astonishing person—of a perceptivity too rarely encountered and a strength almost never. He says you have beautiful eyes—and they are, Cecil dear: tender, blue

lovely as you

much, much love

T

[Collection St. John's College, Cambridge University]

TO ANDREW LYNDON

Forio D'Ischia
[2] May 1949

Andrew darling—

I've had a premonition you were in Macon; well, at least I was right in one particular: someone was away: Harold, according to our beautiful PP

---

[1] Lady Juliet Duff, daughter of the Fourth Earl of Lonsdale, was a friend to writers, politicians, and artists.

[2] Richard Avedon was one of *Harper's Bazaar*'s lead photographers.

[3] Peter Watson was a British millionaire and patron of the arts; Waldemar Hansen, an American writer, Capote's age exactly, was his lover.

[4] Though both his parents were American, Brian Howard, a product of both Eton and Oxford, was quintessentially English. One of the flamboyant Oxford aesthetes of the twenties, he was the model for some of Evelyn Waugh's characters, including Ambrose Silk in *Put Out More Flags* and Anthony Blanche in *Brideshead Revisited*. Borrowing a phrase once applied to Lord Byron, Waugh described him as "mad, bad, and dangerous to know."

[Phoebe Pierce], has been in California: why? Give him a kiss for me, and tell him I'm glad he's home again—I don't like to think of him out there in the land of strawberry-flavored coffee.

Elinor M's party sounds as though it were at least a little amusing: that precious Lee Wiley. And Phoebe says Jordan [Massee] has been in town: how did he seem and why was he there?[1] I had two accounts of MLA's soiree; Phoebe's, and another from Malcolm—he was full of praise for you both—says you are charming and intelligent—calls Phoebe "wonderfully keen and wildly attractive." Poor Malcolm. His romance has busted, and he is very unhappy.

I think the title of Phoebe's new story lovely: A Fall of Rain. And you, sweet magnolia, what are you working on? If you have done a new story, please send it to me.

My book has changed somewhat since I outlined it slightly to you.[2] I feel very much that my writing has grown (though this may be a delusion), and the time has come when I must shoulder some real responsibility; that is, I want for once to pose a problem and provide an answer, too. I do after all profess to some sort of style, and that is something I can hope only to improve upon; but the material and my own view toward it are different from anything I've attempted before. God, what a revolting mess it could be. And may.

I had a letter from Newton yesterday: midway in the text, and with his usual cunning, there were inserted a few lines to the effect that he was dedicating his book to David Lillienthal [Lilienthal].[3] Pretty extraordinary, when you think how often he has inferred the honor was to be mine. Our present circumstances have nothing to do with it; I realize now that he never intended to dedicate the book to me: honestly, I don't care about that, but somehow the symbol is so profound I can't dismiss it. Poor man, he is a true coward; and what is worse, a moderate coward. Moderation is the key to his character. I should be a fool to despise him: so I don't: but I would be a greater fool if I did not despise myself: how pitiful it was of me to have put that vast love into such feeble hands—hands that never closed over it but let it dribble through the fingers like water.

Have you glanced at the new John Horne Burns book?[4] Seen South Pacific, Detective Story or a movie called The Fallen Idol? Did Diable Au

---

[1] Massee was Carson McCullers's cousin.

[2] Summer Crossing.

[3] Arvin dedicated his biography of Herman Melville to his old friend David E. Lilienthal, chairman of the U.S. Atomic Energy Commission from 1946 to 1950. Capote, by contrast, had dedicated Other Voices, Other Rooms to Arvin.

[4] Lucifer with a Book (1949), a novel about postwar life at a coed American private school.

<u>Corps</u> ever open?[1] Did you get Christopher's letter from Leo? What did he have to say? Tell me about these things. Life is so circumscribed here. On top of which I've broken my glasses and so am staggering around absolutely blind.

Jack is fine and sweet as pie. He sends you his best, and Harold, too. I've already sent Harold a kiss, but here are several million more (for which I will have to pay extra postage). I love you, precious baby, darling child, and in my dreams frame your mad adorable face with a wreath of roses

T

[Collection New York Public Library]

TO ROBERT LINSCOTT

Pensione di Lustro
Forio D'ischia
Prov. Di Napoli
Italia
May 6 1949

Dear Bob—
Your letter was too brief a treat, but a treat all the same: there is only one excitement to my day, and that is when the postman comes. Ah, what a joy it is when he has a little something for me: so, even if you don't have time to write, just send me a lot of old circulars.

Except for the customary anxietys [sic], and a stomach that has finally revolted against Italian food, I guess I'm fine. When I finish the chapter I'm working on now I will have done ⅓ of the book—which is making very good time, don't you think? If I can finish a draft of it here before going home, then I probably will have it all polished by the first of the year, which means you could publish it the following June—that is, if you have a mind to. But we will see what happens—it is by so far the most difficult thing I ever tried to do.

<u>Other Voices</u> has appeared here in Italy and has had very good reviews. Did you know it has been banned in Ireland? Marion tells me <u>Tree</u> has sold

---

[1] The French film *Le Diable au corps* (1946) opened in the United States in 1949 as *Devil in the Flesh*.

6300: neither good nor bad; maybe it will sell more.[1] I rather liked the review Leslie Fiedler wrote of it in The Nation.

I hope you are well Bob, enjoying your elegant phonograph and having good weekends on the farm. I shall probably be leaving Ischia around June 6. Write me before then, and give my best to the Messrs Haas, Cerf and Cummins.[2]

Always,
Truman

[Collection Columbia University Library]

TO DONALD WINDHAM

Pensione di Lustro
Forio D'Ischia
May 7 1949

D dear—

A joy forever is a letter: thank you, baby, and for the clipping, too—though that good old standby, the Rome Daily American, had given us a few of the facts. Had a note from 10 [Tennessee Williams] saying he was London-bound: it never occured [sic] to me that Britaneva [Maria Britneva] bitch might be the cause. Maybe they'll be married yet. Ugh.

Auden's [W. H. Auden] arrival has thrown something of a gloom over Ischia. He is furious because anyone other than himself is here—seems to feel the place belongs to him; and is, in fact, downright rude about it. Such a tiresome old Aunty. I'm glad I don't have to see him. But there are quite a few people here now, most of them very nice—though I suppose it is beginning to look like a Meditternean [sic] version of Fire Island. I gave Jimmy [Schuyler] your love and he sends you his and says he is going to write you when he gets a grip on himself. I think he feels rather sad. I like him, too. But Jack so dislikes the Santa Lucia set (Chester's word)[3] and is so disagreeable to them that we don't get together often. Oh dear, I sup-

---

[1] Marion Ives, his literary agent. Linscott replied that sales were actually 6,500 and still moving.

[2] Robert Haas, Bennett Cerf and Saxe Cummins, Linscott's colleagues at Random House.

[3] Chester Kallman, American poet and librettist, W. H. Auden's longtime partner.

pose this is what happens on an island. They, the Santa Lucia set, were dreadfully and overtly rude to 10 when he was here: that is what brought Jack against them.

I'm bored with R. H [Random House]; and the news of your book bores me more: <u>who</u> turned it down? Pat Covici at Viking is an affabble [*sic*] guy, but a little stupid; however, you might be able to come to some kind of understanding with him.

I have a whole new collection of Buffie J. [Johnson] stories—mostly about her Hindu lover: <u>the</u> ugliest man you ever put eye to.[1]

I'm so hungry: go out to Hicks and have a nice ice cream parfait in my honor.

Why did Irene [Selznick] let Sandy go?[2] Is she bringing the whole Chicago Co. intact? Personally, I think Sandy should be relieved: he'll get a lot more out of going to the Cape than staying in a show all summer. Give him my love. And my love to you, honey

    T

<u>write</u>!!!

[Collection Beinecke Library, Yale University]

TO ANDREW LYNDON

[Forio D'Ischia, Italy]
May 8 1949

Darling, darling, darling—

I feel full of love for you today; woke up thinking about you and wishing that it wasn't Sunday so there would be at least the hope of a letter: that was a sweet one from you early in the week. The Lottie episode fills me with disgust—how vulgar can you get? Of course it was only to make eventual trouble between you and Harold: he's tried the same sort of thing with Jack and me. I think you behaved admirably. Excuse my handwriting, precious, but the flies are about to drive me insane—it is just like down home, except they haven't any screens here. I'm glad Harold is back, the lamb. I'll

---

[1] Buffie Johnson was an American artist.
[2] Selznick was the producer of *A Streetcar Named Desire,* in which Sandy Campbell had a part.

<u>bet</u> you missed him. Let all these cunts have their cruising, <u>I'll</u> take the
married life any time. I sure do feel married, honey: I've even started baking that man chocolate cakes—and he is more sweet and wonderful than I
could have ever imagined. He says you have beautiful eyes, and you do, little love. Darling, if the Pisas make me move out, as they are trying to do
(the unscrupulous bastards) then I want Harold to go there and take not
only his things but the chandelier as well. I want him to have the chandelier in any event; but I will let you know what happens.

Princess Margaret came to Ischia yesterday and we threw flowers from
the balcony. Quel camp. And in the evening I gave a dance-ball on the roof
with lanterns to assist the moon and Tears-of-Christ punch to assist the
spirit. Chester Kalman [Kallman] and Jimmy Schuyler and Ralph
Pomeroy[1] came in drag: rather amusing, though I don't like Chester.

A kiss for Harold,
and a thousand tenderresses [sic] darling
T

[Collection New York Public Library]

TO PEARL KAZIN[2]

Pensione di Lustro
Forio D'Ischia
May 16 1949

Poil my Pearl—
Wasn't that clever, the way I got you to write me a letter? But really, darling, you don't know how grateful I am: recieving [sic] mail is a serious
problem when you are as cut off from the world as we are. But little scraps
keep drifting in, such as Mr Pomeroy: an ambitious young man—can he
write? Anyway, he has gone away, but there are others, horrors like B. V.
Winebaum, who says he knows you: <u>wherever</u> from, dear.[3] But Jack and I
live an isolated life—both of us working very hard. I have a good start on
my book, and, with any luck, should have something like a draft finished

---

[1] Ralph Pomeroy was a poet and art critic.
[2] Pearl Kazin was an editor at *Harper's Bazaar*.
[3] B. V. Winebaum, author of *Postcards & Snaps* (limited edition, 1965).

before coming home. Nothing amusing happens: except I've taken to baking cakes—is that amusing? Also, Jack caught a rabbit and we made a rabbit stew. Before that, I had a pet bird, but it flew away before we could find a suitable recipe. Aren't we cruel?

If, as you say, you are happy for no reason, how wonderful. That is the best kind of happy to be: so airless and independent. All other kinds of happiness seem to depend on someone else. But it is a lovely thing, that feeling you describe: like a seagull with a fish in its mouth.

The Pulitzer prizes are as shocking as usual. Peter Viereck, indeed.[1] Thought the Guggenheim list very odd, too. Still, can't get very interested. Have been reading for the first time Miss Austen: loved <u>Emma</u>, got a little wearied with <u>Persuasion</u>, and <u>Northanger Abbey</u> has worn me plumb out. E. Bowen's <u>To the North</u> is a beautiful novel, don't you think?[2]

Who misses you? None more than Truman:

Who loves you? everybody but especially Capote—

otherwise known as →

T

P.S. Write me a sweet letter.

P.P.S. Is Richard Hunter in Europe?

[Collection Pearl Kazin Bell]

TO ANDREW LYNDON

Forio D'Ischia

May 17 1949

My own and most precious baby—

<u>2</u> letters, one right after the other; what joy—but, alas, how sad, for I can't expect another for oh so long. Loved the <u>Look</u> cunt; gave me <u>just</u> the biggest thrill.

You ought to make all those gentlemen in distress chip in and buy you a mink. Really, isn't Newton shocking: that shows such lack of taste and so

---

[1] Viereck won the Pulitzer Prize for *Terror and Decorum: Poems 1940–1948* (1948).

[2] *To the North* (1932), novel by Elizabeth Bowen.

little real regard for you. He doesn't <u>see</u> people, as it were. Having him out of my head is like being rid of a tumor. As for C.I [Christopher Isherwood], I suspected what was wrong; furthermore, I think he is trying to pave the way toward a proposition. Ironical how all these things turn out. But darling, is it [Bill] Caskey[1] or Christopher who is being loud and drunk in cheap dives? There was an ambiguity in your phrasing. That shared income system is <u>screaming</u>! I wish you would write Chris just so we could find out more.

So the Massey-Bigelow's are coming back to Big Town.[2] I should think they would run an excellent book-record shop. Really, it would be the ideal thing for them. How do other people get the money for such things. It would take about $50,000 I should think. You mention Bill Hope; but how is he? Is he absolutely well? Donny wrote me that you ran into Sandy at <u>Diable</u>. Sandy, as you may know, has been fired from <u>Streetcar</u>. And Donny, poor dear, is still without a publisher: <u>everybody</u> has turned down the book. It really <u>is</u> stupid.

Jack survived the cake, and I made toll-house cookies last night. Jack caught a rabbit and we made rabbit stew: it was delicious. My real life, though, seems to have become all involved with the book: it is becoming difficult to say where one begins and the other ends.

I think your witch-idea charming and delightful, perfect for someone's October issue. Do send it to me now. I want to see the result of your operation on Miss Jenkins, too. Don't forget about the bathtub full of potato salad.

A long letter from Sister Pierce—who sounds very chipper. I wish she would finish her story. She doesn't mention it this time.

That friend of George Davis used to spend every summer at Shelter Island.[3] He seemed to like it awfully. I hope you do go there. I'm sorry, though, that you have to go to Macon, especially in June, when it is so hot.

My lungs have about given out under the impact of these manure-filled Italian cigarettes. Though I live to be a 1000, I shall never get accustomed.

The nerve of Fritz Peters! <u>Finistere</u>—is that the title of a <u>book</u>?[4] He makes me vibrate. Someone ought to shake him till his teeth fall out—that, I dare say, they would do very easily.

---

[1] An amusing and good-looking young American, Caskey was Isherwood's lover.

[2] Jordan Massee and Paul Bigelow were companions.

[3] Shelter Island is at the eastern end of Long Island, between the larger island's North and South Forks.

[4] Fritz Peters's gay-themed novel *Finistère* (1951), about an American student in France and his relationship with a teacher.

We leave here June 6, and will be in Paris a week or ten days; I will let you know a new address as soon as I do: it will be somewhere in Brittany, I think. But write me again here, and then American Express, Paris.

Jack says hello! hello! and love to Harold from me. Across the room I see someone in a mirror who says he loves you: who is he? why,
    that's
    T

[Collection New York Public Library]

TO DONALD WINDHAM

    Pensione di Lustro
    Forio D'ischia
    [Late May or early June 1949]

Donny dear—

Indeed, I would be only too delighted to take some pictures of swimmers and send them to you: alas, there are none! These fraidycat wops won't dip their toes in the water until mid-July: our own bathing activities shock them profoundly.

We are leaving here June 14th—and going directly to Paris—then, a week or two later—somewhere (I think) in Brittany. But write me here so that I will hear again from you before leaving.

Whittlesey House used to be rather dreary; but they are vastly rich, and have in the last year decided to go high-brow: they lured away a lot of top-flight people from other publishing houses (including E. C. Aswell from Harpers) and have poured great sums into the project. What about Vanguard—poor but good. Or William Sloan Associates—who are really top-flight.

Saturday's Rome Daily carried a brief item about T. Heggens [Thomas Heggen's] death: it was so ambiguously phrased that I didn't have the slightest notion of what had happened. It sounded like suicide. Was it?[1] Or do you know anything at all about it?

---

[1] According to a medical examiner in Manhattan, Heggen, the author of *Mister Roberts*, which was a novel first, then a play and a movie, was a probable suicide. He was found dead in the bathtub of his apartment. Friends, however, believed his death was the result of an accident—that, as a result of too many sleeping pills, he had fallen asleep and drowned.

There is another war on between the Santa Lucia crowd and the Di Lustro (our) set. Bu Falkner [Boo Faulkner], of the Di Lustro, is under fire from the S.L. because they claim he is overpaying the local trade: he pays 300 Lira and they give 200. Remember those thousands in Venice?

I'm working on an idea for a comic-strip: Super-queen. "It's a bird, it's a plane, <u>it's Super-queen</u>!" Speaking of super-queens, did you hear P. [Paul] Bigelow was coming back to N.Y. to live. He's going to be in the jewelry business: better put everything in the safe, dear.

I love your new song—even though it doesn't have quite the pathos of Don't Speak to Me Before Dark.

Where is Tenn now? I seem to have lost track. Is he in Paris? The [Paul] Cadmus entourage are in Florence, and creeping southward like the plague.[1]

Well, Donny dear (<u>why</u> do you call yourself Don? it's <u>so</u> unsuitable), write me a <u>2</u> page letter. Love to Sandy ("Everyman's Favorite Candy") and oodles of passion from your pasta-weary

Sister

P.S. Salvatore has departed for the army.

[Collection Beinecke Library, Yale University]

TO ANDREW LYNDON

[Forio D'Ischia, Italy]
[3 June 1949]

Baby sister—

That's a shame about the apartment: do you imagine there is some cabal against you? Darling, I hope this reaches you before you get off to Macon—not that I have anything important to say: after all, I'm still here on Forio with a lot of goats and donkeys. We are leaving the 14th. Do you remember that material I told you about in N.Y. and said I would send if I could find any. Well, I've looked here and everywhere else from Venice to

---

[1] Although seven thousand people attended his one-man show in Manhattan in 1937, Paul Cadmus's figurative and satirical style of art was out of fashion amid the abstract expressionism of the forties and fifties. He was a close friend of Jack Dunphy's.

Florence with no luck. However, I did find some stuff to have a summer suit made of (I'm <u>roasting</u>) but I don't think you would be crazy about it. Jack had a nice suit made, but that was in Naples, and I am simply not up to Naples—the thieves of Naples are not merely legend. Weren't you there during the war? An extraordinary city. We saw a "show" in a "house" there last week. Every concievable [sic] kind of fucking: they had an Arab with a cock, believe this or not, that measured a good 14 inches: pretty, too. I'm so happy about all of Phoebe's new accomplishments—can't wait to see her story. She wrote that she was having a party June 3rd in the new apt—that is today, so I hope at this very moment you are all having a rollicking good time. I'm trying to finish a chapter before leaving—but the imminence of departure has upset me. Yes, I know we will like Brittany—if only we can [find] a suitable place: I would like to take a house, and it may be that we will. I don't believe for one minute that Newton <u>ever</u> called Leo: from any angle it is absolutely illogical, don't you think? How goes your witch? Have you polished her off and thrown her into the editorial cauldron? You said you were going to send me a copy. Auden and I are being friends again. He is really very nice. That household of theirs is sompn', though. Phoebe tells me Nina [Capote] asked you to a party—I wish you had gone, it would have amused me to know what sort of people she is seeing—not that I can't imagine.[1] Tell Phoebe that the [Doris] Lilly woman wrote me a letter: yuk yuk, as Doris would say. Whatever happened to Richard Hunter—did he and Bubble-Brain sail for Europe.[2] Europe is so very unchic these days— perhaps I ought to come home: another reason, and a better one, is that Jack's <u>legal</u> wife is on her way here.[3] Those two correspond like mad. But never fear, your little sister is fully fortified: just let that two-bit song-and-dance girl put her paws on Mah Man and ah'll take a tweezer to every hair on her koozy. Which reminds me; in my idle hours here, I've thought up several commercial projects: one is called Kiddie Kits—a Kiddie Kit for a little girl will contain such items as a little cunt-wig, which will be useful for playing grown-up. For queer little boys there will be the Everhard Kid-die Kit—inside, the lucky little bastard will find a Turkish towel and a jar full of real live crabs. Speaking of which, I have a terrible case: what should I ask for in a Paris drugstore? Well, darling, on this sordid note I will leave

---

[1] Nina Capote was his mother.

[2] "Bubble-Brain" was probably Howard Rothschild, whom Capote disliked.

[3] Joan McCracken was Jack Dunphy's former wife. She was a memorable dancer and come-dienne, rising to something near stardom in the original Broadway production of *Oklahoma!*, a mu-sical in which Dunphy himself also had a part.

you. Give my love to Harold: he is mean not ever to write me even a note!
I miss you, darling lamb, and love you

avec tout mon coeur (right? Oh.)

T

P.S. I have another idea—this one for a comic strip: <u>Super-Queen</u>. "It's
a bird, it's a plane, it's . . . Super-Queen!" There's a fortune in it!

[Collection New York Public Library]

TO CECIL BEATON

Forio D'Ischia
June 6 1949

Cecil dear

You are a rascal: not to have let me hear from you for so very long! I
hope this means you have been working frightfully hard, and that you have
smoothed out all your script troubles. As you can see, I'm still here in Ischia—getting fat on pasta and less fond of all things Italian every minute.
But we are leaving here the 14th of June and arrive in Paris on the 17th.
Will be at the Hotel Pont-Royal in the Rue du Bac. I include the address
because it occurs to me that you may be in Paris then: a few days ago I saw
in the Paris Tribune that your very best friend [Greta Garbo] is expected
there June 13th—and I thought perhaps you might be coming over to meet
her. Or was it simply an erroneous report?

News reaches me that Waldemar [Hansen] is once again ensconced at
10 Palace Gate.[1] Ha! Have you noticed, everyone seems to be killing themselves—Tom Heggan [Heggen], Klaus Mann, Owen Davis—do you suppose they all just needed a rest?[2] Speaking of rests, Isherwood writes that
there is a most infamous purge on in Los Angeles—and 3 of his most intimate friends are taking a rest at state expense: San Quentin is not <u>my</u> idea
of a holiday rest.[3]

---

[1] Peter Watson's address in London.
[2] Thomas Heggen wrote *Mister Roberts*; Klaus Mann, one of Thomas Mann's sons, was also a
writer; Owen Davis, Jr., was a movie actor.
[3] They had been jailed for homosexual activity.

I have got nearly a third of my new novel done—to celebrate this I've had myself a most beautiful suit made: grey raw silk. I look almost presentable in it.

Honey, you can see how skimpy my news is—but God, what can you write from this forsaken island? We've been here nearly three months, and our contacts with the real world have long since dried up. I only wanted to send you my love: here it is—LOVE.

Truman

P.S. It is best to write c/o American Express, Paris. Please do.

[Collection St. John's College, Cambridge University]

TO CECIL BEATON

British Post Office
Tangiers, Morocco
[July 1949]

Cecil dear—

Was heartbroken not to have seen you again in Paris—alas, you were always "sortie" when I called the Littré number. The trip through Spain was ghastly—trains that took 9 hours to go 112 kilometres, food that tore my stomach apart etc. But I like Tangiers, a marvelous city really. We are living on the mountain at a place called Farhar—I should not reccomend [*sic*] it to anyone, but it will suffice. Your friend Jessie Green has rented her house to someone else—which makes me wonder, are you still coming? I very much hope so. we've had a few adventures—the most dazzling of which happened between Granada and Algeciras when suddenly everyone on the train began to scream and throw themselves on the floor: bandits! Bullets flying through the air. Only it wasn't bandits—just a group of Spaniards who had missed the train and were firing on it to make it stop: one old man got hit in the head. Lovely country. No doubt by this time you've seen George D [Davis]. He said he probably would see you in England. Isn't his rise in fortune spectacular? And I know the new magazine will be very good indeed.[1] It is an excellent

---

[1] The magazine, *Flair*, had a brief life, beginning publication in February 1950 and ending a year later.

day here, cool and the water crashing on the rocks and the sky classic in its clearness: just below me there is a quite beautiful Arab standing stark nude on a rock. And what a joy it is to be writing you this little note, Cecil dear— for it is almost like talking to you. what do you know about a young English writer named Angus Wilson? He has just published a book called <u>The Wrong Set</u>—and I think he is quite good.[1] Which reminds me—when you come, oh please could you possibly bring a copy of <u>My Royal Past</u>?[2] Do drop me a line, dear, and let me know if there is anything I can do for you here. All love

    T

[Collection St. John's College, Cambridge University]

TO ROBERT LINSCOTT

    Capote
    British Post Office
    Tangiers
    Maroc, Africa
    July 1949

Dear Bob—

How long it has been since I've heard from you—or, rather, how long it has been since you heard from me. Someone writes that it has been terribly hot at home; however, remembering your nice air-conditioned office, I haven't worried about you. Speaking of heat, look where I am: Africa, no less. Don't assume what I'm doing, for I haven't the faintest notion either; at any rate, I have a nice place to live, and am getting on with the book.

I came here by way of Spain (dreadful country), a trip I would not readily undertake again. I was in Paris a week, and had lunch one day with a friend of Bennett Cerf's—Fleur Cowles, who, in conjunction with George Davis, is starting a new magazine—something on the order of Vanity Fair— and I may do a piece for them. Anyway, if you know anyone who is looking for a job, you might send them around there, for I understand they are about to assemble a staff.

---

[1] Angus Wilson's *The Wrong Set* was his first book; it was a collection of short stories.
[2] Published in 1939, *My Royal Past* was Beaton's parody of royal memoirs.

Perhaps this little note (just to let you know I'm alive) will find you in the middle of your vacation; if so, have a good time, dear Bob—and know that I miss you. Love

T

[Collection Columbia University Library]

TO ANDREW LYNDON

British Post Office
Tangiers, Maroc
Africa
[6 July 1949]

Darlingest one,

I've written Phoebe about the journey through Spain, so maybe she has told you; it was, in a word, ghastly. Such a beautiful country, though. I even went to a museum: The Prado, natch. But am mad for Africa; life in the Casbah is quite my cup of tea. I don't think Jack is so crazy about it; he says it is no fun to live in a place where you are frightened to walk in the streets alone. All the shadiest people are gathered here because it is an international city. The most <u>extraordinary</u> people. It's the most exciting place I've ever been. If you and Phoebe were here we could all take a house in the Casbah and go native in a great big way. There is the most divine nightclub here called Parade—La Pierce would lose her mind. The nights are very cool, but the days are fearfully long and hot and mosquito-ridden: a few miles inland it is 137 in the shade—the heat <u>stings</u> your pores. We are living on a mountain in a little tiny house with a fabulous view over Tangiers and the harbor. So I'm settling down and starting back to work. Jack misses Ischia, but I guess he will get to like it here.

Saw George [Davis] in Paris; I think his new magazine sounds marvelous. A letter from Phoebe yesterday said some woman was going to act as fiction adviser to the Bazaar. If she still doesn't know who it is—<u>I</u> do: Marian Ives. But why did Pearl say that was a secret? Or maybe they have decided to make it one.

I'm all a-jitter: a doctor is coming in ten minutes to 1) give me a shot for cholera, and 2) see what he can do about my stomach, which is torn to pieces: god, he's here. (Later) Well, that wasn't so bad, though I nearly fainted at the sight of the needle—like a tiger's tooth it was, magnolia. You should have been here to hold my hand.

I miss you, little bird, it seems a century since we parted. I wish you would write me a 75 page letter. Give my love to your husband; mine sends his best, who loves you?

T does.

P.S. Also saw [William] Saroyan in Paris—in a gambling joint where he was drunk and losing thousands. He has a brain the size of a b.b. bullet. Said he was washed up avec Carol. The only intelligent thing he said.

[Collection New York Public Library]

TO ANDREW LYNDON

Tangiers
[15] July 1949

Blossom-child—

Angel, by this time you are doubtless back in New York, so am writing you there—for some reason I don't trust the Macon mail dept. But what a bore your journey must have been. Still you must have got some good things to eat, and that I envy you. Food. I seldom think of anything else. Arab cooking is the worst of all. No, precious, I'm not visiting Paul Bowles, and yes of course Jack is still with me—shaky in the legs though he be.[1] I haven't the faintest notion what brought us here, but it is quite an adventure and well worth the effort. I work in the mornings, and sleep in the afternoons (it is too hot to do anything else) and carouse around the Casbah in the evening—which I don't think half so frightening as, say, an American town. Paul & Jane [Bowles] are both here, and we see them fairly often. Cecil Beaton says he is coming in August. Darling, isn't this ironic about Christopher [Isherwood]? I told you so. But surely you have written a let-

---

[1] A writer and composer, Bowles lived in Tangier with his wife, Jane, who was both a novelist and a playwright. The Bowleses had an unusual marriage—he was homosexual and she was a lesbian—but were nonetheless devoted to each other. Capote was particularly fond of Jane Bowles; he praised the surrealistic style of a novel like *Two Serious Ladies* and placed her close to the top of his list of favorite American women writers, just below Willa Cather and Edith Wharton.

ter by now. There is so much I would like to say—but I'm never sure who reads these letters. Anyway, I think Ch. is rather a shit—for a good many fairly valid reasons. To get off on another subject, do you remember Waldemar Hansen? I saw him in Paris, and he is a wreck: the poor thing has been ousted by Peter Watson, and it is one of the most fabulous stories you've ever heard. A letter from Newton, who has finished his book, and is going to the Cape.[1] Phoebe seems very happy in her new home—entertaining and whatnot. Tell me, is she still going around with [unclear]? She never mentions him. And is she writing anything? Where are you going in Maine? Are you going to stay in a pension? I've always wanted to go to Nova Scotia. I may go to Timbuktu in a couple of months—you cross the Sahara in a truck: takes three weeks. It all depends. Of course, I am really only thinking of my book: all this travelling seems to be done in a dream. Then, too, I suppose I must think about coming home. I miss you and Phoebe terribly—but that is really all that I miss.

Darling, I am going to do a little work now (the days go so swiftly, and there is so much to be done) so, with love to Harold and the most staggering number of kisses to you, my precious friend, I will fold this particular tent and, quite unlike an Arab (the noisy heathens) silently steal away. Love

T

[Collection New York Public Library]

TO CATHERINE WOOD

British Post Office
Tangiers, Morocco
Africa
July 28, 1949

Woody darling—

Don't scold me, dear: I've been absolutely awful—but, since I left Italy, which was around the middle of June, I've been in almost continual motion: a week in Paris, and then to Spain: traveled all the way down through Spain, stopping off in various cities—Madrid, Granada, Seville, and smaller

---

[1] Arvin's book was his biography of Herman Melville.

places: a beautiful country, but not at all pleasant to travel in, too many restrictions, too much red tape, too many men in uniforms—in fact, almost everyone is in uniform. It is a war-time atmosphere there. At Algeciras, which is at the southernmost tip of Spain, I took the boat here to Africa. I do miss Italy, but it is quite strange and beautiful here, and I like it enormously. I am living with Noel Guiness [Loel Guinness], who has a wonderful house in the casbah; it is really great fun, and promises to be more so, for Cecil Beaton and Greta G. [Garbo] are coming here week after next to stay with us into Sept—she is going then to France to make a movie (Balzac's "La Duchesse de Langeais.")[1] Perhaps I will go back to Paris with them. Meanwhile, I got on with my work, and now have half the main book finished—or almost half. <u>Other Voices</u> came out in France, with an introduction by Maurice Coindreau, in which he mentions you. I will bring you a copy.

It is hot here, but it is a dry, not too unpleasant hot, and there are excellent beaches nearby—though I must say I don't go often.

I bought two parrots; one is pink-headed and the other gold; they are fine company—they twitter and laugh and sit on my shoulders. I also have a little gazelle, which I brought back from an excursion to the Atlas mountains. He is adorable <u>and</u>—he is called <u>Woody</u>!!!

I suppose Margery is in Maine—send her my best love. And oh such a lot of love for you, darling

T

[Collection New York Public Library]

TO LEO LERMAN

British Post Office
Tangiers
Aug 8 1949

Leo, dear mama

I couldn't believe my eyes: a letter from Myrt: practically wept, my pet—and know you must be bored stiff, or you would never have taken pencil in hand.

---

[1] Garbo did not make the movie.

Yes, here we are: and, while Jane [Bowles] is not selling grain in the market place, she is very much in love with a woman who does: an Arab witch who looks exactly like Katina Paxinou.[1]

There is no point in telling you what has happened; there has been so much, and I would leave out the important things anyway.

Saw Richard in Paris—who seemed vaguely disastisfied [sic]—as doesn't he always. But God, what a bore it must be, travelling with that Rothchild [Howard Rothschild]. It was nice, though, seeing him. Do you remember that young sculptor from Canada who lived in your 88th Street apt. for a while?[2] He spoke to me one night in a cafe, said he was living in Paris.

Had the most extraordinary day with George D. [Davis] in Paris. He arrived there under the wing of Mrs Biddle and a curious Mrs [Fleur] Cowles: first off, he gave a luncheon party with a table laid out in solid gold—tout de Paris was there. Then he gave a dinner party that evening at Maxim's that literally must have cost 2 or 3 thousand dollars. So I gather his new magazine has rather spectacular backing. It was fun to see George riding on such a crest of luxury.

But oh how quiet I've been! I read and write most of the day and most all night. I have some sort of grip on a novel and am hoping for the best. Incidentally, I have been reading Angus Wilson's book, <u>The Wrong Set</u>.[3] Do you know his work? I think you should get a story from him. By the way, Newton has finished his book;[4] I wish I could see it.

Such a lot has happened in New York, I'm afraid really to go back, everything will be so different. But you will be there, unchanged: that is your charm, dearheart, and the sight of it is worth a trip across the Atlantic. Of course I miss you, of course I love you, but of course!

mille tenderesse [sic] (ha! ha!)

T

P.S. Ran into Marge, that hussy. She says for you to write!

[Collection Columbia University Library]

---

[1] Oscar-winning Greek actress.
[2] The Canadian, Peter Sager, was actually a painter, not a sculptor.
[3] *The Wrong Set and Other Stories* (1949) was Wilson's first book. His story "Realpolitik" appeared in the debut issue of *Flair*, February 1950.
[4] Newton Arvin's *Herman Melville* (1950).

TO EDITH SITWELL

Truman Capote
British Post Office
Tangier, Morocco, N. Africa
Aug 21 1949

Dear Dr. Sitwell,

For so long I hoped I might be coming this year to England. Alas, it is clear now that this shall not be: a considerable disappointment, for I had expectations of our perhaps meeting again. Meanwhile, and after having spent a beautiful, really golden spring in Italy, I am more or less pleasantly settled in this ragamuffin city, Tangier—writing a novel with one hand and fanning myself with the other: the heat outdoes anything. England, I understand, has had a remarkable summer, and I'm sure you have enjoyed it.

I know this will be a nuisance to you, but I have a request to make, one which, for any number of sensible reasons, you may feel unable to grant. It is this: I am applying for a Guggenheim fellowship, and in so doing one must submit a list of seven sponsors, distinguished persons willing to write a letter testifying to their belief in the applicant's worthiness. The point is, may I use your name? If so, you will sometime in November receive a communiqué from the Guggenheim foundation privately asking your opinion of my abilities as a writer. Of course, it may be that you have none, in which case I should certainly understand a negative answer to this request. In any event, thank you for whatever attention you may give it.

Recently I've read <u>Brave and Cruel</u>, a marvelously gifted book. I remember that it was you who spoke of it to me, and told me also of Denton Welch's death; what a great shame it is.[1]

If Alice [unclear] is in England, and you should see her, do please give her my regards.

I hope some day you will see fit to risk again the danger of a New York winter. It was so much—yes, <u>fun</u>—having you there.

Believe me,
Truman Capote

[Collection the University of Texas at Austin]

---

[1] English on his father's side, American on his mother's, Denton Welch died in 1948 at the age of thirty-three. *Brave and Cruel, and Other Stories* was published posthumously in 1949.

TO ANDREW LYNDON

Tangier
Aug 23 1949

Darling baby—

I was so worried; and really, you were sick after all—what a shame. I'm rather rundown myself, mostly because I'm not getting the right things to eat—the food here is so abominable, it all tastes like candy fried in olive oil. Yesterday was Jack's birthday, and we had the most beautiful party:[1] Cecil Beaton is here, and helped me arrange it; we gave it in the grotto at the Caves of Hercules, there was champagne and an Arab orchestra and it lasted all night. I've gone nuts on the subject of Arab music—Abu Muhud has replaced Billie [Holiday] in my affections. Otherwise everything has been terribly quiet. Work, work, oh God! I think it would be wonderful fun to work on G's [George Davis's] magazine—which, by the way, is to be called <u>Flair</u>: not very promising, that. Tenn & that loathesome [*sic*] Merlo boy are on their way to Hollywood—perhaps Frankie will get into the movies, for I understand all the old Lon Chaney movies are going to be remade, and by hiring him they'd save on makeup. <u>Have</u> you a new apartment, <u>truly</u>? Such exciting news. Am I down on Christopher? Yes, perhaps I was, but I can't remember now why: you know me. I heard about Margaret Mitchell: to have been run over by a drunken taxi driver![2] Peter Watson ran off with someone else, a brickhead from California who had been Waldemar's lover before he met Peter and who W had rejected in favor of Mr Watson! How's that for irony? Give Harold a big kiss, my sweet magnolia, and write me at once, for I miss you from dawn to dawn, and love you like an old Kentucky Colonel loves his rock n' rye.

T

[Collection New York Public Library]

---

[1] Dunphy turned thirty-five.
[2] Margaret Mitchell, author of *Gone with the Wind*, had died in Atlanta on August 16, 1949, after being struck by a speeding taxi five days earlier.

TO ROBERT LINSCOTT

> British Post Office
> Tangier, Morocco
> Aug 30 1949

Dear Bob—

I don't care how hot it's been in New York, it's been just twice as hot here—but I've acquired such a menagerie I can't seem to get away—two parrots, a Siamese and a little green frog, very tame, he is, and hops up and down my arm. In the midst of this, the heat, the birds and beast, I've plunged ahead with my book and am now ⅔rds the way through—at least in draft form—some of it I'm pleased with, some of it not, naturally. I think it will run to about 80,000 words, rather longer than I expected—but then it has turned into quite a different, infinitely more complex novel than I originally proposed, and to pull it into shape will take a monumental effort. I long for you to see it. I have not made any plans yet for coming home, such a problem, but when I finish the chapter I'm working on now I will begin to think about it. Did you get my last letter? Write me, dear Bob. Best

  T

[Collection Columbia University Library]

TO IRWIN EDMAN[1]

> British Post Office
> Tangier
> Morocco
> [1 September 1949]

Dear Mr. Edman—

For three long months I've been in this ragamuffin city whittling away on a novel. You perhaps have had a more agreeable summer—not that I complain, really, it _is_ an extraordinary place; and I stayed from March to

---

[1] A friend of Newton Arvin, Edman was a much respected professor of philosophy at Columbia.

June on Ischia, that lovely island next to Capri—it has the most beautiful spring! At the moment I'm engaged in the national pastime of applying for a Guggenheim: could you help me by letting me use your name as a reference? Please do not hesitate in giving a negative reply to this request. There are any number of sensible reasons why you might feel unable to do so.[1]

My God, aren't Arabs queer? Several weeks ago something happened here which might interest a philosopher. Four Arabs were walking down the road near my house, and one of them suddenly disappeared: he'd fallen down a hidden overgrown water well. And his three friends simply leaned over the well, calling miktoub, miktoub (It is fate). Then, they walked away, calmly shaking their heads. The next day the police passed and nailed a tip on the wall. Nobody seemed to care about the poor man, long since drowned. This is perfectly true.

Best regards,
Truman Capote
Sept 1 1949

[Collection Columbia University Library]

TO ROBERT LINSCOTT

Capote
British Post Office
Tangier, Morocco
Sept 12 1949

Dear Bob—

I have sent a query to the bureau of missing persons: surely they will know what has become of you. Or is this long silence due to overwork—I am making more work for you: if all goes well, you will have a book to read by the first of the year, or somewhere around there. And I am coming home next month; at least I think I am, but it is terribly difficult to get passage. Bob, I'm applying for a Guggenheim; I have quite a good list of sponsors, so maybe I will get it: one of them is E.M. Forster, and he has just written ask-

---

[1] Edman replied that it would give him "real pleasure" to recommend him for a Guggenheim grant. Capote was turned down, however, by the Guggenheim committee itself.

ing if I could send him my book of stories. Could you? E.M. Forster/King's College/Cambridge, England. Thanks so much. Is it autumn in New York? I like it best then, and long to be there. I long to see <u>you</u>, too. There's such a lot to tell! So many funny things have happened. Best always,

    T

[Collection Columbia University Library]

TO ANDREW LYNDON

    Tangier
    Sept 15 1949

Precious baby—

At last report you were still in Macon: surely you are home by now. Did you see the report on Flair in Time? It sounds ridiculous, am too disappointed. Have just come back from a week at Xacun, a strange and poetic little city high in the Rif Mountains; and I bought Phoebe the most wonderful old Moorish ring, it is an amethyst surrounded by uncut emeralds, rubies and moonstones, it's absolutely huge and I can't imagine what it will look like on her silly little hands. And what about the apartment? Have you really got a new one? Jack has an infected foot, and I have a raging toothache, otherwise we are fine. We will be here at least another two weeks, and then will take a boat to Marseille; maybe, if the weather is good, we will stop at Aix-en-Provence a little while before going on to Paris. In the current French <u>Vogue</u> there is a picture of Jack and Joan McC. [McCracken] et moi sitting together at a party: how's that for scandal? Newton has finished his book and it has been a great success with AML[1] people; he writes me constantly; I think I must still love him, alas; but once you truly love someone, I don't suppose you ever really stop. You needn't worry, however: I'll never be caught in that particular trap again. I miss you, sweet heart, and oh what joy it will be to see you. All my love and love to that sweet Harold

    T

[Collection New York Public Library]

---

[1] AML, academic abbreviation for American Literature.

TO ANDREW LYNDON

Paris
Oct 23 1949

Darling baby—

What a joy to have that fat long letter; surely by now you have had the one from me telling about Aix etc. What news from here? Saw "Un Tramway Nomme Desir"[1] avec Arletty—and that, honey, was slaughter—chichi beyond words; for instance, on all those occasions when Stanley is supposed to be getting those colored lights going the stage is flooded with Negros [*sic*] doing belly shakes—ludicrous. As for Arletty, oh such miscasting. Paris empty of Americans, and freezing cold, and mostly I am working. A copy of The World Next Door has reached me; have you tried to read it?[2] Every now and then there are some good things in it—but I've never had the patience to pick raisins out of pudding—and God knows he writes a pudding prose, weak, lazy, hurried. Am so glad to hear about Ernest, maybe now Time will have some good reviews—occasionally I see a Nation and his work there is excellent. I take it that Phoebe has not gone to work for Flair. Someone here told me that George and Fleur Cowles have had a falling out—hope not. Have you any idea what boat is transporting Marylou [Aswell] to Europe? She is a fool to come here at this time of year, particularly if she has had a serious operation. God willing, I will be home the end of next month—just in time for Christmas, so be sure and get me a present. Be sure and write me, precious darling, and give Harold my dearest love.

Bushels of kisses
T

[Collection New York Public Library]

---

[1] *A Streetcar Named Desire.*
[2] *The World Next Door* (1949), novel by Fritz Peters.

TO ANDREW LYNDON

Paris
Nov 1 1949

Sugar—

Paris colder than a nun's cunt; how I long for good old steam-heated, suffocating N.Y. Or do I? Anyway, I will be there the end of this month. Suppose you've heard about George [Davis] et moi.[1] He sent me the most Godawful cable. I guess washing all those diapers has unhinged him. I couldn't be more innocent. But I gather that our Phoebe is working there; alas, she never writes me. But I'm glad she has the job; it might be fun. Saw the most wonderful movie, Carol Reed's "The Third Man." Orson Welles is in it—superbly so, believe it or not. And it has a marvelous musical score— all played on a zither. Jane Bowles is here living with us, and we have a Pekingnese [sic] puppy: cutest thing you ever saw. My room is too cold to work in, so I have ensconced myself at a table in the hotel kitchen—frightfully gay—except the "help" keeping feeding me cognac so usually I'm wild-tight by nightfall: Jack is very displeased. Are you coming to my lecture on Dec 8th?[2] Partisan Review was kind enough to let me know I was giving one. My love to Harold, and write me, sweet one.

Kisses galore
T

[Collection New York Public Library]

TO CATHERINE WOOD

Paris Nov 9 1949

Woody darling—

Thank you for the clippings: poor Greta [Garbo]—but a great deal of it is her own fault. And I agree with you that I should not stay in Paris—but my finances are so mixed up right now that I don't dare make another move

---

[1] Capote and George Davis had a rocky relationship from the beginning. It is unclear what dispute he is referring to here.

[2] On December 8, 1949, Capote was to give a reading, arranged by John Malcolm Brinnin, at the 92nd Street Y in Manhattan.

until my agent gets thing's [*sic*] straightened [out]. I want terribly to go to Sicily—however, unless something happens, I will probably have to come home around the 1st of the year. If only the various publishers who owe me money would pay up I could certainly afford the winter in Sicily. It's such a bore. I recvd. an invitation to Teddy's[1] wedding, and would like to send them a gift, but where do I send it? Both my books are having a great success in Europe, especially France and Italy, and I'm as famous as a movie star—which is sort of fun. I don't know how long before I'll finish my new book, certainly five or six months. Darlin give my love to Margery, and write me very soon. Have a lovely thanksgiving, and know that I love you always.

   T

[Collection New York Public Library]

TO LEO LERMAN

   22, Rue de L'Université[2]
   Paris
   Nov 15 1949

Myrt hon—

   No, pet, your letter (if, indeed, you sent one) has never reached me—so write another, as your ever-loving palsy is dying for Myrt's news. No news from this end—or rather too much—and I'm not up to writing it because 1) I have the grippe, 2) and dysentery—so am very weak. So here I am in bed, surrounded by parrots and pekingnese [*sic*] puppies—don't ask me to explain this last, just take my word for it. Has been a lovely autumn here, though. Lots of smoky chimneys and leaves. Honey, someone wrote that you had given birth. Gave me rather a turn. "Leo has given birth to Speed Lankin [Lamkin]."[3] What does it mean? And is Speed Lankin that boy called Hillyer? Have you read Paul Bowles' book?[4] Terribly thin, really, but I rather liked it. I liked the first twenty pages of Fritz's book, but thought the rest unreadable. There is a young French writer called <u>Mou-</u>

---

[1] Ted Walworth.
[2] Capote and Dunphy were staying at the Hôtel de l'Université, a small establishment on the Left Bank.
[3] Speed Lamkin was a novelist and playwright.
[4] Bowles's first novel, *The Sheltering Sky* (1949).

joudki [Marcel Mouloudji]—he is published by Gallimard, and has not been translated; awfully good, you should be the first to publish him. Hear you are doing fine with Mlle. Do you think <u>Flair</u> will be amusing? Certainly their "dummy" issue doesn't promise much. Give my best to Richard and Gray [Foy].[1] I miss you. Love

    et mille tenderesse [*sic*] (ha ha)

    M

[Collection Columbia University Library]

TO ANDREW LYNDON

    Post Restante
    Taormina, Sicily
    [4 April 1950]

Darling baby—

We were 21 days at sea! and mostly with everyone talking Norwegian and Turkish, oh it was fierce, little lamb, but we have somehow survived the agony of the voyage, which really was not an agony but rather pleasant, and yesterday arrived in Taormina: we think we like it, it is almost too spectacular, every where a bella vista, but it will take a few days to tell. This morning, we are off villa hunting. Gide is living here. He sits in the barbershop all afternoon having his face continually lathered by little boys of eight and nine: but what else can you do at his age? Donny is here too; we were very surprised to find him sitting in the piazza; he is in quite a bad mood because his book has not been reviewed or advertised: is this true? What about Newton's book? I hope you have saved me some of the reviews. Darling, it was a joy to have your letter in Naples. I hope Phoebe doesn't do anything rash, and I must write her immediately. Kelly has proved a most able little traveller . . . though we have had our moments.[2] For instance, yesterday we were put off a train in Catania and had to wait in that Pittsburgh of Sicily five hours until a cattle car loaded with peasants allowed us to board it with our beast. All Italians seemed to be scared shit-

---

[1] An artist, Foy had become Lerman's companion.
[2] Kelly was a dog, a Kerry blue, a breed known for its pugnacity.

less by Kelly's dear little face. I have written a short story that I want so for you and Phoebe to read; it is called A DIAMOND GUITAR. I'm really very enthusiastic about it. Honey, I will write a real letter in the next few days. Love to Harold

and much much love dearest

t

[Collection New York Public Library]

TO WILLIAM GOYEN

Fontana Vecchia
Taormina, Sicily
April 5 1950

Bill dear,

It was a long but amusing trip; we were 21 days at sea and, though most of the other passengers were Turkish and began each sentence with We Turks (think soandso), I enjoyed it: came away feeling much healthier. Also, I wrote a new story, one that I like; it is called A DIAMOND GUITAR, and I wish so much that you could read it: there are so few people that one wants to have read one's work.[1] But dear Bill, I hope that you are in more relaxing circumstances; I long to hear that you are settled and working. And now that I am far away, you please will remember to send me that name you would not disclose previously: does it still proceed?

Sicily is far more spectacular than I had imagined. Greener, steeper, sweeter. I love it. In the cafes the men dance together to the music of guitars, children with sheep sit in fields of wildflowers playing pan-like flutes.

We have got the two top floors of a lovely old villa about twenty minutes walk from the town. It has a view of the mountains and the snow and the sea. It is terribly quiet and pretty and <u>Cheap</u> and we want awfully for you to come here. Why don't you, Bill?

Gide is living here. He goes to the barbershop in town and sits there all

---

[1] "A Diamond Guitar" was published in *Harper's Bazaar,* November 1950.

afternoon having his face lathered by little boys of ten and twelve. He is a nice vague old man.

On the other hand, I sometimes write long letters. But we have walked over ten miles today, and I am plumb tuckered out. I hope you will come here; if not that, do write me, for We Turks miss you.

mille tenderesse [*sic*]

t'amo

T

[Collection Unknown]

TO JOHN MALCOLM BRINNIN

Fontana Vecchia
Taormina, Sicily
April 7, 1950

Honeybunch,

You were very dear to come that last night, and I felt quite guilty about it, especially because I would [have] liked to have seen you alone. The voyage was extraordinary; it lasted twenty one days, and the other passengers were mostly Turkish, some of whom prefaced all remarks with We Turks (think soandso); consequently, I am rather delirious to be here on the steep but solid earth of Taormina: it is almost appallingly beautiful, an unearthly spring. You would like it here, I know, and we have found the loveliest little villa; it is about a twenty minute walk from town, there is a garden, two bedrooms, two terraces, an enormous salon, kitchen, bath, and an aeroplane view of the mountains, snow, sea. It costs fifty a month, which is quite cheap don't you think? Really, you ought to come here. [André] Gide is living here; he sits in the barbershop all afternoon having his face lathered by little boys of ten and twelve; there is rather a scandal, not because he likes to take little boys home with him, but because he only pays them two hundred lire (20¢). Otherwise, the scene is blessedly free of literary folk, or folk of any kind. Write me, lamb, for We Turks miss you; and much much love

t

[Collection University of Delaware Library]

TO WILLIAM GOYEN

>Fontana Vecchia
>Taormina, Sicily
>April 12, 1950

Bill dear,

I hate it that you should be living in this really depraved sounding place: to think that you will be there until the middle of June, however I forbid you to move into the mass of brownstone on Sixty-fifth. Actually, you must come here . . . if only because you can live pleasantly for so very little. If you wanted great privacy we can find you a little apartment for, say, twenty dollars a month. And you could eat with us often as not. Our house is a dream. The water is divine, we go swimming and boating every afternoon. The town is lovely, the people divine, the food heaven. And it would all cost you about fifty dollars a month. What more do you want?

I work in the mornings, and read in the evenings. Did you see The Lady's Not For Burning.[1] I thought in London perhaps you might have. I've been reading it, and some of it seems to me very beautiful. I long for Bob [Linscott] to send me your book; do please remind him that he is supposed to. Night is the only time to work in New York; I used to work at about the same hours you are using. Everything one writes at night seems to have a rather fevered quality.

Do tell me, why did life in Mt Kisco become too complicated? And when, and how, did Horan go to Egypt.[2] It does seem a queer choice. I understand that Carson is not going to Ireland after all; is this true?

We have a little girl working for us; she is charming, very quick, and a reasonably good cook; but she kept wearing the same old pinned-together dress day after day, so we bought her another dress. But the next day she came in the same ancient costume, and we asked her why she wasn't wearing the new dress: oh, she said, that was her good dress now and she must save it.

Perhaps she is saving it for you. At any rate I can promise you a gala welcome here, so please try and arrange it.

I miss you and think of you. You know that I love you.

>T

[Collection Unknown]

---

[1] *The Lady's Not for Burning* (1949), a popular comedy by Christopher Fry.

[2] The composers Gian Carlo Menotti and Samuel Barber owned a house called Capricorn in Mount Kisco, 38 miles north of New York City. Goyen was Barber's lover for a time, and Robert Horan, a talented young poet, was Menotti's.

TO ROBERT LINSCOTT

note the new address

Fontana Vecchia
Taormina, Sicily
[7 May 1950]

Dear Bob,

I recieved [*sic*] your letter about the proofs just as I was sending one about the picture releases, and so scribbled an answer on the envelope which you probably did not notice.[1] I think it best that you do not send the proofs; it would be far too involved.

We have had luck, at least I hope it is luck, in finding a place to live; it is the top two floors of a little villa about twenty minutes walk from Taormina . . . very isolated, but plenty of room and a wonderful view. It is the house where D.H. Lawrence lived for many years. It costs fifty dollars a month, which is rather a lot, at least by Italian standards, but I like it tremendously.

As I guess I wrote you, Gide is living here, and I enjoy him except that he is so vague. Otherwise, the scene is blessedly free of literary folk; in fact, folk of any kind.

I think I will send you parts of my book as they are done; not only because I want you to see it, but it will be safer to have a copy of it elsewhere. I've sent a story to Marian [Ives] that I long for you to see. Write me a newsy letter. Love

t

[Collection Columbia University Library]

---

[1] Capote was referring to his travel book, *Local Color*, which included contributions from several well-known photographers.

TO ANDREW LYNDON

Fontana Veccia [*sic*]
Taormina, Sicily
May 15, 1950

Light of the world—

As I wrote Phoebe, we have a lovely little villa and it is working out beautifully, at least is seems to be. I know it will be hot here, the days already have a certain fire, but the nights are cold, and after supper we have a fire in the fireplace: god, all that fire! So now you and Harold must pull yourselves together and come hither: maybe in the fall. It is a wonderful place to work (I think), and I've written another story, The Bargain.[1] I'm so happy to be writing stories again—they are my great love.

Perhaps there has not been time, at least I've not heard from you since Naples, and I long for your news. Here, very little happens that is newsworthy. On the way down, we stopped a few days in Ischia, and it was the same, except the Auden circle were all adither because the master is writing a movie scenario based on The Odyssey (to be filmed in Ischia) and Ingrid B. [Bergman] was expected to star in it. Oh dear.

Gide's daughter is here to keep him company. She amazes me by being 1) ugly as a wood-stove, and 2) younger than you can imagine, only twenty-three or four. Do you suppose that old goat is really responsible?

Honey, how goes MIRTH? I hope that you are going to talk with Audrey.

Kelly is filled with ticks and burrs. Our spare time is given over to picking them off him. Jack is hale and active: he even manages the half-mile hike down to the sea and back—I've managed it only once, and I thought my heart would stop. He sends you both his love.

Tell Phoebe that I love her, tell Harold, too. Do I need to tell <u>you</u> anything?

T

[Collection New York Public Library]

---

[1] Found among his papers posthumously, a typescript of the then-unpublished "The Bargain" was donated to the archives of the New York Public Library. More recently, the story was included in *The Complete Stories of Truman Capote* (Random House) after making its publishing debut in *The New York Times Book Review* in September 2004.

TO CECIL BEATON

Fontana Veccia [*sic*]
Taormina, Sicily
May 20 1950

Cecil love—

Such a lovely letter, angel—how alive you are! And I do hope Miss Cleghorn will [unclear] the dreamier routines of your life.[1] The costumes and decor for "MRS T" sound charming—indeed, I should adore to wear the orange-lined cloak: I do feel the need of something spectacular for promenading in the piazza.[2] But why are you going to Brittany? Absolutely you must take a holiday here. I love my home, it is very beautiful, but I haven't much chance to enjoy it, for, thank God, I seem to be working all the time. I have written three stories, and am finishing a fourth: one I sold to the New Yorker, another to the Bazaar, and the third I've just sent to my agent. Very soon I hope to be started on my new book. No, dear, I have not read Denton Welch's novel, and I long to, for I do think him infinitely gifted, and his death was a true tragedy. I would be so grateful if you could send it to me.

The Merman thing[3] sounds fun; on the contrary, I think you should do it, especially since it could not fail to bring you quite a lot of dollars—on the other hand, if it would in any way interfere with the production of The Gainsborough Girls, then certainly you must do your own play first.[4] At this point I think it really important that your play be put on, particularly for your own peace of mind. I must say, I don't at all see [Thornton] Wilder's play as a musical, or am I wrong?[5]

My news from New York is uninteresting. Friends who saw the preview of The Glass Menagerie (movie) say it is appalling, and that Gertrude Lawrence is pathetic. Tennessee [Williams], I'm told, has asked that his name be taken off the screen. This morning there was a letter from Janie

---

[1] Louann Cleghorn was Beaton's secretary.

[2] Beaton was designing the sets and costumes for Arthur Wing Pinero's *The Second Mrs. Tanqueray*, a play first performed in 1893.

[3] Beaton had apparently been approached to do designs for Irving Berlin's *Call Me Madam*, which opened on Broadway October 12, 1950, with Ethel Merman in the starring role. In the end, he had nothing to do with it, however.

[4] Beaton's play *The Gainsborough Girls* opened in the seaside resort of Brighton on July 16, 1951. It was a failure, however, and ended its life in the British provinces without productions in London or New York.

[5] It is unclear which Wilder play he is referring to.

[Bowles], who seems still to be in Paris; she suggests that she and Oliver S. [Smith],[1] who is arriving there shortly, are going to Broadchalke to stay a visit—I envy you Jamie, but not the other, especially since I hear he is traveling with his mother (who, of course, may turn out to be charming).

David and friend may remind you of Tatiana [*sic*] and Bottom (which, by the way, is Titiana? not David certainly), but they remind me of the comic strip, Mutt and Jeff.[2] God knows they deserve each other, and after all it is only right for two of the same species, in this case Reptile, to mate. Or am I too harsh?

It delights me to know my roses are blooming on the library wall. You please will not allow anyone to pick them.

Jack is fine, except that he is having to go to the dentist, and my dear after you have faced a Sicilian dentist you could face a firing squad with the merest tremble.

Dearest squire of Broadchalke, I miss you 25-hours a day, and love you like an old Kentucky colonel loves his rock n' rye—which is to say, you are very dear to me, bless your heart

T

Write soon

[Collection St. John's College, Cambridge University]

TO ANDREW LYNDON

Fontana Veccia [*sic*]
Taormina, Sicily
May 24 1950

Magnolia love—

Loved your letter, darling, and thank you for all those clippings. I agree with you that Newton's reviews are especially inane, but perhaps the magazines will do better by him. Did you have a good evening together?; how wonderful it would have been to be with you, the two people I love so

---

[1] Smith was a well-known American set designer.
[2] An Englishman, David Herbert was a longtime resident of Tangier—indeed the Western colony's social arbiter. Titania, the Queen of the Fairies, and Bottom, a weaver who is transformed into an ass, are characters in *A Midsummer Night's Dream*.

much. There is no one much that I love here, except Jack. Heavens no, Donny is not living with us; I'm fond of him, really, but he has become more than a bit of a bore: as Jack says, Donny looks in a mirror and doesn't see Boswell but Johnson. His ego, perhaps because at this point it is wounded, smothers you like some fast growing vine.

I do love the house, and long for you and Harold to come here. Perhaps your script on anti-biotics will do it. Joky as you made that sound, I think it [is] actually a good idea.

I am still working on stories. Marian sold A Ride Through Spain to the New Yorker, and A Diamond Guitar to the Bazaar: can't you ask Pearl to let you see it? I do so want to know what you think. I've sent Marian another story, The Bargain.

Tomorrow I'm having a little lunch party that could be amusing; it is to introduce those two eminent Frenchmen, [André] Gide and [Christian] Dior.

It is getting real hot here, but Fontana is cool enough and the nights downright cold. We have a girl to clean and cook lunch but make supper ourselves; except for gin and cigarettes, and even here we use Italian brands, ugh, we are living economically—and in such style.

Kelly and Jack send their love to Harold, to you. We all miss the Halma-Lyndon's. Write me, my precious heart, for your adoring friend has you always in his thoughts. Many kisses

T

[Collection New York Public Library]

TO ROBERT LINSCOTT

Fontana Vecchia
Taormina
June 14 1950

Dear Bob—

About the Bazaar: I am outraged, aghast—my only arrangement was to credit them, which I did <u>very</u> adequately on the thank-you page. Please do nothing about it—please, that is, do not have the plates altered, as I am sending a letter in this same mail to Frances McFadden, which I think will be effective. Incidentally, those particular Haitian photographs by Bissinger never appeared in the Bazaar. Here are the pictures that were in the Bazaar: Cartier-Bresson's New Orlean's [*sic*] pictures, Bill Brandt's seagull, Bissinger's picture of Spain, and Hoynigen-Huene's [Hoyningen-Huene's] picture of the Spanish castle. None of the within photographs have ever appeared anywhere. All I hope is that nothing has been done about changing these plates—wait until we see what effect my letter has.[1] I am writing Marian to intercede, too.

About Goyen's book: I've just sat up most of the night reading it, and it is beautiful, very extraordinary indeed. I know it will go blowing and howling around in my head for a long time. Such a wonderful ear! Do you think, though, that he will ever tighten his brakes? He can't go on driving over cliffs, especially if he wants to take us passengers with him. But it is so gifted and "seeing" of you, Bob, to have encouraged this book in the way you have; it makes me appreciate you all the more. "An artist, a writer to salute, has made The House of Breath. William Goyen's gifts, understanding, vision, style, are gifts infrequently encountered, and almost never in combination. This is a beautiful book." If you can use this quote, you are welcome.

Bob, I hope you forgive me all the trouble that I cause you. Write me; it is lonesome here.

Always,

T

[Collection Columbia University Library]

TO WILLIAM GOYEN

Fontana Vecchia
Taormina Sicily
June 14 1950

Dearest Bill—

I wish I had the strength to write you properly; but The House of Breath, which I've just finished, having read it all in one sitting, has left me

---

[1] His letter brought an immediate reaction. After demanding credit under each photograph that had first appeared in its pages, *Harper's Bazaar* agreed to a compromise that did not require Random House to spend the time and money to make up new photographic plates.

very exhausted indeed: the exhaustion that only the joy of art can produce. I feel, not unaccountably, as though I'd had a nearly religious experience. Dear God, Bill, I wept, trembled, and as I turned the final page I might have frozen from the chill along my spine. It is a novel of unearthly beauty! If you never wrote another word I'm sure you would always be remembered for having made this important contribution: what a treasure it will be for those who care about feeling, understanding, love, art. Surely you are in a state of grace.

It is worked out with such intelligence, you have really built a house of breath: the wind swoops down the flue, sifts with real music through the shutter; the story-voice mourns and howls with a terrible authenticity; the underwater marriage of Christy and Otey, so perfectly shaped a climax, is one of the loveliest moments in literature. You have blown this house with your own breath—but no one, not even you, will be able ever to blow it away.

How proud I am to know you, William Goyen. What kin are we all to each other, anyway? I can answer you, [unclear]. All the kin in the world. All.

and love
Truman

[Collection Unknown]

TO ANDREW LYNDON

Fontana Vecchia
Taormina Sicily
June 15 1950

Darling—Precious—Lamb,
That lovely letter! Just after I'd written you a scolding card. What you say about Miss Wharton sounds so encouraging, I do hope something marvelous comes of it: you must show it to Audrey [Wood]. It is sad, though, about Phoebe's new story, I hope it doesn't discourage her; the truth is, she has not written enough—if you are as talented as she is, you might write two or three successful stories without, as it were, half-trying; but beyond that you must have a firmer foundation than Phoebe so far has built for herself. I want so awfully for her to realize her really extraordinary gifts. Just now I have finished reading Bill Goyen's novel, The House of

Breath—and really it is beautiful: at last something one can authentically admire. I know you will like it. Random House is publishing it in the fall. By the way, I've read The Lady's Not For Burning, and loved it. It is getting very warm here,—not too bad, though. No, that story about Gide and Donny was not true. I read it aloud to him, just to see him squirm, for I am sure he must have written something like it to someone in New York. Gide has gone, presumably to Paris. Donny was robbed of all his money, and many of his clothes two days ago; some one of his many pickups broke into his room, and made a clean sweep. D. had to give the names of all the boys who had been in his room to the police; my, it was a sordid list. The boys in town are very mad with him. Poor Sandy; he is arriving Saturday in the middle of all this mess; I daresay they will leave as soon as possible. So it looks as though we are going to have Taormina to ourselves. I hope so. Though I wish that you and Harold were here. Darling, I miss you so frightfully; you know how dear you are to me. Kiss Harold. Jack says thanks for the kiss you sent him.

I love you
T

[Collection New York Public Library]

TO ANDREW LYNDON

Fontana Vecchia
Taormina Sicily
June 20 1950

My own precious—

Thank you so much, angel, for taking the photograph to Marian, and Harold, that darling, for making it.[1] It is for my French publ. I'm glad to know you are trying again at Life. You would be so marvelous for them, and I hope that at last they will have the sense to know it.

La Vie en Taormina es tres tranquil. Sandy arrived, but is, I think, much too depressed by the appallingly manifest evidences of D's infidelities to enjoy the bella vista. How would you feel if every other boy you

---

[1] Capote is referring to a photograph of him taken by Harold Halma.

passed on the street was wearing a shirt or tie that once had all been presents from you to your lover? Well, Sandy is keeping a stiff upper lip: poor idiot, he hasn't the imagination to do anything else. I daresay they will leave soon, which is just as well: Sicily for the Sicilians, I say.

Phoebe is a bore about writing. But perhaps I owe her a letter, though I don't think so. And anyway, where would I send it? Is she still at Yaddo?

You mention Jordan [Massee]. Is he in N.Y. now for good—or bad? Please give him my best. I hope he finds a good job, or whatever. How can he bear to be around that ass, [Paul] Bigelow! You don't say whether you liked Wm. Goyen. I do, very much. Linscott sent me his book last week. The first fifty pages are a waste, but from there on, except for vast confused passages, I thought it remarkable. The next to last chapter is wonderfully beautiful.

Darling, I'm so happy that you are very nearly finished with Miss Wharton. I long to see it—on the screen in particular.

Guess what I'm doing? Putting up tomato preserves (in old gin bottles) and fig preserves. They are so delicious, the figs here. Maybe you and Harold will come here this fall or winter and we can eat them together. I try to believe that, because I miss you both so much.

Kelly is full of ticks, lice and burrs, but says to give you his love, and Jack, who is just full of nonsense, sends his. Here is mine xxxxxxxxxxxx—please divide half those kisses with Harold.

Your own
T

[Collection New York Public Library]

TO PHOEBE PIERCE

Fontana Vecchia
Taormina, Sicily
June 24, 1950

Phoebe devil—
Perchè lei non scrittore a me? Bei a molte brute, e is non è piasce! That's telling you. Anyway, little toad, why are you so silent? Yaddo got your tongue? God, what a windy day: can hardly hold onto this paper. Andrew writes that he liked your story The Green Catherine; lovely title—you do have such a title sense—and I would pay several dollars in postage to see it.

Have you written more? Oh what news from here? Well, Donny Windham, who has been here 2 months, is leaving tomorrow, muchly disgusted with Taormina: his room has twice been robbed, and all his money and most of his clothes stolen. It all has, however, such comic ramifications that I have not been able to feel very sad. I go on liking it here. I have been putting up apricot and fig preserves; an unmanly activity, I suppose, but very relaxing and the reward is delicious. Today is St. Giovanni, Jack's name day, and so we are preparing a big feast, and the people working in the wheatfield below are coming up with an accordion and we are going to have a dance.

As you see, my news is simple-minded. I am working on my book and have written a long story (The House of Flowers) that maybe you would like—Marian, the fool, has sent it to Holiday magazine because "it has such a nice Haitian background."!![1]

[Collection Peter Geyer]

TO ANDREW LYNDON

> Fontana Vecchia
> Taormina, Sicily
> July 6, 1950

Darling baby—

Simply can't work this morning: across the hill they are having some sort of military manoeveurs [sic]—much bullet fire etc. When it began we thought it was the Russians. And so have been thinking about the Russians ever since. No one here seems to feel there is going to be a big war; actually, they don't care—are really apathetic. We get our news here so late; I have no idea what is happening. Oh the thought of a wartime America! I hope you will have the good sense to stay out of uniform this time.

I just finished Newton's book, and it is so very wonderful—it came the other day, and I'd not read it front to back before. How was your lunch? What does Newton say about me? I want him to meet Bill Goyen; don't

---

[1] *Holiday* was an upscale travel magazine. "House of Flowers" was published in *Botteghe Oscure* in 1950 and in *Mademoiselle*, April 1951. Published in Rome, *Botteghe Oscure* was a biannual review that featured original poetry and fiction from England, Germany, Italy, France, Spain, and the United States in the original language. Among those who contributed were André Malraux, Albert Camus, Paul Valéry, Ignazio Silone, Robert Graves, Archibald MacLeish, and e.e. cummings.

you think they might like each other?—Bill seems to like older gentlemen. Yes, Goyen is very sweet; I'm so glad that you are seeing each other. Have you read his book? Alas, Phoebe! I'm terribly afraid your friends will never see those issues of Flair. Tell about Doris [Lilly]. I didn't know she was back; and how <u>did</u> she find the apt.?—as if I don't know. I pray for Phoebe; she just could let herself go completely—and seems to want to.

My tomato preserves turned out divine, apricot even better—but the figs were rather a failure. Am going to try peaches Sunday; must do something with all these old gin and wine bottles. Do you know a good recipe for mayonnaise? Chocolate pie?

Currently am waging war against two little girls down the road. They are driving me out of my mind. Why do children always think that I am a child too? I'd like to crack their little heads together.

We have all the equipment for underwater fishing (masks, spears) but have caught nothing so far, though I almost put the spear through Jack's leg. It's fun, anyway; and I'm learning a lot about sea life.

It is so hot here—not humid, just a classic, relentless, Grecian sun— but oh dear, I think sometimes I will just pass away.

Donny & Sandy left—a good thing, for Donny was about to be lynched by the Taormina trade for having given all their names to the police. What a mess! But I promised not to tell about it, so don't you.

I miss you, little heart. A big kiss for Harold. Jack & Kelly send their love. You are my precious

T

[Collection New York Public Library]

TO DONALD WINDHAM AND SANDY CAMPBELL

Fontana Vecchia
Taormina Sicily
July 7 1950

Donny dear, and dear Sandy, too—

I hope this, along with the rest of your mail, reaches you in Palermo. It will amuse you that old Niente at the poste here has been laid off: seems they rotate the jobs, and his place has been taken by a very attractive young man called Mimi. Anyway, I have told him about forwarding your letters.

We had your postcard from Syracuse; it sounded so charming. Are you liking Palermo as well?

Last Monday was too hot to believe; otherwise the weather has been blowing and really wonderful. At last they have added those buses to the beach, so it is a lot easier. We finally bought water-masks etc, and are practicing to be underwater fishermen. Analdo is wild with envy. Everyone asks after you, and though I keep saying you have gone, they always reply: Ah, ritorno, si?

Svedesi is leaving next week (really), followed by the Cacopardo's [sic] themselves: he has got a job cooking in some hotel. So at last we will have Fontana to ourselves.

Nothing much has happened except that the people on the farm above here had a dance to celebrate their daughter's wedding. Practically no one danced except the men, and of course I had a marvelous time. There was a beautiful wierd [sic] old man who played the guitar and sang like a Sicilian Walter Huston.

Oh yes, I forgot. There has been a werewolf scare here. No joke. A boy on the other side of town claims to have been attacked by a werewolf. Graziella[1] says there have been werewolves in Taormina before. I'm sure you will believe that. Anyway, the general opinion is that we won't have to worry about [it] until it is full moon again.

I've been making lime meringue pies—practically every other day: Jack screams when I go near the kitchen.

Had a letter from Jimmy Schuyler, who says he has read your book three times and thinks it is superb.

Kelly misses you. He is worse than ever, and on the beach the other day bit a real bite out of a man who turned out to be your friend De Bonnville. As a result, the police said we must keep him on the leash.

There was an article about Gide in Il mundo [sic], and it mentions your name—at least so Carlo Panarello[2] says. I didn't see the article.

So here we will be,—unless we have to flee before the Russians. I hope you are having fun, and that you are working. Jack sends his love to you both. Please write me, little one.

Meanwhile, best love

T

[Collection Beinecke Library, Yale University]

---

[1] An Italian girl in her late teens who was Capote's housekeeper and cook in Taormina.
[2] Proprietor of an antiques and specialty shop in Taormina.

TO JOHN MALCOLM BRINNIN

[Postcard]

Fontana Vecchia
Taormina, Sicily
July 14, 1950

Sir—

Why have you not answered my letter? I only write letters so that I will get them: please put this on a paying basis. We have a wonderful home here, and if it weren't for the newspapers would be perfectly happy. At any rate, it seems a good place to work, and I am making use of it. Have you read Newton's book? It is a wise, good book. Jack has a story in the July Bazaar, but we haven't seen it. He sends his best. Honey, I hope you are enjoying the American summer; I know it is your favorite time. Prefer winter myself. Wish we could have a long talk. Much love from

T

[Collection University of Delaware Library]

TO DONALD WINDHAM

Fontana Vecchia
[Taormina, Sicily]
July 20 1950

Donny dear—

Have sent a letter (to Palermo) and a card (to Firenze),[1] so hope both of these have reached you. Was much amused by the clipping re T.W.'s [Tennessee Williams's] fisticuffs in Paris. Do you suppose it is true? And if so, who was the other gladiator? Speaking of violence, Graziella came to work today with a black eye, a bandaged arm where she had been stabbed, and black and blue marks head to toe. Her brother had beat her up—because he thought she went to the beach too much. She was really in a bad way, and we made her go home. Italians are just niggers at heart. Fulco [di Verdura] and his friend (Simon, American) came for supper last night, and were very pleas-

---

[1] Firenze is the city of Florence.

ant.[1] Is it cool in Florence; I should think it would be, there in the hills. You won't believe this, but it has gotten downright cold here; we've worn sweaters the last two nights. La vie a Mazzaro is much the same; there are some new people, and The Panther is conducting a wholesale business in a grotto-cave on the island at Isola Bella.[2] A new trade-character called Adelio has thrown himself upon the market: he looks <u>just</u> like our old friend, the soccer-player.

So what is happening in Florence? Do you see Edwin Denby, and any of those?[3] If so, give them my best. We hear no news from N.Y. <u>Everyone</u> has stopped writing—except my old school teacher.[4] In Florence they have beautiful copybooks bound in the Medici paper and many other designs; you can buy them in any good stationers, and I would love you forever if you could send me four of these, and I will send you the money for them. I need new copybooks so badly. Had a letter from Bessie Breur [Breuer] who asked me to congratulate you on your novel.[5]

I hope Sandy is having a good time. Give him my love. Jack sends love; Kelly would too if he wasn't so busy gnawing the furniture. Write me, candy lamb

T

P.S. Nella was sick for a few days, but is alright now.

[Collection Beinecke Library, Yale University]

TO LEO LERMAN

Fontana Vecchia
Taormina, Sicily
July 26 1950

Darling—

Your sweet letter. I love you, too: for the very good reason that I always have, and always will.

---

[1] Fulco di Verdura was the duke of Verdura—the "duke of vegetables," he was called behind his back. A Sicilian aristocrat with a home in Taormina, he was also one of the twentieth century's most creative jewelry designers.
[2] The Panther was a hustler who sold his wares on the beaches near Taormina.
[3] Edwin Denby, American poet who specialized in sonnets; also a noted dance critic.
[4] Catherine Wood.
[5] Bessie Breuer, American novelist and short-story writer.

How wonderful it would be if you could come here, you and Gray. Really you are not going to the Argentine! perché? Someone, I forgot who, wrote that all the editors in N.Y. were there (Buenos Aires), including Cynthia Laffoon, whose profile[1] I so much enjoyed in The New Yorker. Well, 'tis an irony, isn't it? How it's all turned out, George [Davis] etc.?

As they say, Glady's [sic] sounds a treasure. Just what you needed, a good cook. We have a cook, too; she is charming, but Italian food weighs you down after a bit—though actually [I] have never looked better, at least I'm very tan, dark as an Arab. All my teeth are falling out (literally), but what matter?

I'm so happy that you are writing; I would love you to do that book about your family—it could be so sad and funny and sweet. And I would like so much to see Gray's new pictures, for what he does is so much his own, a rare quality indeed.

I've read William Goyen's novel, and parts of it are lovely: have you seen it? But the rest of the books that have been sent here are not at all interesting.

We have Sicily, and Taormina, quite to ourselves; there is not a soul about, just a few chickens and some stray dogs. But I am content, if it were not for the newspapers I should even be happy: I do not seem much to need people anymore, which is the greatest advance I've made toward wisdom, you might say freedom. Of course one always needs one's friends; but then they are not people, they are part of one's self—as you are part of me, dearest Leo; Phoebe, for all her wiles, and a few others.

I am working—thoughtfully. To be an artist today is such act of faith: nothing can come back from it except the satisfaction of the art itself. I think I've kept my head and know now what I am doing. I've written some stories, two of which I feel you would like; and I've got a start on the book that all along I should've known was the one possible book for me—because it is really mine.[2] There is always such a tragic tendency to disregard what is one's own—just as we are often nicer to strangers than we are to our friends.

I think of you, darling, and send you as many kisses as there are scraps in a crazy-quilt. Love to Gray.

mille tenderesse [sic] (ha ha)

T

Write me

[Collection Columbia University Library]

---

[1] By S. J. Perelman.
[2] This book became The Grass Harp, which borrowed extensively from Capote's childhood in Alabama.

TO ANDREW LYNDON

[Taormina, Sicily]
[Late July or early August 1950]

Mia Cara—

Forgive this scrappy little paper (haven't anything else) but want to get a little note off to you, if only to say that I love you. Adored your letter, precious; and was so happy to hear about Phoebe's new story—wish she would send me a copy, but of course she won't. Had such a sweet dream about you and Harold last night: we were having a picnic, and whenever the food seemed about to give out, Harold reached up into a tree and pulled down something new and marvelous. Made me miss you both so much. Had a letter from Newton today, telling about his psychosomatic laryngitis. I don't know that Goyen would be interested; doubt it, really; perhaps something does go on between he and Barber, though he swore to me quite the contrary. See in the paper where the draft is back: be <u>sure</u> that you avoid it. Fulco Verdura is here, but we don't like him much. So [Paul] Bigelow is becoming a producer. Well, I guess it's about time the world did come to an end. Did you see Jack's story in the July Bazaar? Or didn't you like it? I did. Cecil may be coming here, and that would be nice, as long as it didn't interfere with my work, which it would. Some days are cool here, and others are worse than anything I've ever known: this is one of the latter. Are you and Mr Halma taking a vacation? Phoebe sent me the Perelman piece on Cynthia Laffoon: <u>couldn't</u> have liked it more. The New Yorker sent me proofs of the Spain piece; it has been pared down to read like every other lifeless thing in that magazine.[1] Honey doll, write your poor friend, for he treasures you. Love from Jack to you and Harold. My own love, over and over

Mille tenderesse [*sic*], kiddo
T

[Collection New York Public Library]

---

[1] Capote's article, "A Ride Through Spain," was published in *The New Yorker* September 2, 1950. It was the first time the magazine ever published his writing.

TO DONALD WINDHAM

[Postcard]   Fontana Vecchia
                                                Taormina, Sicily
                                                Aug 3 1950

Donny lamb—
    Grazia for the notebook; it is very pretty: quanto costa, prego?
    Cecil arrived—lots of news. Lincoln K. [Kirstein][1] has had a nervous
breakdown: ended up slapping people's faces in London—including one
old lady. Said he'd seen T.W. [Tennessee Williams] in Paris, and that T. had
lost about 25 pounds and was looking very handsome: can you credit that?
We had a letter from the French's [sic] who are in Denmark and maybe are
coming here.[2]
    Got some new records; wish you were here to dance. Wish you were
here period. Seems so hard to believe that it is August, and you have been
gone all this time. There is going to be a beauty contest Saturday to pick
Miss Taormina: if I win will send you a telegram.
    When do you leave for Sirmione? I know Sandy will like it there. I hope
the printing of the story went well.[3] Please write a long letter: am so weary
of hearing Niente at the posta. Love to Sandy et vous from Jack, Kelly
    and
    Me

[Collection Beinecke Library, Yale University]

---

[1] Kirstein was the father of the New York City Ballet, which performed at the City Center for
Music and Drama on West 55th Street in Manhattan. Windham had worked for Kirstein's magazine *Dance Index* in the 1940s.
    [2] American artist-photographers Jared and Margaret French.
    [3] The limited edition of Windham's story "The Hitchhiker" (Florence: Tipografia Giuntina,
1950).

TO DONALD WINDHAM

[Postcard]

Fontana Vecchia
Taormina, Sicily
Aug 7 1950

Donny heart—

Sylvia Bombaro (yr. landlady's dghtr.) won the Miss Taormina contest at Mazzaro last night: of course that didn't do my ego any good. Am so furious, in fact, that we are planning to leave Taormina.

At least we are plotting departure. Hate to leave in a way, but suppose it is not sensible to become another Bobby Pratt-Barlow.[1] So we think we will go to Spain the first of Oct. and get a house on Majorca. Does that tempt you? Anyway, we still will be in Venice in September—at least I will, though Jack may go to Spain before then. Oh I don't know, am so mixed up. Give Sandy a hug, then give him another (from Jack): and no doubt that will land the two of you in bed. Oh the things I put on postcards!

Love
T

[Collection Beinecke Library, Yale University]

TO ROBERT LINSCOTT

Fontana Vecchia
Taormina, Sicily
Aug 19, 1950

Dear Bob—

I was good, and didn't bother you on your vacation. But now that you are back in the old stand I shall start pestering you again. Actually, for the moment, I haven't anything to pester you about. Except I wish you would air-mail me a copy of Local Color—or hasn't it been printed yet? I am sending you about 15–20,000 words of The Grass Harp (2 chapters) the end of this month. It has been hell working in this <u>incredible</u> heat, but you will

---

[1] A wealthy English resident of Taormina.

like what I have done maybe. Newton writes that he had a most enjoyable luncheon with [you]. I may go to Venice for 2 weeks around the 20th of September, but am planning to come back here to go on with my work—I suppose I should come home, what with Russians etc., but this is such a good place for work—what do you think?[1] Give Goyen my best; I wish him all the luck in the world. Miss you. Best—

[Collection Columbia University Library]

TO DONALD WINDHAM

Fontana Vecchia
Taormina
Aug 20 1950

Donny dear—
Thank you for A Sicilian Marriage; as you know, Mr Sladen is my <u>favorite</u> author: right now I have The Gotham hunting up A Japanese Marriage.[2] By mistake, you sent also Sicily, the New Winter Resort. I'm sure, however, that you will want that valuable volume returned.

Surely <u>someone</u> has sent you the <u>disgraceful</u> article by T.W. [Tennessee Williams] that appeared in the Aug 13th Sunday New York Times magazine.[3] In the event they haven't, may I tell you that there is a cartoon by Hirschfield [Hirschfeld] (that man who does the drama things)[4] which is supposed to [be] a scene in a Paris cafe: you (and you don't look remotely like yourself, dear) are seated at a table with Mr. Williams, while I (depicted as a hideous dwarf) am in the hairy embrace of Hemingway. There are others involved: Paul Bowles, Janet Flanner etc. The accompanying article, which is all about what a travelled and sophisticated gentleman T Willie is, reaches the absolute zenith of vulgarity. Here is the paragraph

---

[1] He was probably referring to heightened Cold War tensions caused by the beginning, a few weeks earlier, of the Korean War.

[2] Douglas Sladen, a British poet and travel writer, was the author of the novels *A Japanese Marriage* (1895) and *A Sicilian Marriage* (1906). The Gotham Book Mart on West 47th Street was one of Manhattan's best known bookstores.

[3] "A Writer's Quest for a Parnassus" by Tennessee Williams.

[4] Al Hirschfeld, cartoonist known for his caricatures of Broadway and entertainment figures.

that mentions us: "I have not yet been to Sicily this year. Truman Capote has unfurled his Bronzini scarf above the fashionable resort of Taormina. He is supposedly in D.H. Lawrence's old house. Also there, I am told, is Andre Gide and the young American writer, Donald Windham, whose new novel, "The Dog Star" contains the most sensitive new writing since Carson McCullers emerged ten years ago." Of course there is a plug for your book, but in such a context: the general tone of the piece is infinitely lower—if he turns up here, I'll Bronzini scarf him. But <u>why</u> would he want to write such an article?: it's the lowest form of hack journalism. He really must have lost all his senses of value.

No news from the Taormina front—except De Bonnville skipped town owing over a 100,000 lire. Giovanni Panarello[1] returned, much shocked to find you not here. I will be in Venice on the 20th of Sept. Do hope you are there. I don't think we are going to Spain after all, and will probably return here until after Christmas. I may go to Paris for a week. Hope you have written me about Sirmione. Give Butch a hug and a kiss. Sandy, too. Love from Jack, love from

T

[Collection Beinecke Library, Yale University]

TO ROBERT LINSCOTT

Fontana Vecchia
Taormina, Sicily
Aug 22, 1950

Dear Bob—

Wonderful to have your letter; I had, just the moment before, sent you a little card. Delighted that you think <u>Local Color</u> turned out well; am dying to see it—though, unless one of those 3 copies is coming air-mail, I won't until sometime in October: I think you had best send my other copies to the photographers, or at least the following—

1. Karl Bissinger
   c/o Flair magazine

---

[1] Proprietor of an antiques shop in Taormina, whom he called "Carlo" in an earlier letter.

2. Louis Frances
   c/o Flair magazine
3. Alexander Lieberman
   c/o Vogue magazine
4. Harold Holmes
   919 Third Avenue
   N.Y.C.
5. Newton Arvin
   45 Prospect Street
   Northampton, Mass.
6. Mr. and Mrs. Charles Chaplin
   1685 Summit Drive
   Beverly Hills, Calif.
7. Christopher Isherwood.

It occurred to me that maybe Isherwood would review it for the N.Y. Times. Anyone except that awful Princeton man they gave both my other books to.[1]

I hope Random plans to do some interesting ads for it—especially with the idea of its being a gift.

As soon as I send off these chapters of The Grass Harp, I'm going to catch my breath, then go, around Sept 15, to Venice for 2 weeks. But I think I wrote you this. Send me another of those lovely gossipy letters; it makes me feel we are having a drink together somewhere. How I should like that—both the drink and you.

Always
T

P.S. Thanks for that peculiar drawing. If there is anyone's arm I should loathe to have around me it is Ernest Hemingways [sic].[2]

[Collection Columbia University Library]

---

[1] Carlos Baker, who had written about Other Voices: "The story of Joel Knox did not need to be told, except to get it out of the author's system."
[2] He is referring to the Hirschfeld drawing mentioned in the previous letter.

TO ANDREW LYNDON

> Fontana Vecchia
> Taormina Sicily
> [Late August or early September 1950]

Lover Lamb,

A good thing for you that I had a letter from you yesterday: it forestalled the posting of a time bomb. I don't understand why you haven't recvd any letters from me, certainly I've written them. Phoebe says she hasn't heard from me either, but that must be because she is jumping around just two hops in front of the law.

I suppose you know that Newton has had a crackup and is in the McLean hospital, Waverly, Mass. It happened very soon after his weekend in New York . . . though I doubt that there is any connection. He is well enough, however, to have written me a letter. He speaks of spending the winter in New York. Poor dear, he was not ever made for this world. I have no idea what to do; or suggest. The Morton he called is, I suspect, another of those cockteasing kikes he's so fond of; I'm afraid he's had just too many thoughts about this one.

Yes, I've been snowed under by that cartoon you enclosed. 10 has really gone to pot; imagine writing a piece like that . . . more vulgar than Mary McCarthy. The next time I unfold my Bronzini scarf it's going to be to wrap around his neck. Incidentally, unless things have changed, they sold you-goosed-me for fifty grand, not a hundred, and out of this Windham gets 6 thousand.[1] They, Donny, Sandy and Butch, are all in Sirmione together. You know that Pippin and Melton are no longer sympatico . . . and that Wi-l-l-burr has gone off to be Edward James's secretary: at last the fate he deserves.

I'm surprised to know that Goyen is going to Chicago. I've just had a letter from him saying he was off for Houston, and returning to NY late in the fall. He wrote very tenderly about you, said you were the sweetest, most sensitive person he'd met in a moon's age. I second that. But do you mean he has a lover in Chicago? And so attractive?

Have sent you-all a copy of Local Color. Haven't seen it myself, and don't know when I will, as they undoubtedly sent it regular mail. So let me know how it looks.

---

[1] "You-goosed-me," a play on the title of *You Touched Me!*, the 1945 romantic comedy by Tennessee Williams and Donald Windham.

Oh it is ironic about Phoebe. But I think it might turn out for the best. Standing on her feet in Bloomingdales might finally plant them in terra firma. Would love to see her new stories. She writes that you have done two Video scripts. What about it?

No, I'm not making the grand tour en famille. They are coming here for a few days, then Jack and I are going to Venice around the 15th, planning to be back here the 1st of Oct. Wish you all would lay hold to some cash and come here for Christmas etc. It would cost you nothing except the passage; you would adore the house, and could stay as long as you liked.

Masses of love for that sweet Harold. Jack and Kelly send love. And did you see that shooting comet last night? That was a kiss I was blowing to you

T

[Collection New York Public Library]

TO ROBERT LINSCOTT

Venice
Sept 21 1950

Dear Bob—

Wonderful wonderful wonderful: to have your lovely cable and to know you liked the chapters. I hope you are going to like the book. I suspect it will be a month or two before I send any more. Marian wants to sell the 1st chapter for a story—but I have written saying no; because I don't [want] anyone (outside the family) to read any of it until the day it is published. So please don't show it to anyone, will you, Bob? Had such a sweet cable from Bennett; he was really nice to send it.

Monday night had a glass of champagne to celebrate Local Color. It really is a beautiful book, couldn't have turned out better.

Do ignore Cyrilly Abels.[1] Poor thing, she is simply hysterical with inferiority feelings. Lord knows, she has good reason to feel inferior. Leave me to settle her hash. I will so much enjoy the job.

---

[1] Cyrilly Abels was the managing editor of *Mademoiselle* magazine. She had complained that her magazine had not received credit for one of the photographs in *Local Color*.

It's raining here, as though Venice were not watery enough. Am going back to Sicily in five or six days—and the monastic life. I do feel like such a monk living on that mountain.

Bought here a copy of the New Yorker with the Hemingway profile.[1] Thought it very entertaining—goodness, he's a fool.

Miss you. Write me. Love

T

[Collection Columbia University Library]

TO BENNETT CERF[2]

Venice

Sept 22 1950

Dear Bennett—

It was wonderful having your cable; you were sweet to send it, and it made me so happy to know you and Phyllis liked the chapters. I hope you will like the book. Am going back to the wilds of Sicily next Wednesday, for I'm very anxious to get on with it (the book). Meanwhile, am having a lovely holiday here in Venice: so beautiful this time of year. Don't you think Local Color turned out well? It is marvelous looking, I want to thank all of you. You are so good to me: I hope you know how much I appreciate it. Have not seen Herbert [Wise] after all; I wanted them to come and visit in Sicily, but guess they just couldn't face the primitiveness of that.[3] You and Phyllis would love it. I would almost pay your passage if you would spend your winter holiday there (have a wonderful house, and the climate is better than California or Florida). I am practically the Grand Seigneur of Sicily: there was a contest for the schoolchildren of the island to write an essay on the classic Greek theatre—and, though I protested that I couldn't read Italian, I was supposed to be the Judge; the house is filled with manuscripts, the authorities are awaiting a decision, and I am very nearly

---

[1] In "Portrait of Hemingway" Lillian Ross followed Hemingway and his wife, Mary, around New York for two days, meticulously recording the writer's incessant drinking and sometimes foolish comments. ("I beat Mr. Turgenev," he says at one point. "Then I trained hard and I beat Mr. de Maupassant.")

[2] This letter to Bennett Cerf and the one that follows to his wife, Phyllis, were written separately, but included in the same envelope.

[3] Herbert Wise was Bennett Cerf's uncle.

in tears. Phyllis wrote me about your house (or houses) in P-Town.[1] It must
have been fun. Hope you have a good winter, interrupted by a trip to Sicily

Love

T

[Collection Columbia University Library]

TO PHYLLIS CERF

[Venice]
[22 September 1950]

Phyllis dear—

Have got the gondola shoes, and am sending them by regular mail. My
mother, who was just here, was supposed to take them but forgot. However, I did send you a little trinket by her. She will leave it by Random
House when she gets back to N.Y. next month. I loved your letter, and
wished I could have helped with the painting of those shacks. I don't think
I will be in N.Y. this winter (though one can never tell); but I do think of
you and miss you—how I would love a long four hour lunch. Write me,
honey. Love et mille tenderesse [sic]

T

[Collection Columbia University Library]

TO ANDREW LYNDON

Taormina,
Oct 1st, 1950

Darling—

Had your sweet letter in Venice, and today, arriving back here, found
another letter mailed the 10th of Sept. Of course your news saddens and

---

[1] Provincetown, Massachusetts.

upsets me; I can't believe it is turning out this way: have brooded over it a good deal, and did, despite your admonishment, write to Harold—not to criticize him (or you), but merely to say that I thought it a great waste.[1] Well. Allons.

Honey, there is this: we would like you to have the apartment on 76th Street. You can move in right away. The rent is $16. a month. Call Jack's brother, either at the apt. (Re 7-1085) or at The Wall Street Journal, where he works, and tell him he is to give you the key. Of course we don't know when we will be coming back, but I don't think it will be soon. I offered the apartment to Newton, but I do not now think it would be a good place for him to stay, not in his present frame of mind. He would not like it really, and should be in a place with more obvious comforts. Maybe you could help him. At any rate, let me know at once if you are going to take the apt.

So happy you thought Local Color came out well. Have not seen or heard of a single review: it might as well have been dropped in the ocean. Has Random advertised it at all? Delighted to hear about Doris [Lilly] selling the book, and only hope Phoebe can pull herself together and finish it.[2] And I do hope something good comes of the television scripts. I should think "Petrified Man" would be wonderful.[3]

We had a wonderful whirl in Venice and Rome, many people, much to drink, and have returned to the quiet of Taormina quite pale and exhausted. I'm glad to be back in Taormina, at the same time wish more than a little we were in New York, where there is you and Phoebe and all the things that are really important to me. But I must take my courage in hand and stick it out with the book. Oh it does frighten me, though; this lonely mountain, the wind, and winter coming on.

Do you expect to see much of Harold? What precisely are your relations?

If Goyen is back in town give him my love. I thought the reviews of his book, at least the few I saw, were incredibly dumb and dreary.

I love you, darling; you are my most precious friend, you are always near to me. Many kisses

T

[Collection New York Public Library]

---

[1] The news was that Lyndon and Harold Halma had broken up.
[2] Phoebe Pierce helped Lilly write her book *How to Meet a Millionaire*, which was published in 1951.
[3] "Petrified Man" was a story in Eudora Welty's first book, *A Curtain of Green* (1941).

TO GRAY FOY AND LEO LERMAN

Fontana Vecchia
Taormina, Sicily
Oct. 5, 1950

Gray, Leo, dear ones—

I loved having both your letters, and am answering them together because, Lord knows, I ain't got much news: no sense repeating it twice.

We spent the month of September in Venice, and it was beautiful, exactly what I wanted after a long summer's labor: oh am working hard, and do so hope you will think well of what I am doing. I was so happy, Gray, that you liked The House of Flowers. Well, one night (in Venice) who should come sauntering up but Howard Rothchild [Rothschild]—never an attractive vision, but what has happened to him: his mouth, and general manner, is more bitter-persimmon than ever. But I only said hello, and went my way. Another funny thing: one night in Harry's bar, which is always too crowded to know whether your hand is your own, a tall man leaned over and greeted me most effusively. I couldn't think who he was, except he was English and asked me "how is Leo?" Suddenly I thought—it must be Henry Green[1] (who I met once at 1453).[2] So I introduced him to the people we were with as Henry Green. He asked me to have lunch the next day. I was surprised to find him accompanied at lunch by an obvious piece of Limehouse trade: I'd not thought H. Green "so". I started to talk about books etc, but Mr. Green didn't seem to have heard of anyone I mentioned. Terribly strange. Then finally of course it turned out he wasn't H. Green at all. His name was Peter Wilson. I was quite put out.

What do you make of the Andrew-Harold separation? I never thought Harold would do it.

I must say, Gray, that house where you were staying in Chicago sounded powerfully grim. It upset me to think of you there, away from the coziness of Lexington Avenue.

Now, I want you both to save your pennies and give everyone Local Color for Christmas—I'm afraid its sales will be limited strictly to my friends.

Leo Lamb, I would love to read the book you are working on. The material is so wonderful. I hope you are getting on with it.

---

[1] British novelist.
[2] Lerman's apartment was at 1453 Lexington Avenue.

I'm glad to be back at Fontana; it is lonesome, and strange, but I am really quite content. They are harvesting the grapes now, and the air is sweet with the smell of new wine—I wish both of you were here, we could be so happy. I miss you, my darlings, and send you my tenderest love

T

[Collection Columbia University Library]

TO ROBERT LINSCOTT

Taormina, October, 1950

Great White Father—

Here I am, back at the grind—though it will be a few days before I climb that china tree again.[1] Meanwhile, am <u>struggling</u> through an article for Bazaar on my happy life in Sicily: need the money, my dear. The story, A Diamond Guitar, is going to be in the November Bazaar—please read it.

Have just had the first batch of <u>Local Color</u> reviews. Nearly all of them were good—at least the great chest-pounding he-men spit less venom than usual. God forbid they should ever take me to their hearts; when that time comes, I'd best retire. I do hope somebody is buying the book—I should hate for Random House to have to cut its staff, and put all of you to scrubbing floors.

I've been so happy about your reaction to my chapters. It is very real to me, more real than anything I've ever written, probably ever will. Satisfying as, in that sense, it is, it keeps me in a painful emotional state: memories are always breaking my heart, I cry—it is very odd, I seem to have no control over myself or what I am doing. But my vision is clear, and if I can half execute that vision it will be a beautiful book.

Had a letter from Goyen this morning. I like him so much. I think the title of his new book is good, Ghost and Flesh. In the same mail came the most appalling news: my cousin Gordon Persons has been elected Governor of Alabama—he is a mush-head, believe me.[2] What is America coming to?

---

[1] Several characters in *The Grass Harp* find refuge in a tree house.

[2] Seth Gordon Persons was governor of Alabama from 1951 to 1955. He worked to increase funding for roads and education, but he also supported bills to limit the rights of unions and to discourage blacks from voting.

They are harvesting the grapes now. I went over and stomped a tub or two myself. It was a delicious feeling, sqush, sqush [*sic*].

I suppose you know that Newton had a nervous collapse and will not be teaching at Smith this fall. I think he ought to get out of N'hampton for good.

Write me, dear Bob; I am homesick these autumn days, and would love to be crossing Madison Avenue with you in tow. My best to everyone. With all affection

T

P.S. Phoebe and Doris Lilly finally sold that book—to Putnams.[1]

[Collection Columbia University Library]

TO CECIL BEATON

Taormina, October, 1950

Cecil dearest,

I was so happy, on coming back from Venice, to find your letter. But Lord, honey, you should have stayed in Taormina—away from all that rain, all those frustrations: I hate to think of your garden wrecked—hate now to think of all the trouble you are having over G.G. [Greta Garbo] (funny, has it ever struck you? those initials have double significance). Never fear, little lamb: your day is coming! What a shame, though, that you have never had a chance to wear your lovely suit. Why don't you pop back down here! The sun is still shining ever so brightly, the sea has never been warmer. But I daresay cold weather is on its way—and a lonely winter for me, as really I must stay here working quietly: much as I should like to be in New York, at least for a few months. Ah well, maybe you will come to Italy in the spring. We had a lovely time in Venice—marvelous things to eat which, as you must remember, is not Sicily's strong point. The tea party with Fulco [di Verdura], Simon [Fleet],[2] Juliet [Duff], must have been rather sad: that is, surely Juliet & Jules loathe each other. I would <u>love</u> to read the new play; it could be terribly good, I think: it is most certainly a promising situation. I wonder if you might not send me it, a

---

[1] *How to Meet a Millionaire.*
[2] Fleet lived with Juliet Duff.

carbon; I would return it promptly.[1] I've heard that the reason the Kanins [Garson Kanin and Ruth Gordon] dropped Janie's play[2] was that they, the Kanins, demanded All Rights, and Oliver S. [Smith] refused to let them have it. Am so happy that you thought Local Color turned out well; it is, at any rate, a beautifully made book: maybe it will have some sort of Christmas sale—though that probably is an idle hope. Of all people, who should I have had a letter from but Thermistocles [Themistocles] Hoetis—back in New York, and looking for a job.[3] Frankly, I'm afraid he is one of the unemployables.

Well, my dear, I must return now to my friends in the tree: they do not like to sit too long in one position. Need I say that I miss you? Write your poor loving friend, he cherishes your letters. mille tendresse [*sic*]

T

Jack sends his best; Kelly says he misses your leg.

[Collection St. John's College, Cambridge University]

TO WILLIAM GOYEN

Taormina, Sicily,
October 12, 1950

Bill dear—

I love to think of you knitting and darning, writing at a kitchen table. At any rate, I think you are better off in N.Y.—Chicago, never! I think the title "Ghost and Flesh" is beautiful, please don't change it. It has for me a wonderful evocativeness; and I long to read the stories.[4]

We spent September in Venice—it was exactly the kind of holiday I needed, though, as a result, am suffering tortures trying to get back to work. Am too keyed-up. The reviews of Local Color have been more or less good, but in quite an uninteresting way, and I am very much put-out by the amount and kind of advertising that has been done—believe me, I would

---

[1] Beaton's play *The Gainsborough Girls*.
[2] *In the Summer House*.
[3] A year younger than Capote, Hoetis was a Greek American who lived in Paris for several years after World War II and edited an avant-garde magazine called *Zero*, which published, among others, Samuel Beckett, Paul Bowles, and Jean-Paul Sartre.
[4] Goyen's volume of stories, *Ghost and Flesh*, was published by Random House in 1952.

rather have had <u>no</u> ads than be inserted at the bottom of list-ads (or even at the top). RH [Random House] is so good to me in most ways—but I feel as though I must make a complaint.

So: you are up to your naughty tricks again—why don't you tell me what goes on in your life? All you do is tease. And here I am thousands of miles away.

They are harvesting the grapes here, making the new wine. Sig. Barti, a friend here, let me stomp out a tub or two, and I did enjoy it, jumping up and down on all those fat squshy [*sic*] grapes.

Am very upset about Andrew—I can't think what will happen. He is so charming, so sweet—so incapable. Or do you know that he and Harold [Halma] are finito? H. was no prize—but at least he gave A. a center, not to mention <u>support</u>. A. is now living in Jack's apt. right around the corner from you: 232 E. 76. I hope you will see him.

There was an article in the Italian paper Il Tempo about modern American writers and it contained a long paragraph about you, very flattering. I meant to cut it out, but now can't find it.

We were in Rome for a few days, but did not see Gian-Carlo [Menotti] as I did not feel up to all the nuisance of locating him. What kind of opera is it that you are writing with Sam [Samuel Barber]? I once tried to do one for Aaron Copland but somehow couldn't work up the right kind of interest: vanity, I suppose—I kept thinking how Aaron would get all the credit.

Tell me, have you met Marylou Aswell (or Peters)? I know you would love her. She is fine for hermits like you.

Ah, little Hermit, T misses you, loves you. Write me soon—say, the next 20 minutes. Mille tenderesse [*sic*], precious

T

[Collection Unknown]

TO ANDREW LYNDON

Taormina,
October, 1950

Darling—

So happy you are settled in at 232; I think it is a fun place to live, and I daresay you will not be having to move out because of Newton. He writes that he is going to Ohio to teach in Jan.—which does seem to me a dreary notion.

Here: rain, rain! The kind of rain you can't see through. Kelly won't go out in it to do his toilette—so full of piss, poor dear, that his stomach's twice the size it should be. The rain, they say, is likely to keep up for several weeks, in which case I shall be covered with fungus.

Thank you, honey, for the review and the White parody of Ol' Hem.[1] Have you read T. Williams [sic] novel?[2] Molto volgare, to put it mildly. He is a bad writer.

Gordon Sager has turned up here. A strange, heartless boy; I wish that I could like him, but—Anyway, he has just published a new novel, The Invisible Worm (hideous [sic] title); it's about Taormina.[3] Gerald, the only well-done character, is an astonishingly accurate portrait of Douglas Cooper, the English art critic who was so mad for Bill Lieberman.[4] It's a bad novel—with amusing moments; you ought to look at it.

Next week—Peggy Guggenheim. During a rash moment in Venice I said come on down to Sicily, dear. Lord God, she is arriving next Tuesday.

I'm glad you and Phoebus have got together again. Poor darling, she wrote me of her crisis. But maybe she will make some money out of this Lilly thing.

I've been wanting to ask, what has happened to Marguerite [Young]? Has she ever finished that book?[5]

Would adore to see the Merman show. Have you seen Wolcott Gibb's [sic] play?[6] I would love a first-hand account of that. New York in the autumn—really, it is the only place to be. Well, I guess I shall just have to go on conversing with nature—that is, if this downpour ever lets up and nature appears again.

Honey, collect masses of gossip for me—for instance, is it true that Glenway W. [Wescott] has broken his neck?[7] I heard that in Rome. Incidentally, I've seen the nude pictures of Miss Pittsburgh—Cadmus, who

---

[1] E. B. White parodied Hemingway's 1950 novel, *Across the River and into the Trees*, calling it *Across the Street and into the Grill*.

[2] Tennessee Williams's first novel, *The Roman Spring of Mrs. Stone* (1950).

[3] *The Invisible Worm* centers on the suicide of a rich American woman in Sicily.

[4] Lieberman, like Cooper, was an art critic.

[5] Marguerite Young's massive novel *Miss MacIntosh, My Darling* was not published until 1965.

[6] Ethel Merman was starring in the Broadway musical comedy *Call Me Madam*, which opened on October 12, 1950. Wolcott Gibbs's Fire Island comedy *Season in the Sun* was on Broadway at the time.

[7] Glenway Wescott, who had gained modest fame in the twenties and was a well-known figure in literary New York, was the author of such novels as *The Pilgrim Hawk* and *The Grandmothers*.

was in Venice, had them. Nothing to fuss over: about as big as your little finger.

Love to Harold, the lamb. Jack sends love to you, doll, ditto Kelly. ditto moi.

T'amo

T

[Collection New York Public Library]

TO MARY LOUISE ASWELL

Fontana Vecchio [*sic*]
Taormina Sicily
Oct 30 1950

Precious Mary lou—

I was so happy with your letter. It made me burn with longing to see you. Oh that I could! I hope this book will be half-worth all those sacrifices—like coming home, like being with the people I love.

Darling, you can write to Newton at 45 Prospect Street. He will not be teaching at Smith this year, and I think he plans to be in New York the month of November. But he is going to teach in January at Ohio State—anything, I gather, to get away from Northampton. I pray that you and Fritz will see him.

I'm sorry that Frances [McFadden] is leaving the Bazaar—she has been very sweet to me. Is she going just to take it easy? I hope she liked A House in Sicily—was delighted that you did[1] . . . speaking of houses, <u>where</u> are you living?

Had a letter from Pearl, who is on her way home. There is a nice room for her. Apparently, she does not seem to be taking too well to Europe—except, ugh, England.

Have you seen that wretched Jane Bowles? She has not written either Jack or I since last spring. You tell her to get on the ball.

No one in Taormina, except Orson Welles, whom I like very much. He

---

[1] "A House in Sicily," a description of Capote's life in Taormina, was published by *Harper's Bazaar* in January 1951.

is planning to make a movie here. I think he and Pearlie will hit it off—I plan so, at any rate.

Honey, I know that you are happy and well. Give my love to Fritz, to Duncan and Pidgy—dear God, how grown they must be. Dear God, I am 26—I wanted always to be 25.

Jack sends his dearest love.

Me too,

T

[Collection Aswell Family]

TO ROBERT LINSCOTT

Fontana Vecchia
Taormina
November 1950

Dear Bob—

Everyone says Sicily has a delightful winter climate: I don't care, I'm cold. But it cheers me up to think of you sitting by your Magnavox in your lovely warm apartment. Do write me the delights of civilization.

I've finished a new part of the book, but will wait to send it until I have another. Hope you will like it. Did you read my story, A Diamond Guitar? P.S. I'm glad you liked [sentence incomplete].

Bob, will you do me a great favor? I forgot to send Local Color to my old school teacher, and she is quite incensed. The address is: Catherine R. Wood, Peter's Rd., Riverside, Conn.

For the sake of the book I've made up my mind to stick it out here. Simply the desire to be somewhere else ought to urge me on. But I do like Sicily really.

I miss you. Write me. Love

T

Just at this moment received your letter. Am simply astonished about Phoebe! Why on earth would she presume you would give her $350.? Incredible. Her mother, who is certifiably mad, did some absurd thing on the stock market 2 years ago with most of the money Mr. Pierce left—so no, she hasn't any money. She <u>must</u> be in a state to have done such a fantastic thing. I haven't heard from her in weeks.

I'm disappointed about Local Color. It should sell more, and perhaps eventually will.[1] What did Isherwood's travel books sell?

Suppose you've heard the awful news about Marylou Aswell? I <u>begged</u> her not to marry that horrible Fritz Peters. Insane—you don't have to look at him twice to know that. He tried to kill her by running a car into a tree.

Write me. Give my best to Bennett and Bob Haas.

[Collection Columbia University Library]

TO CECIL BEATON

Taormina
November 1950

Cecil dear—

Have just returned from wild inside-outside tour of the island. A shame you did not see it all while you were here—the mountain towns: so lovely, heartbreaking. We stopped a few days in Palermo, and went to Monreale: the cathedral is as beautiful as you said, such austere opulence. But I am glad to be back in Taormina. Do you think I will ever get away from here? And certainly we must meet in Italy in the spring.

Precious, I hope you had a good holiday in Paris, that you were, so to say, properly distracted. Don't wear yourself out in New York. If you are going to be at the Sherry-Netherland (and I take for granted you are) I will write you there. At least it will be fun getting back in your tower.[2]

A friend who saw "Mrs. Tanqueray" says your sets and costumes are l'ultima—the whole show in fact. Herlie, she said, was a little monotonous.[3] Be sure and report on the N.Y. shows—as well as other things, like: George Davis, H. Brown,[4] J. Bowles ad infinitum.

Strange thing: when Hansen left here, about 2 weeks ago, a regular army arrived bringing me a radio, about 50 books and 200 records—Hansen having willed them to me. What makes it sad is: I never spoke to the

---

[1] At that point, *Local Color* had sold a little over three thousand copies.
[2] In 1950 Beaton designed a suite on the thirty-seventh floor of the Sherry-Netherland Hotel on Fifth Avenue. In return, he received a 50 percent discount when he stayed in the suite and a 25 percent discount at the hotel's restaurant.
[3] Eileen Herlie was the lead actress.
[4] Garbo used "Miss Brown" as a pseudonym.

man—except that one day when I was in a boat with you. Do you suppose he heard me from afar? Another strange thing: Orson Welles asked me to play a part in a movie he is going to make here. Naturally I declined. He (Welles) is trying to rent Bastine, Fulco's house—but there seems to be some difficulty. Are you really such great friends? He talks as though you'd grown up together.

I am getting on with my book, and long to show you more of it. Honey, don't tell anyone about the little bit you read—not that you would have any reason to.

When is the Photobiography coming out?[1] I hope it sells a zillion copies, and maybe it will if one of the book clubs takes it.

This is all for the moment. Jack sends love, and Kelly says he misses your leg to ride against. I miss all of you, leg included. Bon voyage. And love
      T

[Collection St. John's College, Cambridge University]

TO ANDREW LYNDON

Fontana Vecchia
Taormina
November 14 1950

Little heart—

Until your letter I had not heard about Marylou; then in the evening Pearl, who is here, had a letter from Marylou herself—who said Fritz had tried to kill her and had been put away in a hospital. But isn't that exactly what I said would happen? That someday he would try to kill her? Still I get no pleasure from having been proved right. It must be <u>agony</u> for her. I wish that I could be there, at least to try and help her.

I had a letter from Linscott with a disturbing and astonishing paragraph re Phoebe. She came to his office in a great state, told him she desperately needed $350—then settled for $20. which he lent her. But whatever is wrong?

(3 hrs later)

---

[1] Beaton's *Photobiography* was published in 1951.

Just as I finished the preceding page there was a knocking at the door, and who should it be but Robert Horan (of the Menotti-Barber menage).[1] So he stayed to lunch, and was, I must say, very charming, very witty. Apparently he is going to be here for some weeks.

No, sweetie, I have not applied for a Guggenheim. I simply recieved [sic] a strange communique from that man Moe[2] asking for copies of my books. Don't know what it means.

I hope Newton arrived, and that you saw the Fry play.[3] Write me about it. I loved it when I read it—but such diverse folk as Auden and Beaton tell me I was wrong to.

Sent you a card yesterday, explaining we'd just come back from a giro of Sicily. A wonderful trip visually, but very tense on personal scores because Peggy Guggenheim was with us and she and Jack no-like each other. Quite a story.

In Il Tempo, the Rome paper, there was a long story the other day about an American writer, one Donald Windham, who had met two young men at the Coliseum and taken them home with him ("They told me they would show me the sights of Rome.") whereupon he was set upon, bound and gagged and thoroughly robbed. As this makes the 3rd time Donny has been robbed within 4 months, it is getting to be quite a legend. I daresay he will give up this time and head for home—perhaps at the request of the Italian govt. After all, they can't throw every able bodied male into prison. The kid here in Taormina was sent off for 6 years!!!

Precious, it is getting late. I miss you most at these twilight times. Write me, sweetie. Love to Harold. Love from Jack and Kelly

and

Me

[Collection New York Public Library]

---

[1] Robert Horan, an American poet, was the lover of Gian Carlo Menotti.

[2] Henry Allen Moe, chief administrator of the John Simon Guggenheim Memorial Foundation.

[3] Christopher Fry's The Lady's Not for Burning.

TO ROBERT LINSCOTT

Taormina
December 2nd, 1950

Dear Bob—

You write so <u>briefly</u>—I like details: what you're doing, who you're seeing; but, poor lamb, I know you must be snowed in.

In a week or so am sending more chapters—it will be the halfway mark then. That is, I am half-finished. Longing to know what you will think then. If Bennett or Bob Haas want to read the new chapters that is fine; but I really don't want anybody else to. Also, am sending you a small Christmas trinket—so see it doesn't get lost in the mailroom.

Newton writes that he dropped in on you while in the city. Did he seem better to you?

I wrestled with a Thanksgiving dinner and it came out pretty well—except the turkey was too tough.

I grow increasingly alarmed about Phoebe—not only the incident with you, but several other odd stories have reached me. It seems so out of character. Of course she is in a terrible situation—living in one room in some hideous hotel with that crazy mother. Still, most of it is her own fault—she's thrown away two very good jobs. It's so maddening, because I think she has a wonderful talent—but it's as though she's suddenly lost all sense of self.

Mt. Etna erupted last week—a catastrophe that continues still; every day there is a new explosion.[1] I can see Etna from where I'm sitting now—there are seven rivers of fire flowing down from the crater, an astonishing sight, quite beautiful, especially at night.

I miss you, Bob.

Always,

T

[Collection Columbia University Library]

---

[1] Mount Etna's volcanic eruptions from November 1950 to December 1951 produced one of its most voluminous lava flows in three hundred years.

TO BENNETT CERF

Truman Capote
Fontana Vecchia
Taormina, Sicily
December 5, 1950

Dear Bennett—

I understand that in the new musical "Guys & Dolls" there is a song called "A Bushel and A Peck" (I love you a bushel and a peck and a hug around the neck).[1] On page 84 of Other Voices, Other Rooms, you will find this: "I love you, Joel, I love you a bushel and a peck and a hug around the neck." It is quite my own line. And though Oscar Wilde may have gone into the public domain, I've not. In other words, depending somewhat on your view, I intend to bring suit. To what extent would such an action involve Random House?

Several weeks ago a lawyer called Gilbert telephoned my agent, Marian Ives; he said he was the legal representative of G. Schirmer, Irving Berlin etcetera. He wanted to know: where did I get the jingle a bushel and a peck etc. My agent told him she thought I'd made it up: why? Oh just curious, he said.

Now of course I don't think I should let them get away with this. It is so complete a case of plagiarism that I don't even see why I should have to take it to court. But perhaps I am naive about such things. What do you think?

Please show this letter to Bob.

By this same mail I am writing to my lawyer; in the event the Random House lawyer would like to speak with him, he is: Nathan Rogers, 511 Fifth Avenue.[2]

My love to Phyllis; with much affection

Truman

[Collection Columbia University Library]

---

[1] *Guys and Dolls* opened at the 46th Street Theatre in Manhattan on November 24, 1950, and was an immediate hit, with a run of 1,200 performances.

[2] The matter was dropped when Capote's mother called Cerf to tell him that "A Bushel and a Peck" was an old Southern rhyme and that she distinctly remembered singing it to him when he was a baby.

TO WILLIAM GOYEN

Fontana Vecchia
Taormina, Sicily
December 16, 1950

Bill dear—

I was so happy to know where you were—though I don't approve at all: no wonder you have pleurisy, sitting in a cold Chicago basement. Did romance take you there? There could be no other acceptable reason. But if you are working well, then perhaps it is a good thing.

Andrew's address is: 232 East 76th Street. Do write him, I know he wonders about you. And I have given your address to Kinch [Robert] Horan. He is a charming person, I like him very much indeed. He seems quite happy here (came for a week, and has been here nearly two months), and is writing with a vengeance. Unfortunately, he got a terrible leg infection and that has been a great nuisance. I expect you will hear from him in the next few days.

As for my own work: what with war at the window, and a river of lava at the door (Etna, you know, has had the worst eruption in its history) I haven't been able to really concentrate. All the same, I seem to be getting somewhere. I've no idea what to do about coming home; I should hate to, at just this point—Lord, precious, what a generation we were born into.

In addition to all this, I am involved in a lawsuit with the producers of a show called "Guys & Dolls". There is a song in it made completely out of a jingle that I wrote and included in Other Voices. And, though Oscar Wilde may have gone into the public domain, I've not.

Pearl is still here; she says she had a letter from you.[1] I think she is unhappy over her bust-up with Dylan T [Thomas]. But the magic of Fontana seems to be working on her, too.

I was pleased that Faulkner got the Nobel Prize—but am far from pleased with his Collected Stories. With three exceptions they seem to me unwritten, unreadable, absolute frauds. Dr Martino!! An Artist at Home!! Honor!! Oh oh oh. Did you read that, when he arrived in Sweden, he listed his profession as farmer? I'm not so sure he was wrong. And did you see the letter he sent Time defending Hemingway?[2] Ye Gods.

---

[1] Pearl Kazin was a guest at the Fontana Vecchia for three months.
[2] Ernest Hemingway's newest novel, Across the River and into the Trees, had been savaged by the critics. Faulkner came to his defense in a letter to Time.

I hear Elizabeth Bowen is taking a tour with Eudora [Welty] through the South. I would give a lot to be a member of <u>that</u> party.

Well, honey, that's about it. Have a good Christmas, dear Bill—we will be thinking of you. I wish I could send you a present: will all my love do?

   T

[Collection Unknown]

TO ANDREW LYNDON

   Fontana Vecchia
   Taormina, Sicily
   New Year's eve 1950

Precious One—

So happy to have your long and oh so newsy letter. What did Santa Claus bring you? I got a beautiful black and red sweater from Jack, a pair of gloves from Pearl, a book from Newton, a book from Linscott, $25 from Nina & Joe, a gold cigarette case from the Cerfs, et c'est tout. But our Christmas was marred (understatement) by Robert Horan, who decided to kill himself: very nearly did, too: sleeping pills. As a result of all this, I had to take him to Milan (900 miles) where Gian-Carlo Menotti took over the burden, poor guy. It's a sad and sordid story, and please do not mention it to <u>anyone</u>. On the way home I stopped in Rome for 2 days, and that was rather fun. Saw lots of people, including Donny—who has run out of money, but completely, and is on his way home—sailing from England Jan. 30. Got back to Taormina yesterday, and am very happy to be here. I don't know how I shall ever be able to leave for good and all. Is my piece about the house in the Jan. Bazaar? Was supposed to be.

As for Phoebe: I've known her to go through periods somewhat similar, though never <u>quite</u> like this—and I guess during those times what happened was we just called a halt, understood to be temporary, on our friendship. The business of Marguerite and the check is really incredible. You ask what I think you should say or do. Nothing. Because there is nothing. Aside from the hallucinatory part, I wonder if she really is counting on magazine sales: if the book is coming out in April, as I understand it is, they haven't time to sell anything anywhere, for all those monthlys [sic] work at least 4 months in advance.

Thank you, honey, for your "review" of Bless You All.[1] Cecil also wrote me about it—he too said it was dreary.

Yes, I saw what Time said about Newton. I hope he gets the Pulitzer Prize—it would be a disgrace if he didn't.[2] The occasional letters he sends are rather cryptic. How does he seem to you—really? Whatever happened about Morton? Darling, when he was in N.Y. I hope you did have <u>some</u> little fling with him: tell mother the truth.[3] Mother so seldom gets the truth these days.

Pearl is still here. She is not, alas, the most stimulating girl alive, but I guess it is all right—and Jack seems to like her. She is down at the telephone office today, because Victor Kraft[4] is calling her long distance from Rio De Janeiro.

I miss you always, precious; Jack sends love, and to Harold, too. Many kisses,

much love

T

P.S. BUON CAPO ANNO [*sic*]

[Collection New York Public Library]

TO LEO LERMAN AND GRAY FOY

Fontana Vecchia
Taormina, Sicily
January [4] 1951

Dear Gray, dear Myrt,

Who is Leo Gray? Some actor friend of yours? Anyway, <u>he</u> sent us such a lovely Christmas cable, and I want you to thank him very much indeed. And Gray dear, thank you for the beautiful Christmas card; it had the place of honor on our mantel.

I hope old Claus did well by you both. I got a wonderful sweater, won-

---

[1] Harold J. Rome's musical revue *Bless You All* had opened on Broadway on December 13, 1950.

[2] Newton Arvin's biography of Melville won the National Book Award for Nonfiction in 1951 but not the Pulitzer Prize.

[3] Arvin and Lyndon had, in fact, had a fling while Capote was in Europe in 1948.

[4] Kraft was a photographer and the companion of Aaron Copland.

derful gloves, a check for 25 dollars, and the collected stories of Farmer [William] Faulkner, which weren't worth collecting [if you] ask me. Our tree was a giant bouquet of poinsettas [*sic*]; we had turkey with chestnut stuffing and Soave wine and orange-almond layer cake: not bad for the wilds of Sicily. Right afterwards, unfortunately, I had to make an emergency trip to Milan and Rome, which was tiresome because I hate leaving here at all. Alas, alas, I'm afraid I've turned into a real country boy. You wouldn't believe the quietness of our lives; or that we could stand it. Nowadays the weather is very curious, summer in the morning and winter in the afternoon. But spring has already started: fields of daisies, breaking almond blossoms. All that is sad is knowing that we will have to leave here, though I did so want to stay until I finished my book, but—and, too, I had looked forward to the thought you might come here this spring.

I suppose New York is exciting now in a rather grisly way. Having a good time with a vengeance etc. Or is it not like that at all? There is no kind of real war feeling here—at least no tension about it, and no conversation either; or maybe it's just that we don't see enough people.

Pearl is flourishing—though a little frostbitten from time to time. She is working very hard, and I liked the one story I've seen. Leo seems to have been the springboard for the main character, but just that, for really it is not him. Pearl has certain qualms about it for fear people would say it was you, and I daresay they would: the physical facts are so like you: all the same I said she should show it to you and see what you thought, so maybe she will.[1]

From the few reports we hear, Marylou seems to be handling the situation; my instincts about her are good; I think she will live with a great deal more direction in the future.

Jack is fine, and sends his love; so does old Kelly dog. Now both of you write me—long letters full of LOW gossip. I miss you. Love—Love—Love

and

Love

T

[Collection Columbia University Library]

---

[1] Kazin's story "The Raven" was published by *Botteghe Oscure* in 1952 (vol. 9), and people did indeed think that the chief protagonist, Kuney, was a portrait of Lerman. Lerman himself was deeply offended by passages that portrayed him as little more than an intellectual gadfly. "He knew without a doubt the precise moment when the James 'revival' went into decline," Kazin wrote, "that Stendhal was old hat, Cocteau a bore, and Genet the newest, freshest genius of them all. . . . Kuney's spongey availability to shifts of taste and favor, his facility at a one-hour mastery of sophisticated clichés on any subject, his terror that intellectual sobriety might stamp him dull, his brash inside knowledge about every pen and brush and piano in New York—these were the goods the editors bought from him."

TO JOHN MALCOLM BRINNIN

Fontana Vecchia
Taormina, Sicily
January 7 1951

Malcolm dear—

Last week I was in Venice for a few days: so beautiful, a little snow falling on the Grand Canal, piazza San Marco vast and empty, a great burst of warmth when you opened the door of Harry's bar—I thought of you, and meant to send a card. But a letter is best, for I have many things to mention. It is spring here in Sicily: the whole valley is awash with almond blossoms, and we can have lunch on the Terrace again. Pearl [Kazin] is still here—your mutual friend, D. [Dylan] Thomas, has gone to Persia; but apparently he and Pearl are meeting the middle of next month in London.[1] C'est vrai amour.

About Jack: he has been so happy over your interest in his book, it means a good deal to him I think. He has delayed about sending the mss. for several reasons: but mainly it is because we have been so touch-and-go about coming home, and he thought it would be best if he brought it with him. He has written a great deal more, and I believe it is going to be a very extraordinary novel indeed. Now it seems we <u>are</u> coming home: in March. I hate to, but with the war climate so dark I suppose Americans should be in their own country. Anyway, Jack will show you the mss. when we get there.

As you probably know, Newton has gone to the University of Ohio—at an <u>INCREDIBLE</u> salary.[2] I hope he never goes back to Smith.

Marylou seems, at least in the letters, to have a fine hold on herself. Maybe people will listen to me hereafter; after all, everything I predicted, down to the fact that he would try to kill her, came true.[3] Though it is hardly the kind of prophesy [sic] one enjoys having proved. Do you see her at all? I hope so.

We had a ghastly experience here with Robert Horan (only please don't mention this). He tried to kill himself, and very nearly did: sleeping pills.[4]

---

[1] Brinnin followed Dylan Thomas's trips to America and after Thomas's death in 1953 wrote *Dylan Thomas in America,* which was published in 1955.

[2] Ohio State University in Columbus.

[3] "He" was Fritz Peters.

[4] Horan, a young poet from California, became despondent when Thomas Schippers, a rising young composer, replaced him in Gian Carlo Menotti's affections.

I got the brunt of the whole thing, doctors, police,—couldn't do anything else for ten days. Finally we unburdened him on Gian-Carlo M. Poor Menotti—he really has a suffering time. But I feel sorrier for Horan; he's simply hopeless.

I'm somewhat more than half-way through my book. If I am very patient and concentrated, I certainly should finish it this summer.

Everyone writes what a great success your Poetry Center series is. I suppose it is too late to be on the program. I would like to—towards the latter part of April—and provided they would give me 200. If you could arrange it, let me know. I have the most beautiful new suit (olive velvet) and I must have some place to show it off.

Give my love to Bill [Read]. How I wish you both were here—sitting in the sun. Do please write me—return post, hear. Much love, little blue eyes

   T

[Collection University of Delaware Library]

TO WILLIAM GOYEN

   Fontana Vecchia
   Taormina, Sicily
   January 19, 1951

Bill dear—

   I'm so happy you are leaving Chicago. You will like Yaddo, I'm almost certain. And now, I think, would be a good time to go—so few people. I often think of going back to Yaddo—but am a little afraid to because it was such a turning point in my life. But it is a wonderful place to work, I know you will finish your book. Lord that I could finish mine—but I'm no where near; heaven knows when that beautiful day will be. I love your title, Ghost and Flesh. How I long to read it. Tell me, is it a short book? Yes, Pearl is still here, but she is leaving early next month for Germany where she will be a week, and then flying home.

   I don't know where to begin telling you about Bob Horan. He was here about two months, and I grew very fond [of] him. It was obvious on what perilous ground he stood, but through some failure of insight I didn't foresee in what direction this would lead. Suddenly, in early December, his behaviour became, for the first time, really alarming. If we asked him here for dinner he just never would go home. One morning I came downstairs and found him still sitting up in the freezing cold living-room. Also he began showing rather marked hostilities towards Jack—it very nearly reached the point where Jack could not express an opinion. Finally we did not see him for 3 or 4 days—although I went to his hotel and left notes etcetera. One night the hotel sent me an emergency message. Bob had taken a box of sleeping pills, but had got sick and thrown up a lot; also the Doctor gave him caffein [sic] shots. So for several days I was there as a kind of nurse-companion. Bob just kept saying how much he loved Gian-Carlo, wanted to be with him, didn't want to live without him. But undoubtedly you know what that situation is about. Well, we got in touch with G-C, who is in Milan where they are doing his opera tomorrow night, and it was arranged that Bob was to go there—because I could no longer take the responsibility. He was well enough by Christmas eve to come here to Fontana—where he promptly collapsed. For three days I couldn't leave him because he said he was going to kill himself anyway. Frankly, my dear, I was getting <u>tired</u>. I couldn't work, hadn't worked in weeks, and the whole house was in turmoil. On Tuesday, when he was supposed to leave for Milan, he suddenly told me he couldn't possibly do so: dear God, I saw weeks more of it stretching before me. The only solution I could see was for me to <u>take</u> him to Milan. It was a hair-raising trip—I can't possibly write all the details now.

The rest of the story is just too sad and sordid. When we finally got to the hotel in Milan G-C. wasn't there. He was at a rehearsal. I could have killed him. But Bob, for his part, was dramatizing the situation as much as possible. When G.C. at last turned up Bob was incredibly insolent to him—made him out to be a monster of ambition and stupidity. And there was G-C jumping around pretending it was all a joke.

Then came the really sickening denouement. G-C came to my room, his face white as cold cream. All in a burst he said: Bob was ruining his life, that he'd spent $2,000 a month since he'd come to Europe and B's extravagances were taking all his money—<u>but</u> that none of this mattered so long as he did not have to go to bed with him, that for the last few years B forced him to make love and afterwards he, G.C., had to go and throw up. He also said that he was terribly in love with somebody else—some young American boy—and he was terrified of B's finding out.[1]

Well you can see that it was hopeless. Bob kept pleading with me to know what Gian-Carlo had said: did G.C. love him? I wanted to die myself.

---

[1] The young American was Thomas Schippers.

In a sick and twisted way B. does love Gian-Carlo; but he also loves the Mt. Kisco house, the life there. But G.C. says he will do anything in the world for Bob <u>except</u> live with him again.

I couldn't bear anymore, and left the next morning. Since then I've not heard one word from any of them—and I'm a little sore about it, too. Because I had to pack and forward all of Bob's luggage and pay over a hundred dollars worth of debts. I sent Gian-Carlo a bill for it more than 3 weeks ago—not a word. Of course that is an irrelevant detail, and I shouldn't mention it. But the total picture would be incomplete without this squalid little epilogue.

Darling, I hope my account of all this does not strike you as unsympathetic, unfeeling. But the truth is my feeling has been exhausted—and since those concerned are close to you I know you would rather have a straight, rather than sentimental, story.[1] I'm sure I need not say that all I've written is for you alone—though of course I know you will never make any reference to it.

I love you Bill. In this new year I wish all good things upon your dear head. Write me, precious.

T.

P.S. It isn't definite, but I may come home in early April. Perhaps you will still be at Yaddo—or somewhere that won't be too far away. Please write me.

[Collection Unknown]

TO MARY LOUISE ASWELL

Taormina, January 23, 1951

Marylou darling—

After a great deal of switching back and forth, I guess we've arrived at the only sensible conclusion, which is not to come home. I did want so to see you, see my friends; but I suppose it would be idiotic of me to make

---

[1] Goyen had been part of the Samuel Barber–Gian Carlo Menotti ménage in Mt. Kisco, a suburb north of New York City.

such a move before my book is finished. I hope, darling, I've not put you to much trouble—about a house, I mean.[1] I feel a great relief now that we've decided to stay.

I guess you will be seeing Pearl in a few weeks time; that is if she does take the plane-ride. I don't frankly think she should—she has been doing some good work on a novel, and I'm afraid, without more of a head start, all that will go up in smoke when she hits New York.

It is the most beautiful day, ravishingly springlike, with oranges and roses and almond blossoms all sweetening the air. I do, do wish you were here.

Jack has finished ¾ of his book, and it is remarkable—so different from anything he has done and by far the best.[2]

Has Leo returned, and safely, from his junket? I have been very annoyed, not so much with him as with Linscott who, for reasons I cannot fathom, let Leo read some chapters of my book. It makes me really wild! I would like however, in a month or two, for you to see what I've done. I will arrange it after I've finished what I'm doing now.

Darling, I want such good things for you. Did I write you what Franz Warmik [unclear], the wonderful German fortuneteller, said? Yes—I think I did. Please write me. Dearest love

T

[Collection Aswell Family]

TO ANDREW LYNDON

Taormina
Feb 1, 1951

Sweet One,

We are having a sudden cold snap—that is, my fingers are snapping off. So excuse the handwriting and general numbness.

Anyway, we won't be coming home in April—it would be rather ridiculous to interrupt my work at just this juncture. I've no idea <u>when</u> I will go back, but doubt that it will be before late summer. So I hope you will stay

---

[1] They had talked of renting a house together for the summer.
[2] Jack Dunphy's second novel, *Friends and Vague Lovers*, dedicated to Capote, was published by Farrar, Straus and Young in 1952.

happily undisturbed at 232. The only sad thing is I've wanted so to see you. But it will be all the better when I do.

Pearl is leaving on Sunday—going to Germany for a week, then home. She should be there the middle of the month.

Darling, how goes the job? I should think it would be fun, at least at first. But I hope it does not leave you too tired to do work of your own.

This is Carnival week in Sicily; there is a great dance in the piazza tonight, and I am working on a most elaborate mask of feathers and sequins.

I haven't heard from Phoebe in very nearly two months. I don't know her address; could you tell me? Because I do want to write her.

Did you ever see the Agee story in Botteghe Oscure? I've just read a beautiful book called The Face of Spain, by Gerald Brennan [Brenan]—published in England by The Turnstile Press.[1] He is the one who wrote that wonderful piece in the New Yorker last August—about looking for Lorca's tomb.

What happened to the Rose Tattoo?[2] I heard T.W. had bought a house in Key West and was going to live there with Frankie and the mad sister. It's best, I suppose, to have the source of your inspiration right on hand.

Darling, I can't bear it, my hands are ICE! Please write me. I love you so very much.

T

[Collection New York Public Library]

TO MARY LOUISE ASWELL

Fontana Vecchio [sic]
Taormina, Sicily
Feb 21 1951

Darling Marylou—

So happy to have your letter; I began admonishing you for not writing. See that you do, for, as Pearl will tell you, we <u>die</u> for mail; there is nothing more bitter than those fruitless long walks to the p.o.

I wish I <u>did</u> have a story to send you. I long so to write one, and maybe,

---

[1] Gerald Brenan's The Face of Spain (1950).
[2] The Rose Tattoo by Tennessee Williams opened on Broadway on February 3, 1951, and was published the same year.

when I finish the next chapter, I'll take just such a 'vacation'. Jack hasn't written any stories either. I do think you will like his new book. Nor have I read any good new stories. <u>Nothing</u> happens here—or nothing interesting unless you are familiar with all the characters. I guess by the time this reaches you Pearl will be home; I hope, in her new job, she will have time to work on her own writing.

Honey, do you see Phoebe at all? I know the mess she's in is a good deal her own making—but there are, as you know, so many extenuating circumstances. I understand, though I've not heard from her in some three months, that she has had a kind of breakdown. The way some people have deserted and slandered her is shameful. I wish you would have lunch with her. She respects you, and you just might be able to give her some encouragement.

It's really beautiful here now, and I'm getting quite tan again. Poor Pearl, I'm afraid she got the worst of the month. But even where you are, darling, winter is very nearly over—I hope you have a wonderful spring. I hope that because I pass over your terrible problems you [don't] think me indifferent to them: it is only that I feel that, like this winter, they are in the past, and will grow more so: put out new leaves, you can, it is in your nature. I love you tenderly. And love from Jack.

T

[Collection Aswell Family]

TO ANDREW LYNDON

Fontana Vecchia
Feb 28 1951

Darling lamb—

I could shake you, really I could: nearly 2 months and not a peep. <u>Whatever</u> are you doing? Which reminds me: two letters addressed to Phoebe at the Hotel Seville have been returned. Where, then, is she? She hasn't written me since early December.

All goes quietly on this front; I work along steadily, though the going grows more difficult. It is so very difficult to sustain. I have about sixty pages more—but they face me like Kilimanjaro. I wish you were here to encourage me.

I've started myself a new wardrobe—a foolhardy enterprise considering my finances. First off, I sent my measurements to Ferragamo in Florence and he has made me the most beautiful pair of black shoes. I'm afraid to wear them—and anyway Jack won't let me: says I must save them, I don't know for what. Then I've had three suits made out of a strange kind of flat velvet—to <u>die</u>, honey. Trouble is, I've no place to show off this finery.

You remember that famous wooden chandelier, the one Harold bought from me. Well tell him I've bought two exactly like it: $25 a piece. Now if he wants me to buy one for him I will do so.

What happens with your job? It's so mean of you not to have written me any of this.

I read <u>Finisterre</u>, Mr [Fritz] Peter's [*sic*] latest drivel.[1] Mechanical, so poorly written, so predictable—couldn't bear it. And you? Or did you bother? I had a letter from Marylou, who said IT[2] was living in Arizona and getting a divorce. She doesn't know how lucky she is—just to be alive.

We've got to wash Kelly today—it's nice and hot so he shouldn't catch a cold. I'm getting back my tan, which never quite went away. Well, I guess it's almost spring in New York too.

Oh—I had a note from Herr Isseyvoo [Christopher Isherwood] asking your address: that's all he ever writes me for. I obliged him for the umpteenth time. But honey, I <u>wish</u> you would keep your lovers better informed. It's so <u>hard</u> on mother.

Jack sends his love.

I miss you, sugar, and love you always

T

[Collection New York Public Library]

TO ROBERT LINSCOTT

Fontana Vecchia
Taormina, Sicily
Feb 28, 1951

Dear Bob—

It seems a long time, Lord yes, since I've heard from you, oh Wondrous One.

---

[1] Peters's novel was *Finistère*.
[2] Fritz Peters.

I'm typing my chapter five, very long it is; but don't think I will send it until I've finished the next. There is only one more after that, but it will be the longest one—and looms before me like Kilimanjaro. I ought to be finished in early July—now that will be about a year from the time I started, which is not an undue length of time, despite what Marian (and possibly you) say. Anyway, I'm doing my best to make it something we can all take pleasure in.

Thanks for The Disenchanted.[1] I enjoyed it, but rather half-heartedly. He has such a small sensibility, Schulberg; and I would say almost no feeling for language: time and again, during those unpunctuated lapses into 'stream-of-concious,' [sic] I felt the burn of embarrassment. I couldn't believe this man called Manly Halliday ever wrote a word worth reading—because Schulberg catches only the infantile elements of his mind.[2] At the end the young man says, "But Manly you've got to live to finish this book; now you not only know what happened but why," or something of the sort. Aside from being hokum in itself, this denouement provides an ironic comment on Schulberg's own work: see why? If Manly Halliday, despite Schulberg's coarse and pretended explanations, is left drifting in the void. Bob, I don't believe you liked this book.

Why don't you suggest the Modern Library reprint Sarah Orne Jewett's "The Country of The Pointed Firs"? I read it not long ago, and it seemed to me a singularly 'true' kind of book.

My quiet monkish life goes on as usual. It's the height of Spring here, the sun is very hot. Give my best to Bennett. I miss you. Love

T

P.S. Scribner's sent me a ludicrous book called <u>From Here To Eternity</u>. Combines the sillier qualities of Wolfe and the Naked-Dead kind of writing—but I'll bet it is a success. Let me know.[3]

---

[1] Published in 1950, Budd Schulberg's novel *The Disenchanted* was based on Schulberg's experience of writing a screenplay with F. Scott Fitzgerald shortly before Fitzgerald's death in 1940.

[2] Manley Halliday was the character modeled after Fitzgerald.

[3] James Jones's *From Here to Eternity* was both a critical and a popular success.

TO ROBERT LINSCOTT

Fontana Vecchia
Taormina, Sicily
March 1st, 1951

Dear Papa,

I'd just mailed you a letter when yours came yesterday. A joy to have it, too. You'd been so on my mind.

Well now, I do believe I can stick to those dates, pray so . . . though just today the immediate sense of having to is a little paralyzing. And oh Bob . . . I tried last night, I've tried all morning, and it's no Use: I <u>cannot</u> write 100 words, or even fifty, about the book. It isn't possible to "describe" the book. And I don't want anyone else to either. Newton could maybe; I will see that he does by jacket time. But in the meanwhile, as it's just for the catalogue, couldn't we pull that old chestnut: "The longawaited new novel etc"? Besides, it's more intriguing really if nobody knows what the hell it's about.

There are physical things, too. I want to use the same print that was in Local Color. And I want to have Anna Meyerson [Mayerson], the English artist, do a pen and ink drawing for the title page. She is a genuis [*sic*]. Maybe she would do a jacket for me too. She likes my work and I think she would do them for me for very little. All right?

I will send my new chapters as soon as I can.

I'm sorry Goyen is having such a poor time; but when has he not? and a good deal of it, I'm afraid, is his constant need to seem appealing: as though on your sympathy depended his sanity. I am so very fond of him; but I do weary of his adolescence.

I don't know about Phoebe. I've had two letters returned, and never a word from her. I think though that many people, and Leo in particular, have been too unkind about her. I sure would like to see her show them. But.

I'd better get back to work. Love like always

t

[Collection Columbia University Library]

TO ANDREW LYNDON

[Taormina, Sicily]
March 9, 1951

Magnolia my sweet,

Your letter came in the nick of time: now I can tell my lawyers to cancel the breach of promise suit I was bringing against one Magnolia Lyndon. But honey, you don't mention your job at all; for instance, what is old Floyd like—is he SO? I'm happy you're doing a new story; make a carbon, and I will return it. Oh yes, spring is here, but there is a sirocco today, and the whole house is rattling with wind: otherwise I would go out and pick you an orange blossom to enclose. Did you see Newton when he came to town? and the gold medal?[1] and was it pretty? suitable for beach wear, say? I may stay somewhere with him a few weeks in August; but that depends on such a lot of other things. At any rate, we won't leave here until July . . . either sail then, or go to Venice. The worst thing about Phoebe is, she ain't gonna make no $ outa that book, nothing that will make her purse a burden. I'm so disappointed by all this that I'm not sure how easy it will be for me to see her when I do come home. I'm glad that you have new friends, and going out more; but I don't believe that nobody's asked you in days and days—mother knows her child. I'd heard about Agee's heart attack, poor man; but was surprised when you said the Morning Watch was coming out as a book . . . it must be very brief indeed, or is there more to it than appeared in Botteghe Oscure?[2] I agreed a good deal with what you said about it. Scribners sent me that From Here To Eternity shit; and shit though it is, the young man who wrote it looks extraordinarily constipated.[3] Also finally finished Mr William's [*sic*] dame-and-dago drivel about Mrs Stone.[4] It's, well, pathetic. You didn't say much about The Rose Tattoo—what an irritating title; reminds me, I can't think why, of bedbugs. Incidentally, speaking of bedbugs, and thinking of [words missing] what became of the romance involving Ernest J and Howard D [Doughty]? Is Ernest back roaming Times Square in his riding breeches? Jack and Kelly just passed through the room . . . both said give you their love. I want to know about

---

[1] Arvin had won the National Book Award for his Melville biography.
[2] James Agee's short novel *The Morning Watch,* which had appeared in *Botteghe Oscure,* was published in book form (120 pages) by Houghton Mifflin in April 1951.
[3] James Jones.
[4] *The Roman Spring of Mrs. Stone* was a novel by Tennessee Williams.

Harold . . . is he doing all right with his work, how often do you see him? I don't know, I wish the two of you had never separated; I still in my mind can't quite make the division. Oh yes, tell me: do Paul [Bigelow] and Jordan [Massee] live together? Pearl wrote me that she'd had dinner with Leo and was quite revolted by him. She's written a story about him that would take the skin off an elephant.

Darling it [has] gotten so late, I had no idea, so with a millian [*sic*] kisses and all the love in the world for my precious, my only Sister (daughter?)

t

[Collection New York Public Library]

TO ROBERT LINSCOTT

[Taormina, Sicily]
March 11, 1951

Dear Keeper of The Golden Umbrellas And The Golden Keys to Wisdom And Happiness,

You didn't do too badly, Bob; but I have made a few deletions, all for what I think good reasons: call it, as Mr. Carlos Baker would, my stuffiness. Also, don't you think it should be mentioned that I've published two other books?[1]

About Anna Meyerson [Mayerson]. Last summer I saw in a London Art Review some reproductions of her drawings, and was so taken with them, so, in a word, enchanted, that I got the idea then of her doing a jacket and frontispiece for The Grass Harp. I wrote her, and it turned out, she liked my work too. About a month ago she came to Taormina on vacation, and I let her read the mss. She is young, with a great reputation in Europe—Lincoln Kirstein is arranging a show of her drawings in New York. You said you would like to see samples of her work—but that is not possible, as she has never done a book before. Oh Bob, it will be a Triumph! Please let me handle it. As for the cost, what do you pay ordinarily? Anna will not be at all difficult—and the result will be more beautiful than you can possibly foresee:

---

[1] Linscott had sent him a proposed description of *The Grass Harp* for inclusion in the Random House catalog.

she <u>is</u> a genuis [*sic*]. I want it more than I can tell you. Anyway, she is already working on it—will be finished in time for me to send it along with my two new chapters (May 1st). Then I have only the last, and long, chapter.

I miss you. Love

T

[Collection Columbia University Library]

TO CECIL BEATON

Fontana Vecchia
Taormina
March 18, 1951

Darling Cecil—

I was so happy to have the letter and know you were safely home—damp and rainy though it may be: your roses will soon be out. I envy you going to Spain, especially at Easter when there will be the feria in Seville. Though bizarre of Seville—Cornell and G. Mclintic [McClintic] are there, or so the Spanish sector of my international spy system informs me.[1] But worse than that—the Emlyn Williams [*sic*] are <u>here</u>.[2] Imagine my horror when <u>she</u> comes walking up the path. Or are you fond of them? I have them so associated in my mind with those Logan people that I can't quite focus on them.

Am amazed that Simon's [Simon Fleet] nose experiment should have proved such a dud. Funny thing, I was thinking about it only a few days ago and wondering if he'd done it. By the way, honey, it <u>was</u> your idea. But isn't David a little beast to tell everyone!

Very much liked your jacket for The Loved and Envied.[3] But did not care a bit for the book. Or, rather, found it a maddening mixture of good and embarrassingly bad writing. Too bad—because the theme was sound enough. Incidentally, I've read a remarkable book about modern Spain, which certainly you should read before going. "The Face of Spain" by Gerald Brennan [Brenan], published by the Turnstile Press.

---

[1] Katherine Cornell was often called the first lady of the American theater; her husband, Guthrie McClintic, directed most of her plays.

[2] Emlyn Williams was a Welsh actor and playwright.

[3] Enid Bagnold's *The Loved and Envied* was published in 1951.

Had a letter from C. Isherwood, who has given up movie work, taken an isolated house at Laguna and settled down to a novel—all of which is good news. I hope he sticks it out. Am getting slowly on with my opus, and <u>must</u> finish it by the end of June. I think I will leave Taormina then. I do love it here, and I know I will miss it awfully; but there <u>is</u> a limit. I hope so much you will come here before then. I long to see you, and long, too, for you to read my book.

It is wretched of those people to keep you so on tenterhooks; perhaps by now arrangements have been concluded. I did not have an especially favorable reaction to idea of G's being produced as part of the Brighton Festival.[1] It should be an event quite separate from other events—if you follow my reasoning.

You know I seriously think you should solve your servant problem by hiring Italians. A man and wife, you could arrange this through the British Embassy in Rome.

I'm afraid the Palmara (that restaurant) is on the verge of final collapse. Poor Fritz is drowned in debt and threatened with lawsuits. Wherever will Jules spend his evenings.

Don Elder writes me how much he <u>loves</u> you, and says they are expecting a great success with the Photobiography.[2] When's it coming out?

Jack sends love. I miss you, little heart,

Much love

T

[Collection St. John's College, Cambridge University]

TO ROBERT LINSCOTT

Fontana Vecchia
March 20, 1951

Dear, dear, dear, dear Bob
Anna Meyerson [Mayerson] has sent me the drawings for [the] jacket and frontispiece (title page) and they are superb—beyond anything. There were a few corrections to be made, so I've given them back, but you will

---

[1] Beaton's play *The Gainsborough Girls* opened in Brighton, a seaside resort, on July 16, 1951.
[2] Donald Elder was an editor at Doubleday.

have them by the middle of April. It's alright about the $150. But Bob I will not mislead you—though they are not in color, they are "fancy" in the sense that they are exquisitely intricate pen-and-ink drawings, and will require <u>very special</u> reproduction, engraving—which will cost money. The title-page drawing is a two page spread; and then there is the jacket. I don't think Random House can fail to see what an extraordinarily beautiful thing this book can be. However (and I'm saying this to you as a friend) if there is trouble over the cost, I will accept a smaller royalty to make up the difference. Of course that would be a hardship on me—and if you could put it through without my having to [unclear] to this, then I would be eternally grateful. Maybe it seems strange that anyone should put such stress on the "physical" appearance of a book—but there you are, I can't help it. I want to write a letter to that nice man who helped with Local Color, explaining all about Anna Meyerson and what I want—but what is his name? I will try to send my new chapters by the middle of April, too. I'm working really hard—as I calculate, the book will be almost exactly 60,000 words.

Tell Saxe [Cummins] I saw the picture of him (at the National Book Awards) and he looked real sweet.

Had a letter from Isherwood, who says he has quit movie work and settled down to finish his novel—which is good news. Newton writes that he had a very gay time in New York in conjunction with the prize-giving—he even appeared on Mary Margaret McBride's program: if you can feature that![1]

Love from
T

[Collection Columbia University Library]

TO MARY LOUISE ASWELL

[Fontana Vecchia]
[Taormina, Sicily]
March 22, 1951

Marylou dearest,
The situation you spiritually find yourself in disturbs me deeply; but I cannot agree with you on the attempted 'solution' you propose: to go away

---

[1] Mary Margaret McBride had a popular radio program in which she interviewed a wide range of people, from fan dancers to writers and politicians.

and find a 'new center'. If the new center is to be an emotional one, and it necessarily must be, then going away will neither give you that, nor eradicate the past. What you are in for is a wait: the wait between what has been and what will be: and the bridge between those points should, in fact can only be in work, however distracted, in contact, however tiresome. I know the punishment you endure in this workaday world; but at least it is a real thing and I fear for you if you withdraw from it: I fear for you if you withdraw in an illusionary search for a 'new center'—which is what? simply a new sense of security. If security is within oneself, then how can you find it on a leave of absence?—when primarily the result would be not to make you so much absent from a job as from yourself.

This can seem a random and easy proselytizing that does not take account of peril, true pains and doubts. If so, it's a fault of communication; because I do take account—and, having done so, <u>must strongly</u> advise that you take the new job, huckster's role though it may be: that in itself is the kind of hurdle, professional, not personal, that I want for you. You have the resources (as you would surprisingly discover) to meet such a challenge: you do <u>not</u> have reason [unclear] for withdrawal, however limited—because withdrawal requires a sureness of self that for you can be only a point in the future: the reward, I repeat, of a wait. Very well, I have not seen you in some time, not <u>really</u> seen you in a long long time; there can be changes, reactions that I don't know. But I risk the impertinence of saying that I have never been wrong about you. Do by all means leave the Bazaar, darling; and do by all means accept that other job.

I will write Janice [unclear], though I'm not sure that I think she should return to Europe. Give my love to Pearl. Jack sends his. We are fine, Fontana the same as ever. I love you always   T

[Collection Aswell Family]

TO ROBERT LINSCOTT

Fontana Vecchia
April 8, 1951

Dear Bob,
    In the same mail as this I'm sending to Marian my new chapters; when you get them, I wish you would read the whole mss. all the way through. There is now just the long last chapter; pray for me.

Also, in the same mail, I'm sending Anna Mayerson's frontispiece drawing . . . directly to you. It will reproduce beautifully by a process called photolitography [sic]. But I've written Ray Frieman [Freiman] all about this. Anna decided to abandon her jacket design, as we both decided it would be better to have a plain bold jacket like Other Voices, or Tree of Night. But I've also written all this to Mr Frieman [Freiman]. Oh I do hope you will like the frontispiece; I'm <u>mad</u> about it.

I'm in bed with the meanest kind of flu; also, my whole behind is sore and infected due to having been given a penicillin injection with a needle that had not been properly sterilized. Such is the horror of Sicilian medicine.

Can't wait to hear from you about the chapters et al. But haven't got the strength to write any more. Except that I miss you; and love

T

P.S. Bob—on pg. 12 of my mss. would you please change the word "folks" to <u>people</u>. Should read "and people told her he'd had offers" etc.

[Collection Columbia University Library]

TO BENNETT AND PHYLLIS CERF AND HERBERT WISE

Fontana Vecchia
Taormina, Sicily
April 10, 1951

Darling friends: Phyllis, Bennett, Herbert,

Just when you were deciding that I no longer loved you (at 2:11 a.m.), you were no doubt among my tenderest thoughts, for I miss you twenty-five hours a day. Not, I must say, that you've been dazzling correspondents, any of you: many's the night I've trudged down to the post-office, then trudged back empty-handed—thinking, a fine lot they are, whirling from one gay event to another, never giving a thought to poor Truman: far off there on a windswept hill with nothing but the sound of the sea to cheer him up. Oh chilluns, it do get mighty powerful lonesome here. I so long to finish my book and end this exile; another two months, I think.

From time to time people do pop in. Emlyn Williams and Molly were here for a week—chockfull of London gossip; and little [Arnold] Saint

Subber appeared here just in time to have a full scale nervous break-down.

I've concocted the most scandalous parlor game. It's <u>SO</u> educational; and you can slander people right and left, all in the interest of le sport. It's called IDC, which stands for International Daisy Chain. You make a chain of names, each one connected by the fact that he or she has had an affair with the person previously mentioned; the point is to go as far and as incongruously as possible. For example, this one is from Peggy Guggenheim to King Farouk. Peggy Guggenheim to Lawrence Vail to Jeanne Connolly to Cyril Connolly to Dorothy Walworth to King Farouk. See how it works? Peggy Guggenheim had an affair with L. Vail who had an affair with J. Connolly etc. Here is another, and much more difficult, not to say raffiné, example: from Henry James to Ida Lupino. As follows: Henry James to Hugh Walpole to Harold Nicholson [Nicolson] to the Hon. David Herbert to John C. Wilson to Noel Coward to Louis Hay-ward to Ida Lupino. Or: from Aaron Copland to Marlene Dietrich. Aaron Copland to Victor Kraft to Cecil Beaton to Greta Garbo to Mercedes Da-Costa to Tommy Adams to Marlene Dietrich. Perhaps it all sounds rather dreary on paper; but I can <u>assure</u> you that, with a few drinks inside you and some suitable folk to play with, you'll be amazed. Suppose you began with John Gunther . . . where <u>might</u> that not lead one? John Gunther to Mrs Hornblow to Wayne Morris to Jane Wyman to Elia Kazan to Marlon Brando to Tennessee Williams to Frankie Merlo to Joseph Alsop to Bill Caskey to C. Isherwood to Wystan Auden to Ruth Lowinsky to Wolcott Gibbs to Barbara Wilding to Billy Redfield to June Grant to George Bal-anchine to Danilova to Serge Lifar to Diaghalev [Diaghilev] to Nijinsky. Now I'm sure Mr Gunther didn't know he had <u>this</u> connection with Ni-jinsky! Oh the immorality of it all.

Bennett, have you seen the frontispiece drawing Anna Mayerson has done for my book? I'm mad about it. I hope Phyllis and Herbert will see it, too. She is such a genuis [sic], Anna Mayerson.

I have something lovely for you, Phyllis; but it's too fragile to send through the mail; I'll have to bring it. It's an old French watch face that I found in Palermo and had made into a lapel pin: should look wonderful on a trim little suit.

I wish you were all coming to Europe; perhaps Herbert is. But I give up on you other two. I know that if I'm to see you it will be on native soil. I ex-pect to be home around August 1st. Will you be in Provincetown? Newton Arvin is taking a house in Wellfleet, and I am going there until the middle of Sept. That isn't too terribly far from Provincetown, is it?

Well, darling ones, I'd best climb back into my China tree. Kisses, heart's love, et mille tenderesse [sic]

Your own

T

Forgot to include my most favorite IDC: Cab Calloway to Hitler. Cab Calloway to Marquesa Casamaury to Carol Reed to Unity Mitford to Hitler.

Get Moss and Kitty to play this game; I bet they'd be wonderful at it.[1] If you get any good ideas, <u>please</u> send them along.

[Collection Columbia University Library]

TO WILLIAM GOYEN

Fontana Vecchia
Taormina
April 19, 1951

Bill dear,

How good it was to have your letter; but what I don't understand is—did you ever recieve [sic] a <u>long</u> letter I sent you about Horan et al? I'd rather wanted you to reply to it, but since you don't mention it I wonder whether it reached you. It was not anything I would care to have had fall into the hands of a stranger.

So glad that you've been happy at Yaddo. I loved it too—though I'm afraid I didn't really get much work done there. I'm delighted that "Ghost and Flesh" is nearly finished. Bob thinks it's wonderful, a real achievement. I'm mad to read it. Will it be published this fall?

I read Spender's autobiography.[2] What a spurious book—him and his homosexual affairs that were only "undertaken in a spirit of opportunism." I'll say. Seriously, though, it makes me hopping mad. But Henri-Louis de la Grange, who was just here, says that you and Signor S. are friendly as ever.[3] <u>Surely</u> it isn't true.

---

[1] Moss and Kitty Hart.
[2] Stephen Spender's *World Within World* was published in 1951.
[3] Henri-Louis de la Grange was to become the world's foremost Mahler scholar.

I'd advise you strongly against the Gulf coast. I've lived in nearly all those little towns along the coast. They are flat, ugly as tin-roofs; the water is grey soup, the beaches are filthy and so are the people. From May through September all the middle-aged ladies in the South are holed up there. But if you really want to go, there is only one <u>possible</u> place to stay— Pass Christian.[1] Why not one of the little islands off the coast of Georgia? Ask Andrew about those.

I don't know that I will come home in July. In fact I'm pretty sure I won't—maybe in August. But I do want to see you, precious. Of course we will. Write me. much love from

    T

P.S. Give my love to Elizabeth Ames

[Collection unknown]

TO ROBERT LINSCOTT

    Fontana Vecchia
    Taormina, Sicily
    April 21, 1951

Dear Bobolink,

Am in heaven with your praise—you can't lay it on thick enough, honey; cause I just **LOVES** it. Only hope the last chapter doesn't dissa-point [sic] you. Could be.

Am enclosing a little picture you can use if you want—don't I look healthy? Only Bob please let's not use that same biography again—about river-boats and fortune tellers and god knows what all.[2] So I suggest: "Tru-man Capote was born in New Orleans; he is twenty-six. A first novel, Other Voices Other Rooms, established him in the front-rank of younger American writers. His stories, eight of which are collected in A Tree of Night, have appeared in the better periodicals here and abroad, and are frequently anthologized. Last year Random House published Local Color,

---

[1] Pass Christian, Mississippi.
[2] The biography Capote wrote for the dust jacket of Other Voices, Other Rooms was mostly fic-tional, claiming, among other things, that he danced on a river boat, painted flowers on glass, and studied fortune-telling "with the celebrated Mrs. Acey Jones."

a book of Mr. Capote's travel pieces. His work is widely known in Europe, where he has lived the last several years."

Trite—but in the right way. But as for a blurb for the book I give up. Poor Bob, you'll have to do that. Newton could, only he hasn't read the book—or I'll bet Pearl Kazin could do a good one. Ask her. Anyway, it shouldn't claim too much. As for the back flap, I think you should list my other books, alloting [sic] for each two quotes from the reviews. Blah Blah Blah, N.Y. Times. Incidentally, for A Tree of Night you should quote something from the Christopher Sykes review and from Leslie Fiedler's review in The Nation.

Marylou sent me a beautiful cable about the book. Everybody's being so nice. Oh lord, all I've got to do is finish now.

Had a letter from Goyen. Am so glad he got the Guggenheim—I'll bet you are, too.

Bob, is Random going to be good about advertising this time? I mean in <u>this</u> respect you-all have not done such a lot for your child's last two books. I'm not unrealistic; I know they were not the kind of books it repaid to greatly advertise. But with the Grass Harp I certainly am not expecting to be third-down in a list ad. No sir. <u>I'm expecting to bask in the sunshine of a few full pages</u>. And on that ungrateful note I bid you adieu. Except to say that I love you lots

T

P.S. Will airmail the last chapter soon as finished. Did you change the word "folks" to "people"?
P.P.S. Look inside.
P.P.S. Here is a suitable quote from the Sykes review of <u>A Tree</u>.

"Prose at its best. Mr. Capote gives his readers an exhilarating experience—the classic mark of excellence" Christopher Sykes, London Observer.

Also Leslie Fiedler in The Nation.

For Local Color there is that James Hilton review in The Herald Tribune—and that one in the Sunday Times (pretty grey it was, probably nothing there). I can't seem to find these, or I would do it myself.

[Collection Columbia University Library]

TO ROBERT LINSCOTT

> Fontana Vecchia
> Taormina, Sicily
> April 24, 1951

Dear Boss,

As near as I can calculate, the last chapter will be between 8 and 10 thousand words. The mss. as a whole should run to about 172 pages—which, if properly arranged, could print out to 180–190 pages.

I'm told that Tallulah Bankhead has a radio program on which she sang a new song, composed by Joe Bushkin, called "Other Voices, Other Rooms." Surely <u>that</u> is an infringement. I do seem determined to sue somebody.

Love (molto)

T

[Collection Columbia University Library]

TO MARY LOUISE ASWELL

> Fontana Vecchio [*sic*]
> Taormina, Sicily
> April 24, 1951

Precious heart—

You were the dearest of angels to send the cable, and now your sweet letter is here. I am so happy and relieved that you liked the book; I wanted you to, I guess more than anyone. A good deal depends on the last chapter—unfortunately I am very tense with it; I feel as though I were holding my nose under water: when I'm finished, I'm going to take a long gulp of air and do a mile of handsprings. I hope La Neige[1] lets you buy the chapter—I'm more broke than little Orphan Annie.

Of course I can see why you are upset about Fritz returning to N.Y. On the other hand I don't think it likely that your paths will cross—surely no one is going to invite you to the same place. But it is an incompatible feeling, God knows. At any rate, I hear you have sublet a heavenly apartment

---

[1] Carmel Snow, editor of *Harper's Bazaar.*

for the summer. We expect to come home early in August, and we will see you in it. Oh I <u>long</u> to see you—it will have been nearly two years!

Tell me, what is Jane [Bowles] doing? She is so tiresome about not answering letters. I hope she is working on the novel she was writing in Tangier; it seems to me it should have been finished by now.

Darling, Jack sends much, much love. Please do write me, precious. I love you always.

T

[Collection Aswell Family]

TO ROBERT LINSCOTT

[Taormina, Sicily]
[May 1951]

Dear Bob,

A quick, quick note to let you know that I do want a dedication.

FOR MISS SOOK FAULK
IN MEMORY OF AFFECTIONS DEEP AND TRUE

All is going well, I think, I hope. It won't be too long now. Thanks. Love

T

P.S. Sook Faulk is Dolly in the book. She died in 1938. What happiness it gives me to dedicate this book to her!

[Collection Columbia University Library]

TO ROBERT LINSCOTT

Taormina
May 3, 1951

Dear Bob,

As far as I'm concerned, Polly is free to use her own judgement: separate or run-together whatever words she wants.[1] However, I would prefer

---

[1] Polly was a copy editor.

that "Sheriff" and "Judge" remained capitalized. Also I have what are probably incorrect, but certainly very definite notions about punctuation, and I think that, except in cases of blatant misusage, my colons and semi-colons should stay as they are.

The check arrived for Anna Mayerson, and I have given it to her. Molto graçias.

Several problems have arisen in my last chapter, problems of technique; but with a kind of slow anguish I am unravelling them. I guess I'd best get back to it.

Love

T

[Collection Columbia University Library]

TO CECIL BEATON

Taormina, May 8, 1951

Cecil darling,

Wonderful to have your letter; and am as happy to know you at least have the theatre, if not the cast. Franz Werner, the fortune-teller, is back and I asked him if July was going to be a good month for you,[1] and he said yes, but that something astonishingly good was going to happen to you in late August; also, that you are soon going to receive a letter or a long-distance phone call making a proposal which you must accept. It's amazing how many of the things he's told me that have come true already. For instance, he told me that in April I would receive a prize of some kind. And I did: the O. Henry Memorial Award (for "distinguished work in the short-story"; it's the third time I've won it).

Jane Bowles is in Paris—much sturm und drang because she doesn't know where Paul is, and hasn't heard from him in several months. I don't know what will happen to Janie; she shouldn't be floating around this way, especially with all those loathsome Paris characters.

Yes, the E. [Emlyn] Williams' [*sic*] did rather suggest that they were friends of yours. But there were several little things that made me decide

---

[1] *The Gainsborough Girls* was scheduled to open on July 16.

they weren't; one was, that every time I mentioned you they immediately would begin to tell me what a <u>wonderful</u> person Oliver Messel was.[1] But I made my love for you quite clear to them; so to give them credit, maybe that is why they pretended to be fond of you. But they are a fishy pair. Please don't repeat this, because they would know where it came from, but they were asked to leave their hotel here, were, in fact, thrown out: I don't quite know the reason why, and those who do are singularly reticent. He, Emlyn, sent me a play of his called "Accolade." I must say the corn is <u>very</u> green: such incredible trash.[2]

Saw your pictures of Jamaica in Vogue. Liked the one of you and the one of Bea [Beatrice Lillie] with a pickaninny on her back. [Noël] Coward and [Graham] Payn look too "Greenbay Tree" for anything: only you couldn't cast either of them as the <u>young</u> man.[3]

Spring is long since over and it's summer here. But I'm working too hard to enjoy it. But how I wish you could come for a flying visit before we leave. We both hope to be finished with our books in another month, and then we're going to Venice and, early in August, to America. But as soon as the boat docks I'm going straight away to Wellfleet on Cape Cod where I've taken a house through the middle of September. I hope you come to New York sooner than usual this fall.

Tell me, darling, do you know anything about a young man called [Arnold] Saint Subber? He had something to do with producing Kiss Me Kate etc.[4] What is his reputation—professionally, I mean. Because he has made a crazy proposition; wants to give me option money—<u>just</u> in the event I ever <u>do</u> write a play. It's rather mad. I'm tempted only because at the moment I do need money. Should I? What do you think? Is he at all a person to respect?

Jack sends his very best love. I do miss you, little precious. Write me. Much love

   T

[Collection St. John's College, Cambridge University]

---

[1] Messel was also one of Britain's leading theatrical designers and one of Beaton's rivals.

[2] Emlyn Williams's best-known play is *The Corn Is Green.*

[3] A South African, Graham Payn was Coward's companion. Mordaunt Sharp's play of the thirties, *The Green Bay Tree,* had recently been revived on Broadway.

[4] Saint Subber was, in fact, the producer of Cole Porter's *Kiss Me, Kate,* which was a huge hit, running for more than two and a half years on Broadway.

TO ANDREW LYNDON

[Taormina, Sicily]
May 16, 1951

Honey,

T'was about time you wrote me: you owed me two letters. I don't understand why Phoebe hasn't written me (or perhaps I do); still I've had 2 letters returned from addresses where she was Unknown.

You mention so many people that I never heard of. Who is Gene Price? Tell me everything about him. At any rate I'm very glad that Rita [Smith] is having this affair. Oh dear I hope it is a really good thing, and that it makes her happy. And who is Ruth Randall?

By the way, speaking of affairs, did you know that Goyen and K. A. Porter have been doing it for quite a spell? I do like Bill, but he is, as more and more I've discovered, an opportunist nonpareil. Anyway, having got what he wanted from KAP, he now has given her the air, and she is eating her heart out. All this I get from a very informed source—don't pass it on, please.

I should have finished my book in another few weeks—but it only makes me nervous, so the least said etc. It's been one long pull, and now I'm collecting breath for the final climb.

When do you plan to go to Macon? We expect to be home the end of July/first of August. I hope you will have found an apt. by then.

I have a line on a wonderful job for you, and maybe it will work out: American Editor of Botteghe Oscure. Princess Caetani is looking for someone, and I think you would be perfect.[1] It would pay reasonably well too. I expect to see her in Rome next month, so will find out more then.

The weather has been wretched here the last week—sirocco every day. It really is as oppressive as Agatha Christie claims.

I want to know what Harold is up to—give him a kiss.

Are you in love? I sense a reticence in your letter.

Jack is well, and sends you his love. Kelly is covered with ticks and burrs: scratch, scratch. Myself, I do a lot of scratching too—I seem simply to breed crabs.

---

[1] Princess Marguerite Caetani was the editor of *Botteghe Oscure*, a magazine published in Rome, in the authors' original languages.

Write me immediately, darling—as I expect to leave here some 3 weeks hence.

l o v e

T

[Collection New York Public Library]

TO ROBERT LINSCOTT

[Taormina, Sicily]
May 29, 1951

Dear, Dear Bob

I finished the book! Two days ago—and then promptly came down with intestinal grippe, so have not been able to type it yet, but expect to get at it tomorrow. Anyway, you will have the manuscript very soon—in about 10 days.

Have no news at all. My story "House of Flowers" won an O. Henry prize.

But feel <u>so</u> weak—wanted just to tell you the glad tidings; at least I hope it is a glad tiding. By the time you get the chapter I probably will have left here. Let me know at once what you think—c/o American Express, Venice.

If all goes well I'll be seeing you in early August. Have missed you so much

Love

T

[Collection Columbia University Library]

TO JOHN MALCOLM BRINNIN

Venice, c/o American Express
June 24th, 1951

O Radiant One,

Although it was addressed to Jack, I will stoop to answer your letter. Darling, you <u>are</u> a creature of habit; Yaddo, yadddooooo . . . through the

ages; don't you ever get just a wee bit weary of going there? You're going to
end up like Leonard Ehrlich.[1] All the same I can't wait to see your sweet
lollipop face. Which is to say you must come to Venice before July 25th. We
are taking a piccolo palazzo and so can put you and Bill up . . . or at least I
think we are going to get the house; as usual, the landlord is crazy, and
things have not got quite straightened out. But please do come quickly because you'll be going back to Paris anyway. Venezia is more wonderful than
ever, the weather is heaven . . . though some of the current inhabitants
aren't. All the rich international queens are here en force. A thrill of horror
ran through me when I read about Indiana. I don't think it's at all a suitable
proposal . . . of course everything like that tempts you, so probably you are
all set to go. But I hope not. By the way, I never got your book of poems.
I'm so happy about Farrar Straus taking Jack's book. He sent them the last
third of it but hasn't heard. Jack sends love; love to Bill. Now hurry on over
here, my sweet . . . at least do let me know whether to expect you before
we leave Venice.

heart's love   T

[Collection University of Delaware Library]

TO ROBERT LINSCOTT

Venice, June 27th, 1951

Dear Bob,

I was under a strain not hearing from you, a neat little understatement,
but your letter came yesterday and of course it only made me feel worse.

I cannot endure it that all of you think my book a failure; I am stricken
by such an overpowering trinity of opinion.[2] The vagueness of the criticism
makes me feel even more helpless.

Perhaps you are right about the last chapter. Yet I don't see what could
have been done differently. You describe it as tapering off . . . which is exactly what I intended. When they leave the tree-house, that is the climax of

---

[1] Ehrlich was a writer (*God's Angry Man,* 1932) who had several stays at Yaddo.
[2] The trinity was Linscott, Bennett Cerf and Robert Haas. "We all had a slight feeling of let-
down," Linscott wrote Capote, "of the story tapering off a little, with the ending coming too soon
and lacking the profusion of delight that had so entranced one up to that point."

the book; but what point would the book have unless the last chapter were written in exactly the mood it is: the destination of each character has been prepared from the beginning. Then there was the enormous technical problem: having already had my <u>narrative</u> climax, speed seemed to me of the essence . . . what I had left on my hands was a great lot of information, and it seems to me that I arranged this well. I think the end very moving and right. But of course at the moment I am too near to it really to know.

So I wonder if we should go ahead with a fall publication. I wonder if I shouldn't see what improvements I can make.

The proofs still have not arrived. I did not cable this to you because I sent a cable to Rome asking whether they had arrived there and if so why the hell hadn't they forwarded them here. I can't believe they were sent airmail.

I am leaving here July 16th and will be in New York August 1st.

I'm sorry I dissapointed [sic] you, Bob. I know you are leaving now on vacation, so forget the whole thing and have a good time.

Love

T

[Collection Columbia University Library]

TO BENNETT CERF

Truman Capote
c/o American Express
Venice, Italy
July 3rd, 1951

Dear Bennett,

Your letter only just today arrived, for it had been sent to Sicily and forwarded.

I do deeply appreciate what you tell me. Bob had written me about your combined reservations . . . which came as a shock because I'd been so certain that what I'd done was right. But there is no point in going into any of my arguments; obviously there must be something wrong or you would not all feel as you do.

By all means we must postpone publication until I can make improvements.

You say several times that the first half is better than the last half . . . do you really mean "half" . . . or just the last chapter? I can rewrite the last chapter but I don't understand what the criticism is of the other chapters.

As for Verena, it is essential that she be a sympathetic person in the end. In one sense, she has never NOT been sympathetic. The central emotional situation is between herself and Dolly . . . not between Dolly and the Judge. It simply would be psychologically untrue if Dolly did not go back to the house.[1]

But these problems are all mine. Anyway, is it only the last chapter that disturbs you?

I cannot make any basic change in the chapter . . . as to the events and outcome, I mean. What I can do is make it more gradual. I was conciously [sic] using the snynopsis [sic] method as a technical device; but if it <u>reads</u> like a synopsis, then it is on my part a failure in style.

Thank you infinitely, Bennett, for writing me so frankly what you feel.

Please let me know quickly about postponing the book etc.

Give my very best love to Phyllis, and love to you.

Truman

ps. I am sailing the 16th from Genoa, and will be in NY the first of August.

[Collection Columbia University Library]

TO BENNETT CERF

[Telegram]   [Venice]
                                                 [9 July 1951]

HAVE READ PROOFS AND PREFER PUBLISH BOOK AS IS[2]
    LOVE TRUMAN

[Collection Columbia University Library]

---

[1] Verena and Dolly, two old-maid sisters, were loosely based on two of the three female cousins, the Faulk sisters, who lived in Monroeville, Alabama, and who took care of Capote as a child.

[2] Capote did not make the changes suggested by the Random House editors, and Bennett Cerf gave in with his usual grace. "If it is now in the form that you wish to keep it, it's good enough for me," he replied. The critics took Capote's side, and *The Grass Harp* was widely praised.

TO CECIL BEATON

1060 Park Avenue
New York, N.Y.
[Written from Wellfleet, Mass.]
Aug 26 1951

Cecil dear,

I have begun so many letters to you, and then been interrupted. We got back here 3 weeks ago and for the last two weeks I have been here on Cape Cod, but will go back to New York Sept 4.

Of course, I have been mad to know what happened at Brighton. In the "New Yorker" this week there is a description of the opening of G.G's [*The Gainsborough Girls*]—but it is so brief and indefinite that I could not gather anything from it. My interest and my heart have been with you, dear bunny—

The "Photobiography" has had very good reviews here. I thought the paragraph about me was very loving and tender; thank you.

We had a ghastly voyage home—two storms and the captain of the boat committed suicide.

Isn't it extraordinary about George Davis getting married?!!! And to that Lotte Lenya.[1] I've always thought myself a lad of the world; but this beats all—and is in such bad taste, don't you think?

My book is coming out October 1st. I will send it to you. Have you any idea when you will be coming here? I don't think I will be crossing the ocean again until after the first of the year.

I don't suppose you will be going to Venice for Bestiqui's [Beistegui's] big blowout—that is, I expect you are too taken up just now. But if you do go write me a full report—I got so tired of all the fuss about it in Venice, still I want to know how it turned out.

Jack sends his love to you. I long to see you, precious one—much love from your very own

T

[Collection St. John's College, Cambridge University]

---

[1] Lotte Lenya had originated the role of Jenny in the first Berlin production of Kurt Weill and Bertolt Brecht's *The Threepenny Opera*. When Hitler came to power, she fled with Weill to the United States, where he died in 1950.

TO CECIL BEATON

1060 Park Avenue
Nov 12, 1951

Cecil dearest,

I've wanted and wanted to write . . . however, more has been happening than I can tell you and I seem now not even to have the time to sleep. All work, dear . . . no play. Or rather very much Play . . . and that is what I'm writing about.

In short, it seems as though this play of mine is really coming off.[1] I've not finished yet, and do not expect to until early in January. The plans are to go into rehearsal around the first of Feb. and open here in New York sometime in March. Saint Subber is producing it, and the Gish sisters [Lillian and Dorothy] will co-star. We expect Virgil Thomson to do the music . . . and he expects to do it. Now the thing is, I want so much for you to do the sets and costumes. The play is in two acts, there will be two sets, both rather elaborate . . . I fear it will need a revolving stage. It is a real challenge, but I do believe that the second set, the tree and tree-house and forest, could be one of the most visually exciting scenes a curtain ever went up on. I can send you the first act at the end of the month. But are you interested at all? Or could all this not fit into your schedule? So far we have not settled on any director, although [Harold] Clurman and Bobby Lewis etc are all too willing and eager . . . but I don't think they would be good; Subber wrote Peter Brook, who replied that he already had a bursting calendar . . . but I think I will pursue him further; or maybe you will have some brilliant suggestion.[2] Anyway, honey, do let me know whether or not you think you can take this on.

I've seen quite a few plays . . . "Point Of No Return" is the only halfway good one.[3] But there is no news . . . Jack has been writing stories and sold two this last week; he says . . . send you his love.

Despite the long silence, I've not been worrying about you because I read in the paper that you have been entertaining your favorite houseguest [Greta Garbo], and so I know you've had a pleasant autumn.

---

[1] At Saint Subber's suggestion, Capote had agreed to adapt *The Grass Harp* for the stage.

[2] A few months younger than Capote, Brook was considered the rising young British director in both theater and film.

[3] Paul Osborn's *Point of No Return*, based on the novel of the same name by John P. Marquand.

The book has had terribly good reviews here, and seems to [be] selling fairly well.

Write me as soon as you can. When are you coming? I miss you and love you. Mille tenderesse [*sic*]

Truman

[Collection St. John's College, Cambridge University]

TO CECIL BEATON

[Written from Regent Hospital]
[115 East 61st Street]
[New York, N.Y.]

Write to: 1060 Park Avenue
New York, N.Y.
Dec 4, 1951

Cecil dearest

I am sorry to be writing you from a hospital—but had rather a collapse last week—a sort of combination of a virus infection and <u>complete</u> exhaustion. I have been working so hard—and you know what New York's like. However, I am much better, am feeling really rested—and will be out of here in the next two or three days.

Oh precious, I am overjoyed about your doing the scenery and costumes for "Grass Harp"—it will be lovely! I can't understand why you never got the book, however I have sent you another copy—to Pelham Place.[1]

I can't tell you how lovely I think your "Swan Lake" is. You had RAVE notices in all the papers—I'm sure you've had them by now. Everyone has said how wonderful your work is—

Dear Juliet [Duff] is having quite a whirl. I took her once to lunch, and saw her again at a dinner party at the Lunts (not very bright, those two: but fairly gracious—in a rather commercial way).[2] I really like Juliet—I could never say why (she <u>is</u> a bore), but I do all the same.

---

[1] Beaton's London address.
[2] Alfred Lunt and Lynn Fontanne were America's most famous acting couple.

I am so worried about a director for the play. I would like awfully to have Peter Brook—with all modesty, this play would be the perfect American introduction for him. But old Irene Selznick assures me I cannot get him—due to commitments etc.[1] However, I feel that if I could talk to Peter Brook, somehow it would work out. I will be sending you the 1st act of the play on Monday (it's in only 2 acts) and perhaps you could show it to him etc. Then, if he was sympathetic, I could fly to London the 1st of Jan., see him, and come back to N.Y. with you. Let me know.

Whatever happens, it has to be a top-flight production. A great many directors have asked to do it—some of them quite good—but I guess I am wary of anyone who asks to do something.

I liked so much your "Ballet" book—it is charming, and solves any Christmas shopping problems.[2]

The Isherwood–Van Druten play "I Am a Camera" is quite a success—which, having seen it, is something of a mystery.[3] It seems to me so bad—though here and there amusing.

Emlyn Williams sent me a picture of himself as Dickens—can't something be done to stop this?[4] Surely poor Dickens has some still living relatives to defend him.

By the way, Isherwood is sailing for England Dec 14. I hope you see each other. He adores you.

Cecil, my sweet, I am so happy that you have had such a good autumn. Whatever you want, you know that with all my heart I want it for you, too.

Write me—about everything—I do love you

T

P.S. Jack sends much love

[Collection St. John's College, Cambridge University]

---

[1] Irene Selznick was David O. Selznick's ex-wife and a leading Broadway producer.

[2] Beaton's *Ballet,* a short, eighty-six-page book of ballet photographs, was published in 1951.

[3] John Van Druten had adapted Christopher Isherwood's *The Berlin Stories* for the stage. The play was later translated into film, then into the musical *Cabaret,* which in turn became a movie.

[4] Williams gave readings from the works of Dickens.

TO CECIL BEATON

1060 PARK AVENUE
NEW YORK 28, N.Y.
Jan 5 1952

Cecil dearest—

You will have received by now a letter from Robert Lewis—which I can see, reading it over, is not what it should be: between us, he has a certain vulgarity (as in this letter you have no doubt detected)—but, kept within check, I am perfectly certain he is the right director for us—he does really understand the play, has a very real sensitivity and also a strong realistic sense—which, as you pointed out, is so necessary to a play such as this.[1] Of course he <u>knows</u> about the factual things—floor-plans, sight-lines etc. But as for everything else, it must, and will be, according to your own insights. I do agree about Jean Rosenthal, I mean I do think she would be the best person to light the play—do you? I hope you will consider her rather than Peggy Clarke. But of course nothing will be done about this until we hear from you.

I have finished the play, and the last scenes will be sent to you as soon as I have typed and corrected it. I know Subber sent you the first scene of the second act—I have since made cuts in this and will tighten it up even more. This next week I am going to make quite a few alterations through the whole play—but none of them will affect the decor.

It means so much to me to know that we are going to work together on this—all the difference, really. I think you will like the cast Lewis is assembling—we have a wonderful Catherine Creek (Georgia Burke). Mildred Natwick, who is going to play Dolly, may seem a curious choice at first—but I think she will be wonderful. We have a very good Verena, too: Ruth Nelson—you probably don't remember her, she hasn't played in ten years. No Judge so far, and no Collin—but several excellent candidates. I think Alice Pearce is going to play Miss Baby Love Dallas.[2]

Have been so busy with all this that there is no personal news. Jack is very well—I liked very much his story in the January Bazaar. Look at it if you get a chance. Was riding in a taxi the other day and saw G.G. [Greta Garbo] crossing the street—looking very beautiful and with her hair cropped like a boy's. Darling, do hope you are finishing your Gainsborough revisions—Con-

---

[1] Despite Capote's pleas, Peter Brook had declined to direct *The Grass Harp*.
[2] Miss Baby Love Dallas was the only character that had not been in the original novel.

stance Collier was telling me she had seen it in Brighton and liked it very much and was glad you were going to work it over.[1] Have a lovely boat-ride, my precious one—I await you with the most open of open arms. LOVE

T

[Collection St. John's College, Cambridge University]

TO MARY LOUISE ASWELL

[New York]
February 29, 1952

Darling:

I wrote to Paris and I hope you got the letter before leaving for Rome. Jack told me that he wrote you the other day; at least, amid all the confusion we are trying to keep up our end of the correspondence: see that you do. And, by the way, when you see the Princess, talk up Jack to her as I'm trying to get him to send her that story THE FAR COUNTRY. Just for the hell of it Jack wrote a sort of superior thriller script for television and it turned out wonderfully well—I think. Don't know what Audrey [Wood] is doing with it, though.

Hope most of your editorial labors are over and you can have a real rest now. Sounds so wonderful—your coming stay in Capri. Maybe you can convince Tony et al to make a quick whirl to Taormina. Am working day and night to protect your investment, dear. Everything seems to be going quite well (which may or may not be ominous). But, anyway, Virgil's music is ravishing and so is Cecil's contribution. I do so wish you were going to be here, dear.

Jack's book has been postponed again and now comes out the 24th of March. Jane comes round to see us quite a lot, but I keep falling asleep because she stays so late and I am so tired. Wrote a little piece for the Bazaar about Garbo and Dick Avedon has taken a startling and fantastic photograph of Virgil, Cecil and me. Virgil and I look like two little owls and Cecil, in a black bowler hat, is leaning above us like a terribly hungry hawk. Am writing Pearl today, there having been long silence on both sides, though in her last letter she told me she was getting quite fed up with Rio.

---

[1] After a distinguished career on the London stage, Constance Collier became an acting and voice coach in Hollywood, giving lessons to Marilyn Monroe, among many others.

Mrs. [W. Murray] Crane gave a most elegant dinner party last Wednesday night in honor of Dylan Thomas to which I was invited but, alas, could not go—and I really mean alas from a most hysterically funny account of it.[1] It seems that Mrs. Thomas, in a rage of some sort, suddenly picked up Mrs. Crane's two Ming vases, crashed them to the floor with flowers and water spilling all over everything. Whereupon Mr. Thomas, quite drunk himself, knocked her to the floor—loosening four of her teeth and splitting her lip— and then proceeded to kick her in the stomach until she passed out. Whereupon Lolly H. and Louise [Crane], with great cries of distress and sympathy, tried to bring Mrs. Thomas to. At this point Mr. Thomas said to Louise who was bending over the prostrated Mrs. Thomas: "What the hell are you crying over her for? You need just what she got. What you need is a kick in the butt." Whereupon he kicked Louise and sent her sprawling across the floor. Poor Mrs. Crane retired in a state of considerable shock to her bedroom, and that old butler and the maid managed to get Mr. and Mrs. Thomas out to the vestibule; then—and this is my favorite part—Mr. Thomas came back into the drawing room and very politely asked Louise and the company in general, could somebody loan him $2 because he didn't have the money for a taxi! All of this happened in front of the following: Edmond [Edmund] Wilson and his wife, Virgil, Mrs. Otto Kahn, and poor Lady Ribblesdale.

Do write me a long letter, dear, with lots of gossip and news of everybody in Rome. My love to everyone there and a thousand kisses, precious.

[Collection Aswell Family]

TO ANDREW LYNDON

[Tour de Villebon]
[Meudon, France]
[Early April 1952]

Darling Magnolia—

The boatride was revolting—such big waves, such big boring passengers; but now I am feeling fairly rested and calm—staying in the country a

---

[1] Mrs. Crane was a rich, elderly philanthropist and a friend of Andrew Lyndon, who, for nine years, read to her nearly every afternoon from three to six o'clock. Lyndon often took his friends, including Capote, to her apartment for dinner. She allowed Capote to use her apartment for the backers' reading of *The Grass Harp*.

few miles from Paris. We are leaving for Rome Wednesday—I think by car: I've been persuaded to buy a little Renault car on the grounds that I can re-sell it and thereby <u>save</u> money (better not look too deeply into this)—only hitch is Jack can't drive and I haven't touched a car in 7 or 8 years. It's all rather frightening—when and <u>if</u> we ever reach Rome I hope there will be a letter from you at the Am. Express.

Have heard not a word from the Martin Beck set—so do not know <u>what</u> is happening there.[1]

Darling, I hope everything goes well. This is just a note to tell you that I am all right, that I love you with all my heart and miss you.

Your own

T

[Collection New York Public Library]

TO MARY LOUISE ASWELL

Rome May 12 1952

Precious darling Marylou,

How outrageously overdue this letter is; but we only just arrived in Rome after a huge delay in Paris due to my having the flu and etc. I was miserable when your cable came saying that you had to stay in Lon-don . . . actually, we would have come to London to see you except that we had nowhere to leave Kelly and they won't let him on their blessed soil.[2]

Darling, you have no idea what those last two months in N.Y. were like for me . . . I was really off my rocker with exhaustion and that is why you never heard from me. Well, the play closed last week; we had so much working against us and there is no use going into it now. But I'm deeply sorry that you did not see it, for really it was absolutely beautiful, the sets, the music, everything. And of course I'm sorry that you lost your money . . . poor darling, very sorry. But maybe I will make it up to you.

It is awful that you are not going to be with us in Italy as we planned; I feel like scolding you . . . but on the other hand I do understand.

---

[1] *The Grass Harp* had opened in Broadway's Martin Beck Theatre on March 27; it closed on April 26.

[2] The British imposed a six-month quarantine on animals coming into the country.

I'm afraid that we are going to miss [Princess Marguerite] Caetani (which reminds me, bless you for your opening night cable) because I have called her but there is no answer and I expect we will be leaving tomorrow or next day. But I will send her a telegram tonight. I'm not quite sure where we are going . . . we are going to look over a place called Cape Palinuro and if we like it stay there . . . if not, probably we will go to Taormina.

I am going to work on some stories and I hope a new play.

Jack just came in and says he LOVES you. He just today got your letter (forwarded from New York) and he says it was a sweet letter and that he is going to write in the next few days. Perhaps it will be he who sends you our permanent address.

I cannot at the moment think of much New York news. Newton is going to Harvard next year to replace Matthiesen [F. O. Matthiessen][1] . . . I know you will be glad to hear that. A strange thing happened just before we left . . . someone, and it <u>must</u> have been Pearl, tried to call me from Rio, but after a long delay the opeartor [sic] finally said the call had been cancelled. M. Young just called (she is in the same hotel, Lord save us) and said give you her love and tell you Caetani took the chapter.

Darling, write me as soon as you know <u>where</u> to write me. Meanwhile, I love you with all my heart

    T

[Collection Aswell Family]

TO LEO LERMAN

Taormina, Sicily
June 16, 1952

Myrt dear—

Poor baby—all that you have suffered: and I didn't even know it; but I hope all that is behind you now. I hate to horn in on <u>your</u> misery, but have been a little the worse for wear myself—I have three different ailments going simultaneously, one of which put me in the hospital briefly (can you <u>imagine</u> what a Sicilian hospital is like?), but I'm getting a grip on myself because I'm afraid I haven't any alternative.

---

[1] One of Arvin's friends, Matthiessen had committed suicide in 1950.

Darling, I'm very excited about the possibility of you and Gray coming to Italy in the Fall. We could meet in Venice—I would love to see the two of you in Venice: how happy both of you would be!

I don't know any news from anywhere—except I heard that Newton had been appointed to Harvard. But I never see a soul, and my new house (or hotel) is much too far away on the mountain for anyone to walk to. I guess I told you that I bought a little car, and that is pleasant because we can visit all sorts of strange places we never could have gone before.

My various complaints have set me back so far as work goes, but I still hope to have accomplished several things before the summer is over.

I am delighted that Gray is doing the albums for Columbia;[1] I hope he makes a fortune. I can't wait for the two of you to come over here.[2]

Jack is working on a book—he is very mysterious about it.

Kelly has a girl friend—an awful mongrel really, not at all a suitable match, still I shall not interfere.

If you have any long-playing records that you don't want please send them to us.

Are Saint and Robbie together—?[3] Saint never mentions him in the few letters I've had.

Love to Gray, and Love to you, and Love from Jack and Love from Kelly and Love Love Love from

T

[Collection Columbia University Library]

TO LEO LERMAN

Taormina,
July 2 [1952]

Leo dearheart—

At first I didn't know what you were talking about—I'd quite forgotten Pearl's story: and I think you should, too.[4] I maintain what I did when I

---

[1] Foy was doing jacket covers for classical music albums put out by Columbia Records.

[2] Lerman and Foy went to Europe later that year and saw Capote, who had left Sicily, in Rome.

[3] Theatrical producer Arnold Saint-Subber and his young companion, Robbie Campbell.

[4] Kazin's story "The Raven," which was an unflattering portrait of a Lerman-like character, had just been published by *Botteghe Oscure*. For a full explanation, see the January 4, 1951, letter to Lerman.

originally read it: that the story, or essay, is <u>not</u> about you, anymore than a parody of me is about me.[1] This is the sort of thing that happens, though happily you have avoided it until now: I've been bitten so often that anti-serum flows in my veins. Lord knows Pearl has done you a disservice—but mainly an artistic one. I know that you have been hurt, precious, and Gray, too, because he loves you; but if possible I think you ought not to hold it against Pearl—I'm sure she is quite miserable. At any rate, very few people will see the story—not of course that that is the point. What is so wretched is that you should have read it when you have been having so many troubles. Darling, I hope that all your surgery is over, and you can look forward to the rest of the summer in comparative peace.

Taormina is peaceful enough all right: not a bloody thing happening. I work all morning and in the afternoons continue to be the local underwater fishing champion—you'd love me with my water-mask and spear-gun. So butch. Every day I remind myself that you and Gray may be coming here—we can't wait. Jack wants to send love to you both—Kelly would too, except he's off chasing rabbits somewhere. Kisses for Gray.

I love you: so does
<u>all</u> the nation
T

P.S. Write me

[Collection Columbia University Library]

TO CECIL BEATON

Taormina, Sicily
July 1952

Cecil darling—
Am writing in the middle of a fierce sudden storm—hailstones large as your thumb: it seems all very strange, for I can't recall having seen so much

---

[1] He is being diplomatic. He of course knew that Kazin's story was about Lerman, and in a letter to Andrew Lyndon on March 9, 1951, he had written that Kazin had "written a story about him that would take the skin off an elephant."

as a drop of dew during a Sicilian summer. On the whole, the weather has been marvelous—not really too hot at all. We have taken up underwater fishing very seriously—have an extraordinary new mask, as well as the one you left, and shoes, guns—we transport tons of equipment to the beach. I've been a real devotee—awfully solemn about the whole thing.

Darling, I'm so happy everything turned out so well in Manchester. I long to see it, and your sets, especially the clamber-rose. I hope you make <u>stacks</u> of money. Was very amused by Saint sending the Cartier token; I think it was sweet—and can't understand what the Wilsons' [*sic*] mean by saying 'he only does it to humiliate us.' As a matter of fact, I'm really fascinated by this remark—what <u>does</u> it mean?

Just had to go downstairs and help Jack rescue the terrace furniture—all being overturned and blown away. Am drenched!

I wish I <u>could</u> entice you to spend your August holiday with us—after all, it's only a little plane ride. You can have any room you want, and anybody in it—and there <u>is</u> something Really Remarkable stalking the streets.

Would it be possible for you to speak to John Heyward (sp?) and ask him if he would read Jack's book and if he liked it reccomend [*sic*] it to the Cresset Press? The Cresset Press turned it down—but Marylou Aswell said they will probably reconsider if Heyward reccomended it to them.

Thank you for the Avedon snaps—but I look so fat in them—and really I've lost pounds.

I'm working every day on the play—I wonder what you will think. To tell the truth, I'm delighted your play is not going to be done in summer stock—I was always against the idea—but I'm really delighted with the thought of a N.Y. production. Am keeping my fingers crossed.

Honey, pack your clothes and come back here to those who love you: Jack, Kelly.

[Collection St. John's College, Cambridge University]

TO CECIL BEATON

July 12, 1952

Cecil dearest—

We were all delighted with the pictures—Anne especially. I've intended writing you every day, but really so little has happened here—except a carabiniere on a motorcycle ran into the car and partly demolished it. However, it has been fixed now and we are again riding to the beach (Isola Balla [Bella], where we rented a little boat for the summer).

I finished the story, but am not too pleased with it and at least shall keep it a while longer.

Had a two page cable from the Saint yesterday. He is very anxious to come over here and seems to feel he needs a visa from me. Christ! But I just don't want to see him until I have done enough work to feel less vulnerable.[1] Speaking of which, our friend [Arnold] Weissberger telephoned me—but I refused to go to the telephone office.[2]

Darling, at this moment you are probably off battling the Lunts in some remote province. I'm assuming the play has opened. You must write me every tiny detail. I know it will be a great success, and a triumph for you.

Are you going to the states?

The Verdura set have not arrived, but suppose they will be along presently. I wonder what they're going to sleep on or with. The house they've rented hasn't a stick of furniture.

Something far more interesting than the Panther has turned up. Something in fact really fabulous. If you don't go to the states, come back! Come back!

The weather has been really quite wonderful—cool and crystal. Even Anne has stopped complaining.

Did you see [Katharine] Hepburn? What was it like? Please tell me if Constance Collier is still at the Hotel Connaught—and if so what is the Connaught's address?

I miss you, precious one. Everyone sends their love, especially Jack. Write soon, honey.

Love

T

[Collection St. John's College, Cambridge University]

---

[1] Capote was writing his second play for Saint Subber, this time a musical based on his short story "House of Flowers."

[2] Arnold Weissberger was an entertainment lawyer based in New York. The Fontana Vecchia did not have a telephone, and Capote had to go to a telephone office in Taormina to receive calls.

TO DONALD WINDHAM

Taormina, Sicily
August 4, '52

Donny love,
 This long silence was due not to a lack of affection—but infection. I was feeling right porely there for quite a spell. Anyway, I've missed not hearing from you.
 I <u>wish</u> I had read your book, for this way I can really have no opinion, except I hope Rupert Hart-Davis took it. But I'm glad you are working on a new book—you are a real writer. You said you had written a play—I would love to see it; have you shown it to anyone yet?
 You ask about the folks here; it seems all so much the same—except there are more cafés, more tourists, and Carlo Panarello has opened a nightclub. That boy Enzio has gone to Brazil to join his father. <u>The</u> <u>Panther</u> no longer parades the beaches: he got involved in a great scandal by trying to 'blackmail' one of Gayelord Hauser's guests, and the police told him to stay out of Taormina.[1] Chicho, the football player (Sylvia Bombaro's boyfriend) has taken up whoring and according to those who are interested makes himself very available on a trip to see the grotto. Bobby Pratt-Barlow has been very miserable all year, due to two things 1) a really horrible American called Culver Sherrill stole his little boyfriend Beppé—and thus divided the whole town into an absolute war: those for Bobby, and those for Sherrill—Sherrill is very rich and bought a villa here; 2) he is the 'hero' of Aubrey Menen's novel 'Duke of Gallodoro' and Bobby feels very betrayed by Menen—actually, it's a bad and silly book, only worth reading because of one terribly funny scene. The Campbell-Wood's [*sic*] are still dispensing boredom and latte di capra. I have a simply <u>wonderful</u> story to tell you about Giovanni Panarello: but it is very long and I will only do it if you write me a three-page letter. Kelly is biting more dogs than ever, and Jack insulting more people.
 I think we will go to Venice toward the end of September. I don't know whether Merlo and Williams Inc. are in Italy or not—never hear of them, not even in the Rome Daily American—which paper, by the way, is worse than ever: they have a new column called 'Roamin' Forum.'!! ***

---

[1] Hauser was the preeminent diet guru of the fifties, extolling the benefits of such things as wheat germ and yogurt. His book *Look Younger, Live Longer* was a bestseller in 1950.

Love to Sandy, and congratulations on his selling his article to the Bazaar. Love from Jack, and Kelly, and

Me

[Collection Beinecke Library, Yale University]

TO ANDREW LYNDON

[Taormina, Sicily]
[Summer 1952]

Andrew darling—

This morning I woke up thinking about you, remembering all sorts of sweet things, and I thought now today I'm going to write my precious magnolia a letter and tell her how much I love her and miss her.

For in truth there is nothing else to tell you. Kelly has fleas. Jack got a haircut. I'm reading 'To the Lighthouse'[1] and when it's not too hot tinkering with my pen: mostly it's too hot. I _said_ I would never, could never, go through another Sicilian summer—alas, I don't listen to myself: a great failing.

I suppose you've heard about the apparently battle-to-the-death being waged between Pearl & Leo. Because of the really ghastly bad story she wrote about him and published in the current <u>Botteghe Oscure</u>. Leo has vowed to drive her from New York, and according to Pearl he has so far prevented her from getting two jobs. Myself, I have no side. I think they both are quite, quite expendable.

Well, I take it the Robert Dunphys are heading this way.[2] But over my dead body will they ever set foot inside <u>questo</u> <u>casa</u> [_sic_]! I do <u>loathe</u> that Olga woman.[3] I must say she wrote Jack's sister (who sent it to him) an hilarious letter—quite unintentional: a dead-earnest account of spending an evening in the exalted company of Freddie Bartholomew.[4] (!!!)

Dear heart, what has been happening along employment row? If Mary Lou is back, and I don't know whether she is, you might ring her up about the Farrar, Straus thing—because last winter she volunteered to get you a job there if she could.

---

[1] A 1927 novel by Virginia Woolf.
[2] Robert Dunphy was Jack Dunphy's younger brother.
[3] Olga was Robert Dunphy's wife.
[4] Freddie Bartholomew was a child actor of the 1930s.

I read 'Look down In Mercy' (the English Edition) and it ends with the officer committing suicide—it does not sound like the ending you mentioned.[1] How did that end?

I know Walter Baxter—and he is so cheesy (not at all unlike Howard Rothchild [Rothschild]) that it deterred almost any feeling I might have had for the book—which did, amid a lot padding, have many touching and terrible scenes. Write soon. Love from Jack. Love from Kelly. And much, much love from T.

[Collection New York Public Library]

TO CECIL BEATON

[Taormina, Sicily]
August 16, 1952

Cecil dearest—

Bless you for the Angus Wilson—I'd been longing to read it.[2] On the whole I liked it very much, it really has quite a charge for all its slickness. The N.Y. Times has asked me to review it when it comes out there—but I don't believe in reviewing books. Or do you think I should?

It is so sad about Simon's [Simon Fleet] little house—I think there must be a pyromaniac abroad in Wiltshire. Fulco [di Verdura] hints that Simon didn't come here because Juliet [Duff] wouldn't let him—which sounds a little farfetched to me.

As for news from the piazza—Fulco and his crowd seem to me like a rather desperate lot: so longing to have a good time, and yet not knowing quite how to go about it—they seem to sleep all day and play Canasta all night. There are many too many of them, and Fulco never stops complaining. Their house is hideous. I think Fulco is having an affair with a French boy (man) who has dyed blond hair and whose name is Jacque Something. I loathe the man called Hamish Erskine; he is profoundly repulsive. I do like Judy Montague [Montagu], and the young girl Sarah Roosevelt. Judy has a nice hearty openness. There was a woman called Mrs. Alexander who made a fool of herself trying,

---

[1] *Look Down in Mercy* (1951) was a novel by Walter Baxter that portrayed a homosexual relationship between a British officer and an enlisted man, set against the Japanese invasion of Burma in World War II.

[2] *Hemlock and After*, Wilson's first novel.

of <u>all</u> things, to put "in" with G. [Gayelord] Hauser. Hauser gave a huge party and didn't invite any of them—they were mad as hornets. So <u>they</u> gave a costume party night before last. Jack wouldn't go, but I went—much to my regret: it was terribly tacky—nothing to drink except a cheap wine punch and etc.

Saint [Subber] tried to phone the other day, but I refused to go down and sit in that office. I suppose he wanted to tell me he's coming over here. I <u>wish</u> he wouldn't. He ought to get to work—get a play and produce it; <u>any</u> play.

I have a new animal—a Raven. We have got it quite tamed now, and it really is very clever and amusing. It sits on my shoulder every evening on the terrace. Kelly <u>hates</u> it. It's called Lola.

The heat is terrific—I simply pass into a coma every afternoon. But mornings and evenings are fine.

Darling, I wish you would hop a plane and come here next week. For heaven sakes why not?

We are going to be here until the 20th of September, then I want to go to Venice for a week or so. I can't think beyond that—

I'm very sorry indeed to know that your mother has not been well—I do hope she has recovered.

I guess that is all the news for the moment, honey. Jack sends his love. I miss you greatly,

L O V E

T

P.S. Thanks so much about John Heyward; you were an angel to ask him; perhaps some other publisher will like the book.[1] I do hope so.

[Collection St. John's College, Cambridge University]

TO CECIL BEATON

[Taormina]
[Late August or early September 1952]

Cecil dearest—

All quiet on the Sicilian front: the merry-makers have vanished in a cloud of discontent and debt—even La Reine [Gayelord] Hauser departed leaving a string of unpaid bills: I suppose he thought he could get away with

---

[1] In July Capote had asked Beaton to show Dunphy's book to Heyward.

it for, as he told me, he does not intend ever to return to Taormina—a bit of news not received with the grief he might have wished. Fulco and Judy [Montagu] left under rather dismal circumstances, too. The fact is, poor Judy had just gotten out of jail—seems the police in Syracuse were not amused by her habit of speeding round the countryside without 1) a drivers license, 2) a passport, 3) a permisse de Seggiorno—so, along with several of her loutish companions, they tossed her into the jug; and Fulco managed to get them all released just in time to pack their bags, _not_ pay their bills, and catch the plane for home. Well, I was sorry to see Judy go: for all her drawling inanities, her bad taste, her third-rate friends, her offensive clothes, her canasta mentality—for all that, she still seemed to me a thinking person, good-hearted and wanting to please: but then I'm always a sucker for this type: The Ugly Duckling Holding Her Own. So ends the summer. Amen.

After having opened that cable from the mad Saint [Subber], I'm amazed you still do have your young secretary. What I would like to know is: _who_ sends those cables for him? Surely he hasn't the guts to walk into a Western Union office and hand over such a message in person! Bye the bye, I rather fear he will be headed this way toward the end of the month, and I strongly suggest you put up storm windows at 8 Pelham Place. For my own sake, I pray to god he doesn't bring The Tar Baby with him.[1] Because I will _not_, no never again, put up with the boredom of _that_.

Darling, I will be thinking of you on the 12th—I wish for you all a wonderful opening, and a great success.[2] I'm too broke to send you a cable, much less a Cartier token—but you know I love you anyway, don't you? And won't you please give my good wishes to the Lunts?

Lola, the Raven, is in here pecking at my head—she's a violent creature. Kelly is downstairs barking at a horse. Jack is in the kitchen making coffee—I guess I'd better get up and begin the day. Write me soon, precious

Love

T

P.S. We are leaving here around the 20th. When do you go to N.Y.?

[Collection St. John's College, Cambridge University]

---

[1] The Tar Baby was Saint Subber's companion, Robbie Campbell, a boyishly handsome black singer who had won some acclaim in Paris in the late forties singing "Nature Boy" at the Boeuf sur le Toit. "_Jeune vagabond noir!_" passersby would shout as he walked through the streets of the Left Bank.

[2] Beaton had designed the sets for Noël Coward's _Quadrille,_ which starred Alfred Lunt and Lynn Fontanne and which was soon to open in London.

TO ANDREW LYNDON

[Taormina, Sicily]
Sept 6 1952

Dearest Heart—

You've been so long silent—I wonder if a letter from you went astray. Anyway, I've been brooding about you, and missing you and wanting to know how everything is. I want so to hear from you before I leave here—on the 20th—I will probably be in Rome (just for a day or two) on the 22nd and you could write me there. (American Express). After that, our plans are a little vague. We may go to Copenhagen. I don't want to come home until I've finished this play—I wonder if you will like it. To which purpose I know I ought to stay in Taormina—but for the moment I'm really very tired of it.

Two weeks ago Frankie Merlo descended without warning and sans Tennesee [Tennessee] who is off sucking cock in Germany. I thought Frankie would a) never stop talking, and b) never leave. Finally I convinced him to get on a train. Bless Jesus we're leaving before Bob & Olga [Dunphy] can possibly put in an appearance. Have I told you about Lola? Lola is a big black Raven who came to live with us—a mad, marvellous creature, terribly affectionate; we're taking her with us.[1] Kelly hates her.

Darling, will you call Nina and tell her two things. 1) Will she please give my tweed overcoat to Saint to bring to me here, and 2) The Grass Harp is being televised Sept 17th on the Kraft Theatre Hour.

Had a letter from Pearl Kazin who said she'd met Phoebe on the street. Of course Pearl, with her usual generosity, gave a very negative report, but I take it Phoebe is still at the Vendome. What is the Vendome? A restaurant? I do wish I knew her address, as I would like to write her.

Have you heard from Newton? I suppose he is happily established in Cambridge. Here's one bird who'll never visit him there. I wouldn't set foot in Boston if my life depended on it.

Jack is very well and says give you his best love. Write me all your news, precious. I miss you muchly. Love galore

T

P.S. Who is the friend of yours that took B & O's (how accurate those initials are) apt.?

[Collection New York Public Library]

---

[1] Capote's essay about Lola, "A Curious Gift," appeared in *Redbook,* June 1965; it was retitled simply "Lola" in *The Dogs Bark* (1973).

TO ROBERT LINSCOTT

Taormina, Sicily
Sept 7 1952

Dear Bob—

So happy to have your letter; it seemed such a while since I'd had a steadying word from you. I hope, in fact I <u>know</u>, your summer was better than mine. But I shall not go on about it, at least it's nearly over, the summer I mean, and I am leaving here on the 20th—I will be in Rome on the 22nd for two days and you can write me there c/o American Express. I will let you know a more permanent address when I know it myself.

Even so, I have done quite a lot of work. I've written half of a play which I think you will like, and about forty pages of my novel. I would like to finish the play and have a hundred pages of the book before coming home (after Christmas). I may want an advance—I don't know yet.

Of course you know Marian Ives is closing her agency. I am sorry for her—but, well, you know how I feel about it. I do not intend to have another agent—couldn't Random handle my foreign rights? Marian says she is going to hang on till the new year—but I <u>don't</u> <u>want</u> her to make some contract for me with Random, which I'm sure she would expect to do if it were done before she quits. So how can I avoid that? I've endured all these years, I would hate to hurt her at the very last.

What ever happened about Goyen? Not a word from him have I heard. Did Faulkner enjoy his trip to Paris?

Give my best to Bennett and Bob Haas. Write me all your news. Love
T

[Collection Columbia University Library]

TO CECIL BEATON

American Express
Rome
October 5, 1952

Dearest bunny—

I suppose you've wondered at this lengthy silence, but it was rather an ordeal quitting Taormina. Finally, we decided to spend the winter here in

Rome and have found, I must say, a beautiful apartment, a dream, really; I have fallen quite in love with Rome, it's an enchanting city if you simply settle back and don't know too many people. The weather is wonderful—such still crystal October days, and I am working again: I finished, or have nearly finished the first act of the play, and have started a novel—which is perhaps unwise of me, still I could not resist it.

Had just to pause for lunch—we have a first-rate cook! Everything is so different from Taormina—I guess this is the first time in my life I've ever [rest of page missing]

I think I saw most all the reviews of 'Quadrille' and was delighted that you came out with such flying colors.[1] But I know [Noël] Coward must have been dissapointed [sic]: the critics seem just not able to forgive him for past successes—they write like a peck of schoolboy bullies. How did the Lunts take it all? I saw a good deal of Thornton Wilder in Venice; he was very amusing on the subject of the L's. But I daresay you've had your [unclear] of it now. Only do write me what storms, if any, have brewed in cloud Cuckoo land. Speaking of which, or at least of cuckoos, Saint writes now that he is coming over here in December. But I read in the papers where he is producing about three different plays, one by Frank O'Connor, which I hope is true. Jack is fine, and working well; he sends his best love. All our animals are fine, too. Honey, when do you go to New York? Be sure to answer that. It's so sad, really sad, to think of not seeing you this winter—but perhaps I will. Has anything been settled about 'The Gainsboroughs'? I miss you greatly, precious one. Write me as soon as you can, c/o American Express, Rome. Much love

T

[Collection St. John's College, Cambridge University]

---

[1] Beaton designed the sets for Noël Coward's *Quadrille,* starring the Lunts. The critics disliked it, but audiences gave it long runs in both London and New York.

TO ANDREW LYNDON

> c/o American Express
> Rome
> Oct 14, 1952

Darling one—

Was so happy to have your newsy sweet letter. I guess I must have written you that we have taken an apartment here in Rome—very sunny and charming, but alas much too expensive. Anyway, I guess we will be here for the next several months. If all goes well, I mean if I finish the play and anybody likes it, I suppose we will come back to New York in March.

I'm terribly upset about Nina and Joe moving to Cuba. I do hope it works out for them. In the meantime, I'm so afraid of all my books and mss. getting mislaid. Oh well. It seems so terrible that all this should have happened to Joe.[1] I never get a personal letter from either of them, and so don't know exactly what they plan. Is Tiny still at 1060?[2] I wish <u>you</u> would let me know.

Rome is full of old acquaintances. Sister (you remember <u>her</u>? the famous Carson McCullers) and Mr. Sister [Reeves McCullers] are frequently to be observed <u>staggering</u> along Via Veneto. We don't speak—or they don't speak to me, whichever way you care to look at it. The Cow [Marguerite Young] is somewhere in a pensione—she has dyed her hair brick red. And just today I bumped straight into Messrs. [Gray] Foy and [Richard] Hunter. I plan, in the future, to only venture upon the streets when <u>heavily</u> veiled.

Next day—!

No sooner had I finished the foregoing paragraph than the doorbell rang and there were my in-laws: the Robt. Dunphys. Surprise, surprise. They stayed the whole day and half the night—Jack is prostrated. But I must say they were rather touching—recounting all their experiences in the most tedious detail. We are busily trying to convince them that they ought to go to Germany—at once. But I have a feeling that they will be around a good two weeks. Dost thou heart bleed for me?

---

[1] Joe Capote had been fired from the Wall Street textile brokerage firm for which he had worked for many years after it was discovered that he had misappropriated a hundred thousand dollars. To escape jail he needed to repay the money, and he went into business in his native Cuba in hopes of raising the cash. He was unsuccessful, however, and the Capotes soon returned to New York, poorer than when they had left. Truman sent them much of the money he was soon to make writing screenplays.

[2] Tiny, whose formal name was Marie, was Nina Capote's younger sister, who sometimes stayed with her in New York.

Incidentally, when I ran into little Miss Cunter,[1] she told me some wild story about Harold having a rich Texas lover who has set him up in business. Is there <u>any</u> truth in this?

Well, I'm glad you saw Phoebe and she seemed so well. I will write her soon. Two days ago I had a letter from her mother—enclosing my <u>horoscope</u>! All very peculiar.

I miss you so much, little angel. Write me soon. Jack sends love, so do all the animals, so does

T

[Collection New York Public Library]

TO CECIL BEATON

33 via Margutta
Rome
Nov 8, 1952

Cecil dear—

Had your sweet letter yesterday, on the eve of your departure, and so perhaps this will reach the Sherry-N. [Sherry-Netherland Hotel] about the same time as you. Poor darling, how <u>wretched</u> of them to take away your pretty apartment. I think it's just a ruse to get you to decorate another flat <u>free</u>. But I do hate it that we won't be in New York together. Still I'm glad you are there—and away from all your female obligations.

I saw an article in the N.Y. Times that Aldrich & Myers were 'delighted with the alterations' in 'Gainsborough Girls'—and so I hope this means they are going to take the scenery out of storage.

I was offered the job of doing a film scenario for Vittorio De Sica, but hesitated so long that they got someone else. Now I'm just a little sorry, if only because it would have put an end to my financial straits, which grow increasingly severe. But it would have been dishonest of me to have accepted, for I did not feel at all sympathetic to the story they outlined, and besides I <u>must</u>, <u>must</u> get on with my own work.

---

[1] Marguerite Young.

Darling, I hope you can have an easier, at any rate less neurotic, rapport with Greta G. [Garbo] this winter. But I'm afraid she will never be a satisfactory person because she is so disatisfied [sic] with herself, and disatisfied people can never be emotionally serious. They simply don't believe in anything—except their own limitations.

I am still enjoying Rome, it reveals itself to one a little more each day. It is a beautiful city, really—though inhabited by a quarrelsome and cynical race. I do not see any of 'The Big Ball' set—but have become rather friendly with certain of the intelligentsia. Outside of them, I guess the only person I see very much of is Orson Welles—who has grown somewhat pathetic, still he has a point-of-view and so few people do anymore.

I don't know anymore whether or not Saint is coming here. Perhaps your presence will keep him in N.Y. You must be kind to him—I mean, if you are going to give him the axe, then do it by degrees.

I hope (so much) that we can spend your spring holiday together. At any rate, I will try to come to England when you return—when, more or less, do you imagine that will be?

I have exactly half-finished my play—I think just possibly it could, so far, be good, but such a great lot depends on <u>other</u> people, which is the curse of writing for the theatre.

Jack is fine, and sends you his best love. He is working well. But the animals get <u>worse</u> all the time. That dear <u>Kelly</u> bit me yesterday.

You are such a good friend to me, I respect and trust you almost more than anyone I know—and love you exceedingly, which is to say hugely

T

[Collection St. John's College, Cambridge University]

TO NEWTON ARVIN

[Christmas card]   [Rome]
                                                        [December 1952]

Sige dear—
Have been working like a donkey, for, in addition to everything else, I took on a movie job—that is, I rewrote the scenario for the new De Sica picture (he directed 'Shoeshine' and 'Bicycle Thief') and it had to be finished in 3

weeks as the picture was already in production.[1] Anyway, the whole experience had its amusing moments, and I think I did a pretty good job, all things considered. But it meant interrupting my play, and now it is hard getting back. Did you go to N'hampton for Thanksgiving? Are you still going to N.Y. for a while? I think that is a good idea. I had a Christmas card from you yesterday, but it only said your name—not <u>even</u> love. I miss you a lot at Christmas time. Oh anyway, let's forget Christmas, and think about the New Year and hope it will be a good one for us both. Write me soon, my dearest friend. I love you

    T

[Collection Smith College Library]

TO ROBERT LINSCOTT

33 Via Margutta
Rome. Dec 27, 1952

Dear Bob,

I think you must have missed a letter from me, and a Christmas card, too. For I'm perfectly certain that I wrote you about the Dinesen project.[2] Anyway, this is how the matter stands. I showed the story to Garbo, as the whole idea, to my mind, depends on her playing the part. Her opinion of the story was not very coherent (<u>this</u> is an understatement) . . . but she said, quite rightly, that so much depended on the scenario treatment. Anyway, she would not give a definite answer—but then she couldn't very well, and on the whole I got the response I expected. So the next thing to do was interest a producer; because naturally I could not go ahead with such a project unless someone was ready and willing to put the picture in production when and if. I offered it to David Selznick (who has produced other Garbo pictures) and he was enthusiastic at first, then less so; and what was more, we did not seem to see the picture in the same way. I still think I could get Selznick to do it . . . though I'm afraid he would be mainly interested in it as a vehicle for his wife, Jennifer Jones. Which brings us to Roberto Rosselini

---

[1] Titled *Stazione Termini* in Italian, the movie was David O. Selznick's attempt to join Hollywood glamor with Italian realism. Shot in Rome and directed by Vittorio De Sica, it starred Selznick's wife, Jennifer Jones, and Montgomery Clift. Capote was the last of several scriptwriters. Called *Indiscretion of an American Wife* for American audiences, the film was a flop—"lousy," in Capote's estimation.

[2] A movie based on Isak Dinesen's "The Dreamers," one of the stories in *Seven Gothic Tales*.

[Rossellini] (he is the Italian director who did OPEN CITY etc). I'm reasonably certain Rosselini would do The Dreamers . . . but here is the catch: Rosselini will want to star <u>his</u> wife, Ingrid Bergman, and will want to direct. Well I don't think he is the right kind of director for such a picture as this . . . (cause one thing it ain't, it ain't realistic.) I suppose Bergman could be rather good in the part (I would like to know what Dinesen thinks); but after all the whole point, or at least my point, is that this is a picture for Garbo. I guess the thing to do is to find a producer who hasn't got an actress wife. All joking aside, I do still very much want to adapt this story, and if Miss Dinesen will allow me to continue I know that I will find just the right sponsorship. For one thing, I want to speak to Carol Reed (and am going to do so in March) who I know is interested in this whole idea, and who I think would be able to realize it in the most sensitive way possible. But if on the other hand Miss Dinesen would care to take a chance on Rosselini and Bergman . . . then I am perfectly willing to have all rights revert to her, as indeed they would in any case, for I should not want to do the scenario.

Bob I expect to come to New York around the middle of March. I must finish my play first (I think you will like it) . . . and when that is over I'm going to settle down to being a novelist again.

I miss you all the time, and God knows I wish I could talk to you. Give my best to Bob Haas.

always

T

P.S. Bob, would you please see that all mail is forwarded to me c/o Saint Subber, 17A East 57th St. N.Y.C.

[Collection Columbia University]

TO CECIL BEATON

33 via Margutta
Rome
New Year's Day 1953

Cecil dearest—

Here it is, a new year—I want to begin it with letters to those who are closest to my heart: I shall <u>not</u> be over-burdening the postman.

Perhaps this will reach you somewhere on your 'lecture tour'—probably too exhausted to open the envelope. Oh I don't envy you, poor lamb; but I hope you are making a fortune and not having to eat too much cream chicken (those provincial ladies serve <u>only</u> that).[1]

I had such a laugh over the clipping about Juliet [Duff]. But seriously, I think someone has it in for that family: all those fires, robberies—can they be just coincidence?

As for Saint—his personal life is too muddled for me. I can only conclude that he is a masochist: and rather a bore about it, too. What he needs is a dose of <u>dignity</u>—maybe Dr. Jacobsen could oblige. On the other hand, I am touched when he writes, as he does every letter, how much in love with you he is; and I believe him, too. But there is such a lot to say on this subject—best wait till I see you.

We had a very quiet holiday period—the only really good present I got was a Caraceni suit (which I gave to myself). I have been working pretty steadily, and so has Jack; we did not even go out New Year's eve.

Jack is rather put out today, because we saw in the paper where Joan is getting married again. Not that he objects to that—only the person she is marrying, a dancer called Bob Foss [Fosse]. Seems to be a most unfortunate alliance.[2] She has a good part in the new Rodger's [sic]-Hammerstein.[3]

The [Charlie] Chaplins were here last week—amid great ovations. And I acted as their cicerone for several days—it was kind of fun. They were showered with presents—including a miniature Japanese tree, which they gave me, and which I shall probably leave to the landlady—although it's charming, and Lola looks delightful perched on its tiny branches.

I want to come to London in March—Jack & the animals would have to stay in Paris because of the quarantine (on animals, not Jack). But will you be there—around the 10th or 15th?

I miss you, precious one. Write soon, and forgive this dull note—I only want to tell you that I am thinking of you and love you

T

[Collection St. John's College, Cambridge University]

---

[1] Beaton was on his first American lecture tour, visiting several cities in the Midwest.

[2] Also a dancer, Bob Fosse achieved even greater fame as an innovative choreographer. Even as Capote guessed, their marriage ended in divorce.

[3] *Me and Juliet.*

TO CATHERINE WOOD

33 Via Margutta
Rome
[Early January 1953]

Woody darling

Bless you sweet heart for the oh so appetizing can-goods—which arrived a few days ago: we've all been gorging!

Darling, the reason your letters were returned is that you mis-spelled the name of this street. M - A - R - G - U - TT - A.

I had your letter this morning, and my goodness you sound as though you had a gay holiday whirl. Mine was very quiet—just rested up, having finished that damned movie. Yes, you will see it in New York—it's in English. I've been working regularly on the play, and another 2 months should see me finished.

It's <u>freezing</u> here in Rome. I have two electrical heaters but they just barely take the chill off the room. The floors are <u>marble</u>—absolute ice. I can hardly hold this pen—

Princess Caetani arranged for me to have a <u>private</u> audience with the Pope. It was supposed to last 15 minutes, but I stayed more than half-an-hour—an extraordinary man, so really charming and beautiful. I long to tell you about it.

The Chaplins were here just before Christmas, and when I leave Rome (around March 1st) I am going to stop a few days with them in Switzerland, (where they have taken a house) on my way to Paris. Did you see his picture, 'Limelight'? I loved it. I am so fond of them, and it breaks my heart that all this foolishness is happening about him at home. It makes me feel so ashamed of my own country.[1]

Give my love to Margery: I enjoyed her Christmas card. Jack sends his fondest regards. <u>All</u> the animals are fine. I love you with all my heart, precious Woody.

Your own
T

[Collection New York Public Library]

---

[1] In the Red Scare of the fifties, Chaplin, a British subject, was accused of being a Communist sympathizer. When he left the United States for the London premiere of his last American film, *Limelight* (1952), he learned that he would be barred from returning. Embittered, he moved with his family—his wife, Oona, was one of Capote's oldest friends—to Switzerland.

TO ANDREW LYNDON

33 Via Margutta
Rome
Jan 7 1953

Dearest Bunny—

I was so relieved to have your letter—I'd begun really to be alarmed. Anyway, I hope you enjoyed the holidays—ours were very quiet.

I expect you must have seen Nina when they came back at Christmas to close up the apt. Heaven knows <u>where</u> I am going to keep my things— much less <u>live</u>—when we get back to N.Y. If you hear of a nice sublet from April 1st let me know.

As for the movie—I don't think very much of it. The actual making of it was a helluva lot more interesting. I got started on a great feud with M. [Montgomery] Clift—for six weeks we really loathed each other—but then (this is for your eyes alone!) we suddenly started a sort of mild flirtation, which snowballed along until it reached very tropic climates indeed. Nothing <u>too</u> serious—I'm not breaking up house and home—but it <u>has</u> been rather fun, and anyway he is really awfully sweet and I like him quite a lot. He is leaving next week—going to Hawaii to be in 'From Here to Eternity'— Or 'Horseshit' (as you say)? So I guess everything will cool down—and I'm glad in a way because, for obvious reasons, it's all been <u>too</u> nerve-wracking—

And not at <u>all</u> good for my work! Still, I am making headway—and with Great Effort should have the play finished by the time we leave. As for J. [Jennifer] Jones—I don't want her in the part: she is all wrong for it, I feel a little badly about it, because I really have gotten to like her—<u>but</u> she is an extremely neurotic girl, and would have 12 nervous breakdowns before rehearsals had hardly started. Besides, I want an all colored cast—or nearly so. Why was Alice P. so upset at the thought of Eartha Kitt? Of course I've never seen her—have you? If not, I wish you would and write me. By the way, when does Alice open at the Blue? I'd like to send her a cable.

Another thing, darling—<u>where</u> is Tiny? I asked before but you didn't answer and of course none of the Capotes ever write.

Jack sends love—(when you write, be discreet about certain items mentioned in this letter as Mr. D. always wants to read your letters). I love you, too, my precious one

T

P.S. What I wouldn't give for one of our long tête a têtes just now.

[Collection New York Public Library]

TO CECIL BEATON

33 via Margutta
Rome
Jan 21, 1953

Dearest Cecil—

I'm in bed with a cold—am sitting here sipping tea laced with rum, and have read six books in two days: it is all so very cozy: such a pleasure to be ill once in a while.

But I must tell you <u>how</u> I got the cold. It's all Mr. [Saint] Subber's fault. I had a message from the telephone office to come to their headquarters as there was a call for me from New York. It was a huge icy marble barn of a place and I had to wait there, sitting on a freezing slab of stone, for over <u>two</u> hours. Of course, when the call finally came, it was only Saint, who had really nothing to say, but was in great high spirits, rather like a manic-depressive in an up phase. I do seriously wish I could talk to you about Saint—I am, for my own sake, in a quandry [*sic*] about him. His behavior pattern is, if you are fond of him, irritating enough—<u>but if</u> he is involved with one professionally it gives <u>real</u> pause. I wish with all my heart that I could feel more confidence in him as a producer—I feel so much the need of a firmer, surer hand. What should I do?—try just to rely on myself? oh, ma mio caro [*sic*], one does get so weary of being a pillar of strength.

Darling, what about Margaret Phillips for your play? I think she is one of the two or three best young actresses.[1] By the way, when I suggested D. [Diana] Lynn, it was, you'll remember, for a summer theatre foundation and your producers wanted a film name—and <u>she</u> was looking for just such a job. But really you might investigate the possibility of M. Phillips. Or Audrey Hepburn—or, and this is an odd suggestion—Cathy O'Donnell. I've only seen her in one picture "Best Years of Our Lives" and she isn't a star, but she has a very charming quality. I met her here in Rome not long ago, and was rather struck by her.

Incidentally, I'm going to have an awful time finding the exactly right girl for my play. Eartha Kitt is too old, too soignée for the part—though there is another part I think she would be wonderful in.

No, I've not been anywhere near Switzerland, much less with the Selznicks. Actually, they aren't so bad—and David has some really quite admirable qualities; but others, need I add, less so. But I have such a lot of

---

[1] Though others also admired Margaret Phillips's acting, her career never took off.

amazing things to tell you about them; and about Montgomery Clift, too. I've seen quite a lot of the Rosselini's [Rossellinis], too. This is a sad story.[1]

I was interested in what you write about Constance [Collier]—especially because I am trying now to write the little article about her. I'm glad you took Greta to see her—a friendship with Constance would do her a lot of good I think.

How delighted I am that the lecture tour is going so well—perhaps it will become an annual event: the club ladys [sic] will await you like the Spring swallows. I'm sure you must be enjoying it—are you booked for Town Hall?[2] On the lecture circuit, that's like playing the Palace.

Jack is fine—he has written really the most beautiful short story. He sends his best love.

I am looking so longingly to the time when I will see you. It probably will not be till early April. Actually, I hate the idea of going to N.Y. just then—maybe I won't, who knows. I love you and miss you, precious one

T

[Collection St. John's College, Cambridge University]

TO ANDREW LYNDON

[Ravello, Italy][3]
[February 1953]

Andrew darling

Your letter caught me in the midst of an article (for the Bazaar, about Constance Collier) which I finished twenty minutes ago and so now hasten to write my own true sorella. It is JUST awful about the apartments . . . Jack has written his tenant and his sister to see what can be done about storing our junk. By the way, the apartment at 1060 [Park Avenue] is still there. This is between us: but I have been paying the rent of that apartment, and it is paid through April 1st—not for myself, but Joe, in case his business in Cuba

---

[1] The affair and subsequent marriage of Ingrid Bergman and the Italian film director Roberto Rossellini had scandalized much of America and torpedoed Bergman's once-flourishing career in Hollywood.

[2] Town Hall is on Manhattan's West 43rd Street.

[3] Capote was in Ravello, writing the script, together with the director John Huston, for *Beat the Devil*.

didn't work out; but I can't go on doing it, I'm rock-bottom poor, and no joke, for reasons you perhaps can guess. What all this boils down to is, I don't see why you can't go and stay at 1060 as long as it's empty. If you want to, please write Nina (P.O. Box 536, Havana) saying you would like to take refuge there a month or so. Do you think I should try and keep that apartment? Most of all, do you think it's really true about Feb 27 and 232[1] . . . isn't there a possibility of its dragging on a few months? If only there were some place to go when we get off the boat. Because I don't see how we can come home before the first of May. I haven't finished the play, and it would be ace-stupid of me to go there before doing so.

The last few weeks here have been filled with peculiar adventures, all involving John Huston and Humphrey Bogart, who've nearly killed me with their dissipations . . . half-drunk all day and dead-drunk all night, and once, believe it or not, I came to around six in the morning to find King Farouk[2] doing the hula-hula in the middle of Bogart's bedroom. Jack was disgusted with the whole thing; and I must say I breathed a sigh when they went off to Naples.

There is a wonderful thunderstorm going on outside. All the buildings are a beautiful color . . .

I was interested in what you wrote about Eartha Kitt. I was never too serious about her, and anyway I think she is much too old for the part.

You didn't tell me . . . is Rita [Smith] back with her boyfriend or not? Did you see Eudora [Welty] at the Poetry Center . . . what was it like?

I feel so sorry about Tiny [Rudisill].[3] What a rotten thing. She ought long ago to have tried to recreate her life . . . well, no sense going into that.

Had a letter from Newton . . . very happy about his life at Harvard.

Lola is over here trying to yank the paper out of the typewriter. God, she's tough. You can brain her with a rolled-up newspaper and faze her not the slightest.

Precious heart, write me **at** **once** about all our problems. Jack sends his love. I miss you all the time.

dearest love

t

[Collection New York Public Library]

---

[1] 232 was Lyndon's street address in New York, which he was supposed to vacate by February 27, 1953. Capote was suggesting that he find temporary refuge in the Capotes' apartment, which they were also soon to vacate, at 1060 Park Avenue.

[2] King Farouk of Egypt.

[3] Capote's aunt.

TO ROBERT LINSCOTT

Rome
May 20, 1953

Dear Bob—

This is Truman: remember me? I shouldn't be at all surprised if my name had gone quite out of your head. I'm sure I deserve to be forgotten—but I've been in a whirl of one kind and another, sometimes several whirls simultaneously.

I've just come back from a month in London—and am leaving Rome Sunday—the best address to write to me is—

c/o American Express
Florence, Italy

Because I'm not altogether sure yet where I am going to spend the summer. I've finished my play (in a sense) but I want to put it aside and then spend about six weeks revising it. I don't suppose you've gone to see the revival of 'The Grass Harp'—some people thought it was rather good.[1]

Bob, my novel is really a long short story, and I want to publish a book of stories next winter or spring—I think I will have enough by then. I <u>need</u> to write short stories now, partly because they interest me and, perhaps more importantly, I am entering a new area of style, developing a different cast of characters and theses—and only when this is set in my mind can I really write a novel. I <u>have</u> a novel to write—but I want to try, with short story, trial and error, to set my guns right.

You ask what to do with the paper-back copies of 'Harp'. I suppose you could send them to 1060 Park Avenue (my mother is back there)—or, if this is easy please to keep them at R.H., I would be grateful if you did that.

I am coming back to New York in the fall. Give my best to Bennett and to Bob Haas. Have a good summer on the farm and write me soon.

Love
T

[Collection Columbia University Library]

---

[1] Almost a year to the day after it had closed on Broadway, *The Grass Harp* saw another production at the Circle in the Square Theatre in Greenwich Village.

TO ANDREW LYNDON

Rome
May 20, 1953

Dearest—

Bless you for your sweet letter, and the clippings. We have just come back to Rome, after a month in London. We had a fine time in London, except that I had to work every day—did you know that I wrote the script for Huston's new picture? Called 'Beat The Devil'. It's a mad camp—I had fun doing it. We saw all the plays, including Graham Greene's 'The Living Room'—which is a great success but a very bad and spurious play (I think): Jack liked it.[1] Alas, we have acquired a new dog, a little English bull puppy called Mr Bunkum—a present from Huston. But we lost Lola—she flew out the window and couldn't find her way back—it was very sad. Kelly is fine, however. Jack has finished his new book. We are going to Portofino or Camogli for the summer (depending where we can find a suitable house) so that I can finish 'House of Flowers'. We are leaving Rome next week— you can write me c/o American Express, Florence.

Darling, do you like your new apartment? I shall miss it so much, all of us living together that way. We are coming to New York in the Fall (Sept. or Oct.) but god knows where to live.

I don't suppose you ever see Phoebe—I never hear from her. Or Newton.

My intuition tells me you are having an affair—a good sexy one. Who is it? What does he look like? What does he do? Please, dear—sua sorella is interested.

Such extraordinary things have been going on the last three months. Jack blossomed out in London—was a great hit with all the movie-stars and 'nobility'. But oh the tales I have to tell—!

Do you see Nina at all? I talked to her on the phone from London. What is your <u>frank</u> impression of the situation?

I wish we could have a huge long talk just now. Darling, I love you very much—you are always dear and close to me. Write me as soon as you can. Jack sends love. So does

T

[Collection New York Public Library]

---

[1] Graham Greene's first play, *The Living Room*, ran at London's Wyndham's Theatre.

TO MARY LOUISE ASWELL

> Fermo Posta
> Portofino
> June 19, 1953

Marylou darling—

We were so happy to have your sweet letter. I hope you are going to have a good time in Folly [unclear] Cove—the name, at least, is wonderful. I wish I <u>did</u> have a novella to send you—oddly enough, I might—if you were waiting until December. As for 'Summer Crossing' I tore it up long ago—anyway, it was never finished. Jack has written a really beautiful short story—the one the Bazaar reneged on—and I wish you would get it from Audrey [Wood] with one of your future anthologies in mind. It's called 'Light on the Square'.

This has been the strangest winter, have been mixed up with such extraordinary people. I enjoyed very much working with Huston—he and his family have come here to spend the Summer with us (though, thank God, they have taken their own home). It's heavenly here, we have a little boat and I am working on the play—everything would be fine, except for the terrible and constant worry about my mother and father—but I will not burden you with that.

Jack has nearly finished his book. I'm sure you will like it—I hope all goes well at f.s.& g.—they really are such goons.[1]

I think it's fine about Dunny [Duncan Aswell]. With that kind of drive, he should go a long way. Tell him to make pals with dear old Daisy [Daise] Terry—and he should have no trouble at all.[2]

I'm glad you liked 'Harp'. Frankly, from what I've read about it, it sounds as if it had been directed all wrong <u>again</u>.

Darling, we are coming back to New York the middle of October. I guess we will have to find an apartment—three-four rooms, not more than $150 or $175. If you hear of anything, cable. Would it be possible for Jack to stay with you for a few days when we first arrive? Everything will be such confusion. If it's inconvenient, or any kind of a problem, just say so, honey. Maybe he could stay with Janie.

---

[1] Farrar, Straus & Young, which became Farrar, Straus & Giroux, was the house that published Dunphy's novel *Friends and Vague Lovers*.

[2] Aswell's son Duncan had apparently taken a job at *The New Yorker*. Daise Terry was the magazine's office manager. Famous for her terrible temper, she had nonetheless befriended Capote when he was one of the magazine's office boys.

I miss you so much, sweet one. Jack sends love. So does Kelly. So does your own

T

P.S. A kiss for Pidgie. Tell her if she's as pretty as ever, I'll put her in the movies.

P.P.S. I think folks at the Bazaar have lost their minds. You should have <u>seen</u> what Helen Eustis did to an article of mine! I wrote them a letter that would have tickled your heart. Anyway, they are now publishing the original. Oh God!

[Collection Aswell Family]

TO JOHN MALCOLM BRINNIN

Fermo Posta
Portofino (Genoa)
Italy
[Early summer 1953]

Malcolm dear—

A bolt from the blue!—actually, I've meant to write you for months (and months) but we have been so movemente [sic], to understate, that it hardly seemed ever the right moment. However, we've settled in Portofino for the summer—and am catching my breath. You would love Portofino—or do you know it? I am finishing a play, and a story, and Jack is finishing a novel—how we ever reached the point of finishing <u>any</u>thing is beyond me.

But we don't know your news and you don't know ours; and I want to—know your news, I mean. I've had a curious winter in Rome and in London—part of it spent making a movie with John Huston (just your type)—the whole thing was kind of fun and the picture ('Beat the Devil') is at least the camp of all time. Other than that have been working on the above mentioned.

Is there any chance you will be coming to Italy this summer? Malcolm, why haven't you written us? I hope it is not because of Goyen. By which I mean people at Random House, and others, have written me that he said (many months ago) some terribly harsh things about me—which amazed, even rather hurt me. I have always been aware that Goyen was an opportunist non pareil—but at least there was some quality about him I liked, so remained silent on <u>this subject</u>. He had no reason to be anything but grateful to me—the little fool. If you are still seeing him, then of course it is in the poorest possible taste for me to write in this vein—all the same, I prefer to risk that, because I prefer your friendship to most people's—Now we have <u>two dogs</u>; I got a bull puppy in London and the whole thing is <u>madness</u>. We are coming to New York the middle of October. Write me soon, my dear. I miss you. Much love from T

P.S. Give my regards to your mother.

[Collection University of Delaware Library]

TO DAVID O. SELZNICK

Fermo Posta
Portofino
June 23, 1953

Dear David—

It's wretched of me not to have answered your long nice letter sooner—but oh dear, the complications of getting settled here—not only me and mine; but also Ricky [Ricki] Huston, who suddenly dumped herself and family on my doorstop.[1] I found them an enormous, quite wonderful villa (though have <u>never</u> been able to find anything for myself, only an apartment—but rather attractively situated). Poor Ricky—when you've said that, you've said all. But she <u>is</u> a sweet girl—though incapable of dealing with <u>any</u> situation. Apparently John is coming here July 1st—I hope he brings a whole entourage with him, for God knows I'm not up to constituting their social life; am neither mentally nor physically qualified. At any rate, Ricky has made great pals with Rex and Lilli [Lili] Harrison, who live next door to her.[2] I don't think they will be John's cup of tea—whatever happens, I'm determined to stay well out of it.

---

[1] He was responding to Selznick's letter of June 5, 1953. Ricki Huston was the wife of movie director John Huston, with whom Capote had collaborated on *Beat the Devil*.

[2] Lili Harrison was also known as Lili Palmer, an actress with both beauty and talent.

On the whole I like Portofino—at least enough to get through the summer. It's not a bad place to work, and I've been making progress with 'House of Flowers.'[1]

I recieved [*sic*] the picture frame, and am sending it to California.

The little bull dog fell off the boat today and nearly drowned, but I pulled him out, shook him upside down, and tonight he seems fine. He has turned out to be the sweetest little creature.

I miss Jennifer—my old comrade in arms! Ah, where will we ever find the like again? Nowhere, I trust. Though someone (Jack Clayton) who had seen a rough-cut of 'B the D' wrote me that it was 'very good, surprise! surprise!'[2] John told Ricky on the phone that it was 'good.' But who knows?

David, have you finished cutting 'Terminal'? I long to see it—but it was no good my seeing it in London: I was too <u>distrait</u>.

Well, I wrote Binkie Beaumont—as suggested.[3] He answered very nicely indeed—so I sent him a copy of 'Harp', but he has not had time to reply. Bless you, David, for taking such an interest—you have always been so good to me, and I am very grateful indeed.

Friday, June 26th

Am still holding on to this, wondering where to send it—can't find your letter with all the addresses—don't even know where you are. California, I suppose. I know you will have a good summer there; I wish I were going to be able to come for a visit. I have passage on the Queen Elizabeth, Oct. 8—maybe you and Jennifer will be coming to New York by then. For many reasons, mostly personal, I dread going to N.Y.

There are some simply extraordinary people in Portofino—the place is rampant with the kind of Goings-on Jennifer never really believes Go-on. There is an Australian girl who ran away with her step-father—and a Swedish mother and daughter who share a fisherman between them etc. But these are very ordinary instances. Altogether, the place is fraught with peril.

As you can see, I'm a little thin in news just now—but I daresay I shall be able to correct this deficiency later on.

Love to Jennifer, and love to you David—always—

T

[Collection the University of Texas at Austin]

---

[1] He was trying to translate his short story into a full-fledged Broadway musical. He was writing the book, Harold Arlen was writing the music, and they were collaborating on the lyrics.

[2] 'B the D' was *Beat the Devil*. Jack Clayton was the associate producer.

[3] Binkie Beaumont was a theatrical producer, a major figure in the British theater.

TO LEO LERMAN

Fermo Posta
Portofino
[30 June 1953]

Dear Myrt love—

Your letter was so chucklesome (how is <u>that</u> for a repulsive phrase). <u>Any</u>how, have been traipsing all over the place since last I seen-you (don't ask <u>me</u> what's happened to my vocabulaire!)—but have now settled in Portofino for the summer. A fine place, Myrt—especially if we were the girls we used to be. Yachts and millionaires everywhere. But it depresses me a little: we have a <u>little</u> motorboat, and that cost a fortune, and we have a lovely apartment over the harbor, and <u>that</u> cost a fortune—but the Life around is So Rich, and <u>that</u> is tiresome to contemplate. The Huston's [sic] (John) have taken a house here—and the Harrison's [sic] (Rex) go speeding by in a big yacht (I kind of like her) and the Vanderbilts (Alfred) are parked outside the door—and I don't know, but somehow it's so gloomy. But am enjoying other aspects of the view—and am on the road to health again, it having been ruined in London—where we <u>did</u> have a good time. I'm sorry to have missed your Strawberry Birthday.[1] <u>What</u> is L. Kronenb etc. play?[2] Didn't know he'd written one. Who was in it? The 'Terminal Station' movie is a stinker—haven't seen it myself, but everyone says so. Thought it would be. The other one 'Beat The Devil' is pretty good—fair. Saw 'The Living Room'—phony. Jack liked it, though. Saw 'Quadrille' and 'Applecart'—both dreadful. Loved 'Venice Preserved' and 'The Way of The World'.[3] Have you ever read Mrs Gaskell's 'Life of Charlotte Bronte'?[4] You must. Is poor [John Malcolm] Brinnin still seeing [William] Goyen? Think it wonderful about all the work Gray is doing: maybe the day will come when we can all lie back and let him support us. You would love my new puppy. So beautiful. There is a hammock and nice garden furniture and a lovely brass bed in

---

[1] Lerman's birthday was May 23. He had given himself a party in the garden behind his Lexington Avenue apartment building, serving strawberries and cream to his guests.

[2] Louis Kronenberger's adaptation of *Mademoiselle Colombe* by Jean Anouilh, with Julie Harris in the title role, opened on Broadway on January 6, 1954.

[3] The plays Capote saw in London were *The Living Room* by Graham Greene, *Quadrille* by Noël Coward, *The Apple Cart* by George Bernard Shaw, *Venice Preserved* by Thomas Otway, and *The Way of the World* by William Congreve.

[4] Capote might have been reading Elizabeth Gaskell's *The Life of Charlotte Brontë* (1857) or Margaret Lane's *The Brontë Story: A Reconsideration of Mrs. Gaskell's Life of Charlotte Brontë* (1953), which contained the best of the original work plus significant updated material.

'House of Flowers'—it isn't true that I've finished it: I just tell people that, because I'm so tired of them asking. But Jack has just about finished his book—haven't read it since he started revising, but liked the first draft very much. Darling, I hope you and Gray have a good summer. I miss you such a lot. Jack sends love

So does

T

[Collection Columbia University Library]

TO MARY LOUISE ASWELL

Portofino
July 11, 1953

Darling Marylou—

So there you are in dear old Folly Cove: I wish we could change places—I love the fast life, but honest to God Portofino is too fast for me. Jack gets up at dawn (literally) in order to have a quiet swim before the Rest of the World (in its entirety) appears à la plage. Still, I manage to go on working, though am getting a little desperate now—as time is getting very short and the play isn't finished. It just must be before we leave here.

While I think of it—no, that story of Jack's 'The Comedian' is not 'Light on the Square'. Heaven forbid. 'Light on the Square' is a really good story—by far the best he's done. That's why I seriously wanted you to read it.

Darling, it would be wicked of me to have you postpone your collection of novellas with the idea of my 'coming-through' by December. There is a novella I want to write, and have wanted to for over a year now, and I think it would be fine in the context you outline—because it is 'funny' in a rather grim way. It's called 'The Wrong Mrs. Rockefeller'—about an American woman who rents a villa in Italy and tries to get people to come and live with her. Perhaps that doesn't sound too promising—but what I have in mind is rather more diabolical than this. It's something I really have to do—but with all the various pressures I don't think it would be fair of me to promise it for any specific date. How much do Ballantine plan to pay for the novellas? Will you do a second collection? Why not one of short stories?

You are an Angel to say that Jack could stay with you—it would not be for long: just so he has some place to go to when we get off the boat. He is so pleased and grateful and will be writing you soon (he's finishing his book—I'm going to read it tomorrow—I liked the first draft so much).

As for Huston! You know the Bea Lillie song: 'Maud [unclear], You're Rotten to the Core.' Well. But I do have an admiration and a real fondness for him—Except he and his whole family have come to spend the summer here (so that we can all be so near each other!) and oh dear—that is the main reason I'm so desperate about my work. Poor Jack. He's been sweet, so far, but keeps threatening mutiny. Darling, am I to spend my whole life in that kind of situation? Is it really all my fault? Yes, I suppose it is.

As I think I wrote you, we are sailing Oct 8 (Queen Elizabeth). I'm looking forward to New York, mainly because of seeing you and Jane and well—practically no one else. But am more than usual dreading it, too—not for the customary reasons but because of the insolvable Nina and Joe problem. How can I keep all that up and be a writer, too? Obviously I can't. I loathe writing for films—the fact that it is undermining is no mere myth. I think the bit I've done so far has done me a certain kind of good (though neither of the pictures is any good at all—but that isn't what I mean)—but that is as far as it should go. However, no point talking about this—I just must hope, and do the best I can.

Kelly is the same old Kelly—always fighting with other dogs. You will love Bunker—my little (but growing) English bull. So Sweet, so ugly!

Darling, give my love to Pidgy and Dunny (or Duncan, now that he's a working man)—I love and miss you so much. Jack sends his dearest love.

Many kisses, precious one from your own

T.

[Collection Aswell Family]

TO JOHN MALCOLM BRINNIN

Portofino (Ligure)
August 1, 1953

Malcolm dear—

I was touched, relieved, and worried by your sweet note today. Worried because of what you say about your health. I hope (so much) that you are feeling better now, and that there will be no delay in your trip. Because by all means you must come to stay with us in Portofino. It is very charming; the swimming is wonderful—we will be here until Sept 3rd. Please let us know, with some degree of accuracy, when to expect you.

I do regret this Goyen business, particularly as it affected you, and consequently me; but on the whole regret it more for his sake—not mine (which may sound a little saintly, or even pompous, still it is what I mean). I'm afraid he's set fire to too many bridges—Linscott, for instance, to whom he owes nothing but gratitude. Linscott sent me a letter G. had written him about <u>me</u>. Really astonishing; really insane. But actually, you know, I don't think I was an especial obsession of his; or if so, in <u>what</u> sense? I think it's just my turn had come for his customary, paranoid, <u>sudden</u> blitz-style vilifycation [sic]. It happens finally to anyone who shows him sympathy: Sam Barber, [Gian Carlo] Menotti, Eleanor Clark, [Stephen] Spender, Stephen Green ad infinitum. But we can talk about this later.

Jack sends his best love. I love you too, dearest M.—always—

T

[Collection University of Delaware Library]

TO ROBERT LINSCOTT

Fermo Posta
Portofino [Ligure]
Italy
August 3, 1953

Dear Bob—

It seems so long since I last wrote you—this is just to find out how <u>you</u> are; and to let you know that really I am quite well. I hope you had a good holiday in the 'hills'—I always remember the day we went to pick blackberrys [sic].

I wish so much that I could talk to you right now, Bob—about my work. I have so many plans, ideas—maybe you could help me sort them out. I do need counsel—no two ways about it. I could <u>write</u> it all, I suppose—but it would take 50 pages. However, I am coming to New York the middle of October—then you really must devote some time to me. I'm looking forward to seeing you far, far more than anyone else! Would you like me to bring you something—any European records that are difficult, or more expensive, than there? Please send me a list—I'd like so much to bring you a present.

Drop me a note; tell me some news—

always

T

[Collection Columbia University Library]

TO DAVID O. SELZNICK

Portofino
Sept. 2, 1953

Dear David—

Bless you for your letters and the photographs etc. I can't <u>tell</u> you what Portofino's been like the past August—really rather fun, if you just abandoned yourself to it. More of that later.

Firstly, Binkie [Beaumont] and John Perry were here for about 3 weeks and I saw a great lot of them.[1] I like Binkie very much, and John Perry too (the real power behind that particular throne). I talked to him (Binkie) about you and Jennifer many times; he seems to be very fond of you both, and enthusiastic about Jennifer's quality as an actress. He read 'House of Flowers'—which is nearly finished now—and assuming he meant the things he said, was most flattering about it. But he did not think J would be suitable in the part. In any event, it is unlikely the play will be done before next fall, so I am determined Peter Brook should direct it, and it <u>may</u> be impossible for him to do so before then. I don't know anything definite yet.

Our own little household has been amusing the last month. Cecil and John Gielgud came to stay most of August; now Noel C. [Coward] and Graham P. [Payn] are here—in other words, the Lavender Hill mob in force. At any rate, we've managed to jazz up the joint considerably.

Went to Venice last week on Arturo Lopez's yacht (shades of Gentlemen P. Blondes[2]) and was no sooner down the gangplank than who should rear his head but Friend Huston—there, I gather, for the Film Festival.

---

[1] John Perry was a theater manager, as well as Beaumont's companion.

[2] *Gentlemen Prefer Blondes* was Anita Loos's comical novel about a lovable gold digger.

Which reminds me; I've met a lot of people who, for one reason or another, seem to have seen 'Beat the Devil'—apparently it is rather good. But who knows? Anyway, they all say Jennifer is excellent and 'speaks' so well—whatever that means! Her accent, I suppose—[1]

I don't know why Mr. Arthur Jacobs sending me the telegram upsets you.[2] It struck me as a perfectly reasonable suggestion. I should be delighted to write such a piece—if I had some particular point of view; but the main thing is at the moment I don't have much energy to divert—because I must have my play in order before I go to New York. Am dreading the ordeal of that—and the complications that are going to fall in my lap when I get there.

I read somewhere that you are going to do 'Bell, Book and Candle.'[3] It seems to me a good idea—at least a charming part for Jennifer.

I hope you both had a good summer; more than that, I hope I see you in New York or somewhere soon—I miss you greatly. Write me ALL your news; meanwhile

Much love

T.

P.S. Will be here until the end of Sept.

[Collection University of Texas at Austin]

TO CECIL BEATON

Portofino, Sept 4, 1953

Dearest Cecil—

Thank you for my shorts—such a compromising sort of package. By the way, there are a pair of yours here. Also, your shirt is finished and looks very handsome. I shall hold on to all for the time being.[4]

---

[1] Jones's character was English.

[2] Arthur Jacobs was a publicist Selznick had hired to promote *Indiscretion of an American Wife*—and Jennifer Jones. Jacobs had written Capote to ask if he would be interested in writing a magazine profile of her.

[3] John Van Druten's comedy *Bell, Book and Candle* was later made into a movie. Selznick was not the producer, however.

[4] Beaton had visited Capote in Portofino in August; the two had then gone to Venice together.

It was so sad leaving you in Venice. You must write me the juicier details of the party et al. Lili's only comment was: 'Well, you know my dear, I'm just too old for that sort of thing'!![1]

My friends were here when I got back. And no sooner had I set foot in the door than who should come clambering up the stairs but—M. [Margaret] Case![2] She'd come back on a <u>hideous</u> yacht, large and dour and Victorian and reeking of creosote, with her Political Associate. Also here, Noel C. [Coward] and G. [Graham] Payn—raising Hell with the Harrison's [sic] speed boat. Noel tried hard to charm Jack—went about it in <u>the</u> strangest manner: something I can't write—will have to tell. One amazing thing. Madame Luce said to Noel: "why don't you boys take Maggie swimming with you?"

Noel said: "I'm afraid we'd spend the whole time dunking her."

"If you did," said Mrs. Luce, "she'd only come up with three well-known fishes."[3]

But they've all gone, and it is very quiet here—beautiful days, and I am working hard again. All I want to do is finish the play—beyond that I don't know what my plans are, where we're going or when.

Not a word from Saint. That episode, for all its frivolous side, has left me with a rather seriously odd feeling. It's as though Saint, instead of being any kind of help, had become Another Burden, Another Problem. And my God, I have too many.

Darling, I hope you are happy and quiet in the Country, reading, working as you want. It was so wonderful being with you here. I'm sure you know how warm and real my respect and love for you is. Jack sends his best love. Write Soon.

Your own

T

[Collection St. John's College, Cambridge University]

---

[1] Lili Palmer (Harrison).

[2] Margaret Case was an editor of *Vogue* and an influential figure in New York society.

[3] Clare Boothe Luce, the playwright and wife of Henry Luce, the proprietor of the Luce magazine empire, was the American ambassador to Italy.

TO ANDREW LYNDON

Portofino,
Sept 12, 1953

Dearest One—

Forgive me, dearheart—I'm long overdue in writing you: one thing, I lost my address book—hence, am sending this to Lenox Hill, with the hope it will find you.[1]

Obviously, we still are in Portofino and will be until early October. We have passage on the Queen E. Oct 8, but I doubt that we will make it; if not, perhaps a boat shortly after. All my plans are more up in the air than ever. It depends somewhat on the play—I keep not <u>quite</u> finishing it. Saint, who came here to get it, and left in a rage, expects to do it this season. But I very much want Peter Brook to direct it—and it is very unlikely he will be available before next Autumn. For myself, I'm willing to wait; but really I don't know what will happen—anyway, don't mention all this to anyone.

I've liked it here and have done a lot of work, but in August everything became too social—and I <u>do</u> mean social—the Windsors (morons), the Luces (morons plus), Garbo (looking like death with a suntan) the Oliviers (they let <u>her</u> out)[2] Daisy Fellowes[3] (her face lifted for the fourth time—the Doctor's [*sic*] say no more),—then Cecil and John Gielgud came to stay with us, and we went to Venice on Arturo Lopez's yacht—whence I've just come back. Oh yes, I forgot Noel Coward—he fell in love with Jack. Jack hated it <u>All</u>. For a town with a population of less than a thousand, Portofino has been quite a place.

I've not heard from Newton since early summer, have you? I hope it does not mean more of the same.

Do you think Jack could get a flat in your bldg.? We have no idea where we would stay in N.Y. I don't know what to do about 1060. I don't know what to do about so many things. I wish you could tell me.

I miss you always, little angel. Write me here. Jack sends love. So does
Your own
T

P.S. Hope you had a good rest in Macon.

---

[1] Lyndon was working at the Lenox Hill Book Shop.
[2] Laurence Olivier was married to Vivien Leigh, who had various emotional problems.
[3] Daisy Fellowes, the Hon. Mrs. Reginald Fellowes, was an heiress to the Singer sewing-machine fortune.

P.P.S. T'is [*sic*] Sept 14—will mail this today for sure. Jack wants to know did the city ever pay you for 232. He hasn't heard from Marcia Van Meter. Love and Love. Oh, I found your address. Another thing: some time ago P. [Pearl] Kazin wrote that Harold [Halma] had had a nervous breakdown. Is this true? Why? Give him my love if you get a chance.

[Collection New York Public Library]

TO JOHN MALCOLM BRINNIN

Portofino
Sept 22, 1953

Malcolm dear—

Was delighted, and startled, to have your letter this morning: it seems as though you were here only a week-end ago—now you are back in Boston or Conn. or New York: wherever it is you <u>do</u> live. Perhaps it's only that time is so peculiar here—it's beautiful now, the piazza deserted and the sea like 'shook foil.' [unclear] I have been working very well (for a change); and Jack is doing an amazing thing with his book—it is, in fact, a different book.

I believe I talked Noel [Coward] into appearing at Poetry Center. The magic word is 'serious'. So when you write him, little phrases like 'emphasize the serious nature of your contribution' should be freely sprinkled. Speaking on this subject—or, rather, speaking of my own proposed Appearance, I've decided I really must have a more 'generous' honorarium (not for naught was I once a faculty-wife) than 250. In fact, Poetry Center must pay me 400—which seems to me only reasonable and correct, all things considered. I suppose I should have said so at the time, but I did not think about it until afterwards; and if P.C. is not willing to pay this, then certainly it is not too late to cancel out.

The dogs are full of fleas—we've spent all morning bathing them in some odd South African ointment. We still have no carnet[1] for the car—heaven knows how we'll leave here, or when. Not until the middle of October, in any event.

I hope you had a good time at Chateau [unclear]; you <u>do</u> go to the

---

[1] A customs document allowing a car to be driven across international borders.

damdest places—I wonder if anyone has ever had, over a prolonged period, a more extraordinary love-life: possibly Marilyn Monroe.

Had a fine offer last week from Carol Reed to do the film script for 'A High Wind In Jamaica.'[1] Does it make you happy to learn that I turned it down?

Darling, it was wonderful seeing you, having you here—I always love you very much. Jack sends his love. Write me—

T

[Collection University of Delaware Library]

TO ANDREW LYNDON

Portofino,
Oct 14, 1953

Darling—

Bless you for your birthday letter—no one else remembered, not even Jack (who, rather late in the day, I truculently reminded); so I <u>was</u> touched.[2]

I've finished 'House of Flowers'—or as much, as you can testify, [as] a play is ever 'finished'. I don't expect I will come to New York until a composer is chosen and ready to work—I've written all the lyrics (9 songs) but I suppose they will need 'adjusting'. I long for you to read it—

We are fairly weary of Portofino—the skies are dark and the water is cold. So we are leaving here Monday—going to the mountains, St. Moritz etc. for a spell; I want to finish a story. But you can write me c/o American Express, Paris—they will forward.

You are an angel to offer to find an apt. in your place; under the circumstances, with plans so grotesquely uncertain as ours, I don't feel it is right to put you to the bother. There is a delightful apartment, very cheap, that we can have on East 63rd Street—but <u>not</u> until the 1st of April!

Did you hear about R. Lowry?[3] Trying to murder (really) his wife and

---

[1] Richard Hughes's novel, first published in 1929.
[2] Capote had turned twenty-nine on September 30.
[3] Robert Lowry was a writer and poet who was diagnosed as a schizophrenic and given electric shock treatments.

being put in an institution? There was an article about Doris Lilly in a London paper the other day—I meant to send it: she is cutting a wide swath, and 'her' book is being serialized in the Daily Express—a detail I'm sure that would interest Phoebe. <u>Whatever</u> has become of Phoebe? I'm glad it was all hogwash about Harold—that Pearl!

'Tea and Sympathy' sounds most unsympathetic.[1] Or what? Have you seen 'The Little Hut'?[2] Hear it got poor reviews. I thought it was amusing, especialy [sic] the decor.

Tenn. & Frankie & P. Bowles were all here the other day—on their collective way to Tangier. Tenn. wanted to know if you have a lover. I said I didn't know. I don't. Do you? Well, darling, you always have your own
T

P.S. Love from Jack!

[Collection New York Public Library]

TO NEWTON ARVIN

Portofino,
October 16, 1953

Darling Sige—

Was so relieved and happy to have your letter—I've meant to write you every other day, though actually you did owe me a letter; except all this dreariness about 'owing' letters is such a bore. The truth is, I've been working with zombie-like concentration the last 2 months (after having squandered most of the summer) and have put everything else out of my mind. I finished my 'House of Flowers' play (if indeed a play is ever 'finished') and am working on some new stories—what a pleasure to return to the sanity and 'space' of straight prose! I've not heard yet about 'House of Flowers'—whether it's going to be done this spring or next fall; I prefer the latter—it's enough of a risk without rushing.

---

[1] *Tea and Sympathy,* Robert Anderson's drama set in a New England boys' school, had opened on Broadway on September 30, 1953.

[2] André Roussin's desert-island comedy *The Little Hut* opened in New York on October 7, 1953, but closed by the end of the month.

I'm sorry, darling, really sad that you had such a wretched summer; it seems to me almost anything would be preferable to staying in Northampton—I think, right now, you ought to start plotting next summer in Italy. Or Spain or Austria: they're both so cheap—you could live beautifully on $200. a month.

Odd, I seem to think about money all the time; I used not to ever. But the whole Nina-Joe situation has given me such a jolt; and it goes on and on—and I have to pay straight down the line because I don't know what else to do. You have rather a talent for lame-ducks; but I am <u>the</u> genuis [sic]. But no sense raging on about this—

As you see, I'm still in Portofino but am leaving Monday for Switzerland and the Mountains. That does not sound too promising, but I have been having trouble with my throat and chest, nothing serious, and I think the altitude will do me good. I'm not sure where I'll be stopping, whether St. Moritz or some smaller place. But I will let you know where you can write me.

Please give Wendell [Johnson] my love.[1] I don't know why he should feel badly about not writing me—there's no reason why he should (except, of course, I would enjoy hearing from him).

I love you, precious Sige; as for crossing you off my list—you are still at the top of it. Sempre [sic]. Ciao, carissimo

T

P.S. Gracia [sic] tante per la photographia [sic]—though I look like a near-sighted Jewish half-wit: so different from <u>real</u> life!

[Collection Smith College Library]

---

[1] Arvin had persuaded Johnson, to whom he was attracted, to leave Ohio State University and teach Victorian literature at Smith.

TO NEWTON ARVIN

> Hotel France et Choiseul
> Rue St. Honoré, Paris
> Nov 20, 1953

Darling Sige—

Was so happy to have your letter. Have been in Paris about ten days, and will be here (at the above address) until January—when I expect to go to New York to work with the composer on the music for the play. Alas, it has become increasingly clear I have to rewrite the last half of the play stem to stern.

Paris is cold and yellow, not very exhilerating [*sic*]; but I dread the thought of N.Y. so much I'd hawk hot chestnuts in the Tuilleries [*sic*] sooner than set sail a moment before necessary.

Dreadful rumpus in London over gents who interfere with gents. Paris is a-glitter with escaping royalty. As you probably know, John Gielgud was arrested.[1] He came to stay with me last August in Portofino, and I got really terribly fond of him. I talked with him on the phone last week, and he seemed to be bearing up with a good deal of bravery and 'style'. Still it was a shocking thing to have happen, malicious and stupid. Did you see the article E. M. Forster wrote in The New Statesman: if <u>that's</u> the best he can do—why did he even bother?

Was interested by your report of Carson's [Carson McCullers] call. I should say Reeves [McCullers] is <u>not</u> with her. He is right here in Paris— if alcohol hasn't killed him off in the past 24 hours. He and Carson are the center of a left-bank scandal. The L.B, by the way, is a place to be avoided: I moved over here to the Place Vendome—and nothing could induce me to cross the River again. Well, the reason Carson left Paris so precipitously is this: dear Reeves cashed several huge checks with a certain money-changer (the favorite money-changer of the cognoscenti) and Carson cabled her bank to stop payment on these checks. Unfortunately, Reeves had already recvd. the Francs—which left the money-changer holding the bag. When Carson refused to honor the debt, he made a huge outcry and such folk as Janet Flanner were outraged. So Mrs. McC. took the first plane out. Of course in a way I think Carson was right. Still she left owing many other large sums, and all her friends here are being hounded by her creditors.

---

[1] Gielgud had been arrested on October 21, 1953, for trying to pick a man up in a Chelsea lavatory, an incident that instantly made the headlines.

Some people say Reeves is going to be arrested. Carson should have long since clipped his wings—Janet Flanner says she has finished a novel and it is very good—so maybe she can start a new life.

I think by all means you should do the text-book for Random House. And with Wendell to collaborate, I daresay it would not be drudgery. Give him my best love.

And my very special best always love for you, Sige lamb. Write me soon, dear-heart—put in some news about the Aarons and the Fischers [Fishers][1]—I spent the night in Dijon on the way here: it made me laugh to think of Al's 'glamourous' diploma from that quite hideous city.

Kisses galore

T

P.S. I read your Forster review in the Times, and thought it excellent.[2] Didn't you adore that picture of him in Indian drag?

[Collection Smith College Library]

TO ANDREW LYNDON

Hotel De France et Choiseul
239/41 Rue St. Honoré, Paris
[27 November 1953]

Darling—

Am writing in the maddest rush—and maybe should wait till later to write at all, but have been thinking about you this morning and wondering why you had not answered my last letter.

Am going to Reeve's [*sic*] funeral—which is an odd circumstance, all things considered, but Janet Flanner insists that I go with her. Of course

---

[1] Daniel Aaron was a colleague of Arvin's in the English department at Smith; he and his wife, Janet, were among Arvin's closest friends and supporters. Poet Alfred Young Fisher, another Smith colleague, spent three years at the University of Dijon with his first wife, gastronomic writer M.F.K. Fisher.

[2] He is referring to a review of E. M. Forster's *The Hill of Devi*, a memoir of his stint in India as private secretary to the maharajah of Dewas in 1921.

I'm sure you know that Reeves killed himself in a hotel here last Saturday.[1] The whole story is rather fantastic—and I seem to have a genuine feeling of sadness about it.

We are definitely coming to New York in January. I'm making an enormous revision in my play and adding an Act—I don't think I can possibly accomplish all of this before we leave.

Paris is grey and cold and more expensive than New York.

Had a letter from Newton—who seemed to be very well.

Darling, I hope you are having a good winter. I miss you muchly. Jack sends his love. Write me to the address above.

Love Love Love

T

[Collection New York Public Library]

TO LEO LERMAN AND GRAY FOY

Hôtel de France & Choiseul
Paris
Christmas Day [1953]

Leo dear and sweet Gray

Was so distressed to know about the eye infection (my God, you have the worst luck) and have meant every day to write, but there have been so many problems and such bedlam on all sides. Anyway it is Christmas day, and I wish we could be all together—but wonderful wishes for the New Year for you both.

Have just been a week in London, and saw most of our friends and quite a few others. Went to the theatre a good deal—the cast of 'A Day By The Sea' is marvellous, but the play is a boneless, shapeless jellyfish.[2] By

---

[1] Carson McCullers's estranged husband, Reeves, committed suicide by taking an overdose of barbiturates in a Paris hotel on November 19, 1953. Capote was one of the few mourners who attended his funeral a few days later.

[2] Ralph Richardson, John Gielgud and Sybil Thorndike starred in N. C. Hunter's play *A Day by the Sea*.

the way, John Gielgud has survived his ordeal in fine style. He is a wonderful person, first-rate in every way. Saw the Oliviers: hideous, both them <u>and</u> the play.[1] "Confidential Jerk" is a better title for a very dreary item indeed.[2] Only thing I liked was a little musical called "The Boy Friend."[3] Really charming.

Speaking of theatre, I opened the Paris Trib yesterday to find a prominent letter denouncing me in what I assume the author considered a witty style. And just <u>who</u> was the author of this epistle? Our old friend <u>Dorothy Wheelock</u>!!![4] Seems she objected to the fact that in an interview in [the] Paris Trib I'd said I'd once written drama criticism for Harper's Bazaar!!! The last line of the letter says "I'm afraid our little Truman was indulging in a <u>daydream</u>. I'm surprised you were <u>taken in by it</u>." Can you believe it? Well, at least it's been something to laugh about.

Did you both get lots of delightful items from Cartier? Our haul was very meagre indeed. 1 cigarette lighter (silver-plated) and 1 bottle of cologne (I bought the cologne myself). I don't know what the world's coming to when a girl can't do better than that. Jack's family sent him lots of lovely things—but that doesn't count, does it?

I went to Reeves McCullers funeral. Oh God it was sad. I went with Janet Flanner; there were only about 4 other people. But I would rather wait and tell you about it—it's a terrible story.

There is all kinds of news, but since we are coming to New York the end of next month I suppose it will wait. I long to see you both. I hope you will be all better by then, darling Myrt. Jack sends love. Me too

Kisses galore

T

[Collection Columbia University Library]

---

[1] Laurence Olivier and Vivien Leigh starred in Terence Rattigan's play *The Sleeping Prince*.

[2] *The Confidential Clerk* was a play by T. S. Eliot.

[3] *The Boy Friend*, musical by Sandy Wilson set on the French Riviera in 1926.

[4] Dorothy Wheelock was a mystery writer, the author of *Murder at Montauk* (1940) and a Greenwich Village murder mystery, *Dead Giveaway* (1944).

TO CECIL BEATON

300½ East 65th St.
New York, N.Y.
Feb 7, 1955

Darling Cecil—

Bless you for the Sweet letter—it is more than I diserve [*sic*], for I should have written you long ago, but these last months have left me rather unnerved, and I am only just coming back into focus. The whole experience with "House of Flowers" was so unbelievable, really excruciating, and the only good thing about it is that I may make some money as the show seems to be quite a hit.[1] But at least my sense of humor has survived, and I can regale you endlessly with little anecdotes concerning one and All.

I went to Jamaica with the [William] Paleys for a holiday, which was very pleasant but did not last long enough.[2] Then I went to California for a week—stayed with David [Selznick] and Jennifer [Jones, his wife]: she is back in fine spirit and has gone to Hong Kong to make a film.[3] Now I have no plans at all until May when we leave for the summer in Italy and where I hope you will plan to spend your annual holiday!

I saw Greta [Garbo] last night at a party—looking extremely well—though her hair seemed a peculiar color: sort of blondish lavender. I think she must have dyed it.

It is <u>freezing</u> in New York—especially in this house. I'm afraid the house has been a mistake.

Lincoln Kirstein has had a great quarrel with the City Center and resigned his post.[4]

How goes the 'Winter Garden'? I long to see it. Speaking of gardens, Irene S. [Selznick] seems all set now to go ahead with the play. Peter Brook read the new version and told her it was one of the worst plays he'd ever read and that she was 'insane' to put it on. All of which fazed Irene not a bit. She is giving me the script this week.[5]

---

[1] *House of Flowers* had opened at Broadway's Alvin Theater on December 30, 1954. It was not a hit, however, and though it had some fanatical admirers, they were not numerous enough for a long run. The show closed May 22, 1955.
[2] William Paley was the head of CBS, the television and radio network.
[3] *Love Is a Many-Splendored Thing*; Jennifer Jones's co-star was William Holden.
[4] Kirstein was the prime force behind the New York City Ballet.
[5] Enid Bagnold's *The Chalk Garden* opened on Broadway on October 26, 1955, and closed on March 31, 1956. Selznick produced and Beaton designed the sets and costumes.

Someone told me you are going to Portugal. I hope you have a good trip, darling. I miss you so much. Give my love to your Mama. And to Eileen H., too.[1] Write me soon. Jack is fine and sends his best,

Love et mille tenderesse [*sic*]

T

P.S. Everybody <u>loves</u> your Isak Dinesen picture in the new Bazaar.

[Collection St. John's College, Cambridge University]

TO THE DRAMA EDITOR OF THE NEW YORK TIMES[2]

[New York]
[13 February 1955]

Last Sunday, you printed a letter by Members of The Friday Drama Group in Montclair, N.J. These ladies wished to "protest vigorously" the theme of "House of Flowers." So far, no quarrel. * * *[3] The picture conjured of the Friday Drama Group, their offended sensibilities at a Stradivarian pitch, sitting down all in a huffandpuff to write a letter to The Times, is, come to think of it, rather endearing.

But then the picture changes, a shadow falls across the cheerful scene of busy scribblers, and you realize that here after all is not a Hokinson idyll, for suddenly there occurs an ugly theory to the effect that the production of "House of Flowers" is harmful to "racial relations."[4] Now I don't like this. * * * Surely chauvinism is the last fault that can be claimed against our musical. If this were not true, then a host of intelligent and talented artists, including Pearl Bailey, Juanita Hall and Frederick O'Neal, would not be connected with it. As far as "racial relations" are concerned, the only possible damage that could be done by "House of Flowers" is if it bored you: boredom is fatal to all relations; and somehow—don't ask me why—I have the oddest feeling the ladies from Montclair were not that.

TRUMAN CAPOTE.

---

[1] Eileen Hose was Beaton's secretary.
[2] This letter was published in *The New York Times*, February 13, 1955, under the heading "Protest Answered."
[3] The *Times* apparently cut Capote's letter, inserting starred ellipses to indicate its deletions.
[4] Set in Port-au-Prince, Haiti, *House of Flowers* had a cast that was almost entirely black.

TO JOHN MALCOLM BRINNIN

> As from—
> 300-½ E. 65th St.
> October, 1955

Dear M—

Despite the (to me) startlingly unjust contents of your Portofino card, I hopefully assume it was intended as some sort of good-friend, stern-critic comment.[1] If it was meant otherwise, and your words were weighed, then frankly, dear-heart, I don't know what the hell you are talking about. You have, and will always, a most particular place in my affections. If I have dissapointed [sic] you as an artist (as you suggest), that is one thing; but certainly as a person, as a friend, I have done nothing to deserve your misguided candor. If memory serves, this is the second time you have rounded on me; on the previous occasion I correctly deciphered the clumsy hand of Mr. Goyen. But I am not a detective by profession, and so shall have to leave the clues to this latest attack untraced. However, rest [assured] in the knowledge that you are on the popular side; my stock in all quarters is very low, and if the numbers of folk I have apparently offended were laid end to end they would girdle the globe.

As for Jack (about whom you are so bitter), Jack is Irish. He talks. He talks for the fun of it, and for the moment: and no one is immune—me (least of all), his family, his friends, himself. You know that. And really, dear, I have to laugh: I think you're more than a bit of an ass, a jejeune [sic] jerk, if you start getting riled over Dunphy's little sallies at this point.

I've had a quiet, working summer. Moreover, I lost thirty pounds: am just a svelte bag of golden bones. We're going back to the city next week.

Please reconsider, and write your perhaps unworthy, but still loving, very loving—

> T

[Collection University of Delaware Library]

---

[1] This letter was the answer to a curious postcard from Brinnin. According to his memoir, *Sextet*, Brinnin disapproved of Capote's increasing involvement with the glamorous sets of Broadway, Hollywood, and London. He was in Portofino when he saw a photograph in *Time* magazine of Capote dancing with Marilyn Monroe. Furious, Brinnin wrote a postcard that, in his words, was designed to scathe: "Was *this* the Portrait of the Artist as a Young Man?' 'Joyce's motto was, Silence, exile, and cunning. What's *yours?*' " Brinnin then signed his card: "Reader of *Time.*"

TO JOHN MALCOLM BRINNIN

[Telegram]   [New York]
                                                             [November 1955]

I THINK YOUR BOOK[1] IS WONDERFUL LOVE
    TRUMAN

[Collection University of Delaware Library]

TO CECIL BEATON

[New York]
Nov. 12, 1955

Darling Sizzle—

Miss you! The weather here is wonderful, fresh as the first bite of a macintosh. I hope you got a thorough rest on the boat ride. You'll be amused to know that 'Chalk Garden' has become the rage: people can't afford not to see it. Your article was in The Tribune today, and the play itself is getting terrific publicity.

I went up to Boston with Audrey [Hepburn] and Mel [Ferrer] to see Julie Harris in 'The Lark.'[2] Julie is playing St. Joan like 'Member of the Wedding' in a pair of B.V.D's. Will be a hit, though.[3] Went to the opening of 'The Vamp'—dreadful, including Carol Channing.[4] And not long for this world, I daresay. Am going with Ina [Claire] to see J. [Joyce] Grenfell tomorrow night. Ina is going to start giving acting classes! She is buying an apartment in New York.

Ann Woodward continues to occupy the front pages—but those who

---

[1] Brinnin's book was *Dylan Thomas in America*. In his capacity as director of the Poetry Center, Brinnin brought Thomas to the United States and arranged all his American readings. Thomas died in New York on November 9, 1953, after a bout of drinking, and Brinnin's book was an account of his experiences with the poet. A Broadway play, *Dylan*, followed in 1964.

[2] Hepburn and Ferrer were husband and wife.

[3] Jean Anouilh's *The Lark* opened on Broadway on November 17, 1955, and ran for 229 performances; Julie Harris won that year's Tony for best actress.

[4] *The Vamp* was a flop; it opened on November 10, 1955, and closed after sixty performances.

discuss it have had to move to L'aiglon since Mr. Soulé closed the Pavillion.[1] L'aiglon has upped its prices.

I am still working on my various stories, and Audrey Wood is still trying to decide to whom she should submit Jack's play. I've lost five pounds more, and though I've given up dieting, can't seem to stop losing weight. Very odd.

Ran into Herman Levin, who told me how <u>thrilled</u> they all were with your 'Pygmalion' designs.[2]

There is other news, much and lots, but I have to start typing now. My love to your mother, and please give best regards to Eileen [Hose]. All the love in the world, precious one

T

P.S. Poor Bob Sherwood died this morning.[3]

[Collection St. John's College, Cambridge University]

TO DONALD WINDHAM AND SANDY CAMPBELL

[Postcard]   Leningrad[4]
                                                [27 December 1955]

Dear-hearts—

Love to think of you, cozy and warm. It's thirty below here. But Leningrad very beautiful, like an arctic Paris. Am returning to Moscow next week. Whole experience pretty extraordinary. Miss you. Love

T

[Collection Beinecke Library, Yale University]

---

[1] In October 1955, Ann Woodward, a former showgirl, claimed she mistook him for an intruder and shot and killed her husband, Bill, one of the bluest of New York's blue bloods, in their house on Long Island's Gold Coast. Although a grand jury exonerated her, most of Bill's friends regarded her as a murderer. Capote recounted the case in fictional form in his short story "La Côte Basque," which *Esquire* published in October 1975. After reading an advance copy, Ann Woodward swallowed a lethal dose of Seconal.

[2] Levin was the producer of *My Fair Lady,* for which Beaton designed the costumes. The show was a musical adaptation of George Bernard Shaw's *Pygmalion.*

[3] Robert Sherwood was a successful playwright—*Abe Lincoln in Illinois* was one of his successes—as well as a speechwriter for President Franklin D. Roosevelt.

[4] *Porgy and Bess,* the first American theatrical production to tour Russia, opened in Leningrad on December 26, 1955. Capote traveled with the cast and crew; his account, *The Muses Are Heard,* was serialized in two issues of *The New Yorker,* October 20 and 27, 1956, and published in book form by Random House on November 8, 1956.

TO JACK DUNPHY

[Postcard from the Hermitage Museum]
   Leningrad, Dec 27 [1955]

Dearest—such a pity the Hermitage is being wasted on me (how you
would adore it) though I do love to go and stare at the jewels. Did I write
that I'd bought you an Astrakhan cap? Tell Joan [McCracken] there is no
such thing as a "little peasant" coat.
   Love
   T

[Collection Gerald Clarke]

TO CECIL BEATON

   [New York]
   May 15, 1956

Cecil dearest—
   It was a terrible disappointment to me not to have had a little holiday
with you <u>somewhere</u>. But then, just as I was arranging to meet you in Paris,
I got a cable that made it imperative I return here at once. I had only two
weeks to finish my Russia articles (which are coming out as a book in
September) if I wanted the New Yorker to run them. But that was the least
of it—too involved to go into here.
   I didn't know about Peter's death until your letter came, and it touched
and grieved me very much.[1] I know what a tragedy it has been for you to
lose a friend, and a friendship, that has meant all he has meant in your life.
Especially in the spring, when one is so longing for beginnings, continua-
tions; not endings. Your letter made me inexpressibly sad; for you, for Peter.
He loved you, Cecil: you were his youth, as much as he was yours. The last
time I saw him, in Rome, 1954, he told me you were more marked by "tender honesty" than anyone he'd ever known. I remember because I liked the
phrase "tender honesty," and knew what it meant.

---

[1] Peter Watson was found dead in his bathtub on May 3, 1956. Watson was the love of Beaton's
life, Beaton confided to his diary, though apparently the two had never actually engaged in sex—
Watson's choice, not Beaton's.

My summer plans are still a little vague; there is a charming house on the Connecticut shore that we will probably take. But I do not expect to get away from here before the middle of June. Jack's play is being produced, supposedly in the Fall, by a new company, Horne & Lloyd—who seem very clever without being shady, and who seem to be well capitalized.[1]

I miss you, dear heart. I admire you as a man as much as anyone I've ever known. But more importantly, I deeply love you—

T

[Collection St. John's College, Cambridge University]

TO CECIL BEATON

3 Gold Street
Stonington, Conn.
June 21, 1956

Dearest C.—,

At last, a moment to breathe. Finished my "New Yorker" pieces (I will send the issues; it's coming out as a book "The Muses Are Heard" in Sept.), and a few days ago settled down for the summer in this really charming old seaport village. You would adore it. The most beautiful trees and old houses. We have a huge, rather amusing house with wonderful views. We will be here until the end of Sept. Then we are moving to Oliver [Smith]'s Brooklyn Heights abode, 70 Willow Street. You've seen that house? I love it. We rented the floor that leads onto the garden; it can be made into something very attractive. There is another apartment on the top-floor— terribly pretty—and Oliver is determined to install <u>you</u> there. So am I. Think it over; dear-heart. It is both a fun—and a <u>practical</u>—thing for you to do. You can be anywhere in Manhattan in fifteen minutes, and you have your own kitchen et al. <u>Please</u> come live with us, my love.

---

[1] Dunphy's play *Light a Penny Candle* was performed off-Broadway.

I saw "My Fair Lady" 3 times. It's probably the best show I've ever seen, and I was so proud of your work: you, Rex and Moss (and Shaw!) are the heroes of that production.[1] Went to the openings of "Shangri-La" and "New Faces"—gruesome, both of them.[2] Read the new Carson McCullers play that Saint is producing: have read worse, but can't recall when.[3] Am reading Forster's book about his aunt: delightful.[4] Saw Huston's movie "Moby Dick"—uneven, poorly acted, but remarkable all the same: superb photography. By the time you get this, Marilyn M. [Monroe] will have married Arthur Miller. Saw them the other night, both looking suffused with a sexual glow; but can't help feeling this little episode is called: "Death of a Playwright." She is greatly excited about going to London. Went to a dinner-party at your friends the [Winston] Guests. You're right about her: she does have quality.[5] And he has a sort of bumbling sex-appeal. But the rest of the gathering were all huntin', shootin', fishin' types—and I left indecently early. They are still trying to find a director for Jack's play. The Paleys say they saw you in London, looking fine. Hope you are enjoying Redditch [Reddish House]. My love to your mother. Write me. Come to 70 Willow. Jack sends love. Miss you, my dearest friend.

    mille tendresse [*sic*]

    T

[Collection St. John's College, Cambridge University]

---

[1] Rex Harrison played Henry Higgins, Moss Hart directed, and George Bernard Shaw wrote the play from which the musical was adapted.

[2] *Shangri-La,* based on James Hilton's novel *Lost Horizon,* lasted only twenty-one performances; *New Faces of 1956* ran for 220.

[3] *The Square Root of Wonderful* opened on Broadway on October 30, 1957; it closed after only forty-five performances.

[4] E. M. Forster's biography of his great-aunt was titled *Marianne Thornton.*

[5] Born into Boston society, C. Z. Guest worked as a showgirl and posed nude for Diego Rivera before marrying Winston Guest, a leader of Long Island's monied, horsey set.

TO WILLIAM SHAWN

[Princess Kaiulani Hotel]
[Waikiki, Honolulu]
[1 January 1957]
New Year's Day

Dear Mr. Shawn—

Just to let you know that I have got as far as here, and that tomorrow I forge on to Japan.[1] Meanwhile, I've had two outstanding experiences: 1) as I was getting into an elevator the <u>steel</u> doors went haywire and slammed into my head, knocking me cold: now my face is the most interesting colors of blue and green and puce and mau-mau black; and my left eye is closed tighter than a miser's fist. And (2) Japan Air Lines has managed to lose ALL my luggage—clothes, my work notes, reference books, everything. I am down to one tweed suit, a very Dirty Shirt, a pair of snow-boots and a just-purchased tooth-brush. Otherwise, am fine. More from Tokyo. Until then, best regards and Sayonara—

Truman C.

as from: Imperial Hotel
         Tokyo

[Collection New York Public Library]

---

[1] Capote was traveling to Japan, in the company of Cecil Beaton, to write an article for *The New Yorker* on the making of the movie *Sayonara,* starring Marlon Brando. A problem with visas delayed his arrival, however, and he and Beaton spent two weeks in Hong Kong, Thailand and Cambodia. More problems arose in Japan, and when Capote finally arrived in Kyoto, the director, Joshua Logan, barred him from the set. To be polite, Brando, whom he had known in New York, invited him to a long dinner he later bitterly regretted. The result was "The Duke in His Domain," a Brando profile that one columnist labeled "a vivisection" and another called "the kind of confession usually confined to an analyst's couch."

TO LEO LERMAN

[Postcard]   Hong Kong
                                                  [11 January 1957]

Dearest Myrt— Sad to say, I've been through many vicissitudes since last
you heard from me—can you believe that your lovely golden Marge has
ended up as a dance-hall hostess in Hong Kong?! Well, things are tough all
over. A white-slaver is shipping me to Bangkok next week. Pray for your poor
    Marge xxx

[Collection Columbia University Library]

TO WILLIAM SHAWN

    The Kyoto Hotel
    Kyoto Japan
    Jan. 25, 1957

Dear Mr. Shawn,
    Dizzy with exhaustion is no mere phrase. When I finish a day (beginning
at 5 a.m.) of keeping tabs on this outfit, I just lie down and SPIN. Hence, my
long silence. That, and the difficulties of giving you any proper idea of the situation: a feat impossible short of twenty single-spaced pages. But here, most
briefly, is how things stand. The objections to my doing this story never involved Brando (who has been extremely straightforward and obliging) but
stem entirely from [Joshua] Logan himself. He of course was anxious that I
not discover this, preferring to hide behind the producer, [William] Goetz,
and Brando: oh it has been a regular little Chinese box of hypocrisy.[1] The
trouble has been to keep a sense of humour and balance, despite the Logan-
contrived obstacles and discouragements. I'm not quite sure how the story itself is working out; I think maybe Yes. In any event I'm enjoying Japan, and
shall bring back several souvenirs (some, let's trust, on paper).
    Best regards,
    Truman C.

[Collection New York Public Library]

---

[1] Marlon Brando was the star of *Sayonara;* Joshua Logan was its director and William Goetz
its producer.

TO CECIL BEATON

[70 Willow Street]
[Brooklyn, N.Y.]
[15 May 1957]

Dearest—

I started a letter to you three weeks ago, lost it, found it again yesterday, saw that it was nothing but a list of complaints, so will start again.

Quite a few of your pictures are in the new Bazaar, and very handsome they are, too. Finally had mine developed at that Hoffman Lab—and a splendid job they did: <u>too</u> splendid—I nearly dropped dead when they handed me a bill for almost $300. Lord, I had no idea photography was so expensive.

Adored your items about Peter B. and Cyril. But I hope P.B.'s novel <u>does</u> get published. Just to have the last laugh.

Oliver [Smith] no sooner arrived back then he had to fly out to California because his mother had a stroke.[1]

One of Jack's plays is going to be done at the Westport Playhouse this summer.[2]

'New Girl in Town,' the musical version of "Anna Christie," opened last night.[3] The first-act is excellent; there isn't a second, none at all. But it's a big hit. I went to see Wendy Hiller in "Moon for the Misbegotten".[4] Hated every long, windy minute of it. Have you seen the Genet play?[5] And? Saw Audrey H's [Hepburn's] new film, "Love In the Afternoon". Much the best picture she's made. René Bouché (what a <u>hideous</u> little man he is) has painted two portraits of me—one very light and witty and really quite good; the other a big pretentious nonsense. The Logans are back in town; they asked me out for a weekend: I certainly didn't go—I'm still working on The New Yorker piece.[6] I've finished a children's book, a story, and an article. But I expect to work better when we go to the beach in about ten days— no new address needed, mail will be forwarded from here. One <u>very</u> sad thing has happened—poor Kelly has gone blind.

---

[1] Oliver Smith, the set designer, owned the Brooklyn Heights town house in which Capote and Dunphy had an apartment.

[2] Dunphy's play was titled *Saturday Night Kid*.

[3] *Anna Christie* is a play by Eugene O'Neill.

[4] *Moon for the Misbegotten* is also by O'Neill.

[5] Jean Genet's play was *The Balcony*.

[6] "The Duke in His Domain," his profile of Marlon Brando.

So you <u>are</u> going to do "Gigi".[1] Well, you will do it beautifully. In a quite subtle way I brought up "Madame Butterfly" to Bill Paley. A look of interest flickered in his eyes, but he did not commit himself. However, now that the idea has been planted, I think [Rudolph] Bing should ring him up.[2] Darling, I hope you are having a lovely spring. It's already summer here— we never saw the spring. I miss you lots, and love you tenderly

T

P.S. Look at the envelope. <u>I remembered</u>.

[Collection St. John's College, Cambridge University]

TO CECIL BEATON

[70 Willow Street]
[Brooklyn, N.Y.]
[Late November 1957]

Dearest C.—

I am waiting for Ina [Claire]: she is on her way here for dinner. So, since she is always late, there seems a good chance to fire you a note. I hope you are enjoying the long golden autumn you envisioned. N.Y. is moving into high winter-gear. But the theatre continues a dud. "Time Remembered" got rave reviews, but S. [Susan] Strasberg and Miss [Helen] Hayes irritated me so that I could not sit through it.[3] Went to the Coward opening: he really laid a bomb.[4] So did Jack Wilson—by falling down dead-drunk in aisle.[5] My piece came out—M. [Margaret] Case said she was

---

[1] With music and lyrics by Lerner and Loewe, the team that created *My Fair Lady, Gigi* was a movie musical based on a story by Colette. Vincente Minnelli directed; Maurice Chevalier, Leslie Caron and Louis Jourdan starred; and Beaton was the costume and production designer. The film opened in 1958 and was a box office success.

[2] Rudolph Bing was the general manager of the Metropolitan Opera. Beaton and Capote apparently hoped that Paley's company, the broadcast network CBS, would underwrite a new production of *Madame Butterfly* for which Beaton would design the sets.

[3] *Time Remembered*, by Jean Anouilh, opened on Broadway November 12, 1957.

[4] Noël Coward's *Nude with Violin* opened on Broadway November 14, 1957, and ran for only eighty performances, closing February 8, 1958.

[5] An American, Jack Wilson had been Coward's lover and business manager.

sending it to you, so I did not.[1] It has been rather a sensation. Brando told
the papers he was going to sue me for libel; but I have good reason to doubt
it. I had a telegram from the [Joshua] Logans' [sic] telling me how much
they "loved" the piece. What a pair of hypocrites![2] Your publishers have
been advertising your book splendidly (full-page ad in New Yorker etc.).[3]
Everyone loves it. Your friend Alan Lerner and his former wife had a terrific
scene in El Morroco [sic]—tears, screams: they transferred to the street,
where it lasted an hour. Liked your jacket for the new Mitford, and rather
enjoyed the book, though felt I'd read it all before—which indeed I have.[4]
Very dissapointed [sic] by the Angus Wilson stories.[5] Your picture of Jack
[Dunphy] was in the Bazaar: he was so pleased. His play opens Jan 15.
Read "Vanessa" and thought it a BORE—hope you can save it.

Am back working on my short novel.[6] The [Rex] Harrisons are living in
your Ambassador apartment—they love it. She has dyed her hair grey and
looks god-awful. Since pater's death, Irene S. [Selznick] looks radiant: he
left her $500,000.[7] Edie was disinherited.[8] Irene refused to let her ride in
the family car to the funeral. Everyone is anti-Irene and pro-Edie. TWO
DAYS LATER: well, Ina came and went in a whirlwind of chatter, leaving
behind a sable scarf which I now have to deliver. Went to a birthday party
last night for Clifton Webb; Whitney Warren was there, and what a two-
some they make.[9] Saw an excellent film yesterday "The Bridge Over the
River Kwai." Understand it is playing in London, so be sure to see. Dearest
boy, give my love to your mother and Eileen.

Hugs

T

[Collection St. John's College, Cambridge University]

---

[1] The piece was "The Duke in His Domain," Capote's long profile of Marlon Brando.
[2] Logan had barred Capote from the set of Sayonara and had advised Brando not to talk to
him.
[3] The Face of the World.
[4] Nancy Mitford's new book was Voltaire in Love.
[5] Wilson's collection was titled A Bit Off the Map and Other Stories.
[6] Breakfast at Tiffany's.
[7] Irene Selznick's father was Louis B. Mayer, the longtime head of Metro-Goldwyn-Mayer.
[8] Edie Goetz, who was married to William Goetz, the producer of Sayonara, the movie Capote
had gone to Japan to write about.
[9] Whitney Warren was a rich bachelor and one of the fixtures of San Francisco society.

TO CECIL BEATON

> [70 Willow Street]
> [Brooklyn, N.Y.]
> May 2, 1958

Dearest—

All is changed—or, rather, changed back. We sail May 18 on the Vulcania: for <u>Greece</u>! Am negotiating about several island houses—but plan to do nothing definite until we get there and can take a look. Anyway, hope you will plan to have your summer holiday with us. I'm sure a little blue Aegean is just what we all need. Please try and drop me a note before we go.

Have finished my short novel, "Breakfast At Tiffany's." The Bazaar is printing it in their July issue—though they are <u>very</u> skittish about some of the language, and I daresay will pull a fast one on me by altering it without my knowledge. That whole place has fallen to pieces. [Alexey] Brodovitch is leaving as of June 15. I doubt Diana [Vreeland] will last much longer.[1]

The Lunts open Monday.[2] I had two invites, one from P. [Peter] Brook, the other M. [Margaret] Case. And accepted the latter. So you see! Press reports say "M.F.L." was a huge success. They all credit you with scenery & costumes. Poor Oliver [Smith] not a mention![3] Jane Bowles, having been thrown out of Tangier by the authorities (Paul, too) back in New York—alone, very ill, very penniless. Tennessee [Tennessee] and I are giving a joint reading to raise some money for her. Jack's play opens here May 15.[4] Saw Leland's movie "Old man and the sea".[5] <u>Pretty</u> good. Still haven't glimpsed "Gigi"; though God knows <u>every</u>body else has: and <u>raves</u> about your work—but not too excited by the picture as a whole.[6] Saw a very funny inscription on a men's room wall: someone had written "I am 7¾, meet me here on Monday night." Underneath which a second party had scribbled: "Yes, but how big is your prick?"

> Love
>
> T

[Collection St. John's College, Cambridge University]

---

[1] Brodovitch was art director for *Harper's Bazaar*. Diana Vreeland was its fashion editor; in fact, she remained at the magazine until 1962.

[2] In Friedrich Dürrenmatt's *The Visit*, directed by Peter Brook.

[3] The London production of *My Fair Lady* opened on April 29, 1958. Many people did, in fact, believe that Beaton, who had designed the costumes, also designed the sets; that credit belonged to Oliver Smith.

[4] Dunphy's play was *Light a Penny Candle*; it soon closed.

[5] *The Old Man and the Sea*, starring Spencer Tracy, was based on Ernest Hemingway's novel. It was produced by Leland Hayward.

[6] Beaton did both the sets and costumes for the movie *Gigi*, which, like *My Fair Lady*, had words and music by Alan Jay Lerner and Frederick Loewe.

TO GLORIA VANDERBILT[1]

> *Vulcania* [ship]
> [Lisbon, Portugal]
> [May 1958]

Darling G—

The trip (so far) is vile—rain, black skies and <u>curvy</u> seas. But oh! but ah!—my clock, my little golden clock, is beautiful. No, G., you shouldn't have! But I'm <u>so</u> glad you did. Because it is lovely, because it is here to remind me of you: and you, my darling friend, are a someone this someone wishes to be reminded of. I love you.

T.

P.S. More: when I have a harbor to report from.

[Collection Gloria Vanderbilt]

TO BENNETT CERF

> Villa Meltemi
> Paros, Greece
> [June 1958]

Dear Bennett—

While in Athens, I received a long cable, followed by a phone call, from Clay Hill of Esquire—still pursuing "Breakfast At Tiffany's." They offer: they would buy the story from Harper's and pay me an additional thousand dollars.[2] From what he said I gathered he must have spoken to you directly and you were not opposed to their publishing it. Anyway, I said yes—though with some qualms. I hope I haven't done a stupid thing.

---

[1] Gloria Vanderbilt, an heiress, artist and fashion designer, was one of the three women—the others were Carol Marcus and Oona O'Neill—Capote palled around with as a teenager in New York.

[2] *Harper's Bazaar* had promised to publish *Breakfast at Tiffany's* in the summer of 1958, a few months before it appeared in book form. Not long before publication, however, Capote's old friend and *Harper's Bazaar* editor, Carmel Snow, was booted out, and a new team decided *Breakfast at Tiffany's* was too racy and reneged on Snow's promise. The novella was published by *Esquire* instead, but Capote never forgave *Harper's Bazaar*. "Publish with *them* again?" he said. "Why, I wouldn't spit on their street."

This is quite a remote, and lonely place I've picked to spend the summer (no other foreigners at all etc.). But it is very beautiful, and I hope it will be good place to work: God knows, there's nothing else to do: <u>you</u> would lose your mind.

Love to our mutual girl-friend. I miss you both.

Best—

Truman

[Collection Columbia University Library]

TO CECIL BEATON

Villa Meltemi
Paros, Greece
June 18, 1958

Dearest C.—

We love it: never liked anyplace more. Absolutely beautiful. Just sun, sea, and serenity. No tourists to speak of. The town is dead white—with blue courtyards and walls covered with morning-glory vine and terraces roofed with grape arbor: like a clean, coral casbah. And it is <u>cool</u>, by the way; even sometimes chilly—we sleep under a blanket. The food is fairly good, the wines delicious.

We are living in a very clean and delightful hotel. There is a little villa next door that we are trying to acquire. But really I don't care if we do—because we have such a quiet pleasant apartment with a terrace overhanging the sea and a flight of stairs going down to a nice-enough little beach. All very comfortable; and if you come—<u>if</u>? you <u>must</u>—we will make a good arrangement for you.

Yes, you must come. It is a perfect place to rest and work and swim and nosey around. I'm afraid there won't be much amour—the inhabitants being singularly unsophisticated. The island is 8 hours by boat from Athens—Try not to take a weekend boat as they are <u>very</u> crowded. The boat leaves Pireaus at 2 in the afternoon and you are here at ten in the evening. Not a bad trip.

Have so much to tell you—undoubtedly you've heard, or <u>read</u>, about my war with H. Bazaar. But am so completely unwound and relaxed that I can't go into all of that just now.

Let me hear from you as soon as possible, dearest one. I long to see you.
Love et mille tendresse [*sic*]

T

[Collection St. John's College, Cambridge University]

TO NEWTON ARVIN

Villa Meltemi
PAROS, Greece
July 16, 1958

Darling Sige—

No, I am very happy here. And your amusing sweet letter made me
more so. Hope you are again in correspondence with Hope. Actually, his
letter to me consisted mostly of questions pertaining to you. Where did I
meet you? when? the exact circumstances? etc. Well! I merely replied that
you were a friend of many years, a brilliant and charming and loyal person
to whom I owed much. Which is no more, and perhaps less, than the truth.
But I doubt that I shall hear from him again; for, while my reply was most
civil and pleasant, it was not quite what he may have hoped to encourage.
Anyway, I'm sure more watermelons will arrive on Prospect Street.[1]

Dear boy, what are these Springfield pleasures? Boites pour les garçons
gai? Or—quel? Tell.

Here, in the islands, all the men dance together—you never see a lady
in the taverns. All very innocent, though—or so I think. But Athens! You
can't walk a block without being accosted ten times! No exaggeration.
There is a bookshop, right on Constitution Square, that specializes in photographs and literature of a particular nature. I bought quite a satchel, and
will pass it on to you, especially a volume called "The Sexual Life of Robin-
son Crusoe."[2] You wouldn't believe what went on between the Old Boy and
Friday! The whole notion opens vistas of pornographic possibility. Why
not, à la Jane Austen, a pamphlet on what transpired between Mr. D'Arcy
and his friend Bingley? or what happened when at last Mr. D'arcy got Elizabeth to bed. Or Topsy and Little Eva: muff-diving each other, while

---

[1] Arvin's address was 45 Prospect Street, Northampton, Massachusetts.
[2] Probably Humphrey Richardson's erotic version of the Daniel Defoe classic.

Simon and Uncle Tom buggered them both.[1] And you can't tell <u>me</u> that Tom Sawyer wasn't in love with Huckleberry!

Haven't read "Home from the Hills."[2] Will, though. Did read a book by a Dutch woman that I liked very much, "The Ten Thousand Things."[3] F. Buechner can write, but he can't. Miss Grau <u>is</u> a bore.[4]

Listen, Sige. I am doing the commentary for a book of photographs by Richard Avedon.[5] Am stumped by a portrait of T. S. Eliot. Don't know anything to say about him. Is there, in his work, a stanza, a few lines, that you would say were self-describing? If I just could quote him, <u>that</u> would get me off the hook.

I said I was happy. I am; except about my work. Simply because I'm not able to work at what I want. I'm on some dreadful treadmill of having to do dollar-making articles: because of my internal revenue troubles, the Joe Capote problem (who, aside from <u>all</u> else, has now married an invalid who is living in a hospital at <u>my</u> expense); and, I suppose, my own past extravaganze [*sic*]. Meanwhile, I have a novel, something on a large and serious scale, that pursues me like a crazy wind: <u>but</u>! How did I ever work myself into this cul-de-sac? I have a very rich friend who I think, in fact know, would see me through (writing the book). I've never been in that kind of debt; I don't want to be. Moreoever, it might ruin the friendship, which I value. Should I? Sorry to ask your advice on such an impossible subject; but you are one of the few I could ask. So forgive me.

Hope your researches, your writing goes well. Give my regards to Wendell. Happy Springfield! I love you, Sige, and always will

T

P.S. Yes, something more <u>did</u> come of the Bazaar mess. After I'd left the country, those <u>swine</u> sold my story to "Esquire". To <u>Esquire</u>!!! And there is <u>nothing</u> I can do about it.[6] When copies of the book are ready, I will have one sent you.

[Collection Smith College Library]

---

[1] Mr. Darcy, Mr. Bingley, and Elizabeth Bennet: characters from *Pride and Prejudice*. Topsy, Little Eva, Simon Legree, and Uncle Tom: characters from *Uncle Tom's Cabin* by Harriet Beecher Stowe.

[2] William Humphrey's *Home from the Hill*.

[3] Maria Dermout's *The Ten Thousand Things*, a novel of life on an Indonesian island when it was ruled by the Dutch.

[4] Frederick Buechner's novel *The Return of Ansel Gibbs* and Shirley Anne Grau's novel *The Hard Blue Sky* both appeared in 1958.

[5] *Observations* (1959).

[6] Capote was not telling the truth, perhaps because he thought Arvin would disapprove of publication of *Breakfast at Tiffany's* in *Esquire*. He had of course given his approval to the magazine.

TO DONALD WINDHAM

[Postcard]   [Páros, Greece]
                                                Aug 10, 1958

Jack, too, has temporarily taken to his bed; but you, I hope, have risen from
yours. Summer at its height here: figs ripe, grapes bursting, melons splitting at the merest touch; Kelly full of burrs, Bunky scratching all the time,
me brown as I'm going to get; but the sunsets are ending sooner, and
September sends cool messages at night.

    Love T

[Collection Beinecke Library, Yale University]

TO DONALD WINDHAM

[Postcard]   [Páros, Greece]
                                                Aug 18, 1958

So happy you're on your feet. Poor lamb, what a miserable experience. But
I'm sure you'll be ripping by the time I get home. Better be. [Christopher]
Isherwood had the same thing; is fine now. Have just finished "Playback",
the new Chandler in which P. [Philip] Marlowe gets married.[1] Am back
with Proust. How sad, how strange about [William] Aalto.[2] Well, [Elia]
Kazan hasn't shown up on <u>this</u> inaccessible island. Still like Greece, but
have my doubts about the Greeks: the <u>children</u> are so horrid: have learned
only five Greek words, in order to say: "Shut up, fat girl" and "Shut up, fat
boy." Bless you, sweet one, and love from all 4 of us—

    T

[Collection Beinecke Library, Yale University]

---

[1] *Playback* (1958) by Raymond Chandler. Capote believed Chandler's talents had not been
properly recognized by the literary establishment.

[2] William Aalto, whom Capote had met on Ischia in 1949, had died of leukemia.

TO DONALD WINDHAM

[Postcard]   [Páros, Greece]
                                                    Aug 28 [1958]

This is a village in the mountains. Jack rescued a kitten some cruel people had thrown into the sea, and he's made it live, a miracle.[1] So now we are 5! Can't think how we will ever get home. Hope you are now as strong as ever. Send a note. Love
        T

[Collection Beinecke Library, Yale University]

TO CECIL BEATON

        [Páros, Greece]
        Sept 4, 1958

Darling Cecil—
        Guess what? It's <u>raining</u>!—oh, or rather it <u>was</u>: now, after 2 minutes, the sun is coming back.
        How we miss you! It was so wonderful while you were here. In some ways the nicest of all our annual hols [unclear]. After you left, that night Jack suddenly said, "Cecil is a wonderful man." High praise from him; but not a tenth what you rate from me.
        Adored your Athens letter. Imagine bumping into all that crew: like going on the cruise without having to go.
        Nick is very excited about his impending life in Wiltshire.[2] You'd scarcely been gone 24 hours when he asked if I'd had a letter. He is full of questions: how long will it take to get the Labor [unclear] permit? After that, what shall he do? Who should he contact at the British Embassy? Will he go to England by plane? He is quite set to depart as soon as the papers are in order. I think he is going to work out fine for you—as long as he has access to the T.V. (I mean that seriously).

---

[1] Jack Dunphy named the cat "Diotima," after the Greek priestess who taught Socrates the philosophy of love.
[2] Nick was a Greek whom Beaton apparently had promised a job in England.

Kitty is fine, though last night she produced a crisis by dissapearing [*sic*] for several hours. We went out with flashlights and found her.

I'm afraid I shall have to abandon thoughts of London, and even Venice. It just isn't fair to leave Jack to cope alone with all these lives and all this junk—even though he is willing.

Never fear, I shall not mention the diaries.[1] And, though I perfectly understand your qualms, I think you will discover that the only persons truly offended (though many will <u>pretend</u> to be) are those not included: that has been my experience in reporting.

Write now. Let me know what to tell Nick. Love from all 5

T

P.S. Paddy and that gloomy Glenn finally left. No one here now except the painters.

[Collection St. John's College, Cambridge University]

TO WILLIAM SHAWN

PAROS, Greece
September 29—1958

Dear Mr. Shawn—

All these island-months I have been intending to communicate; and now in a few days I am departing—sadly, for it has been the perfect working place and pleasant in other ways as well.

Speaking of work, you may recall, dimly, dimly, I am writing a piece presently entitled "A Daughter of the Russian Revolution." By mid-July I had finished a version of it which I thought rather good, enough so that I nearly mailed it; but, reading it again and again, I realized that, solid as it seemed, it did not accelerate with the right rythmn [*sic*], and had to admit I'd shirked the job by not casting it in its proper form: it required a straight narrative line with backwards and sideways movement. Instead I'd used the easier episodic, anecdotal method; and it was successful—but my conscience, that unkind creature, kept hollering away. I thought: oh God, I

---

[1] Beaton was planning to publish his diaries. The first volume—*Cecil Beaton's Diaries: 1922–1939*—was published in 1961.

just <u>can't</u> do it again; but I knew I must, though most of August went by before I could face it. Well, I have been working on it since then. In the original draft, the better part of it concerned one evening: now I begin with that evening and, so to say, slide in and out of it. I hope you will like it; I do. I can't say when it will be finished—a long-time commitment to write the text for Avedon's book of photographs, due Jan 1st, is an irksome stumbling-stone. But I think it could be ready for February publication.

It was very saddening to hear of Wolcott Gibbs' death, and I was most touched by Mr. White's tribute.[1] If it is true, as someone wrote me, that my old friend [Kenneth] Tynan is to be drama critic, the department is in lively hands.[2]

I hope this finds you well, and on your way to being a Brooklyn Heights house-holder. I will be back in New York October 23rd.

Best regards

Truman Capote

[Collection New York Public Library]

TO BENNETT CERF

Paros, Greece
Sept 29, 1958

Beloved B.—

I very much appreciated your cable; and how thoughtful of you to have sent it—I was so longing to see the book, and know when it would arrive.

Yesterday a policeman came and said the local chief would like to see me in his office; but wouldn't say why, just that I should accompany him. It was all rather sinister, rather like something happening to Miss Golightly; I couldn't think what I'd done. When we arrived at the head man's office, I saw, sitting on his desk, an airmail package from Random House— the chief, and the local postman, were hovering over it as though it contained heroin. Which is why I'd been hauled there to open it in their presence: they wanted to be certain I was <u>not</u> importing heroin—or at least some article on which I should have to pay tax.

---

[1] Wolcott Gibbs, the humorist and drama critic, had died on August 16, 1958. The tribute was by his fellow *New Yorker* writer E. B. White.

[2] Tynan did indeed become *The New Yorker*'s theater critic.

And so it was under this odd surveillance that I first saw the book. But nothing could detract from the pleasure it gave me; for it is beautiful, indeed it could hardly be more handsome; and, as always, I am grateful to have such tasteful and considerate publishers. Moreover, reading it through, I liked my own work—an event to be expected I suppose, still it does not always turn out that way. I have no quibble at all: except that I wish I'd proofed it myself, as there are several heartrending errors. Anyway, bless you and thank you, dearest Bennett; you are a good man.

And I hope your goodness will encompass what I have to tell next; for, to turn from the mood sublime to despair abysmal—I have not written Sindbad.[1] Yes, that is what I said: no, I have not. I tried to; I wasted a week in July, wrote five pages and came to a standstill; I tried again last month. But, well, it bored me so: an unprofessional excuse, still I can make no other.

Of course I intend to return the advance; or it can be applied against either one of the two books on which I am working: a large novel, my magnum opus, a book about which I must be very silent, so as not [to] alarm my "sitters" and which I think will really arouse you when I outline it (only you must never mention it to a soul). The novel is called, "Answered Prayers"; and, if all goes well, I think it will answer mine. The other book, nonfiction, is called "A Daughter of the Russian Revolution, And Other Personalities"—I will explain about it when we meet. That is, if you'll speak to me. I will be home Oct. 23rd. Love to the wife of my favorite editor; and love to him, too.

Truman

P.S. You need not answer this; I am leaving here in four days—sad, it has been a wonderful working-place.

[Collection Columbia University Library]

---

[1] Capote had planned to write a children's book for a series Phyllis Cerf was editing.

TO JOHN MALCOLM BRINNIN

[70 Willow Street]
[Brooklyn, N.Y.]
[October 1958]

Dearest M—

On the whole, I rather wish you would introduce me; it quietens an audience and focuses their attention—last year, at Chicago, they decided not to have an introduction, and I suppose it was "effective" but it took me ten minutes to get the audience in a listening mood. However, you do what you think best.[1]

I doubt that I will get in the Ritz, so will go gladly to the Copley—if they will have me.

I will take a morning train, arriving early afternoon; please don't meet me. Will go to the hotel: will you come there at three? so that we can talk before going to this Advocate party? Speaking of which, would you ask them to invite a young friend of mine, a student at Radcliffe—

Frances Fitzgerald[2]
Briggs Hall
60 Linnean [Linnaean] St. Cambridge

I see in the paper you will be at Poetry Center Dec. 4th.[3] Please give me a ring. Longing to see you—

Love
Truman

[Collection University of Delaware Library]

---

[1] On December 14, 1958, Capote gave readings from several of his works at Harvard's Sanders Theater. Brinnin, who had arranged the reading, introduced him to an audience of about a thousand.
[2] The daughter of Capote's friend Marietta Tree, Fitzgerald went on to write such acclaimed books as *Fire in the Lake* and *Cities on a Hill*.
[3] Brinnin was director of the YMHA's Poetry Center, otherwise known as the 92nd Street Y in Manhattan, from 1949 to 1956.

TO JOHN MALCOLM BRINNIN

[70 Willow Street]
[Brooklyn, New York]
[Early November 1958]

Malcolm dear—

A most beguiling letter, Mon cher; you <u>do</u> have charm.

If you are coming to New York soon, let me know; the telephone is TR 5-0388.

As for Frank Murphy and Mr. A. [Arvin], I think they sound perfectly mated, both enjoying, as they do, such immaculate insolence.

Please yes, reserve for me a Ritz room for December 14th: I will take a morning train; then we can have a drink, and go to the reading.

Blessings and love

T

P.S. This was written a week ago and just now getting off. I've changed plans and will be coming to Boston on the 13th. So make reservation for 13th <u>and</u> 14th.

Did you see Mr. Goyen's "review" of my book in last Sunday's Times? How is that for a piece of sour grapes bitchy?[1] <u>What</u> a psychopath.

Hugs + kisses

T

[Collection University of Delaware Library]

---

[1] William Goyen's review of *Breakfast at Tiffany's: A Short Novel and Three Stories* appeared in *The New York Times Book Review* on November 2, 1958. He disparaged Capote as "perhaps the last of the old-fashioned Valentine makers" and accused him of dwelling in a "doily story-world" entirely of his own making.

TO WILLIAM SHAWN

[70 Willow Street]
[Brooklyn, N.Y.]
Saturday
[15 November 1958]

Dear Mr. Shawn,
    After several days of trying to accept the matter as an incident of a kind that has happened to me many times, I find I cannot, and that I remain hurt and dismayed by the very contemptuous and gratuitously insulting manner in which my book was "brushed off" in the current issue of the magazine.[1] I would not be upset by an unfavorable notice; however, I take my work seriously, I spent several years on these stories, and believe myself to deserve something more than a condescending paragraph that concludes with an unserious, an unjust and meaningless wisecrack the reviewer does not attempt to explain or substantiate. Truly, I am shocked that "The New Yorker", with which after all I do have some association, would not only treat me in this style, but seemingly go out of their way to do it. Because the writer is anonymous, the voice of the magazine appears to be speaking, certainly condoning—which is very crippling to the pride and self-assurance I once had as a contributor.
    With best personal regards,
    Most sincerely
    Truman Capote

[Collection New York Public Library]

TO KENNETH SILVERMAN

[Brooklyn, N.Y.]
[26 May 1959]

Dear Mr. Silverman,
    This is not an answer to your very kind letter; it is merely an acknowledgment: I am in the midst of work that does not leave me the time to reply

---

[1] A brief, unsigned review in *The New Yorker* (November 15, 1958) dismissed *Breakfast at Tiffany's* as empty nostalgia.

in the manner you deserve. For what it is worth (not much) I made a few remarks on the subject of style which appear in the book "Writers At Work."[1] Of course I am extremely sympathetic to your interest in the question: so few writers, much less readers, are, or even know that it exists. But there is really no <u>practical</u> help that one can offer: it is a matter of self-discovery, of one's own conviction, or working with one's own work: <u>your</u> style is what seems <u>natural</u> to <u>you</u>. It is a long process of discovery, one that never ends, I am still working at it, and will be as long as I live. So must you.[2] With every good wish for your health as an artist, and otherwise—

Most sincerely,

T. Capote

[Collection Kenneth Silverman]

TO CECIL BEATON

[Clarks Island]
[Duxbury, Mass.]
June 12, 1959

Dearest Cecil—

In my not very humble opinion, your agent and his reader are wrong one hundred percent; and wrong in such a wholehearted, pigheaded way that I, for one, cannot talk back to them: which is the whole point: either you appreciate the diary as it is, or you just don't—it isn't anything you can <u>argue</u> about, anymore than you can argue with a person who doesn't like asparagus. I realize their sincerity, and quite see that many people, a majority perhaps, would agree with their view. But the value of the diary is in its honesty; if you tinker with it it will become something other than yourself. These critics are simply asking you to be something other than you are: something that conforms to <u>their</u> idea of what is Proper, Tasteful, Interesting etc. I say fuck them; such people would never like the diary regardless of what you did.

---

[1] *The Paris Review's Writers at Work* series, vol. 1.

[2] Silverman did. He became a biographer and won the Pulitzer Prize in 1985 for *The Life and Times of Cotton Mather.*

I was terribly dissappointed [*sic*] not to be able to see you, or even talk to you, while you were in New York. But I have to go to the mainland for a telephone, and it is all very complicated. The house is wonderful—big clean light and breezy, surrounded by beautiful tree-filled lawns sloping down to beaches—much the best place we've ever had. Wonderful for work. I hope we will still be here when you come back, I long for you to see it. How did you like "Gypsy"?[1] Oh dear, it is upsetting about Nick; he could learn so much, he is such a fool not to take advantage. Or perhaps that is just what he is doing, taking advantage. All the animals are well, so is Jack, everyone sends love. Write soon, I miss you, dearest friend.

Always

T

[Collection St. John's College, Cambridge University]

TO CECIL BEATON

Clarks Island
Duxbury, Mass.
15 July 1959

Dearest C.,

I so enjoy the picture of you sunning the Gainsborough costumes in the garden: well, it *is* exciting news that at least the play will be done![2] I think Donald Wolfit will be excellent—have you cast the daughters yet? I long for all the news—when it opens, where. It would be nice (for me) if I could arrange a quick flight over to see it. Who knows!

I have not heard from Slim [Hayward] since early June, at which time she was in Spain; I believe she is still in Europe, but lately I had become very concerned by her silence—so your item about Leland [Hayward] and Pam C. [Pamela Churchill] <u>stunned</u> me; I'd heard nothing about it![3]—Babe

---

[1] The musical *Gypsy* had opened on Broadway May 21, 1959.

[2] Beaton was still trying to make a success of his play *The Gainsborough Girls,* which had been renamed *Landscape with Figures.* As before, the play toured British provincial cities; but, as before, it was not successful enough to find a home in either London or New York.

[3] New York society was riveted by the breakup of the marriage of Leland and Slim Hayward, brought about by Leland's love affair with Pamela Churchill, the onetime daughter-in-law of Winston Churchill.

[Paley], who is in Biarritz, did not mention it [in] her last letter, though that reached here several weeks ago. Toward the end of May, just before I came back, I saw Leland and Mrs. C., in tete-a-tete at a restaurant—and I kidded them, and said I was going to write Slim (who had already left for Europe, where Leland was supposed to join in a week—but never did). As a matter of fact, with my usual gaucherie, I _did_ write Slim asking if she knew her husband was running around with the notorious Mrs. C. Oh dear! Are you sure it's true? Has he really left Slim? _Please_ write me what you know. I am devoted to Slim, I'm amazed she hasn't written me, I must find out where she is at once.—Everything here goes well, really love the house, and am working hard. Jack sends best. All good luck with the play, my darling friend. Love

T

[Collection St. John's College, Cambridge University]

TO BENNETT CERF

[Duxbury, Mass.]
23 July 1959

Dearest Both,[1]

Bless you, at least bless _Bennett_, for the nice letter, and of course I want to do, or re-do, the children's book. L. Boriss sent me the mss. and I have been thinking about it. But, since the word limitation has been removed, I wonder if this is the right story. At any rate, I've thought of another one which seems to me delightful. Well, I'll do one or the other. This is a picture, blurry though it be, of the house—it's really very nice, a perfect place to work, I wish I were rich and could buy it. Anyway, I _have_ been writing, _and_ writing on my novel and on a long short story. I hope you have been having a lovely Mt. Kisco summer. I am very worried about Slim; she was really shocked over Leland and dear Pam; she has been staying with the Paleys in Biarritz, but now they are coming home, and I hope she does too; I wish she would come and stay with me. Please send me a copy of Moss Hart's book (I guess I'm the only actual gossip who _hasn't_ been sent it).[2] I doubt that I will come home before Oct. 1st; but my goodness I do

---

[1] The letter was intended for Cerf and his wife, Phyllis.
[2] _Act One_, a memoir of Hart's early life in the theater.

miss you! Oh—I've lost 6 pounds! And will settle for ten. Don't do anything spectacular—wait for me.

    LOVE

    T

[Collection Columbia University Library]

TO WESLEY HARTLEY[1]

[Postcard]
                                          [Clarks Island]
                                          [Duxbury, Mass.]
                                          [23 July 1959]

I should say a student does well to remain one as long as he can. It seems to me very doubtful that formal education could ever harm a potential artist—of course, it won't make him one either.

    T. Capote

[Collection unknown]

TO WILLIAM SHAWN

    [Clarks Island]
    [Duxbury, Mass.]
    18 August 1959

Dear Mr. Shawn,

    After a total of some eight months work, I am still not satisfied with my article, "A Daughter of the Russian Revolution." I seem to have lost faith in the piece, or at least in my ability to do it. Therefore, I am returning the

---

    [1] Wesley Hartley, a high school English teacher, wrote many authors, posing the question: "How important to you was your high school education, and is college experience necessary for creative writing?"

money for plane-fare the magazine gave me. If we can arrange another project for me, I will try not to dissappoint [*sic*] you (or myself).

Sincerely,
Truman Capote

[Collection New York Public Library]

TO GLORIA VANDERBILT

Clarks Island
Duxbury, Mass.
20 August 1959

Darling Friend,

Forgive my delay; I've been gone for ten days, during which time the play arrived.

Now I've read it twice. The scenes are a series of poetic mosaics, each very evocatively inlaid: your eye is fine, a painter's eye that sets loose an extraordinary montage of haunting or humourous images, and each, taken separately, successfully projects its color and mood. But it seems to me these moods, these vignettes, are too separate—or, perhaps, too alike. I feel that in most writing, but especially dramatic writing, fantasy, particularly psychological fantasy, must be framed with very realistic detail: otherwise it does not quite come alive—poetry cannot be all poetry, it needs the contrast of mundane matter. The thematic line of "Cinamee" is perfectly clear; but, as a play, it leaves me dissastified [*sic*], for its characters seemed to me insufficiently fleshed, and their movements, in the sense of character continuity, too arbitrary. It is a ballet with words: I do not say that in criticism, quite the contrary, for it is a remarkable accomplishment, probably one that could not have been achieved using any other method than you have. The writing throughout is gifted and poetically inventive, and I would extremely like to see this play acted. At the same time I would like to see you write <u>another</u> play—one in which you deliberately suppress your natural talent for atmosphere and "choreographed thought": a naturalistic, unexperimental play using your very sharp insight into everyday matters. I know you could do it, and it would strengthen your other gifts manifold. You have real talent; and, just as important, great discipline.

Darling, I hope you are having a good summer. Mine is quiet; I write, I

read, I sit on the beach a bit: c'est tout. I <u>miss</u> you very much; will be back
Oct. 2nd and hope to see you soonest. Write just a line. My love always

T

[Collection Gloria Vanderbilt]

TO CECIL BEATON

[Clarks Island]
[Duxbury, Mass.]
24 August 1959

Dearest C—

As I don't know where "Landscape with Figures" (I like the new title) is
opening, or when (though I think it should be out very soon) I hasten now
to send you the most heartfelt good-wishes.[1] So does Jack. I know you
must be in a swivet, and I do not envy you—but really know that my hopes
are very much with you.

Have just returned to the island from a week's visit with the Paleys in
New Hampshire. It was the first time I'd been away, but I do not enjoy
households overrun with children, so it was delicious returning home to
this with isolation and peace; I would not mind living here all the time, and
just making forays into the world. But I'm afraid that is not physically fea-
sible. From having been the most gregarious of persons, I seem increasingly to require huge doses of privacy. At the Paleys (who, by the way, are
in great spirits and beautiful shape) there was much talk about what is
termed "Topic A"—the Hayward-Churchill fandango. I had a long letter
from Slim, very touching, very regretful, but full of good-sense; it seems
that Leland has never asked her for a divorce, though Mrs C. tells everyone she will be Mrs H in November. The whole thing has caused a "situation" among the Cushing girls:[2] Babe and Minnie have vowed undying

---

[1] Beaton's play opened in Newcastle on September 7.
[2] The three Cushing sisters were the daughters of Harvey Cushing, a Boston doctor who had
transformed brain surgery from an art into a science. They had all married rich, glamorous men—
all more than once. Betsey, the oldest, was now married to John Hay Whitney; Minnie, the middle sister, had married Vincent Astor before finding love with James Fosburgh, a socially
connected artist; and Babe, the youngest, was now married to William Paley, the head of the CBS
television and radio network.

enmity to "that bitch," while sister Betsy [Betsey] is Mrs. C's greatest partisan (so grateful is she that the threat to her own happy home has been removed). Tout New York is divided into warring camps—the pro-Slim contingent, led by Mrs. Paley with Jerome Robbins and Mainbocher as seconds in command, have already sent Mrs. [Leonora] Hornblow to the firing-squad because she gave a dinner for Leland and Mrs. C.—which <u>was</u> odd, considering she has always been so close a friend of Slim.[1] No doubt Mrs. C. will be the winner in the coming contest. Needless to say I am a Slimite to the death. Of course the whole story is sad and stupid; I feel endlessly sorry for Slim, and the hurtful role she has to play. It is something she could have been so easily spared, except for Mrs. C's blabbermouth tactics. Anyway, she is coming home Sept. 15th to face the music. It has been beautiful weather here, and today has the blue burning clarity of Greece, though autumn can be felt when you stand in the shade. Dear heart, could Eileen [Hose] look in the London phone book and send me the address of <u>The Bolton Studios</u>?[2] I hear that Harold Arlen's score for "Saratoga" is excellent; but the cast, as announced in the paper, sounds dismal. I wonder if you'll get to Clarks Island? Somehow, it doesn't seem likely, which is a pity—I so wanted you to see it. Isherwood (who I believe is on his way to London to see his ailing mother) has taken a teaching job in California. We return to New York Oct. 1st. Write when you can; I miss you; love

T

[Collection St. John's College, Cambridge University]

TO RICHARD AVEDON

[Clarks Island]
[Duxbury, Mass.]
27 August 1959

Beloved Collaborator,[3]
    You did <u>handsomely</u> with our little tale, and thanks for sending the pictures. They are fresh and amusing and God! how all of you must have

---

[1] Hornblow was the wife of Arthur Hornblow, Jr., a film producer.
[2] Hose was Beaton's secretary.
[3] Capote and Avedon were collaborating on *Observations*; Capote wrote the text and Avedon took the photographs.

slaved. I hope the trip, and the giro de [unclear] was a bit of recuperative fun, and that this finds you ready to tackle some chores as regards The Book.[1]

1) Get Simon & Schuster[2] to try and arrange interviews for you with Maurice Dolbier, who writes a book column in the Sunday Tribune, and the Speaking of Books column in the Sunday Times. They have never interviewed a photographer, so far as I know, and for that reason I think they might. Also, arrange for an interview with Martha MacGregor, who runs the book page in the New York Post. Also, W.G. Rogers of [the] Associated Press. These things would be very helpful.

2) See that copies are sent to—
Irving Hoffman
        (who feeds all book information to [Walter] Winchell)
Dorothy Killgallen [Kilgallen]
Ed Sullivan
Leonard Lyons <u>and</u> Richard Watts[3]
Be <u>sure</u> to include cards saying "with the compliments of the Authors." This will pay off, take my word.

3) Arrange to appear on the Dave Garroway program. Jack Paar sells books, too; the rest, from our point of view, don't matter too much.[4]

4) As we've said before, it would be pleasant if Time and Newsweek, but especially the former, would give the book some sort of spread. See if you can find out whether they are planning, too.

I know I don't have to emphasize how important these matters are, so buckle down.

I am still leading my monastic and silent life, working on my novel and short story. I will be back Oct. 1st.

Love to Evey [Evie] et vous.[5] Your friend
T

[Collection Richard Avedon]

---

[1] Avedon had been in Sicily.
[2] Simon & Schuster published *Observations*.
[3] Winchell, Kilgallen, Sullivan, Lyons and Watts were all widely read columnists.
[4] Garroway was the host of *The Today Show*, a popular morning program; Paar was the host of *The Tonight Show*.
[5] Evie Avedon was Avedon's wife.

TO DONALD WINDHAM

[Clarks Island]
[Duxbury, Mass.]
8 September 1959

Dearest Donny,

Sorry about the heat, and the burst water pipe; but all your other news was certainly good—really it is <u>wonderful</u> about Forster: an introduction by him is bound to impress reviewers and call particular attention to the book.[1] You should feel very set up: <u>I</u> would, god knows.

Of course you may use me as a Guggenheim reference; I should be delighted to tell those boneheads how gifted you are in several hundred dazzling adjectives. But academicians, <u>college</u> professors, seem to be what they put their faith in. Do you <u>know</u> any you could ask? Well, there's R. P. Warren (I've read, or tried to read, his new one, The Cave: oh it is so dull, dull, and so self-concious [sic]). And Glenway [Wescott]? The Baroness [Isak Dinesen]? Forster, of course. Carson [McCullers]? Get as many as you can.[2]

I have been very blue. Kay Kendall's death truly shocked me.[3] She was a fine, dear girl, and I was awfully fond of her. I'd been told over a year ago that she had leukemia, but I didn't beleive [sic] it. Also, my friends the Haywards are getting a divorce, and I feel worried and sad for her. My work isn't going too well, either; but then, it never does. If only I were a writer that could write, not just rewrite: self-criticism is good, but not when it reaches the proportions it has with me—then it is just a tumour draining away all one's confidence. I've written fifteen pages in the past ten weeks, and I've worked <u>every</u> day.

We will be home Thursday, October 1st. I long to see you.

Hope you have luck with The New Yorker.

Love to Sandy,

et vous,

T

[Collection Beinecke Library, Yale University]

---

[1] E. M. Forster contributed an introduction to Windham's book of stories, *The Warm Country* (1960).

[2] The writers Capote suggests are Robert Penn Warren, Glenway Wescott, Baroness Karen Blixen (Isak Dinesen), E. M. Forster and Carson McCullers.

[3] A superb comic actress and the current wife of Rex Harrison, Kendall had died of leukemia on September 6, 1959.

Four Murders and a Ball in Black and White

ON THE MORNING OF MONDAY, November 16, 1959, Capote read a one-column story buried on page thirty-nine of *The New York Times*. WEALTHY FARMER, 3 OF FAMILY SLAIN, read the headline. "A wealthy wheat farmer, his wife and their two young children were found shot to death today in their home," the story went on to say. "They had been killed by shotgun blasts at close range after being bound and gagged." Going on nothing but that short newspaper story, Capote convinced *The New Yorker* to send him to Kansas. His intention was to write an article about the effects of the murders on the small community of Holcomb and neighboring Garden City, in which the Clutters—the murdered family—had lived.

Taking with him Harper Lee, his friend from earliest childhood, he set out for a part of the world that was, for him, as alien as the Soviet Union had been. Nor did the good folk of Garden City take to a creature—short, oddly dressed and with a little boy's voice—who was alien to them. A kind invitation to Christmas dinner gave an opening to the Capote charm, however, and the town was soon his. Five days later, on December 30, the killers, Dick Hickock and Perry Smith, were arrested; two and a half months after that, in March 1960, they were tried, convicted and sentenced to death. With their capture and conviction, Capote realized that he had more than an article; he had a book—and possibly a great book at that. He titled it *In Cold Blood*.

Finishing his basic research in Kansas, he returned to Europe, where he and Dunphy rented houses on the Spanish coast for a couple of summers. For the winters they bought a small condominium in the Swiss village of Verbier. In Europe Capote slowly and painfully wrote his book. "I suppose it sounds pretentious," he told Donald Windham, "but I feel a great obligation to write it, even though the material leaves me increasingly limp and numb and, well, horrified—I have such awful dreams every night." Eventually he completed everything but his concluding chapter, which could not be written until the condemned men had exhausted the last of their many appeals. Month after anxious month he waited for the final verdict of the final court. That came at last, and on April 14, 1965, with Capote watching, Hickock and Smith were hanged.

The New Yorker published *In Cold Blood* in four installments in the fall of 1965. Random House followed with the hardcover in January 1966, and the reception was what every writer dreams of—almost universal praise, stupendous sales and a fame usually reserved for movie stars. *In Cold Blood* was the publishing event of the decade, and Capote was the man of every hour.

After so much work, Capote wanted to play, and the book of the decade was followed, in the autumn of 1966, with the party of the decade. On the night of November 28, a rainy Monday, the rich and famous, as well as many lesser mortals whom he liked, walked into Manhattan's Plaza Hotel for a masked black-and-white ball. As *The Washington Post* wrote, the Capote name, "coupled with a guest list that reads like Who's Who of the World, has escalated his party to a social 'happening' of history-making proportions." The little boy from Alabama had come, he had seen and he had conquered.

With the exception of Robert Linscott, who had retired from Random House, Capote's correspondents during this period remain much the same, with two significant additions—Alvin Dewey, the detective in charge of the Clutter case, and his wife, Marie. Many of his letters to the Deweys include requests for information—his debt to them is obvious—but it soon becomes clear that the friendship is more than convenient. Indeed, he all but adopts them—and they him. "Precious Ones" is how he addresses them in one letter; "Dearest Honey Funny Bunnies" in another. Katharine Graham, the publisher of *The Washington Post* and the guest of honor of his black-and-white ball, also makes an appearance as "Precious KayKay." So, briefly, does Perry Smith, who had asked him for the words of a poem he remembered. Capote found it—it was written by Robert W. Service, a once-popular Canadian poet—and he may have noticed that the words applied equally well to both of them:

> *There's a race of men that don't fit in*
> *   A race that can't stay still;*
> *So they break the hearts of kith and kin;*
> *   And they roam the world at will . . .*

TO CHRISTOPHER ISHERWOOD

[New York]
23 November 1959

Dear Chris—

You would be pleased (I think) by all the enthusiastic comment I've heard about the excerpt from your novel published in The London magazine.[1] That issue evaporated from the counters so swiftly that I had a helluva time locating it. Well, really it is <u>very</u> good; as good as people say it is—I long to read the book.

I understand you <u>did</u> leave Random House; I guess you did the right thing—it's a pretty shabby crew around there.

The last time I heard from Don [Bachardy], and that was too long ago, he said you were going to teach in a college, where?[2] What is it like?

Cecil was here until a week ago—working (sets and costumes) on a musical called "Saratoga." I saw it in Philadelphia.[3] Dreadful. Except for Cecil's contribution. The Selznicks are here—he has been very ill; she (of all things) is studying at the Actor's [sic] Studio; they are looking for a house here—say they are selling the one in California. Tenn. and Frankie are back from their round the world hegira. Saw his movie, "Suddenly Last Summer." Quite good. Also saw the movie they made of "Orpheus Descending" (with Brando-Magnani). A real stinker. Ran into S. [Speed] Lamkin: failure has improved him. Also (same night, different place) ran into G. [Gore] Vidal—and we had WORDS. Saw your friend, Julie H. [Harris] in her play—she charming, play but nothing.[4]

---

[1] *Down There on a Visit*, published in 1962.
[2] Don Bachardy, a young artist, was Isherwood's longtime companion.
[3] With music by Harold Arlen and lyrics by Johnny Mercer, *Saratoga* opened at the Winter Garden Theatre in New York on December 7, 1959, and ran for eighty performances.
[4] Joe Masteroff's *The Warm Peninsula* opened at the Helen Hayes Theatre on October 20, 1959, and ran for eighty-six performances.

Oh I could run on forever—write me, and maybe I will. Love to Don. I miss you both,

T

[Collection Henry E. Huntington Library]

TO ALVIN DEWEY[1]

Hotel Warren
Garden City, Kansas
[6 January 1960]

Dear Foxy,
After your long and heroic journey, we are certain you will appreciate a long swig of this.
So: welcome home!

From your ever faithful historians
Truman
Nelle

[Collection New York Public Library]

TO CECIL BEATON

[Brooklyn, N.Y.]
Jan 21, 1960

Dearest Cecil—
Returned yesterday—after nearly 2 months in Kansas: an extraordinary experience, in many ways the most interesting thing that's ever hap-

---

[1] Alvin A. Dewey, Jr., led the Kansas Bureau of Investigation team investigating the Clutter murders. His relationship with Capote had a rocky start, but Capote soon became friendly with Dewey, his wife, Marie, and his two sons. Capote called him "Foxy" because he refused to give him privileged information. Dewey's "long and heroic journey" had been to pick up the two killers in Las Vegas, where they had been caught, and return them in handcuffs to Garden City. Capote and Harper (Nelle) Lee attached this note to a bottle of J&B scotch.

pened to me. But I will let you read about it—it may amount to a small book.

I wonder if you are still in St. Moritz, wherever you are, I envy you—it is so cold and black here, and everyone has gone away to the snow or the sun.

I am surprised that "this person" was surprised when you "popped the question." And amazed that she hesitated: but think this speaks <u>very</u> well for her; and if it eventually works out, I'm sure it will be a better and happier thing for the thinking-over. Actually, to me it sounds more promising now than earlier. However, we shall see.[1]

How appalling that Stratford et al should have fallen through in that tiresome and wasteful fashion. I <u>hate</u> the theatre—except that it does bring you to New York; am so looking forward to your March return.

No news, no gossip of any sort, at least, having been out of circulation so long, I know none.

Will write more again when I'm unpacked and more collected.

Love and hugs

T

[Collection St. John's College, Cambridge University]

TO ALVIN AND MARIE DEWEY

[Brooklyn, N.Y.]
22 January 1960

Dear Marie and Alvin,

We had a rather longish trip to New York (Super-Chief [2] six hours late in Chicago, which meant we had to stay there overnight etc.)—but finally arrived Monday night.

---

[1] "This person" was June Osborn, a widow, many years younger, from an aristocratic background. She turned down Beaton's proposal of marriage, and it is not hard to see why. This is the wording of his proposal speech, as recorded in his diary: "For a long time I've been wondering if I dare ask you if you would marry me, as I think it would be such a good thing for me although there is every reason why you shouldn't want to." Refusing to accept "no," he later tried again, even more ineptly. "Have you thought any more about our being spliced?" he asked her. "Oh don't put it like that," she replied, and the answer was still no.

[2] The Super Chief was a luxurious train that the Santa Fe Railway ran between Chicago and Los Angeles.

I have had long talks with the staff at "The New Yorker", and with Random House. Just today I signed a contract for the book.[1] Everyone is very enthusiastic. When we come back, I very likely will bring with me Richard Avedon,[2] who is quite easily the world's greatest photographer (because we may use a few photographs in the book—and I'm afraid those in existence are not quite good enough). Speaking of pictures—do glance at the new Feb 2nd issue of "Look" magazine: somewhere around pg. 83 there is something that may amuse you.

Nelle and I parted at the Railway terminal, and haven't seen each other since, but we've talked on the telephone, and she misses you, all of you, Paul and Dewey and Pete,[3] very much. So do I.

I will ring you soon.

Meanwhile, much love—

Truman

And come to New York!

[Collection New York Public Library]

TO ALVIN AND MARIE DEWEY

[Mid-Atlantic, aboard the
French Line ship] Flandre
Easter Sunday
[17 April 1960]

Dearest Folks—

Finally managed to get aboard (with 25 pieces of luggage, 2 dogs, 1 cat, and my good friend Jack Dunphy)—and here we all are, mid-Atlantic. At least, and at last, I am getting a good rest: slept 12 hours last night.

Forgive my handwriting: despite what I say on the card about the sea's calmness, there is still quite a bit of a roll.

---

[1] The book was *In Cold Blood*.
[2] Capote and Avedon had collaborated on the book *Observations*, published by Simon & Schuster in 1959.
[3] Paul and "Dewey" (Alvin Dewey III) were the young sons of Alvin and Marie Dewey; Pete was the Dewey family's cat.

We reach Le Havre next Thursday, the 22nd (I will mail this from there).[1] Then we drive down to Spain, which should take about 3 days. Here is the address again, just to be sure you got it straight—

c/o J. Y. Millar
Calle Catifa
Palamos (Gerona)
Costa Brava
Spain

I was so happy to have your 'Bon Voyage' call: so sweet of you. But then you <u>are</u> sweet, and I love you all.

This just a scribble; but will send cards en route and really write when I reach Palamos.

Hugs and love,

T

[Collection New York Public Library]

TO ALVIN AND MARIE DEWEY

28 April 1960
c/o Millar
Calle Catifa
Palamos (Gerona)
Costa Brava, Spain

Dearest Deweys,

How nice to have Marie's sweet letter waiting to welcome me here. So sorry about your mother; I do hope you can visit them this year. But that <u>was</u> hilarious about the burglary in Syracuse: I am keeping the list of stolen objects—I may use it in the book—which, by the way, I <u>really</u> started writing this very morning.

It took us four days to drive down here through France. A lovely trip, spring everywhere, green fields and wild flowers and beautiful weather. We

---

[1] Postmarked from Southampton on April 21, 1960.

had picnic lunches every day—just lots of bread and cheese and cold wine. Then at night a <u>huge</u> meal. I must have gained 5 pounds.

But the food is not very good in Spain—unless you like everything cooked in olive oil. Which I don't. However, my house is quite charming. This is a fishing village and the house is right on the beach—the water is as clear and as blue as a mermaid's eye. I get up <u>very</u> early—because the fishermen set sail at 5 a.m, and they make such a racket not even Rip Van Winkle could sleep through it. But that is good for my work, n'est-ce pas? All my animals, both dogs and the cat, survived the journey very well. They love riding in cars, especially the cat. She keeps disappearing and we always find her sitting in the car.

I have rented this house only until June 15th. After that, will move somewhere else on the Spanish coast or perhaps go to Portugal. Or Italy. Or France. Who knows?

Hope Dick[1] has sent the pictures. It takes him <u>forever</u> to make his prints—he is so finicky. I have all of the pictures here with me. How delightful you all look. Because you <u>are</u> delightful. And I love you very much. Hugs for Paul and Dewey—write me

T

So glad the Grapevine article turned out well!

[Collection New York Public Library]

TO ALVIN AND MARIE DEWEY

[Postcard]   [Palamós, Spain]
                                              May 3rd, 1960

Dearhearts—

Book going well. Have found another house and am moving there June 15th—so will be in Spain until Oct.

Alvin, something <u>very</u> important! Nancy's[2] diary had entries for the last

---

[1] Richard Avedon.
[2] Nancy Clutter was one of the two murdered Clutter children.

four years. I need the entries for Sat. Nov 14th in 1958, 1957, 1956. Urgent! If you no longer have diary, who has? Miss you all. Love

   T

Wrote Perry [Smith], but letter returned.[1]

[Collection New York Public Library]

TO ALVIN AND MARIE DEWEY

[Palamós, Spain]
17 May 1960

Dearhearts—

So happy to have Marie's letter: and relieved, too—not having heard from you in almost a month. Bless you for sending the diary entries.

Am glad you liked Dick's pictures; I think they are marvelous—so alive, witty and charming.

We move into the new house June 1st—I'm sure I sent you the address, but here it is again: c/o Klaebisch, "Az-Zahara", Condado de San Jorge, Playa de Aro, Costa Brava, Spain. It is a beautiful house right on the sea. My God, I wish you could come here instead of L.A. Speaking of which, please let me know at what hotel you will be staying: I have certain Hollywood friends (especially David Selznick and his wife Jennifer Jones) who would be delighted to arrange movie-studio excursions for you etc. Please don't be shy about this: they really would enjoy doing it, and they know all about you, too. So let me know the address immediately. I will write the Selznicks today. Their address is: 1400 Tower Rd., Beverly Hills.

Small questions in connection with book continue, and will continue, to arise. For instance, according to my notes, the Clutters built their house in 1943: but this does not seem possible; was it 1943 or 1953?[2] Also, how many miles is it from Holcomb to Colorado border? Has a new date been set for carrying out a sentence? (As you can see, all my G.C.[3] Telegrams are accumulating unread in New York).

---

[1] Perry Smith had been convicted, along with Dick Hickock, of murdering the four Clutters.
[2] The year given in In Cold Blood is 1948.
[3] Garden City, Kansas, home of the Deweys.

Hope Dewey's allergies are under control: <u>and</u> Pete's fighting instincts. Love to Paul, Love to all—

    T

[Collection New York Public Library]

TO DAVID O. SELZNICK AND JENNIFER JONES

c/o Klaebisch
"AZ-ZAHARA"
Condado de San Jorge
Playa de Aro
Costa Brava, Spain
24 May 1960

Dear hearts—

David's letter finally forwarded from New York.[1] Have lovely house here by the sea, and will be staying until the end of Sept. However, don't plan returning to New York until my book is finished, and, as it is so complicated, so very long, that will be at least a year from now. God knows I'm working hard—not seeing anyone: though I <u>think</u> Slim [Hayward] is coming to visit a few days some time in June.

Speaking of the book, the "hero" of it is coming to Los Angeles in July. His name is Alvin Dewey, and he is an agent for the Kansas Bureau of Investigation, the man who was in charge of the case and the person chiefly responsible for solving it. He is <u>charming</u>, so are his wife and 2 sons: they will be with him on this California holiday. I know you would find Alvin interesting, and I hope, while he and his family are there, you could give them a ring, arrange for them to visit a studio (or something). Later on, I will send the dates and name of hotel where they will be staying.

Do you remember my story, the one I made a record of, "A Christmas Memory"? I would like very much to make a film of it, something about the length of "The Red Balloon"—35 minutes, and costing about (at most) $50,000. It would be entirely visual, with a boy's voice reading the story and a musical score by, say, Virgil Thompson [Thomson]. It is something Jose

---

[1] Selznick wrote on April 12, 1960, reminding Capote that he expected to see galleys of *In Cold Blood* (not yet titled) in hopes of acquiring film rights to it.

Quintero could do very well (I think).[1] It <u>could</u> be beautiful, if done <u>very</u> simply, and as successful as "The Red Balloon." Several independent producers are interested, one very much so—but could you let me know if this project at all appeals to you?

Slim wrote what a comfort you were to her in California, and said Jennifer looked "ravishing."[2] Give my love to that other ravishing lady, Mary J.[3] I miss you all.

Hugs—

T.

(Truman Capote)

[Collection University of Texas at Austin]

TO DAVID O. SELZNICK AND JENNIFER JONES

"Az-Zahara"
Condado de San Jorge
Playa de Aro
Costa Brava, Spain
[Early June 1960]

Dearest David and Jennifer,

Just a quick follow-up to my letter of the other day. About my friend Alvin Dewey (the hero of my book) and his family (wife, two sons, aged 11 and 13): I told you that they are coming to L.A. from Garden City Kansas for a week's holiday, and that I would very much appreciate it if you can contact them and arrange some studio tourist-stuff for them? Well, they are arriving July 19th and will be there until the 25th, and you can get in touch with them via Mrs. Dewey's uncle: EDWARD STOLL, 2516 Veterans Avenue, Los Angeles, 64. I took the liberty of giving them your address, but I think they will be too shy to use it. They are very nice and I am terribly indebted to them. If you should meet them, please don't say anything caustic about me.

---

[1] Quintero was a theatrical director best known for his productions of the plays of Eugene O'Neill.

[2] Hayward was going through a divorce from her husband, Leland Hayward.

[3] The Selznicks' daughter, Mary Jennifer.

Have never worked so hard; but it is going to be a very fine book . . . though, God knows, a long one.

I miss you and hope you will have a good summer.

Love and hugs

Truman Capote

P.S. On July 11th, Lippincott is publishing a delightful book: TO KILL A MOCKINGBIRD by Harper Lee. Get it. It's going to be a great success.[1] In it, I am the character called "Dill"—the author being a childhood friend.

[Collection University of Texas at Austin]

TO WILLIAM STYRON[2]

"Az-Zahara"
Condado de San Jorge
Playa de Aro
Costa Brava, Spain
7 June 1960

Dear Bill—

I read your book[3] this past week, and do want to congratulate you; really, to have maintained such control, to have sustained such a difficult vision, is an achievement in itself; but, aside from its artistic first-rateness, what I admire most is the book's bravery, the courage with which it plainly states unpleasant (and unpopular) truths. I don't know what sort of press it will recieve [*sic*] (and probably never <u>will</u> know, since I am leading such an incommunicado life), but I suspect, in fact I am darn sure, this novel will arouse the meanest sort of wrath in certain quarters.

I hope it does—final proof you have <u>done</u> something. However, you

---

[1] His words were prophetic. *To Kill a Mockingbird* won not only critical acclaim, including the Pulitzer Prize for fiction in 1961, but enormous commercial success as well.

[2] William Styron and his future wife, Rose, were on their first date in late October 1952 when they first met Capote—with Lola perched on his shoulder—at the bar of the Hotel Excelsior in Rome. At the time Styron was the author of a single novel, *Lie Down in Darkness* (1951). Capote and Styron held each other in high regard and always commented favorably on each other's works.

[3] Styron's novel *Set This House on Fire*, about American expatriates in Italy in the 1950s, was published by Random House on May 4, 1960.

have never been subjected to any concentrated critical abuse, and it can be exceedingly painful: I know, God knows I do. If such happens, simply remember that you are the rarest thing going, a good artist—which is why you will upset a good many so-called colleagues. But perhaps I am mistaken; perhaps for once the Enemy will lay aside their weapons and give a good writer the praise he deserves. But either way, and whatever happens, you win. Again, my very real congratulations—

Truman

P.S. I have a quite charming house (in case you come to Spain). Will be here until end of Sept. Please give my regards to your wife.

[Collection Perkins Library, Duke University]

TO ALVIN AND MARIE DEWEY

[Playa de Aro, Spain]
[Mid-June 1960]

Dear ones—

As you can see, the Selznick Co. is at your service.[1] Shirley Harden is David's assistant, a wonderful girl. So, even if they are not in Hollywood, she will arrange everything. Have her arrange for a special tour of CBS' Television City. Anyway, you are in very good hands and I know it will be fun.

I love your letters, Marie. They are so evocative—I can hear, smell, see everything you're all doing.

Very interesting about Perry. Please let me know everything you hear about the two of them.[2]

Alvin was so right when he said "How are you ever going to make a book out of this chaos?" Well, it may take years, but it will be one. But it is like doing the finest needlework—

I love you each and all. Special regards to Mother Dewey. Hugs—

T

[Collection New York Public Library]

---

[1] This letter was written at the bottom of a letter to Capote, dated June 14, 1960, from Selznick's assistant, Shirley Harden.

[2] The "two of them" were Perry Smith and Dick Hickock.

TO DONALD CULLIVAN[1]

"Az-Zahara"
Playa de Aro
Costa Brava, Spain
20 June 1960

Dear Don—

May I bother you again?

First, news: for the last 5 weeks Perry has been on a hunger-strike, having announced: "Dick can wait for the rope, but I'm going to beat it." He has touched neither food nor water, has lost 40 pounds and is in the prison hospital being fed intravenously.

Now, here is my problem, which is a technical one: no part of the book is narrated in the first-person—that is, "I" do not, and technically cannot, appear. Now, toward the end of the book, I want to include a long scene between you and Perry in which I will use some material from my <u>own</u> conversations with Perry—in other words, substitute you for me. This specific scene will revolve around the quail-dinner (?) Mrs. Meier[2] served you in his cell. What I need from you is a detailed physical description of the scene—what did Mrs. M. serve, how was the table set etc. All and anything you remember. Also, it is during this scene that Perry will tell, as he did tell you, his last and final version of what happened in the Clutter house.[3]

As I wrote, the work goes well but very slowly. It is like doing the finest needlepoint. I have now promised to deliver the final manuscript a year from this October. I have a short story in the July issue of "Esquire" which may amuse you.[4]

Hope this finds you well—

Best

Truman

[Collection Donald Cullivan]

---

[1] Donald Cullivan was a Boston engineer and former army acquaintance of Perry Smith. Cullivan befriended Smith when he was in jail and served as a character witness at his trial.

[2] Josephine Meier was the wife of Finney County undersheriff Wendle Meier.

[3] This scene appears in *In Cold Blood*, pp. 288–292 (Random House, 1966).

[4] "Among the Paths to Eden."

TO BENNETT CERF

"Az-Zahara"
Condado de San Jorge
Playa de Aro
Costa Brava, Spain
27 June 1960

Dear Bennett,

A suggestion: Cecil Beaton, who is free to go to any publisher, has put together a huge book made up of excerpts from his diary; I've read it, and it is very indiscreet, very funny, sometimes quite touching, and relentlessly honest: spares no one, especially himself. I think RH should be interested. So why don't you write him: 8 Pelham Place, London.

I'm all right. Living quietly; see literally no one; and am totally concentrated on IN COLD BLOOD. My enthusiasm is as high as ever. No, higher. It is going to be a masterpiece: I mean that. Because if it isn't, then it's nothing, and I shall have wasted two or three years. But—I have great confidence; and that is not always the case.

I have a story in the July "Esquire" . . . if you have time, please read it.

I liked Styron's book, or rather I liked much of it, and am surprised that it should have had, on the whole, such a poor critical reception.

Haven't recieved [sic] my June royalty statement; hope it was sent to Spain and not to Brooklyn . . . though I suppose it will eventually be forwarded.

And how is my darling Phyllis, my bright particular treasure? Give her my love. Best to Don K [Klopfer].[1]

Affectionately,
Truman

[Collection Columbia University Library]

---

[1] Klopfer and Cerf were the co-founders of Random House.

TO NEWTON ARVIN

> "Az-Zahara"
> Condado de San Jorge
> Playa de Aro
> Costa Brava, Spain
> [25–31 July 1960]

Sweet Sige—

Not 'Branca': 'Brava' (the wild coast): otherwise, all correct, and your gratifying letter arrived safely. "Az-zahara" means 'blossoming'. So here I am blossoming on the wild coast—a strange part of Spain, which is a strange country in any event. I will be here until October, then going else-where, maybe Switzerland. Because I don't want to go home until I have finished my Kansas book, and as it is very long (I should think 150–200 thousand words) that may take another year or more. I don't care—it has to be perfect, for I am very excited about it, totally dedicated, and believe, if I am very patient, it could be a kind of masterpiece: God knows I have wonderful material, and lots of it—over 4,000 typed-pages of notes. Some-times, when I think how good it <u>could</u> be, I can hardly breathe. Well, the whole thing was the most interesting experience of my life, and indeed has changed my life, altered my point of view about almost everything—it is a Big Work, believe me, and if I fail I still will have succeeded.

Sorry to have run on so! I hope you have got launched on the Emerson. Will you be going away at all this summer? Perhaps with Ned [Spofford]?[1] Give Ned my good wishes—I like him very much. By the way, I <u>was</u> in Kansas until mid-April, and after leaving, came almost directly here. I have a short story in July "Esquire"—rather slight, but you might look at it if you have time. Write me when you can, dearest Sige. Meanwhile, hugs and much love

> T

[Collection Smith College Library]

---

[1] Ned Spofford was a colleague and intimate friend of Arvin's at Smith.

TO DONALD CULLIVAN

[Playa de Aro, Spain]
27 July 1960

Dear Don—
Perfect: that was exactly what I wanted—very well observed, and written. Thank you (once again!).
As for the Meiers—no, their kindness only reflects upon them favorably. Don't worry.
Will send more news of Perry when it arrives—I now have a direct-line of communication with him. But he is quite incoherent, and I think it probable he will be declared insane.
My regards to your wife; gratefully, and always
Truman

[Collection Donald Cullivan]

TO ALVIN AND MARIE DEWEY

[Postcard]   [Playa de Aro, Spain]
                                              July 29 [1960]

Dear ones,
Hope California was great fun. Have sent (via a friend, who will mail it from N.Y) the matador sword for Dewey. But please be careful—it is very sharp. Am going to London for 3 days to talk to a psychiatrist from Menningers who has been examining Perry & Dick and who is now on vacation in England. Will write letter about it. Love
    T

[Collection New York Public Library]

TO ALVIN AND MARIE DEWEY

[Playa de Aro, Spain]
12 August 19[60]

Darling hearts—

So glad you enjoyed your California trip. Had a letter from Jennifer, who adored you both; so did David.

Just back from London, where I went to talk to Dr. Joseph Satten of the Menninger Clinic. Gave me some new material on Smith and Hickock; quite interesting. He says he knows for a fact that Docking is going to commute the sentences if he is re-elected.[1]

I bought the bullfight sword for Dewey and sent it via a friend who will mail it from New York. It is a dangerous little weapon, so please be careful.

Nelle's book is high on the best-seller list; she has gone home to Monroeville for a month. And yes, my dear, I am Dill. The first two-thirds of the book are quite literal and true. The trial, no.

More later. Much love

T

[Collection New York Public Library]

TO CECIL BEATON

15 August 1960

Dearest—

Rcvd. your letter after I'd come back from London; hope you are having or have had, a luxurious rest on Capri. I was in London only two days, and spent most of them talking to the psychiatrist in a horrible room in a horrible hotel called the Cumberland: however, he was very helpful. Had a drink with the Messel-Hansens (Vaughn: "Well, you can imagine, my dear: one morning we woke up and found ourselves the uncle of queen and all that sort of thing.[2] So no one can top us now, not in England. We're getting

---

[1] George Docking, the governor of Kansas, was not reelected.

[2] Oliver Messel, who had designed the sets for *House of Flowers*, was the uncle of Anthony Armstrong-Jones, who had become the earl of Snowdon after his marriage to Princess Margaret a few months earlier, in the spring of 1960. Vagn (not Vaughn) Riis-Hansen was Messel's Danish companion. Professional rivals, Beaton and Messel were, by an odd coincidence, London neighbors. Beaton lived at 8 Pelham Place, Messel at No. 17.

10,000 pounds just to do Liz's clothes for Cleopatra[1] etc & etc.") and a dinner with Jamie Hamilton—oh, the <u>boredom</u> of him![2] And that was that. I did miss your not being there, and do wish you could come here before going to N.Y., but guess you've used up all your holiday. Have had several letters from various sources making mention, mostly flattering, of That Person:[3] "Everybody in London knows that he (you) is in love with her, but she has several suitors and seems undecided; her friends think he will wait awhile." So I gather matters are still where they were. The weather here is wonderful (but London, my God: rain, rain, I thought it was <u>winter</u>), and my work goes well. We are negotiating for a little chalet, or apartment, in VERBIERS [sic], which is not too far from Lausanne—and will move to Switzerland in early November. So I hope you will come to see us in the snow. Try to send a line before setting off for N.Y. Jack sends love. Mille tendresse [sic]

T

[Collection St. John's College, Cambridge University]

TO ANDREW LYNDON

[Playa de Aro, Spain]
6 Sept 1960

Angel,

I should not have thought it possible to be shocked without being <u>surprised</u>: still, that was my reaction to this tragic news.[4] For it is tragic, and so inexplicable: why, indeed, did he have to tell ALL, especially why implicate by name all these others (poor Ned Spofford, a gentle, charming, gifted boy:

---

[1] Messel was designing the costumes for the movie *Cleopatra,* directed by Joseph Mankiewicz and starring Elizabeth Taylor and Richard Burton. He was, however, later replaced.

[2] Jamie Hamilton was Hamish Hamilton, Capote's British publisher.

[3] That person was June Osborn.

[4] The tragic news was the arrest of Newton Arvin. Acting on information from a raid on a publisher of pornography, on September 2, 1960, police broke into Arvin's home in Northampton and discovered more than a thousand items, stories and photographs of a homosexual nature, outlawed in the Massachusetts of that era. He was arrested and charged with being "a lewd and lascivious person in speech and behavior." Though he received a one-year suspended sentence rather than jail time, he was nonetheless removed from his teaching position at Smith College. He suffered a nervous breakdown and entered Northampton State Hospital, "Dippy Hall," as Smith students called it. He avoided prison by ratting on two younger gay faculty colleagues, Joel Dorius and Ned Spofford, who were untenured; both were fired by Smith in 1961.

much the nicest friend Newton ever had)? The situation might have been "contained" if he had not done that: but now—I wonder. The last time I saw Newton, two winters ago, I rather thought that sex had taken over—do you remember my telling you about the enormous amounts of money he was spending on photographs, films, erotic objects? And I suppose the police have got hold of those famous diaries, <u>and</u> that great collection of indiscreet letters: perhaps it's just as well yours truly is living abroad. Well—what to do, how to help: I shall write Newton at once. If there is any more about it in the papers (and I have a ghastly feeling there will be a <u>great</u> deal more unless Smith can somehow silence the constabulary) please send it pronto.

Our summer has been even quieter than yours. I have been working constantly, and with great intensity, on the Kansas book. I dread it, dread having to live with this material, this "force", day after day, but am absorbed by it, dedicated to it, emotionally involved in a sense that I have seldom been before.

No, Harper is not here; not long ago she wrote that she was going to Alabama for a few weeks rest-up: poor darling, she seems to be having some sort of happy nervous-breakdown.

Dear one, I am delighted that you have been making real progress with the long story—"gloomy" or not, I long to read it: perhaps, when it is finished, you will send me a carbon?

Jack is working, but on <u>what</u> I know not: he's being <u>secretive</u>. All the animals okay. We are staying here until Oct 25th, then going to Switzerland, though exactly where is still undecided. I want to stay abroad until I've finished the book, so probably won't be home until next fall.

Write at once! I do miss you, dear heart; Jack sends love, so does

T

[Collection New York Public Library]

TO NEWTON ARVIN

[Playa de Aro, Spain]
6 September 1960

Dear Sige,
I have had a letter half-written to you for several days; then this morning, in a letter from Andrew, who enclosed a clipping from a Boston paper,

I learned of last week's unfortunate event. Well, what's happened has happened; and it has happened to many others—who, like Gielgud, took it in stride and did not let it be the end of the world. All your friends are with you, of that you can be sure; and among them please do not count me least: aside from my affection, which you already have, I will be <u>glad</u> to supply you with money should the need arise. This is a tough experience, and must be met with toughness: a calm head, a good lawyer. This combination has won-out over and again for others similarly involved. I am certain it will all blow to sea; but, meanwhile, I am most awfully concerned for you, Sige: so, if you can, please send some word.

    Love,

    T

[Collection Smith College Library]

TO ALVIN DEWEY

[Postcard]   [Playa de Aro, Spain]
                                                15 Sept. 1960

Dear Foxy—

    What a surprise! Hearing from the Master <u>him</u>self! Bless you for your help with Logan Green:[1] the result was excellent. <u>When</u> am I returning? <u>Not</u> until the book is finished: you'll probably have grandchildren old enough to read by then. Seriously, the book is going well and I think it is <u>good</u>.

    Love to Marie and the boys; always

    T

[Collection New York Public Library]

---

[1] Green was the assistant prosecuting attorney in the trial of Hickock and Smith.

TO ANDREW LYNDON

[Playa de Aro, Spain]
15 September 1960

Dearest One,

Damn it to hell—I wrote you a long letter immediately upon receiving that appalling clipping—and I <u>think</u> I sent it to Nelle's address, which is also a 403. I also wrote Newton that same day: very difficult, what can one <u>say</u>? But of course have had no reply. Have you heard any more about it?

When my letter comes back, I will simply mail it again, as it contained our news, not that there is any. I figure my book may take almost two years more, and I don't know that I can live with it that long without having a crackup; moreover, it is so painful I don't know who will ever be able to read it. As I wrote you, we will be here until the end of October, then going to Switzerland, where am negotiating for an apartment in a little town called Verbier. But nothing definitely settled.

My God, what a time you must be having in New York, what with hurricane Donna, and now Kruchchev [Nikita Khrushchev] and Co.[1] As Estelle [Winwood] said to Tallulah [Bankhead], "We're well out of that one, dear."

Had a letter from Donny, who is visiting the Baroness in Denmark.[2] With Sandy, of course: Christ, what a suck that Sandy is. I gather they are both rather peeved with me because I wouldn't write a blurb for that boring novel of his about T.W. [Tennessee Williams].[3] Still, I will always like Donny.

Darling, I hope your long story goes well; write me soon, real soon. All animals are fine, and send you a lick. Jack says hello and love. Many, many hugs, dearheart—

T

[Collection New York Public Library]

---

[1] Khrushchev, the Soviet Union's premier, was attending a United Nations conference in New York.

[2] The baroness was Isak Dinesen, the Danish author of *Out of Africa* and a friend of Capote's.

[3] *The Hero Continues.*

TO NEWTON ARVIN

[Playa de Aro, Spain]
Sept 16 1960

Dear Sige,

Was not only happy to have your note this morning—it also <u>made</u> me happy: of course your friends are crowding round—you are very much loved. I wish I were in America, so that I could come to visit you.

I am hanging on here until October 25th—hoping to reach a certain point in my work; and then am going to some quiet village in Switzerland—I think Verbier: but am not certain. In any event, I will be in touch, and will write you long before I leave.

Take care! Love,

T

[Collection Smith College Library]

TO RICHARD AVEDON

Playa de Aro
Costa Brava,
Spain
22 September 1960

Dickaboo—

Your silence has been noticed, and <u>noted</u>. Though I'm sure you have adequate excuse: read where you had taken <u>all</u> the photographs in the September Bazaar, and, aside from that, have done so most stunningly.

Finally received those due-last-April royalties from Simon & Schuster—had decided they were either crooked or bankrupt. (something wrong with this pen).

I have been working steadily; it couldn't be more difficult, or go more slowly, but what I've done so far seems to me quite good. Am in constant, almost daily, contact with Kansas, and much (too much to tell in a letter) has happened.[1] Perry and Dick are still awaiting the outcome of their ap-

---

[1] Earlier that year, in March, Avedon had joined Capote on a trip to Kansas, where he photographed Perry Smith and Dick Hickock.

peal—but Perry has been starving himself, has gone from 168 pounds to 112, and may not live to hang: in any event, he has lost his mind: believes that he is in continuous communication with God, and that God is a great bird hovering above him and waiting to wrap him in His wings. Poor old Mr. Hickock died—of cancer. What an appalling and terrible story it is! This is the last time I am ever going to write "a reportage."

I will not be in New York this year as I want to stay abroad until I finish the book. We will be here on the Costa Brava until [the] end of Oct. After the 1st of November, the address is:

Poste Restante
VERBIER
Switzerland

Have you read Nelle's book "To Kill a Mockingbird"? When last heard from, she was headed for Alabama and a sort of happy nervous breakdown.

Dearest love to Evie. Send a line before I leave here. Miss you. Love
T

[Collection Richard Avedon]

TO NEWTON ARVIN

[Playa de Aro, Spain]
2 October 1960

Dearest Sige,

Well—at least it's over. If, as you say, you must resign from the college, I hope it is not without compensation—that would be most unfair: after all, in a few years you would have retired. And am I wrong in thinking you will recieve [*sic*] other teaching-offers? Being "on probation" doesn't mean you have to stay in Northampton, does it? Earlier in the summer, you mentioned a book you wanted to do on a subject you thought would surprise me: might it not be a reasonable idea to go to Yaddo for a while and start work? Of course, I know how hard it is to work when the future seems insecure and uncertain—or perhaps I don't, since I have always felt insecure, and simply let the future take care of itself.

Speaking of which (my future), I will be here another 3½ weeks; after November 1st, the address will be:

Poste Restante
VERBIER
Switzerland

Verbier is a quiet little village high in the French Alps; I have taken a small apartment in a chalet until the end of April, by which time I hope to have my Kansas book half finished.

One thing, Sige: when and if you need money, <u>please</u> say so; I have some, I really do, and it would not inconvenience me at all.

Everything will start to sort itself out soon. Meanwhile, know that I am thinking of you and love you very much.

Mille tendresse [*sic*]

T

[Collection Smith College Library]

TO MARY LOUISE ASWELL

[Playa de Aro, Spain]
3 October 1960

Darling Marylou,

Loved your letter. No, we never got the letter from Greece—anyway, so glad you had such a fine voyage.

I don't know—"holing up for the winter" in New Mexico sounds to me very cozy and delightful (I never remember whether it's warm there or cold—or simply <u>healthy</u>). Actually, we, both of us, are looking forward to Switzerland—at least it will be a change of <u>diet</u>. Not that I've any real complaints against the Costa Brava—it's been a fine place to work, and in fact I've done a tremendous amount on my Kansas book—whether it is worth doing remains to be seen: I think it is going to be "good"—but it will have to be more than that to justify ALL I HAVE GONE THROUGH.

Yes. Yes. Poor sweet Newton. I had a letter from him 2 days ago: he will have to resign his Professorship, and says he "doesn't quite know which

way to turn." What's to be done? I know he would appreciate hearing from you: 45 Prospect Street
Northampton, Mass.
After Nov. 1st our address will be—
Poste Restante
Verbier, Switzerland
I don't know <u>what</u> Jack is writing: very secretive. But he is fine, in very good spirit, and will write you himself. How are Duncan and Pidgy? Love to dear Aggie[1] and for you, precious one, hugs
more hugs
and
kisses galore
T

[Collection Aswell Family]

TO WILLIAM SHAWN

[Playa de Aro, Spain]
October 5, 1960

Dear Mr. Shawn—
I am leaving here the end of this month, and after the 1st of November my address will be: Poste Restante / VERBIER / Switzerland.
Verbier is a very remote and quiet village in the French Alps: should be a good work-place. Shortly after I get myself settled there, I will send you part one of my manuscript. I'm not sending it now because a) I still have tinkering to do and b) I am a coward, and want to postpone that nerve-wracking period of waiting to hear your opinion. Meanwhile, I am working on Part Two.
Have recently acquired a treasure-chest of supplementary material: the FBI's official record of ALL interviews connected with the case. I knew most everything they contained, but not in such rich and surprising detail. How I finally got these documents is quite a tale: suffice to say that correspondence with my various Kansas informants takes up half of every day.
I hope this finds you well, with all good wishes—
Truman Capote

---

[1] Aggie was Aswell's companion.

P.S. In [a] recent issue of the magazine, I notice that the writers keep comparing this and that to "soap operas"; and in the Oct. 1st issue, this occurs in no less than three departments: Theatre, Cinema, Books.

I liked very much "The Yellow Bus."[1]

[Collection Unknown]

TO ALVIN AND MARIE DEWEY

[Playa de Aro, Spain]
10 October 1960

Dear Ones—
Bless you for the birthday greeting!
Had a note from Nelle—who is now "hiding out" in Conneticut [*sic*]. Poor thing—she is nearly demented: says she gave up trying to answer her "fan mail" when she recieved [*sic*] 62 letters in one day. I wish she could relax and enjoy it more: in this profession it's a long walk between drinks.

Yes, I knew the Selznicks were Europe-bound, and I may see them in Switzerland. Did I tell you that I have finally taken a house there? A little chalet high in the French Alps. I leave here for there Oct 28th. After 1st November, and until the end of April, the address is:

Poste Restante
VERBIER
Switzerland

Be <u>sure</u> to send <u>at</u> <u>once</u> the results of the elections in Kansas—as regards Gov. Docking.

Thanks for the Audrey Hepburn clipping. They are all in New York now shooting some scenes for the picture.[2]

Question for Foxy: who found Nancy's wristwatch in her shoe—Beverly

---

[1] Lillian Ross's article in the August 20, 1960, issue of *The New Yorker* followed a group of Midwestern high school students on a bus tour of New York City.
[2] The film of Capote's *Breakfast at Tiffany's* was released in 1961.

or Eveanna?[1] Which of these two was with Mrs. Helm[2] when they realized Kenyon's[3] radio was missing?

Had a hurricane here a few days ago. Blasted windows, flooded floors, drove a large British freighter on to the beach. Otherwise the weather has been perfect: blue and still, sunny as an Autumn in Kansas.

Did you see the Sept. issue of Harper's Bazaar? Dick Avedon did <u>all</u> the pictures in it—quite fabulous.

I miss you; all four of you. Much love,

hugs too,

T

P.S. I have finished Part One of the book (which is now in 4 parts), and it is over 35,000 words—which, by itself, is more than half the length of the average book!

[Collection New York Public Library]

TO DONALD WINDHAM

[Playa de Aro, Spain]

Poste Restante
VERBIER
Switzerland
17 Oct 1960

Dear one—

Thanks again to Sandy for sending the book; I sent a card when it arrived, but think I used the wrong address. Be sure and send your London address to Verbier.

<u>Very</u> happy that you have finished a new story, and happier still that [William] Maxwell likes it.[4] Am looking forward to reading it—we get the magazine every week.

---

[1] Beverly and Eveanna, the two surviving Clutter daughters.
[2] Mabel Helm, the Clutters' housekeeper.
[3] Kenyon Clutter was the second of the Clutter children who were murdered.
[4] William Maxwell was fiction editor of *The New Yorker*.

I have finished, or just about finished, Part One of my book, and it is over 35,000 words. The whole thing will run approx. 125,000 words—or twice again the length of an average book. So I wonder if The New Yorker will ever be able to run it. Never thought that I, of all writers, would ever have a length problem. But actually, it is very tightly written, and really can't be cut (I've tried). Well, if I can't come to terms with Shawn (and I can see that they might hesitate to devote 4 full issues to this enterprise—especially since it is not "pleasant" reading, and not very "entertaining", as the word is used) my only regret will be that I have spent over $8,000 on research, which I will not be able to recover. But I shall go right on with the book, regardless: I suppose it sounds pretentious, but I feel a great obligation to write it, even though the material leaves me increasingly limp and numb and, well, horrified—I have such awful dreams every night. I don't know now how I could ever have felt so callous and "objective"—as I did in the beginning.

You are quite right: don't do anything about dramatizing "Hero" unless you get a good advance. But perhaps it would make a play—do you think so? Don't understand why the book hasn't had more reviews—I suppose it was because it was caught in the autumn tide; and, obviously, Crowell has done nothing to help.[1]

Sorry you are having so much rain. Wonderful weather here, but I am in bed with a disgusting cold.

Hope you have a delightful boat-ride to London, and that you enjoy your month (or so) there. Write me to Switzerland. Love to Sandy, bless his heart. I miss you.

Hugs

T

[Collection Beinecke Library, Yale University]

---

[1] Crowell was the American publisher of Windham's novel *The Hero Continues*.

TO JOHN MALCOLM BRINNIN

as from: Poste Restante
VERBIER
Suisse
19 Oct 1960

Dear one—

Am still in Spain, but we leave next week for above address—good until next spring. So if you <u>do</u> go to Denmark!—speaking of which, they've just published a collection of my stories with a nice introduction by Isak Dinesen.

About Newton. Have had several very brave letters from him. He has had to resign from Smith, has no money, and feels, I'm afraid, very lost. How appalling it all is. Stupid and sad. What do people in "Academia" say? Does this mean he will not be able to get another teaching job? He wanted to take refuge at Yaddo, but the board of directors, notably Morton Zaubal [Zabel], vetoed it: can you <u>imagine</u>?[1] I really want to know what the general feeling is—if you can tell me.[2] It would help in writing him if I had some idea of the real situation. I am helping him to pay the so-called fine (between us)—but I wish I could do more.

Working hard on my book and think it is good (so far). Write me to Verbier. Don't understand your reference to Cyprus. Much love—T

[Collection University of Delaware Library]

TO NEWTON ARVIN

[Verbier, Switzerland]
9 Nov. 1960

Sige dear—

Do hope this finds you free of the hospital—and, perhaps, free of Northampton, for I think you will feel very much better once you breathe a different atmosphere. I suppose we will have to be satisfied with the set-

---

[1] Zabel was a literary critic, an authority on Henry James and Joseph Conrad.
[2] Brinnin taught at various colleges and universities, including Vassar and Harvard, and would have known what people in "Academia" were saying about the Arvin affair.

tlement the college has made; but you will certainly have to take up book-reviewing in a serious style. But at least, and at last, your time is your own; and, as you have wonderful work ahead of you, that is most definitely the other side of the coin. Why not ask Maxwell about doing some reviews for the New Yorker—they pay well.

Verbier is a very pretty, very remote, very healthy, extremely snow-bound and unutterably <u>boring</u> village. But I didn't, as they say, come here to be amused: just to try and get on with this book—I've now written 35,000 words with 70,000 to go: all uphill work, and the air is getting very thin. This is my last attempt at reportage; and, in any event, if I manage to bring this off, I will have said all I have to say about the particular technique. My interest in the form was always entirely technical; it didn't, and doesn't, seem to me as though it had ever been given serious artistic attention. I think "In Cold Blood" (title of this book) has a fair chance of being a work of art—alas, I am rather too much involved emotionally with the material: God, I wish it were over. For one thing, I'd rather like to come home, but I promised myself I wouldn't until the book was finished.

Don't bother answering letters, dear Sige. I only want you to know that I am constantly thinking of you, and am right here if you want anything at all. As always, and always,

Mille tendresse [*sic*]

T

[Collection Smith College Library]

TO DONALD WINDHAM

Poste Restante,
Verbier, Suisse
9 November 1960

Dear Donny,

Do hope you had a nice crossing, and this finds you snug and cozy in your London 'flat'—as for us, all I have to say is Sir Edmund Hillary is looking for the Yeti in the wrong place: it's here—and <u>I'm</u> it.[1] Actually, though,

---

[1] Edmund Hillary, the first person to summit Mount Everest in 1953, led an expedition in 1960–61 that failed to find any evidence of the legendary Yeti, otherwise known as the "abominable snowman" of the Himalayas.

it's very nice: if you like lots of snow and spectacular scenery—which, as a matter of fact, I rather do. Of course Jack loves it: this sort of thing is his spiritual home. We have a <u>tiny</u> chalet, but at least (once you <u>get</u> to it: the road ends a mile away and you travel the rest by eagle) it's very warm and so forth.

Frankly, I don't think you should let Crowell do "The Warm Country."[1] If a publisher won't back you at all, then it doesn't matter how many blurbs or reviews you line up. You should withdraw it, and use your New Yorker stories as bait to lure another publisher, one with a future. If "Warm Country" is published by Crowell, and fares no better than HERO, it will do you more harm than good, and will scare off other editors. Blurbs and reviews don't mean a thing unless they are combined with promotion. If I were you, I would dismiss this phony bird-in-hand, and count on two in the bush: I think it would pay off. As for my reviewing the book—I don't quite know how one goes about getting a book to review, since I never have; but I am willing to try, though I suppose the Times would look upon a direct request with some suspicion.

Anyway, I hope the book has the English reception that it deserves, and I'm sure [E. M.] Forster's Introduction will be a great help. I missed your last story in the New Yorker, but I guess the issue will turn up soon.

We had so much luggage that I left almost all my books in Spain, and so now have nothing to read. I ordered Ackerley's book but it never arrived.

Where do you go when you leave London? We are going to spend the Christmas holidays in Munich (Dec. 18 to Jan. 8), mainly because I am going to do two Readings there (sponsored by the State Dept); then we return here for the rest of the winter.

Write soon; I want to hear all about London. My love to Sandy; many hugs—

T

[Collection Beinecke Library, Yale University]

---

[1] The American edition of Windham's *The Warm Country* was published by Scribner.

TO ALVIN AND MARIE DEWEY

> Poste Restante
> Verbier
> Switzerland
> 10 November 1960

Dear Ones,

Listened to the election returns on the Voice of America and picked up my ears considerably whenever Kansas was mentioned. So Gov. Docking was ousted! Now what? It would be rather fitting if the Court heard the appeal next Monday, the 15th of Nov.[1] Actually, when will they? And what is the probable date for the final drama? I hope you will be going, Alvin; I shall certainly require your description.

As for Verbier—they are looking for the Abominable Snowman in the wrong place: he's here, and I'm it. I have a little chalet, very cozy and warm, perched almost on the top of an Alpine peak: the view is spectacular—rather like living in an aeroplane. I have a few friends living not too far away—Noel Coward, Charlie and Oona Chaplin, one or two others. Anyway, I feel very healthy here—the air is marvelous.

Important question: What is the first name of Myrt Clare's mother, Mrs. Truitt? Is it Sadie? And when did Homer Clare die? You will die when you read the scene in Part One between Mother Truitt and Myrt![2] Very funny. Mr. Shawn was very excited and pleased by Part One—which is 35,000 words, more than half the length of an ordinary book. Am now working on Part Two, and Alvin is all over the place, and so, for that matter, is Marie.

I shall never bring up this matter again; but I am furious about that damn sword. I wrote a very testy letter to the person to whom I entrusted it, so perhaps, if he was hording [sic] it somewhere, he has sent it by now. If not, I will never trust anyone again.

I miss you. Do write soon. Love to All—

T.

[Collection New York Public Library]

---

[1] The first anniversary of the Clutter murders.
[2] Myrtle Clare, the widowed postmistress of Holcomb, Kansas.

TO ALVIN AND MARIE DEWEY

[Verbier, Switzerland]
Thanksgiving Day
[24 November 1960]

Dearest Ones—

Was so happy to have Marie's good letter. And the clippings were <u>very</u> useful. Do let me know what ruling is made as regards Hickock and the clemency hearing.

Poor Foxy: it <u>does</u> sound as though they are keeping <u>you</u> on the run. Hope things are quieter now: more time for a cozy evening with a glass of scotch.

But am sure you are all together today—around a groaning board. Jack Dunphy (a friend who is living here with me) arrived from Paris yesterday with a turkey and some cranberry sauce—so we feel right at home.

I drove down to Lausanne (60 miles) last weekend to stay a few days with Oona and Charlie Chaplin. He has grown very old—but Oona, who is a wonderful girl, seems happy, and she has <u>seven</u> beautiful children. On the way home I skidded into a truck on a mountain-pass—no damage to me, but the car got quite a dent.

Sent a congratulatory telegram to the Kennedys, and recvd. a reply from Jackie who said that at first they thought it was from Harry Truman until they realized a) Harry wasn't in Switzerland, and B) wouldn't have signed it "love and hugs."[1] Ha!

Have you seen Nov. issue of McCalls? Has an article called "World's Most Attractive Men." Think it will amuse you. It did <u>me</u>.

Haven't heard from Nelle in several weeks. She's trying to get started on a new book. I don't envy that: no harder task.

Yes, Part 3 (of <u>our</u> book) will be as long as Part I; and the other 2 parts are not short. As for their relative difficulty—they are <u>all</u> hard, as far as I'm concerned.

Goodness, I miss you. Write soon. Love to Dewey, Paul, Pete, and whatever is left over belongs to you—

T

[Collection New York Public Library]

---

[1] John F. Kennedy had been elected president earlier in the month.

TO WILLIAM STYRON

[Pension Biederstein]
[Munich, Germany]
[29 December 1960]

as from: Poste Restante
VERBIER
Switzerland

Dear Bill—

Some stationary [*sic*]! As you can see, I am staying in a <u>very</u> inexpensive Pension. Have you ever lived in Germany? I do dislike it so; but am stuck here, abed with the flu. Next week, or as soon as I get on my feet, am returning to the above address. But I did want to thank you for your note and Christmas good wishes.

I am <u>delighted</u> about the proposed film-version of 'Set this House on Fire,' especially since it is being done by such reputable people.[1] So many people have told me how much they admired the book. You are very well known here in Germany, by the way. You, J. [James] Jones and N. [Norman] Mailer (<u>if</u> you can bear the company). Though poor Mailer—!

Many thanks for the encouraging words Re my Clutter book. It is very slow going; I think it will be my last reportage—too frustrating a form.

A wonderful New Year.

Affectionately,

Truman

[Collection Perkins Library, Duke University]

---

[1] The film of *Set This House on Fire* was never produced.

TO JOHN MALCOLM BRINNIN

> [Poste Restante]
> [Verbier]
> [Switzerland]
> 14 Jan 1961

Dearest M—

We don't seem to have much luck—because I won't be here in February but in <u>London</u>. Have interrupted work on my book for 6 weeks to do the film script of "Turn of the Screw," which is being made in England—hence the London trip.[1] Oh dear—well, someday we will get together.

Your tour sounds exhausting, but fun: especially since you will not be travelling alone.

Send cards and let me know how it goes.

Much, much love

T

[Collection University of Delaware Library]

TO ALVIN AND MARIE DEWEY

> [Verbier, Switzerland]
> 16 Jan 1961

<u>Dearest</u> ones,

Forgive the silence; but the trip to Munich—as you know—was an ordeal, and to top it all my bulldog, my much beloved Bunky, died while we were there. I'd had him eight years, and loved [him] more than anything in the world. It was like losing one's child, and I wept till I could weep no more.

We returned to Verbier last Tuesday—and now I feel much better; it is such a marvelous climate, and I am already brown again from the sun.

The package you sent me (you <u>shouldn't</u> have: but how very sweet) hasn't arrived, but I'm sure it will.

---

[1] *The Turn of the Screw* is Henry James's dark novella about a governess who believes her two young charges are haunted by a former governess and valet. Directed by Jack Clayton, the movie version was titled *The Innocents*. Capote considered it his best film script.

So sorry to hear about Roland Tate.[1] I do hope he is better. He is a fine man; I like him extremely.

Have started work again on the book—I now have contracts for it with 7 foreign publishers: England, France, Italy, Spain, Germany, Poland, Japan. So all the Deweys, including Pete, are going to be world-famous. I think you'll like yourselves in the book—you're awfully nice. But I'm not so sure others will be too pleased.

Please write soon; I so value your letters, your friendship—indeed, everything about you. Love to the boys,

Many embraces

T

[Collection New York Public Library]

TO ALVIN AND MARIE DEWEY

[Verbier, Switzerland]
[27 January 1961]

Dearest All—

Am <u>thrilled</u> with my Christmas package. I love my beautifully-initialled pillow-cases, and immediately put them on my bed. And the book, aside from being the perfect souvenir, is an excellent source of information for my book. Bless you, and thank you.

Am working hard—but feel terribly restless <u>because</u> I've had to give up cigarettes (on Doctors Orders). But after 20 years of chain-smoking, it is far from easy—I can't think about anything except this horrid craving for a Chesterfield. I hope Paul and Dewey never get started.

Am off to London Monday (this being Saturday), and will be there a week.

Love to all, and many hugs

T

[Collection New York Public Library]

---

[1] Judge Roland H. Tate presided over the trial of Hickock and Smith. He died on November 9, 1963, nearly a year and a half before their execution.

TO ALVIN DEWEY

[Postcard]   [Verbier, Switzerland]
                              [Late January or early February 1961]

Dear Alvin—
    Considering that I have 2,000 pages of notes, it's amazing what I left out—but what is the name of the secretary in the Sheriff's office.[1]
    Best— Truman

[Collection New York Public Library]

TO CECIL BEATON

    [Verbier, Switzerland]
    Feb 10, 1961

Dearest one—
    Arrived back from London yesterday—and oh how glorious it seems here: such <u>sun</u>, <u>skies</u>, silence, <u>air</u>. I really do love it. If you want to come back, I have a place for you now—we <u>bought</u> a charming little apartment not far from the Parc Hotel. Am furnishing it now, and it should be ready in a month—I decided it was a wise thing to do: it gives me a European base, and is a good investment and anyway we both love Verbier.
    About London. I was there 8 days, finished the script, and saw Dr. Gottfried 5 times. I like him, and trust him. He says my pain <u>is</u> (was) angina-spasms caused by a bad case of nicotine poisoning. I have stopped smoking completely (agony!!!), and take 30-odd pills a day. I <u>still</u> have the pains— sort of like having an endless series of little heart attacks—but Dr. G. seemed very certain that I would recover. Incidentally—he said it was a damn good thing I'd been drinking those martinis as they acted as an antidote to the poison.
    I called up Eileen [Hose] and asked if I could stay at Pelham Place; alas, someone else was staying there, and she sounded so <u>nervous</u>, that I could tell it wasn't convenient. Sonia Pitt-Rivers came for dinner; I gather

---

[1] The sheriff's secretary was Edna Richardson.

the marriage is <u>not</u> a success.[1] K. [Kenneth] Tynan called by with his lady-love, Penelope Gilliatt.[2] Rather liked her. Too busy for theatre etc. but <u>did</u> see "Dolce Vita."[3] Honestly, my sweet, how <u>could</u> you have liked it? <u>So</u> pretentious, fake arty and <u>BORING</u>! actually, have many little tid-bits to tell about my London visit—but will save them for anon. Write soon. Miss you. J. sends love.

    T

P.S. Don't tell anyone about my buying apt. here. Prefer to keep that a little secret.

[Collection St. John's College, Cambridge University]

TO BENNETT CERF

    Poste Restante
    Verbier
    Switzerland
    12 Feb. 1961

Dear B—

Still here, and still working—though greatly hampered by having had to give up cigarettes (following a severe case of nicotine poisoning that damaged my heart). However, the book progresses and I continue to be completely absorbed by it.

Bennett, I must get my income-tax done. So could you please tell Somebody to send me an account of all monies paid me by Random during 1960? Thank you.

I suppose, at just this moment, you and my favorite girl, the classic Phyllis, are somewhere sipping something under a coconut tree. Anyway I hope so. I miss you both, and love you both—

    Truman

---

[1] Michael and Sonia Pitt-Rivers were Beaton's neighbors at his country house in Broadchalke.
[2] Gilliatt was a novelist, screenwriter and film critic.
[3] *La Dolce Vita* was a movie directed by Federico Fellini. It starred Marcello Mastroianni, who played a journalist who descends into the debauchery of "the sweet life"—the English translation of the title.

Several folk have written me about a dinner-party (at Afdera's); seems you sat next to C.Z. [Guest]—and the resulting conversation, as I'm told, was very amusing. C.Z. herself wrote me about it—said she thought you were "very attractive, but quite a bully!" Now really: what do you mean bullying a poor little idiot like Mrs. G.? And what did you say to her?

[Collection Columbia University Library]

TO MARY LOUISE ASWELL

[Capote]
[Poste Restante]
[Verbier, Switzerland]
2 March 1961

Darling One—

My advice is: enjoy this little junket to N.Y.—and then quietly return to Canyon Rd.[1] At any rate, my love, how can I help: much as I would like. If you were going to write the true story of Carmel and how she was pushed out of the Bazaar (and was no longer allowed to sit at the best table in the Pavillon)—ah, that is high drama![2]

Seriously, though, my entire knowledge of Carmel consists of a few dinner parties, and a half-dozen Pavillon lunches (during which I couldn't understand half of what she said—the fault, on both sides, of the many martinis).

Of course the book could be really very, very interesting: if Carmel would tell the truth about advertising, and Hearst, and the whole fashion racket. Anyway, the people who know her best (that I know) are Dick Avedon and Diana Vreeland. Both, as you know, very gabby types. Lord, I wish you luck. But if you don't really find it working out—don't be a fool: say so, and quit.

Our own news is a mixture. The worst news is—Bunky, my darling bulldog, died. It knocked me out. Jack, too. After all these years it was like los-

---

[1] Aswell lived on Canyon Road in Santa Fe, New Mexico.
[2] Aswell was helping Carmel Snow, the editor who turned *Harper's Bazaar* into a model of excellent writing, design and photography, write her memoirs. *The World of Carmel Snow* was published in 1962.

ing a child. Jack is fine—skis a great deal and looks wonderful. I am always working on my book, so don't look too great.

Give my love to Gray and Leo. They are wicked never to communicate.
Hugs and kisses
T

[Collection Aswell Family]

TO ALVIN AND MARIE DEWEY

Grand Hotel, Venezia
Sunday, March 26 [1961]
Venice, Italy

Dearest All—

Have come down from the mountains to see Spring, and spend Easter in this lovliest [*sic*] of all cities. It is so beautiful here—fruit-trees in flower, birds swooping about. We will stay perhaps a week, then go back to Verbier until April 20th; then am going again to Spain (will send the address) but not for the whole summer, only until early July.

If you are <u>sure</u> that a cuckoo clock is what you want for the new house, then I shall find one for you. They make them in Switzerland, though I believe the best ones come from Austria. The new house begins to sound as though it were almost ready to move into. When do you?

Had a long letter from Nelle, who said she was writing you, so I daresay you've heard her news by now.

Aside to Alvin: Here is a question that I can find no answer to, at least not among my notes. Which is: in Reno, when the patrolman spotted the car, and recognized the licence number, how did he know it was <u>the</u> car, <u>the</u> licence number. I mean, how did <u>he</u>, or <u>you</u>, know what the licence number was? After all, Dick and Perry stole this car, and then stole a Kansas licence plate in Kansas City. So how did you know what kind of car they were driving or, more importantly, how did you know the licence number?

All the above is rather awkwardly phrased, but I think the question is clear.

Marie, you were very dear to drive out to Valley View. I'm so glad the graves are now being marked. It haunted me that they had'nt [*sic*] been.

That was good news about Judge Tate. Though I was rather surprised, for I understood he was incurably ill.

So Lillian Valenzuela is having a baby. Well—as long as it doesn't look like the father.

It is now almost a year since I last saw you. I've missed you the <u>whole</u> time. Love to you both and the boys—

hugs

T

[Collection New York Public Library]

TO ALVIN AND MARIE DEWEY

Verbier

4 April 1961

Dear ones—

Wrote you from Venice, but came back here today and found Alvin's note, with clipping, about the May 8th hearing for S. & H. One line of Alvin's disturbed me—about the possibility of a Federal Judge giving them a "stay of execution": as with Andrews.[1] The problem is: I have reached a point in my book where I must know how the book ends! Now—do you think it <u>possible</u> that the sentence will not be carried out? I know it is an impossible question to answer—but what is your opinion? <u>Real</u> opinion?

I am going back to Spain (Casa Millar, Calle Catifa, Palamos, Costa Brava, Spain) on the 20th of April; but mail will be forwarded from here, in case you write before then.

I am looking for a really pretty cuckoo clock. Saw <u>one</u>—an antique— but it has an <u>owl</u> instead of a cuckoo. Would you like that?

This just a note. Love to all and many hugs

T

[Collection New York Public Library]

---

[1] Lowell Lee Andrews, a schizophrenic University of Kansas student who murdered his family and sat on death row at the same time as Hickock and Smith. Andrews was executed by hanging on November 30, 1962.

TO DONALD WINDHAM

[Verbier, Switzerland]
as from: Casa Millar
Calle Catifa
Palamos
Costa Brava
Spain

14 April 1961

Dear Boy—

We went to Venice for a few days—<u>very</u> few, because Jack had to leave Italy (by request): the whole thing is too much to go into, except that it is all some stupid mistake that has nothing to <u>do</u> with Jack. Anyway, the American Embassy seems to have at last straightened it all out—only who cares. Well, I no sooner got back here (Verbier) than I had a relapse and have just spent a week in a hospital in Lausanne—where my ailment was given an entirely different diagnosis from what they said in London. Seems I have a crushed spinal nerve, and that is why I am in such continuous pain. We had planned to go to Spain from now till end of June, and I have decided to go ahead with it and trust my condition will improve. Anyway, we will come back here in July, and maybe you and Sandy would like to come and visit. I <u>long</u> to see you—though I must say I'm no pleasure to be around. Only maybe everything will be better by then—God, it has to be.

Suppose you have seen a lot of the French-Cadmus trio. Hope it didn't interfere with your work—since you said it was going well. Do you know James Stern, English critic? He loved "The Warm Country."[1] Funny—I ran into Jimmy Gardiner in the airport in Geneva and he asked if you weren't a friend of mine.[2] But he didn't say he and Bobby L. [Lewis][3] were doing your play. I hope they <u>do</u>.

As usual, I've done nothing but complain. Please forgive your tiresome but always <u>very</u> loving

T

[Collection Beinecke Library, Yale University]

---

[1] James Stern was an Irish writer and critic, as well as the translator of Kafka's letters.
[2] James Gardiner was a British collector of gay photographs and ephemera, and author of books and articles on gay male culture.
[3] Robert Lewis directed *The Grass Harp*.

TO ALVIN AND MARIE DEWEY

[Palamós, Spain]
April 23, 1961

Dearest D's—

Recvd. Marie's bulletin and Foxy's "real opinion" just before leaving Verbier. Many thanks for both. As for the "opinion": I shan't be angry if it proves incorrect—I shall simply make Alvin rewrite my book, that's all.

I sent you a cuckoo clock—a modern one, rather small, not a good one, but still the best I could find: hang it in the kitchen—if anywhere. This is definitely <u>not</u> your housewarming present: I shall find something <u>really</u> good.

Took 2 days to drive here via France: lovely trip, all the fruit-trees in flower, and fields of poppies blooming everywhere.

Have taken this house until June 23rd, and am trying to find another for July and August. But a really pleasant house is rare here, and the rents are too high—I had to pay $1,000 a month last year, but if I can't find something <u>much</u> cheaper this year I won't stay. Looked at a <u>very</u> small (2 bedrooms, 1 bathroom, living room, kitchen) and rather drearily furnished beach house this afternoon and the owner wanted $600 a month! They really are mad.

Anyway, I must get down to work. I absolutely must have this book at least past the midway point by 1st July.

Marie, I liked the fabric-samples you sent, especially the flower-pattern.

Dick Avedon was in Paris the other day, and we talked on the telephone; we talked about you, and he sent his best love. He sounded as cheerful (and as <u>frantic</u>) as ever.

I know the boys must be looking forward to the end of school.

I miss you all. Love and hugs

    T

[Collection New York Public Library]

TO ALVIN AND MARIE DEWEY

2 Calle Catifa
Palamos, Costa Brava
Spain
22 May 1961

Dearest Both—

Was very pleased today to have Alvin's note, the clippings, and the Brief
(though you ask for the return of the latter, I don't guarantee that it will be:
can't "The New Yorker" buy another?). Speaking of which, I noticed you
spent $2.40 in postage. Why should you? Let's let the magazine pay for
these things! Hence the enclosed check: because, postage aside, I want
you to send me a telegram when, and if, the Supreme Court sets a date of
execution.

I am now half-way through the book, and have never mentioned Duane
West <u>once</u>. Of course, I guess I'll have to—when it comes to the trial. By
the way, Alvin—do you mind if I insert an occasional "Hell" or "Damn" into
your dialogue? Because, in some of your scenes, you sound too like a choir-
boy.

Well, and wasn't it fine about our dear little Nelle winning the Pulitzer
Prize?[1] She has really swept the boards.

The Selznicks are here (in Europe), and I expect to see them in July.
Jennifer is making a film on location in France and Switzerland: "Tender Is
The Night."[2]

Please send me a snapshot of the new house.

I miss you. A hug for the boys, and love to all—

T

[Collection New York Public Library]

---

[1] For *To Kill a Mockingbird*.
[2] The 1962 film version of F. Scott Fitzgerald's 1934 novel.

TO LEO LERMAN

Calle Catifa
Palamos, Costa Brava
Spain,
5 June 1961

Sugarplum,

So pleased to have your affectionate missive; though <u>very</u> sorry to hear about your leg—even if it does mean you walk now with a stick and look too distinguished. As for my own ailments—gosh, it's all so complex, different doctors say different things, anyway I have my ups and downs but am getting along fairly well at the moment. Good, I'm glad Gray has a Guggenheim (he ought to have five); though I wouldn't necessarily urge him to spend it in Europe. At least not during the summer. Crowded, everything overrun with Germans and Cockneys and grumbling, white-haired Americans. Except Greece, which hasn't been altogether chewed and spit out. You ask if it is expensive here on the Costa Brava; not really, no—but Portugal is both cheaper and far more delightful. Switzerland can be either very expensive or very not—it's quiet, a good place to work, and one does feel healthy there (though, come to think of it, I've never felt sicker in my life than I have this past winter, most of which was spent on an Alpine peak). As for September, I will be right here in Palamos until the 23rd: why don't you and Gray come and stay with us—we have an excellent cook (Oh God, since I had to stop smoking I've gained fifteen pounds). After that, we're going back to Verbier (Switz.). Actually, I'd like to come home; on the other hand, I promised myself I wouldn't until I had finished this book. Has Mina [Curtiss] gone in for politics: I mean, why else would anyone buy a house in Georgetown?[1] Jack just asked me to send you his kind and affectionate good wishes (he did really; as the years go by, his nature seems to be sweetening). Well, dearheart, I think of you often, and always hope that you are well and happy. Write soon; love to Gray,

Hugs,

T

[Collection Columbia University Library]

---

[1] Mina Curtiss was Lincoln Kirstein's sister. She did not go into politics.

TO MARY LOUISE ASWELL

> Calle Catifa
> Palamos, Costa Brava, Spain
> 6 June 1961

Dearest Darling Dearheart,

Yes, of course I will write, will <u>try</u> and write, a cameo-something about Carmel [Snow]. What I'd <u>like</u> to write about is the last time I saw her: it's such a good little study in the meaness [*sic*] of New York. No longer was she seated at the best table in the Pavillon, a restaurant she'd done a lot to create . . . oh no, she was shoved into an obscure little corner by the cash-register.[1] I'd like to write about all that, this marvelous little woman and what happened to her after she was kicked off the Bazaar. Naming names. But I don't suppose you want anything like that. I suppose the book will end on a note of continuing fame and success. But if you want the other, believe me I'd love to do it. Anyway, when must you have this? Right away; or end of summer; or what?

Jack is going to the post-office this instant; since the place is never open, I'd best take advantage. Sorry about Agi [Aggie], but hope she is feeling better. Don't work <u>too</u> hard. Jack sends much love.

So does

T

[Collection Aswell Family]

TO ALVIN AND MARIE DEWEY

> [Palamós, Spain]
> 29 June 1961

Dear hearts—

Arrived back from London yesterday, and found Marie's letter containing the pictures. The house looks <u>very</u> handsome indeed, almost as handsome as the family installed there. Does seem charming and cozy and I am

---

[1] Opened in 1941, for many years Le Pavillon was the premier restaurant in New York.

happy that you are so pleased with it. So looking forward to visiting you there.

It _was_ nice talking on the phone. If Spainish [*sic*] telephones weren't so hopeless I'd call you again.

Marie, would you please use the enclosed check to buy a bottle of Chanel No. 5 for Dolores Hope?[1] With my compliments? In honor of her 5th child. Perhaps $10. is not enough; let me know if it is more.

Yes, I was in London to see a doctor. I have been not really well since last January. However, am feeling much better now—in body, if not in spirit: I am _so_ _depressed_ by the thought of another year or more of waiting for the case to resolve itself. Please let me know at once what happens July 8—not, I suppose, that it really matters anymore, since it seems certain Dick will appeal to the Federal Court. However, I don't understand why Alvin keeps referring to the Andrews case—I don't see _any_ comparison.

Had a letter this morning from Nelle—who said she was writing you. She seems to be in very good spirits.

Much love to you and the boys and Pete. I miss you—

T

P.S. Hope you had a good visit with your mother and father.

P.S. Congratulations on solving the wheat-swindle so swiftly: that's our Foxy!!

[Collection New York Public Library]

TO ANDREW LYNDON

Palamos
4 July 1961

Dearheart—

Yes, I _am_ feeling better; have just come back here from two weeks of treatments in London, and the Doctor seemed pleased with me. Did not go

---

[1] Dolores Hope was a columnist for the *Garden City Telegram*. It was Hope, whose husband, Clifford R. Hope, Jr., was one of the town's leading lawyers, who invited Capote and Harper Lee to Christmas dinner in 1959. That invitation broke the ice for Capote in Garden City, and people who had ignored him until then were suddenly vying for his presence, along with Lee's, at their parties. Clifford Hope was the lawyer for the Clutter estate, and he later advised Capote on legal matters. He is thanked in the acknowledgments for *In Cold Blood*.

to the theatre, except one night, when saw "Beyond the Fringe," a revue that all London is mad about.[1] Perhaps I'd heard too much about it—anyway, thought it rather dreary.

The copy of 'B. at. T.' you sent has not arrived.[2] If I had one here, I'd send it to the Georgia address—but I don't.

We have a little bulldog puppy; I got him in London, his name is Charley and he's a relative of dearest Bunky.

The nicest thing about the Costa Brava is that it is <u>so</u> unfashionable. No one comes here, or <u>wants</u> to come here—except a lot of Limey milkmen and German trolley-car conductors. Will be here until September, but plan to sit-out the Berlin Crisis in VERBIER.[3] The book is half-done, and I <u>think</u> I might stay abroad until it is finished; but perhaps not.

I've not read anything by James Purdy, except, several years ago, a book of short stories, which I thought (to quote his opinion of G. Brenan's[4] novel) "interesting but unsuccessful [sic]." He (Purdy) was once a friend of D. Windham, and I remember D. telling me that Purdy was "a real little bitch." Is he? No, I guess he couldn't be or you wouldn't like him.

I've not heard from Newton since last December. I must try and find out what is happening to the poor guy.

So glad you have a place of your own up there, not only because it may induce you to work but—<u>isn't</u> there some sort of <u>naval</u> installation nearby? Seriously, my sweet, I do hope you get a lot of writing done.

Jack is fine. <u>Looks</u> great. Trim, brown, and golden haired. <u>I've</u> put on weight. Am, in fact, fifteen pounds heavier than when last seen by you.

Oh—I <u>forgot</u>. Herr Issyvoo [Christopher Isherwood] came to see me in London. Gave me the mss. of his new novel.[5] Liked it <u>very</u> much. Sort of "Goodbye to Berlin" brought up to date. It's almost <u>too</u> frank.

I miss you. I love you. Write soon.

Hugs—

T

[Collection New York Public Library]

---

[1] Dudley Moore's musical comedy *Beyond the Fringe* opened May 10, 1961, at the Fortune Theatre in London.

[2] *Breakfast at Tiffany's.*

[3] The Berlin Crisis was another episode in the Cold War. It culminated in the erection, on August 12, of the infamous Berlin Wall, which divided East and West Berlin until Germany was reunified in 1989.

[4] Gerald Brenan.

[5] *Down There on a Visit* (1962).

TO BENNETT CERF

11 July 1961
Palamos
Costa Brava
Spain

Dear B—,

I should have thought my last letter, written perhaps two months ago, would have required a reply: but no, nothing, mere gloom and silence. Ah, well—I'm still fond of you, and fonder still of dearest Phyllis; and I hope you are having a fine summer, Chris and Jonathan, too.[1]

I have a friend who wants to buy a complete set of the Modern Library. Could you please have this sent to him, along with the bill—

PATRICK Guinness
10 Avenue de la Gare
Lausanne,
Switzerland

Some idiot, <u>real</u> idiot, has been forwarding my mail from Random House addressed as follows: c/o Millar, Calle Catife, Palamos, Spain, <u>without</u> my name, <u>any</u> name: just c/o Millar. As I no longer live at the Millar house, the postman has simply been tossing these letters into the court-yard, where I found them the other day rain-soaked and illegible. Perhaps this is why I've not recvd. a June royalty statement. Please, dear Bennett, put a stop to this stupidity.

My book is bit by bit becoming a book. If it had not been for my illness, I would be further along than I am; still I am not dissatisfied; but oh dear, the amount of <u>correspondence</u> the whole thing entails—I'm in closest <u>daily</u> communication with some seven or eight Kansans.

Hugs for Phyllis and love to you both. I miss you <u>very</u> much—
T

P.S. Will be here until end Sept. Then returning to that lonely Swiss mountain: God, how you would hate it. So do I really. But—<u>art</u>!

[Collection Columbia University Library]

---

[1] Christopher and Jonathan were the Cerfs' sons.

TO ALVIN AND MARIE DEWEY

[Palamós, Spain]
[July 12, 1961]

Dearhearts—
Was very glad to have Alvin's cable, and eagerly await the details etc. Well—now we shall see. Oh I hope (hope? I <u>pray</u> on bended knees) that it doesn't go on to the Federal Court. But I daresay dear Dick is already busily filing a petition. Did you <u>read</u> the brief he presented to the Kansas Supreme Court? I got a copy of it—really, it is too absurd. I especially liked his complaining that the sentence was unconstitutional because it meant "deprivation of life."

Am sure you enjoyed the visit of Marie's Ma and Pa. How nice that they could come so soon after you'd moved into the new house.

Did I tell you—I have a new little puppy. I got him in London. A bulldog. I adore him—but my cat doesn't; and, of course, he is chewing the house down. I did move to another house, it is right on the beach, very nice. The address is just: Palamos, Costa Brava, Spain.

By the way, please send me your new telephone number.

I suppose the boys are spending a good deal of time at the swimming pool. I miss you, my best love always
T

[Collection New York Public Library]

TO MARY LOUISE ASWELL

[Palamós, Spain]
18 July 1961

Darling Marylou—
Since haste is the order, I hurry to obey: but, as you can see, it is really written without thought or form.[1]

---

[1] Aswell had requested from Capote a contribution to the book she was writing with Carmel Snow; Capote's recollections of Snow follow the letter.

Jack is fine, and I am okay. I hope you will get a rest after the book is turned in; also, hope you make some money. By the way, Carson [McCullers] was a friend of Carmel's: why don't you get hold of her? And Cartier-Bresson: he is writing his memoirs, so—

Love to Agi [Aggie]. Hugs and kisses—

T

Let me know if you receive this. The mail here has been very erratic.

CAPOTE'S RECOLLECTIONS OF CARMEL SNOW:

My memories of Carmel, my visions of her, seem all rather fugitive, I suppose because our meetings were far apart, and in different unconnected places: lunch in New York, a year later dinner in Rome. It was during one of the latter that I suggested she pay a visit to Ravello, a mountain village south of Naples where a film was being made, or at any rate improvised. I was working on the script, John Huston was directing it, Humphrey Bogart, Jennifer Jones, Gina Lollobrigida, Robert Morley, Peter Lorre were all in the cast, and the title of our small comedy was "Beat the Devil."

So Carmel came, and greatly increased what was already rather a houseparty atmosphere: Huston danced attendance, Bogart whispered dreadful things in her ear, oh she was having a "perfectly divine time, darling"; not only that, but she had taken charge of the picture—"aspects" of it. She said Miss Jones' costumes were wretched; Miss Lolloetc's worse. Her young new discovery was sent for: a pale boy seven feet tall—Hubert Givenchy, who arrived from Paris with his own small entourage. Ever gayer grew the gathering; ever grayer the producer's face. And Carmel, who had come for a weekend, stayed a week.

Then one morning she left. Just like that. No one knew she was leaving. We were quite surprised when she appeared white-gloved, and with a bonnet pinned to her lavender coif, and behind her a boy carrying her luggage. Bogart said, "Why, honey, what's wrong? Ain't we chic enough for you?"

She said, "My dear man, compared to you my life is lived in a salt-mine. No, it's just that now I must straighten my face and stop having fun." She got in her car; Bogart leaned in, and said: "Well, remember, I like you, honey. You're a very ballsy-type type." Mrs. Snow, the Mrs. Snow, regarded him coolly for a moment, then said: "Am I? Well, so are you. Bye-bye, tough boy." He said: "Bye-bye, tough gal." That was April, the Spring of 1953.

I must have seen Carmel two-dozen times over the next half-dozen years; but she remains clearest to me departing into the shine of that far-gone April day. Somehow those two automatically associated themselves in my mind, Bogart and Carmel. Is that odd?

Not really. If you think about it.

[Collection Aswell Family]

TO DONALD WINDHAM

[Palamós, Spain]
[August 1961]

Dearheart—

I was in London quite a long time (the enclosed photo is of my main acquisition there, Charlie J. Fatburger, aged now 4 months; he's a lighter-color than Bunky, and will be rather larger), but I wish I'd known you meant to stay so long in Rome—because maybe I could have got you here after all.

Anyway—<u>there</u> you are. The new apartment sounds pleasant and convenient. So glad you're not moving to the West side. Though really I don't see why you didn't just stay in Rome. Forever.

As for us, we will be here until 23rd September, then returning to Switzerland and, I suppose, will spend most of the winter there. I'm afraid I have at least another year's work on the book; with great industry, and nothing but solid luck, I might be able to finish it a year this September.

I hope, by this time, you have assembled a lot of material for [William] Maxwell, and sold every page of it. (Did you read his new book "The Chateau"? Talented, but tedious. However, after reading Mrs. McCuller's [*sic*] latest birthing "Clock without Hands" <u>every</u>thing seems brilliant.[1] Now I understand the phrase "shockingly bad." For I <u>was</u> shocked—it is unbelievably awful—the real disintegration of a mind. Truly depressing.)

Give love to Sandy. I miss you, my good and angel friend. Many hugs

T

[Collection Beinecke Library, Yale University]

---

[1] Both Maxwell's *The Chateau* and McCullers's *Clock Without Hands* were published in 1961.

TO ALVIN AND MARIE DEWEY

Palamos
16 August 1961

Dearhearts—

Thanks for the "Ruth Reynolds" story, but yes, I had already recvd. it and, as a matter of fact, was about to send it to you. This is a syndicated column that appears each Sunday in several newspapers; the subtitle is <u>always</u> "Was Justice Done?"—that, in fact, is the name of the series. It is just hack-work journalism. However, the writer does produce one piece [of] information new to me. Which is that Floyd Wells[1] <u>did</u> recieve [*sic*] the reward. True?

While we are on this subject—Marie, do you remember telling me that the first time you ever heard of Hickock and Smith was when Alvin came home one night and showed you their "mug-shots," the ones with the vital statistics on the back? Well, I want to do this as a "scene" between you and Alvin. Can you remember anything more about it (not that I mind <u>inventing</u> details, as you will see!)? Also, can Alvin send me the statistics that were on the back of the photographs? <u>Bless</u> you both.

The enclosed check is to cover expensive postage or a cable if something important comes up. When will the Court announce on the Second Appeal? Oh Lord, if only I knew when the whole damn thing would end! By the way, I am certainly going to be there <u>for</u> the end—if and when. How do I go about arranging that?

I hope you had a fine four days in Cuchara; sounds so cool and charming.[2] At the moment, I rather wish we were back in Switzerland—<u>am</u> returning there end of September, and suppose will spend the winter there, with maybe a month in Paris. Meanwhile, my house is just <u>sitting</u> in New York, costing a mint, all because I refuse to go home until the book is finished, and I <u>can't</u> finish the book.

Charlie J. Fatburger is out on the beach chasing Sister (cat)—she's not afraid of him, when she gets tired she just turns and swats him one.

---

[1] Dick Hickock first learned of the Clutters from Floyd Wells, a fellow inmate who was once employed by Herb Clutter as a ranch hand. Wells told Hickock that Clutter kept a large amount of cash in a safe at home, and described the layout of the Clutter house. Wells testified for the prosecution in the trial of Hickock and Smith.

[2] Cuchara is a resort in southern Colorado.

Summer is going, and I guess the boys will soon be back in school. Give them my love. I miss you all. Hugs

Your very own

T

[Collection New York Public Library]

TO ALVIN AND MARIE DEWEY

[Palamós, Spain]
4 Sept 1961

Dearest All—

Bless you for the letter with the beautifully <u>detailed</u> answers to my innumerable queries. I shall try and put them to good use.

So glad the Colorado trip was such fun. At last the tourists have left here and today we had a great storm—the waves are rolling across the beach almost to the front door. However, plan to stay here now until Oct 15th or 20th.

I shall write Cliff [Clifford R. Hope, Jr.] a letter about arranging for me to attend, to use Marie's excellent phrase, 'the final scene.' I do hope Alvin is right, and we will reach that date sooner than later.

Enclosed is another portrait of Mr. F.[1]—he's still chasing Sister and vice-versa. I don't [know] what I shall do when we get back to Switzerland—because then they'll both have to stay indoors most of the time.

The film of 'Breakfast at T.' opens Sept 20th in New York at Radio City Music Hall. I could have had a free trip to N.Y—the producers wanted me to come to the opening. But I decided I'd best stay here in Kansas (which, mentally, is where I am most of the time). Had a letter from Jennifer J. [Jones], who asked about you and said to give you her regards: she's just finished her picture, "Tender is the Night." Not a <u>word</u> from Miss Lee, however—not since early August.

My love to the boys. I miss you, and love you, each and all. Hugs—

T.

[Collection New York Public Library]

---

[1] Capote's bulldog.

TO ALVIN DEWEY

> Poste Restante
> VERBIER
> Switzerland
> 2 Nov. 1961

Dear Alvin,

Since writing two days ago—and after starting work again on Our Volume—I discover that a bit of Dewey Lore is unaccountably missing. Which is: prior to L'Affaire Clutter, what other murder cases have you investigated or been involved with? Other than the Bandshell Case[1] (incidentally, just very briefly, what is the outline of that case: a boy killed a transient in a lavatory and then buried him and reburied him? Alas, I didn't make notes on it and it is rather hazy in memory). I don't want <u>details</u> about other murder cases (except Bandshell), just want to know how much or little such matters have figured in your career. Mr. Shawn, who has read 60,000 words of the mss. (which is slightly less than half) and thinks it is "much the best work" I've ever done, asked me in a letter the other day: "Are those Deweys, all five of them (including the cat) <u>really</u> so charming and intelligent and warm?" The answer is: yes, of course.

Another thing: whatever became of Jonathan Daniel Adrian?[2] Was he given a sentence—or finally let go (what date?).

Hope you will be able to answer this soon, as I am actually writing the part that requires the Great Detective stuff.

---

[1] In what became known as "the band shell murder," Wilmer Lee Stebens killed Walter Mooney, an itinerant farm laborer, in the bandstand at Stevens Park in Garden City, on June 24, 1949. Stebens buried the body, then two days later dug it up and reburied it fourteen miles away. The state proved that robbery was the motive, although Stebens claimed that Mooney had made a homosexual advance toward him. In *In Cold Blood* (pp. 151–152, Random House, 1966), Capote has Stebens (spelled Stebbins in the book) bury and rebury his victim repeatedly.

[2] Adrian was a drifter bound for New Mexico who broke into the Clutters' house and was an early suspect in their murders. A shotgun and a hunting knife were found in his car. He was sentenced to ninety days in county jail on a charge of carrying a concealed weapon, but was released to relatives just four days later on January 9, 1960.

Love to all Five
From your old Friend
[Self-portrait drawing of Capote with bow tie, eyeglasses, and a halo]
↑
Namurt Etopac[1]

[Collection New York Public Library]

TO CECIL BEATON

Verbier
Switzerland
3 Nov. 1961

Dearest heart—

Jack had a cable this morning saying Joanie (McCracken) had died.[2] I always was very fond of Joanie—I cried. But after reading the cable, Jack went right on doing what he was doing (eating an apple). Which means he will be having some serious reaction later on.

Was so happy with your letter. I'd written Eileen [Hose] a few days ago (thinking you were still in America) saying G. [Gloria] Guinness had told me you were Lausanne-bound, and I wanted you to come here. But you do not mention this. I wish you could. As I have 2 apts. here until Dec 20th—our little place, and a larger apt. next door that I've rented to work in. You would like it and be comfortable. And I won't be here the whole month of January—I'm going—to Kansas for 2 or 3 weeks (research work) and New York for a few days. But you could come in February—except you'd have to stay at the hotel.

About my health. I am taking care of myself. I scarcely smoke at all—at most 3 or 5 cigs a day. I drink [unclear] by the gallon. And at the moment I feel okay—but I have, during the summer, had several "spells". And I do believe in our dear Dr. G.—but my finances are not in very good shape at the moment, and Dr. G. is terribly expensive, at least the bill he gave me for my treatments last June seemed to me very high indeed (and even so, he said he was not charging me his full regular fee!). But please don't mention this matter to him.

---

[1] As he had done with Newton Arvin, Capote would occasionally spell his name backward for fun.

[2] McCracken, Dunphy's ex-wife, died on November 1, 1961, of heart disease.

Do you mean to say Waldemar [Hansen]'s play really got produced?[1] Christ! Adored the Withers-Selznick story: she is the ultimate. I had a letter from her this summer that—well, to call it the Ravings of a Maniac is a real understatement. I read reviews of F. [Francis] Rose's book making hideous fun of it. Months ago I wrote your publisher, Mr. George Weidenfeld (who happens also to have published "Observations") and asked him to send me a copy of the Murder dictionary by Colin Wilson that he was publishing. He never even acknowledged my request—much less sent the book.[2] If you see him tell him my address here and that I would very much like to have the book.

Was much amused by the Douglas Cooper stabbing.[3] They ought to give the soldier a medal. Incidentally, does anyone know why Arthur J. [Jeffress] cooled himself?[4] (or was it simply that he took a good long look in the mirror?).

Why do you want to go to S. America? Sure, I'll meet you in Kano—if you'll tell me what and where it is.[5]

Weather here is glorious. Snow. Brilliant hot sun. And the air. I don't understand how you sea-level people can endure living down there in those dank pits!

Too bad about the Tiffany film. I doubt that I will ever go to see it.

So sorry to hear your mother is in the hospital. Why don't you give the dog to Eileen? It could come to work with her every day. Charlie J. Fatburger is (as Diana V [Vreeland] would scream) deevine.

I love you.

T

[Collection St. John's College, Cambridge University]

---

[1] Hansen had helped Beaton in several writing projects, including the diaries he was currently publishing.

[2] Capote is referring to Colin Wilson's *Encyclopedia of Murder,* which was published in 1961. But its publisher was Arthur Barker, not Weidenfeld, which may explain why Weidenfeld did not send him a copy.

[3] Cooper was a rich English art critic and art collector who lived in the south of France. He had picked up a young Algerian for sex, then refused the Algerian's demand that he hand over his watch and all of his money. Pulling out a knife, the Algerian proceeded to make three slashes in his large stomach, one vertical and two horizontal—the pattern of the Gaullist Cross of Lorraine. Though the wounds nearly killed Cooper, he recovered and lived on until 1984.

[4] Arthur Jeffress was a rich Englishman who had spent much of his life in Venice. When the duchess of Windsor asked him for a ride home after a grand Venetian ball, Jeffress was embarrassed to discover that his two gondoliers were off carousing and thus unavailable. He fired the gondoliers, who, in retaliation, denounced him to the police as a homosexual. The Venetian authorities, who were trying to rid the city of homosexuals, thereupon forced Jeffress to leave the city he loved. Brokenhearted, he went to Paris and committed suicide, leaving much of his fortune to a home for sailors, for whom he had always had a special affection.

[5] Kano is a historic kingdom in northern Nigeria. Capote never went there.

TO LEO LERMAN

Poste Restante
Verbier
Switzerland
5 Nov. 1961

Leo dear,
    Your cable arrived without a signature; even so, I was quite, and instantly, certain that it came from you, and I want to thank you, and so does Jack; it was most kind and tender and thoughtful of you. Poor sweet Joan. When I told Jack, he didn't say anything, nothing at all, He went right on doing what he was doing (eating an apple). It was a bitterly cold day, and snowing, and after an hour he went out in the snow, and he didn't come back, and didn't come back, and finally it got dark: I was very worried—but when he finally appeared I saw, I could <u>tell</u>, that he had had a long, long cry. But still he did not mention it, and still hasn't, except last night he said quite suddenly—"God, I'm glad she spent that winter on Fire Island!"
    You are a real and dear friend. I think of you often, and at the oddest moments. Like: this summer I saw a very happy looking man standing on a beach with a pet <u>owl</u> on his shoulder: and I thought of you for hours.
    My love to Gray; and always to you
    Truman

[Collection Columbia University Library]

TO ALVIN AND MARIE DEWEY

Verbier
Switzerland
21 Nov. 1961

Dearhearts—
    I am going to London tomorrow for a week—to see the doctor and attend the world-premiere (as they say) of my film "The Innocents" (<u>very</u> good; be <u>sure</u> and see it). However, I wanted at once to thank dear Alvin for the detective information and also for sending me that extraordinarily vulgar magazine containing the preposterous Hickcock [Hickock] Nations

contribution.[1] Dear God!—and to <u>think</u> that I was worried about Mr. Nations. However, some few details are interesting (from my point of view). Also, it is obvious that this 'article' has been cut out of a much longer mss. I would certainly be interested to see the original Hickcock [Hickock] mss. before Nations tampered with it.

Marie, I am so very glad to hear that your father is improving, and I hope he will be able to travel soon.

Blessings on you both, and love to the boys—

T

[Collection New York Public Library]

TO ALVIN AND MARIE DEWEY

[Verbier, Switzerland]
3 Dec. 1961

Dearhearts—

My thoughts are very much with you this weekend: I hope that the journey to New Orleans was without great difficulty, and that Marie's mother and father are safely and happily with you in Garden City. I know it must have been an ordeal for all concerned—but I'm sure it is for the best, and how nice that you were able to find a suitable house so near your own. I very much look forward to meeting them when I come to Garden City—though I'm not exactly <u>sure</u> when that will be, probably sometime between Jan 15 and Feb 15. It is wonderfully sweet of you to want me to stay with you, and I greatly appreciate it, but I think I'd better go back to my old room at the Warren, as there are quite a few people I want to talk to and it will be easier to conduct the interviews in a hotel etc.

About Nelle. I am rather worried about her. <u>Just</u> <u>between</u> <u>us</u>, I have good reason to believe that she is unhappily in love with a man impossible to marry etc. And this, combined with several other things, has reduced her to a highly nervous condition. Which is why neither you nor I have heard

---

[1] A ten-page account of the Clutter murders entitled "America's Worst Crime in Twenty Years," bylined "Richard Eugene Hickock as told to Mack Nations," appeared in *Male* magazine, December 1961.

from her in a very long while. I don't know where she will be at Christmas, but I should think with her family in Monroeville. I have written her sister, Alice, to see if I can find out what is really wrong.

Also, am quite distressed by the newest developements [*sic*] in The Case. The strange court order, and the emergence of this Wichita lawyer, Russell Schultz [Shultz].[1] These uncertainties, delays, endless draggings on—it makes me absolutely desperate.

Do hope Meme[2] survived the trip and Pete is being kind to her.

When last I wrote I was on my way to London for the opening of my film "The Innocents." I had a pleasant few days there, and the picture got wonderful reviews etc.

It is snowing here today, and skiers are beginning to arrive.

Love to the boys and love to both of you—   Hugs,
Namurt Etopac

P.S. Is Lansing in Leavenworth County?[3]

[Collection New York Public Library]

TO BENNETT CERF

Poste Restante
Verbier, Switzerland
4 December 1961

Dearhearts,

Recvd. B.'s dear letter this morning, and hasten to answer. Phyllis was quite right: as long as I live I will always be at Random House! Leave my loved ones? Quel nonsense! But I think I know (though actually I may be wrong) from whence this rumour sprang. Last summer in Spain a McGraw-Hill editor was visiting that ghastly Robert Ruark, who lives near

---

[1] Russell Shultz was the lawyer appointed to investigate Dick Hickock's allegations of an unfair trial; Shultz later resigned from the case.

[2] Presumably Marie Dewey's mother's cat.

[3] Lansing, home of the Kansas State Penitentiary for Men, where Smith and Hickock were imprisoned and eventually hanged, is in Leavenworth County.

me.[1] Anyway, he came to call (the editor) and told me all about this tax-dodge set-up they have called Manuscripts Inc. I told him it sounded very interesting, but that I had been at R.H. since I was a <u>child</u>, and was happy, and had no intention of leaving. He said well okay but I ought to think about it and that he would write me a letter with a "very good offer." I never thought anything more about it, until I recvd. the letter saying M.H. would give me, if I would come to them, $25,000 outright, as a sort of gift, and all manner of other benefits, higher royalty rate etc. That was in Sept, and I never answered it until about a month ago when I came across it and wrote him and said I appreciated their interest but that etc. So maybe this guy, counting his chickens before they hatched, told somebody he had lured me there etc. Anyway, that's the only thing I can think of.

Oh yes, I <u>did</u> get my stock dividend, and was very pleased and excited. Gosh, I wish I had bought some stock when it was first on the market.

Think you will like my version of Turn Of The Screw, "The Innocents." It opens in New York the end of the month. Send me the reviews if you can remember. No, I was paid very little for it, and only did it because I've always thought it would make an excellent film and (mainly) because the director is a great friend and someone I admire.[2] But I <u>am</u> such a fool—

Saw Bob and Arthur in London, had dinner with them in fact, and they both seemed very dandy, though (apparently) not too wild about the film he is making.

Yes, I would love to stay with you en route to Kansas. But I'm not exactly certain when that will be. I <u>think</u> around the 15th of January. About Kansas etc.—I am deeply in the dumps. There has been a wretched new development. It has been a year and a half since the boys were sentenced, and now, suddenly, because of some legal snafu, it seems as though there may be a NEW TRIAL. Which means it may be another <u>two years</u> before the damn thing is finally settled and I can finish the book. All so damn depressing. But we shall see.

I miss you both and love you with all my heart,

hugs

T.

[Collection Columbia University Library]

---

[1] Robert Ruark was the author of such books as *Something of Value* and *Uhuru*.
[2] Jack Clayton.

TO ALVIN AND MARIE DEWEY

[Verbier, Switzerland]
9 Dec 1961

Dearhearts—

Do hope this finds you all together; Marie's parents safely there and settled.

Alvin, it was <u>very</u> thoughtful of you to take the time, on the eve of your New Orleans journey, to write me a note and send those clippings.

I am sure you can imagine my reaction. Or perhaps you can't. Because <u>if</u> there is a new trial, and the whole situation looks as though it would drag on another two or more years, I will be forced to abandon the project. It is an appalling decision, after all the tremendous work and time and money spent (<u>and</u> the book already more than half finished!) But I cannot afford, even with The New Yorker's financial assistance, such a long delay; nor could I endure it mentally—this sort of sustained creative work keeps one in a constant state of tension, and when one adds to it all these other uncertainties and anxieties the strain is just too much. I'll tell you something: every morning of my life I throw up because of the tensions created by the writing of this book. But it's worth it; because it's the best work I've done. Lord, I don't know <u>what</u> to do. For the time being I intend to forge ahead—wait, and see what happens. And I still intend to come to Kansas next month—I certainly don't intend to give up unless I'm forced to.

Forgive me for sending so complaining and depressing a note. But I <u>am</u> depressed, so why fight it.

Let's see. Can't I think of <u>some</u>thing cheerful? Well, yes. It's cheering to think that before long I shall be seeing your dear kind faces. That, and the thought that we might (indeed, <u>must</u>) get very, very drunk together.

I love you all
T

[Collection New York Public Library]

TO MARIE DEWEY

[Postcard]   [Verbier, Switzerland]
                                              [13 December 1961]

Marie dear—

A quick note to say that what I wrote you about Nelle was unfounded; her father had a heart attack and she has been in Monroeville the past 2 months nursing him. She is coming with me to Kansas.

Love to all
T

[Collection New York Public Library]

TO CECIL BEATON

VERBIER
. Switzerland
9 Feb. 1962

Cecil dearest—

Arrived back yesterday from my <u>exhausting</u> junket to New York, California and (mostly) Kansas. Anyway, found your sweet letter—I am sorry about your mother, I know how anguishing it must be to watch her linger on like this. I wish you <u>could</u> come to Verbier—it would do you a great lot of good. And god knows I have much to tell you.

Two days after I left here to go to the states Jack broke his leg skiing. And the idiot didn't cable me. He's been here <u>all alone</u> trying to take care of the dogs etc. Just a nightmare. He won't be able to take the cast off for another three weeks.

I visited the murderers at Lansing Prison—an extraordinary and terrible experience. But I cannot write about it—it's something I'll have to tell you.

Don't know what to do about the summer. Am inquiring about houses on Corsica. Have you been there? Will you come? I gather it's very wild and beautiful. Anyway, I don't want to go to Spain or Greece—but somewhere I've not been.

Dr. G. is in Zurich—and I would go see him, but I can't leave Jack.

It just seems to me incredible that workmen are still in your house. Like some wierd [*sic*] comedy.

Oliver S. [Smith] is in India for 3 months. Of all people in the world, he is designing the debut party for Babe's daughter:[1] I [unclear] the model— ugh! But of course I kept my mouth shut. Had lunch one day with a new friend Princess Lee [Radziwill] (My God, how jealous she is of Jackie: I never knew); understand her marriage is all but finito.[2]

More anon.

Hugs and love

T

What happened about your trip to [unclear] & S. America?

[Collection St. John's College, Cambridge University]

TO BENNETT CERF

Verbier
Switzerland
14 Feb. 1962

Dearest B.—

Cannot say how much I enjoyed being with you and Phyllis in New York and how much I appreciated the sweetness and hospitality of you both. I hope this finds you all brown and rested from your holiday. As for me, I arrived back here to find everything rather a shambles—Jack with a broken leg (ski-accident) and etc. However, I think I've got things sorted out now, and in any event am back at work.

Now, to start with minor matters and work up—

1. It is only by a miracle that [I] recvd. my January royalty statement— it was sent to an address in Spain where I have not lived for 2 years (the same house where I found all those letters melting in the courtyard). Why,

---

[1] Amanda Mortimer was Babe Paley's daughter by her first marriage.
[2] Lee Radziwill was Jacqueline Kennedy's younger sister. She lived with her second husband, Stanislas Radziwill, and their two young children, in London. As a naturalized British subject, Radziwill had no legitimate claim to his Polish title, and neither, of course, did his wife.

when I have complained so often about this, <u>why</u> can't these people get my address straight? <u>Please</u> tell them to send everything to Verbier.

2. I am sending under separate cover the thermofax mss. of "In Cold Blood"; I would like to have this typed triple-space. Three copies. The master copy I would like to have sent to me—air-mail. The other two you keep at Random.

3. The contract with Verluisant has been signed and returned. It is the opinion of my advisor, Mr. Kurt Haller, that it would be better if Random House advanced me some money now. He suggested $15,000. Could a check to that amount (made out to Verluisant, S.A., of course) be sent to Vaduz, Lichtenstein? Mucho graçias [*sic*].

4. Enclosed, in this <u>bulging</u>-little envelope, is my stock share and the Manuscripts Inc. stuff. The Ginny referred to in the first paragraph is Mrs. [Robert] Ruark and the Bob is the Munster himself.

5. Enclosed also is the proposed contents for '<u>Selected Writing</u>.' This was not done off the top of my head. I've analyzed everything and thought it over carefully. As you see, I've included "The Grass Harp." I know that you do not like this book—but I do, really; and so do many people. Moreover, it is out of print.

Please ask Miss [Daise] Terry at <u>The New Yorker</u> for tear-sheets of the Brando piece, "The Duke In His Domain."

Ask "Holiday" for tear-sheets of the Brooklyn article. They published it under a title I've forgotten. But in the book I want it called: "A House on the Heights."

The story, "Among the Paths to Eden" was published in Esquire July (I <u>think</u>) 1960. Ask Rust Hills at Esquire to send tear-sheets.

6. About Mark Schorer writing an Introduction.[1] Before contracting him, please write me what <u>you</u> think of the proposed contents. And wait until I have replied. Then we can get in touch with Schorer.

If I write any more I won't be able to get this into the envelope. Why don't I get a <u>larger</u> envelope? Answer: this is all our simple kiosque sells.

Outside, a huge blizzard is blowing about. But I shall put on my snow-boots and try to reach the post-office. If you receive this you'll know I got there. Otherwise—

Dear Bennett, your enthusiasm for the Work In Progress was the great-

---

[1] Mark Schorer was a biographer and literary critic. His book on Sinclair Lewis—*Sinclair Lewis: An American Life*—was published in 1961.

est encouragement I could have had. I thank you truly, and only hope the
final book will be worthy of your faith.

And so—back to work!

My special love to you both

Always,

T.

[Collection Columbia University Library]

TO ALVIN AND MARIE DEWEY

Hotel Continental
Paris
[20 February 1962]

Dearhearts—

Coming over the Jura mountain-pass between Switzerland and France
the car went into a skid on an icy road, turned around twice, came to a
stop, then was hit head on by a truck that, coming behind us, had also gone
into a skid. The miracle was no one was hurt. And at least I don't have to
worry about the car anymore. From now on I travel by train.

Paris is cold and rainy—but a lot of friends here, and so I am enjoying
my little holiday. Audrey Hepburn is here making a movie[1] with Cary Grant
(who talks about <u>nothing</u> but hypnosis and vitamin pills: says they are the
two things keeping him eternally youthful.) Go to London Monday and
will report from there on the palace-visit.

Charlie J. <u>loves</u> Paris—he <u>races</u> along the streets delirious with all the
delicious other-dog smells. And everybody turns to stare at him—he really
is both comic and beautiful at the same time.

I was amazed by the clipping about Lee Andrews. I thought it would be
another few months before we got around to that again. Please send word
as soon as you know—it could have great bearing on H & S.

Love you all and miss you.

T.

P.S. Yes, am going back to 70 Willow Street[2]—it's being repainted now!

---

[1] *Charade*, released in 1963.
[2] Capote's apartment in Brooklyn Heights.

But find a nice cabin for me in Colorado and I will buy it and you can all use it. I mean it!

[Collection New York Public Library]

TO CECIL BEATON

VERBIER
25 Feb 1962

My darling friend—

When one is in the grips of raw, hopeless grief there really are no consolations, none. I have always dreaded this for you: the moment when you lost your mother.[1] I am <u>so</u> sorry, my dear. She had a very long life, and you did all you could to make it a happy one.

I am very glad that you will soon be going on your trip to Africa.[2] It is the best thing possible. When do you return? My own plans are not too definite. But fairly definite. We expect to be here until early April, then go to Corsica. Henri-Louis de la Grange (remember him?) has a house there, an old convent he turned into a villa, and he is looking for a place for us. He seems quite optimistic. Anyway, if we do get a decent place, please plan on a holiday there.

As I wrote you, most of my trip was spent in Kansas. Altogether, I was in New York only 5 days, 2 of them in bed with a virus. However, Babe gave for me a large-style party, so I had a swift glimpse of about a hundred familiar faces. Somehow they, it, the whole thing seemed quite unreal, remote. The only thing that seemed real was Kansas, and the people there—I suppose because of my work. Actually, it is rather upsetting—the degree to which I am obsessed by the book. I scarcely think of anything else. The odd part is, I hate to work on it; I mean, actually <u>write</u>: I just want to think about it. Or rather—I don't <u>want</u> to; but I can't stop myself. Sometimes I go into sort of trance-like states that last four and five hours. I figure I have another 18-months to go. By which time I should be good and nuts.

---

[1] Beaton's mother, Etty, had died a few days earlier.
[2] Beaton went on a safari to Kenya with two unlikely companions, Raymond Mortimer, an aesthete like himself, and Lady Lettice Ashley-Cooper, who was deaf.

Jack is supposed to have his cast taken off Monday.

Slim Hayward is in St. Moritz. She is going to take a flat in London, and thinks she might settle there. I do wish a nice man would come along.

I love you very much, Dearheart. Write me when you can—

T

[Collection St. John's College, Cambridge University]

TO NEWTON ARVIN

Verbier
26 Feb 1962

Dearheart—

Blessings for your sweet letter. I am so happy about the book, your book; do long to read it.[1]

No, I did not know Howard [Doughty] had at last finished, and published, his magnum opus.[2] Am not the least surprised to hear it is a first-class book—I always thought it would be, if ever he finished it. However, how fine that he is getting properly enthusiastic reviews. I must send for the book. Meanwhile, tell me his address [and] I will write him a congratulatory note.

Did you [read] Carson's novel?[3] If so, what did you think of it? I don't know why you haven't heard from Andrew [Lyndon] (yes I do: he never writes anybody)—but I can assure you it has nothing to do with the so-called 'avalanche.' I saw Andrew in N.Y. the other day and he spoke of you, as always, with interest and affection. Poor boy, his whole life is taken up by Mrs. Crane: he really loves her, though.[4]

My life is even quieter than yours—if you can believe it. I see no one month in and month out. Except, of course, Jack. I expect to stay abroad

---

[1] Arvin's *Longfellow: His Life and Work* was published in 1963.
[2] Doughty's biography of Francis Parkman, the great nineteenth-century historian, was published in 1962. It had taken him more than twenty years to write.
[3] *Clock Without Hands* (1961).
[4] Lyndon read to Mrs. Crane nearly every afternoon.

until my book is done. God knows when that will be. I may take as long as Howard.

I love you very much, my dear. And always will—

T

[Collection Smith College Library]

TO ALVIN AND MARIE DEWEY

[Verbier, Switzerland]
29 Feb 1962

Dearhearts—

Was much amused by Marie's letter today—especially the Mack Nations news! <u>Do</u> tell me more. Is it serious? Will he go to jail? I certainly hope so. Now why can't they get Shyster Shultz on the same deal? <u>He's</u> a tax-dodger—you can bet your bottom dollar.

Also, very intrigued by developements [*sic*] in the Coffin Case. Perhaps I'll have to write a book about that, too.[1]

Yes, I knew Jackie was doing the T.V. tour, and am delighted to hear it was such a success:[2] it was very thoughtful of you to write her, Marie. She knows all about the Dewey family—we've discussed you at length. She really is a very sweet girl, and is doing a good job—considering that originally she hated the whole idea. I think she loves it now.

The enclosed check is for my petty-cash account. Also, am returning the driver's application—could you send it to the people with the required 50¢ and have them send the license to me <u>in care of you</u>. That way it won't get lost. As you see, it has been notarized by a Swiss Notary.

Am still so sad about Kelly. But then, it has been a year since Bunky died and I still grieve for him. But Charlie J. and Sister are great fun—though they quarrel all the time.

---

[1] Alvin Dewey had told Capote about a bizarre series of murders in Nebraska that Capote eventually wrote about in the novella "Handcarved Coffins," published in Andy Warhol's *Interview* magazine in 1979 and collected in Capote's book *Music for Chameleons* (1980). This "nonfiction account" was actually heavily fictionalized and set in the 1970s.

[2] *A Tour of the White House with Mrs. John F. Kennedy* had aired on February 14, 1962. The television broadcast reached nearly eighty million Americans and won an Emmy award.

I miss you each and all. Hugs and kisses

[Self-portrait drawing of Capote with bow tie and eyeglasses]

also love from Charlie J.

[Drawing of a paw print]←his mark

[Collection New York Public Library]

TO BENNETT CERF

Verbier

4 March 1962

Cher B—

Was happy to have your sweet note from Palm Springs—however, do hope the weather improved.

First off, some Kansas news. It is now quite definite that the Kansas Supreme Court will reject the appeal for a new trial. The hearing was a fiasco as far as Smith and Hickock are concerned. I understand their lawyer never intended appealing directly to the U.S. Supreme Court. Isn't it absurd? Oh yes—one very amusing item: Remember Mack Nations, the newspaper bastard who has caused me so much trouble? The one who said Random House was publ. his book? Well, he has been <u>arrested</u> for income tax evasion!

Now about Mark Schorer.[1] Doubleday is publishing a book about American writers since the war; each chapter is by a different critic, and the chapter about me was written by Schorer. Which is why I originally thought of him to do an Introduction. However, he now writes me that 1) he cannot do it in 6 months, 2) he won't have anything new to say other than what he has written for the Doubleday book. Well, I don't want to wait six months etc. Perhaps we should just forgo having an Intro. (though I can see a good reason for having one). Can you think of anyone that would seem both suitable (solid critical reputation) and sympathetic (likes my work). John Malcolm Brinnin is the latter, but is he the former? Perhaps

---

[1] Random House was planning a Modern Library edition of some of Capote's writing, and he had asked Mark Schorer, a noted critic, to write an introduction.

Jason Epstein can think of someone—he seems to specialize in these types.[1] Or, as I say, shall we just drop the Intro.?

I will discuss the lay-out and appearance of the book in another letter.

The reason I have not yet sent the "In Cold Blood" mss. for copying is because I have not yet recvd. the thermofax copy that was being made for me. However, it will be along.

Verluisant sent back the contract with only two changes to be made.

Will write again within the next few days. Am working hard. Tell Phyllis I love her—anyway, she knows I do. Love—

T

[Collection Columbia University Library]

TO BENNETT CERF

[Verbier, Switzerland]
14 March 1962

Dear B.

Today, under separate cover, I mailed you the "In Cold Blood" manuscript. Please do not send my copy of this until I tell you to. That is, keep it until I need it.

I am writing you a separate letter about the Selected Writings—this is just a quick note to explain the cable I sent you this afternoon regarding Mrs. Currey's deal with the German publisher Kindler. This amazed me— to say the least. First off, I am devoted to my regular German publisher, Limas-Verlag [Limes-Verlag]. They have kept all my books in print, have worked tirelessly for me with the newspapers and critics, and succeeded in building for me an enormous reputation in Germany. I know everyone at Limas-Verlag [Limes-Verlag] personally and they have been wonderful to me. What is more, they will equal any offer Kindler has made. Aside from all else, Kindler is a very vulgar house—the equivalent of Bobbs-Merrill. It has not a single quality writer on its list. I'm not criticizing Mrs. Currey, I'm sure she thought it was for the best. Still, she ought to have asked my opinion. Whatever she has done, she will simply have to undo—because I have

---

[1] Jason Epstein was a Random House editor.

no intention of leaving Limas-Verlag [Limes-Verlag], any more than I would leave Random House. Not just for money, in any event.

Will send other letter tomorrow. I <u>miss</u> you and my sweet Phyllis—
Love to you both
   T

[Collection Columbia University Library]

TO BENNETT CERF

[Hotel Ritz]
[Paris]
5 April 1962

Dear B—

Fine. Out goes 'The Grass Harp'—but I do not like the idea of coupling it with 'Other Voices—'; I'd much rather they were separate paper backs.[1]

Alas, yes—Verluisant is down the drain. The whys are too complicated to go into in detail—it boiled down to the fact that, had I gone on with it, I would (literally) have been paying twice as much tax as someone living in the heart of Kansas. In a way, I'm not sorry. I hated the cooped-in feeling of being a tax-refugee. The hell with it. Now I can come home when I want to. And I will—soon as my book is finished, or virtually finished. Believe it or not, I am working on it every day here in Paris. I <u>thought</u> I longed to have a holiday from it—but the truth is it's the only thing I ever really think about—that truly interests me.

Have been having lots of attention—pictures, stories in all the Paris papers. All of which I enjoy.

William Styron is here—though I haven't seen him. Don't know where he's staying. 'Set This House on Fire' has just been published here, and the reviews were <u>excellent</u>.

I gather from your letter Mark Schorer did not get to read any of the 'In Cold Blood' mss. Do hope by now the Introduction business is settled.

Did you see the story in the N.Y. Times about Manuscripts, Inc.?

---

[1] He was referring to what should be included in his book of selected writings.

To get back to Verluisant. The check and content will be returned to you. Now (poor Mr. Harper!) a new contract should be negotiated directly with me, not only for "In Cold Blood" but also for the "Selected Writings." In both instances, I would like the contracts altered to give me a straight 15% royalty. However, I no longer want the $15,000 advance on "Cold Blood"—at least not any time soon. However, I would like a $3,000 advance on the Selected Writings.

About Germany: Limas-Verlag [Limes-Verlag] have offered the same terms as Kindler. Also, would you ask Mrs. Currey please to continue working with my French agent Odette Armand? I like Odette, and she is a great help to me.

Gallimard is giving a party for me tonight—at Maxims (pretty jazzy, huh?). Random House never gave a party for me—at Horn & Hardarts or anywhere else. Well, a prophet in his own country—

It is cold here, and rather rainy; and I'm afraid it will be the same on Corsica—nevertheless, I set forth a week from today.

Hugs and kisses for my angel Phyllis. Love to you both—

T.

[Collection Columbia University Library]

TO BENNETT CERF

Celui, Corsica, 26 April [1962]
as from: Poste Restante
Palamos
Costa Brava
Spain

Dear B.—

Well, as I wrote Mrs. Currey, this Corsican experiment has not worked out, so am leaving here Sunday, and, in desperation, returning to the above address—a place I really do not like, but at least I will be able to get back on a proper work-schedule, and that is all that matters. I am hoping to have the book eighty percent done by, or shortly after, Christmas; and if so I will come home for (more or less) good. Take a chance on finishing it there. Anyway, I want to be nearer to Kansas. You know, I truly am homesick; nothing could make me lead this ghastly lonely life except this book. Dear God, it had better be a masterpiece!

About the 'Selected Writings': I would like to include one more story—
"The Headless Hawk" (1946) from "A Tree of Night." Please? One reason
is, all the college kids who write me invariably mention this story. Also, I
rather like it.

About a year ago, I wrote you asking you to send the complete Modern
Library to: Patrick Guinness, 10 Avenue de la Gare, Lausanne, Switzerland.
Perhaps the letter went amiss. Anyway, Patrick has not recd. same and he
is very anxious to have the books. And, of course, he intends to pay for
them. So could they please be sent?

My love to dearest Phyllis. I miss you both excessively.

Even under the present trying circumstances, have continued working
hard, and maybe some day you will be proud of me.

So much love

T

[Collection Columbia University Library]

TO BENNETT CERF

[Palamós, Spain]
28 April 1962

Dear B—

Sent you a letter this morning, at the same time rcvd. your note about
Mark Schorer (very pleased), and the physical appearance of the book.

About the latter—

(1) I would like a black <u>cloth</u> binding.

(2) Jacket—do you remember the jacket for "Local Color", which I designed myself? It was certainly very striking and I would like to duplicate it
here. Same colors.

About my little foreword—I will send it by the first of June. At the mo-
ment am deeply imbedded in a very difficult (and very exciting) section of
"In Cold Blood." Also, there is the difficulty of getting resettled in dreary,
Ruark-ridden Palamos. Ugh.

The Kansas Supreme Court has denied the appeal, and the Judges are
expected to set a new hanging date the first week in July. Of course that
leaves the Federal Courts—but I understand the defense lawyer is drop-
ping the case. So don't know what will happen. The consensus of legal

opinions is that some final disposition will be made within the next twelve months.

I had a really fantastic, 50-page letter from Perry Smith, who somehow persuaded a guard to smuggle it out of Lansing and mail it to me.

Love to you both—

T.

P.S. If you have objections to the jacket design just say so.

P.P.S. I _did_ see Styron in Paris. I like him very much, I always have, and I hope he got home in one piece (drinking far too much). He loves you and Phyllis—but not as much as me: who could?

[Collection Columbia University Library]

TO ALVIN AND MARIE DEWEY

Poste Restante
Palamos
Costa Brava
Spain
5 May 1962

Dearest All—

Am so happy to have seen the last of Corsica (and so, I'm sure, was Napoleon)! Ugh. To top everything, someone at the hotel where we staying stole from my briefcase an envelope containing $500. in cash (my 'emergency' money), and I did not miss it until I'd already got on the boat. Do so wish Old Sincerely would trot over and make an investigation.[1]

Anyway, am back in Spain and working again, which is all that matters.

It does seem a tremendous age since I heard from either of you. Of course I know Our Alvin has been very busy giving heart-attacks to poor old ex-governors etc. And Marie, angel one, is that wretched Mr. Hope running you ragged?

Not a word from Nelle—though I read in a magazine that she'd "gone into hiding" and was hard at work on her second novel.

---

[1] "Old Sincerely" was one of his several nicknames for Alvin Dewey.

Think it's very exciting about Dale [Corley] running for Governor. Do hope he wins, but I realize the difficulties.[1]

It must be beautiful in Kansas (<u>Western</u> Kansas) just now—spring at its best and the wheat already quite tall (?). The next time I come, I hope it will be during the wheat-harvest.

Marie, I hope your mother and father are happy in their new place. It sounds a much better arrangement. Give them my best; and love to Mother Dewey. <u>And</u> the boys—I know they must be happy now that school is almost out.

I love you both. Write soon—

T.

[Collection New York Public Library]

TO PAUL DEWEY

[Palamós, Spain]
5 May 1962

Dear Paul—

As I cannot make this dinner, I thought perhaps you might like to go in my behalf. But even if you can't go either, I thought you might like to have the invitation as a souvenir.[2]

I miss you and Dewey; much love to you both—

Truman

[Collection New York Public Library]

---

[1] John Anderson, Jr., was elected to a second term as governor of Kansas in 1962.
[2] Written on the verso of an invitation to a state dinner at the White House on May 11, 1962, honoring author André Malraux, France's Minister of Culture.

TO BENNETT CERF

> Poste Restante
> Palamos
> Costa Brava
> Spain
> 14 May 1962

Dear B.

I cannot write a foreword. I've tried. I've wasted four days making false starts. There are several reasons for this, but the main one is that I am imprisoned by "In Cold Blood"—and I doubt if I will be able now to write anything else until it is finished. It is like an illness—I cannot bear to be "away" from it, as it were; and for the last four mornings have wakened with a feeling of awful sadness—knowing I must try and Concentrate on Something Else. Alas, the plain truth is I can't. I'm sure you understand.

And anyway, I think an Introduction <u>and</u> a Foreword are rather too much, though I perfectly see the commercial advantages of having the latter. I suggest the book-jacket read—

Chosen by the author; and with an Introduction by Mark Schorer.

That takes care of the fact that I selected the contents myself.

A kiss for Phyllis, and love love love to you both—

T.

[Collection Columbia University Library]

TO BENNETT CERF

> [Palamós, Spain]
> 14 May 1962

Dear Sir—

Want you to know that, at a cost to Random House of $10.82, I just rcvd. 10 copies of "Invisible Man" by Ralph Ellison in <u>Japanese</u>! Please let me know if you wish to have these books returned. Meanwhile, I remain

Most sincerely yrs.,

T. Capote

(A disgruntled stockholder)

[Collection Columbia University Library]

TO DONALD WINDHAM

Palamos, Costa Brava, Spain
3 June 1962

Dearheart—

Such a lot of good news! No, I did not see the Times reviews (and would like to); also, am delighted about the story, "Myopia" (good title).

Am working again, though for a month or more my life was upside down indeed. Corsica was a nightmare—I can't <u>begin</u> to tell you: Charlie-dog nearly died of bronchitis—and in fact has been ill ever since; somebody at the hotel stole $500. in cash out of my suitcase—and those were the <u>least</u>, the <u>very</u> least, of what happened. And the people: they combine the worst characteristics of both the wops and the frogs—ugh. I suppose it's beautiful—in a dry, grim, forbidding sort of way.

We have a <u>sensational</u> house here—very remote and right on the water. Jack has been swimming since early May but it is still too cold for me.

Was also glad to hear about Sandy's [E. M.] Forster piece. Please send me a copy when it comes out.

We may come home after Christmas. I'm not sure. It rather depends on how things go in Kansas. Just fantastic how the case drags on and on. Nothing could ever compensate me for the amount of work and true suffering that has gone into this book.

Love to Sandy. et vous. And hugs, too
T.

[Collection Beinecke Library, Yale University]

TO BENNETT CERF

Palamos
Spain
15 June 1962

Dear B.

Just rcvd. your letter containing Mark's introduction. Well, I like it. I think it's okay, though rather brief. No, I think it's all right about his mentioning In Cold Blood.

What have you decided about publication date? As I wrote you, I don't care if it is postponed until March. Indeed, I'd much rather it were rather than have it get lost in the autumn rush.

I want to have a dedication page, please. And I want it to read as follows—

For Phyllis and Bennett

I am working every day and seeing no one. The Kansas Supreme Court is supposed next week to set a new execution date for Perry and Dick, presumably the first of October. However, I'm sure they will get another stay. Most lawyers seem to think they can keep alive another eight months or so.

Isn't it wonderful about Slim marrying Kenneth Keith? He is a fine man. Very good-looking, only forty-five but a highly successful banker, rich—well, it just goes to show. She is terribly happy.

I miss you and angel P. I wish we were sitting by the pool in Mt. Kisco. Love to you both.

T.

[Collection Columbia University Library]

TO NEWTON ARVIN

[Palamós, Spain]
27 June 1962

Funny Honey Bunny—

Well, I'm happy to know your neglect was unintentional. Anyway, am delighted to know the book is done and want to hear what the publishers thought. I long to read it.

About the enclosed. Random House is doing a large Selected Writings book which they intend eventually to put in the Modern Library. They asked Mark Schorer to write a brief introduction. Will you please give me a hard, honest opinion of it? Do you think they should use it or not? What about the reference to "In Cold Blood" (Random let Schorer read the mss., or the half of it they have in their possession); does that seem to you a mistake?[1]

---

[1] Schorer wrote, "The next change [in Capote's career] will become evident when he publishes the book at which he is now at work—*In Cold Blood,* the re-creation of a brutal Kansas murder and its consequences. Thoroughly unpredictable, it will be the most remarkable change of all, and the most exciting."

As for the book itself, I've a long long way to go, another year, maybe two: oh it goes so slowly—I think you'll see why when you read it (I will give you the mss. when I come home, which I expect to do soon after Christmas).

I would like to see the P. de Vries parody of Miss P.[1] Actually, I've not seen the book yet—except the parts that appeared in magazines over the years.

Hope you had a pleasant few days with Bob L [Linscott]. He's an enigma, really; but quite a dear.

Don't bother to return the Schorer. But _would_ like your opinion soonest.

Love to you, Sige. And hugs

T.

[Collection Smith College Library]

TO ARCH PERSONS

Palamos
Costa Brava
Spain
27 June 1962

Dearest A.—

Your letter, forwarded from New York, was received this morning, and I was very pleased to have it. It is quite true that I wrote you twice to a Mississippi (sp?) address, I believe a hotel in Jackson, and had you received those letters, and replied to them, perhaps this present misunderstanding would not have occurred, and you would not think me so neglectful. Truly, I feel only affection for you and love, and I think you rather misinterpreted a letter that I wrote you previously.

I'm afraid what Seabon [Faulk] said about my returning to America in July is not true.[2] I plan to stay the summer, here on the Spanish Coast, then go to Switzerland until after Christmas. When I do go to the States,

---

[1] Peter De Vries's parody of Katherine Anne Porter's *Ship of Fools.* De Vries once famously wrote, "Every novel should have a beginning, a muddle and an end."

[2] Seabon Faulk was Capote's maternal uncle.

which will be sometime in February or March, it will be for a long stay, and I'm sure we will see each other then.

Also, it is not true that I have been working 7 years on my new book. Just three; with another year to go. It is very long, and my publishers think it much the best work I've ever done. Also, Random House is publishing this fall (or perhaps next Spring) a large volume of 'Selected Writings.' So you need not worry about my career; it has never been better.

Your reference to Seabon makes it sound as though you'd heard from him recently; or perhaps seen him. If so, how is he? He has had such a bad time, such rotten luck.

Really, I don't think you should be so pessimistic: all this talk of dying friends etc. Are you ill? No. Are you old? No. At least I don't think you could be more than 62, and I know a number of gentlemen far older than that who work all day and 'Twist' all night.[1] Seriously, though, I <u>am</u> sorry your work entails such hard physical demands. At any rate, I do very much hope this finds you feeling reasonably well and rather more cheerful.

As for me, I'm all right. I was too thin, now I'm too fat (Spanish Cooking), and will have to do a diet. Enclosed is a recent photograph from a French newspaper, so you can see for yourself.

Please give my good wishes to Blanche.[2]

A hug, a kiss, and <u>much</u> love from

T.

[Collection New York Public Library]

TO CECIL BEATON

[Palamós, Spain]
6 July 1962

Dearheart—

Rcvd. yr. sweet letter just now and hasten to say that if you prefer coming sometime toward the end of August then by all means do so. Do as you like. Any time is okay.

---

[1] Born on September 1, 1897, Capote's father was actually sixty-four. He died in 1981 at the age of eighty-three.
[2] Arch Persons's wife.

I lead such a monastery life—have no news at all. The Paleys are coming here for a few days next week. Perhaps they will have something to tell. Oh yes—I had a telephone call from New York (incidentally the no. is PALAMOS 45): a frail little voice came wavering over the wires: none other than Gloria V. [Vanderbilt]—who wanted to say that she was 1) divorcing Mr. [Sidney] Lumet and 2) coming to Europe for a month.

I hear varying reports about Slim's banker. Babe met him and thought him very nice, but said others (the Trees, for instance) thought otherwise. Well, it doesn't matter. As long [as] <u>she</u> likes him.

Could you send me the Oscar Wilde letters?[1] <u>Not</u> as a gift. I'm sure it's expensive. I will repay in pesetas.

Miss you. Love you—

T

P.S. Had a letter from Oliver S. [Smith], who said Irene S. [Selznick] had come for dinner, got plastered, and passed out for <u>Ten</u> hours!

[Collection St. John's College, Cambridge University]

TO ARCH PERSONS

[Palamós, Spain]
11 July 1962

Dear A.—

Have just rcvd. your letter concerning Seabon's difficulties. I am very fond of Seabon [Faulk] and I agree that if I intend to help him I should do so immediately. But I can't. All my money (and it isn't so much as everyone seems to believe) is in Swiss francs in Swiss banks and, for reasons too complicated to explain here, it would [be] very dangerous for me to convert any large sum of Swiss francs into dollars. I keep a very small bank-account in the U.S.A.—just enough for my personal needs. Even Joe Capote, who has gotten many thousands of dollars out of me in the past nine years, has learned that this is no longer possible. Truly, I am very sorry about Seabon's situation; and I think it's very sweet of you to want to help him.

---

[1] *The Letters of Oscar Wilde* (1962), edited by Rupert Hart-Davis.

I had a charming letter from my grandmother. Really, she is an exceptional person. Thinks clearly, writes clearly.

I hope you are having a good summer. My best wishes to your wife. Much love

T.

[Collection New York Public Library]

TO NEWTON ARVIN

[Palamós, Spain]
18 July 1962

Darling Sige—

I wish you <u>weren't</u> so modest. I would like to have seen what the reader wrote about the mss. I <u>know</u> it is a brilliant book, a real achievement, and I am happy for you as I can be.

Was glad to have your opinion of Schorer's little introduction. I was not happy about it, and I don't know quite why, but have told Random House to use it.

Was much amused by your saying Granny [Granville] Hicks thinks <u>every</u> novel is 'great'. I know he is practically your oldest friend (after Dave L. [Lilienthal]) but honestly, he is an idiot without an iota of taste or talent. Now tell the truth: don't <u>you</u> think so? Anyway, I haven't read the novel in question: Jimmy Baldwin's.[1] I loathe Jimmy's fiction: it is crudely written and of a balls-aching boredom. I do sometimes think his essays are at least intelligent, although they almost invariably end on a fakely hopeful, hymn-singing note (glance through them, read the last paragraphs, maybe you'll see what I mean.).

I've heard of the young Spanish writer but never read anything by him.

I don't like it that you are spending <u>such</u> a solitary summer—Excellent for work though it is. Where is Al [Fisher]? He hasn't <u>married</u> again?—I hope. And Dan [Aaron]? Have they all gone away.

Remember Duncan Aswell? Marylou's little boy? Well he's 25 now, and quite extraordinary: <u>so</u> bright. And attractive. And queer, of course. He's teaching at Columbia next winter.

---

[1] *Another Country* (1962) by James Baldwin.

Write soon, dearheart. Much, much love—
T.

P.S. What was wrong with Corsica? Everything; but most particularly the Corsicans, who combine the worst qualities of the Italians and the French. Than which etc.

[Collection Smith College Library]

TO CECIL BEATON

[Palamós, Spain]
26 July 1962

Dearest C.

August 25th will be fine. Let me know the flight number and time of arrival and I will have a car meet you.

Guess who is here for a few days visit? Gloria V., accompanied by a lady-in-waiting in the form of Tammy Grimes—who wears <u>mink</u> eyebrows and a leather bikini.[1] Last week the Paleys were here for a few days, so we have been far, far more social than usual.

I hope you are having a quiet time in the country.

The Wilde letters arrived, for which a multitude of thanks. It <u>is</u> an incredible book. A Revelation. Must talk to you about it.

So longing for our visit!

Hugs & Love
T.

[Collection St. John's College, Cambridge University]

---

[1] Grimes was an actress who gained fame in the title role of *The Unsinkable Molly Brown*, whose long Broadway run had ended earlier that year.

TO ALVIN AND MARIE DEWEY AND FAMILY

[Palamós, Spain]
3 August 1962

Dearest Family—

I had hoped to have a cable (about the Date) by now, or a letter—but perhaps something is on its way. When do you go on your vacation? And where? To Colorado?

Well, Gloria has come and gone and we had a 'real nice' visit. There is a new man in her life. It's supposed to be a great secret, but I will tell you because I must tell somebody: it's so fantastic. Nelson Rockefeller! Heaven knows what will come of it—it would certainly be a strange thing if they got married. Have had no other new guests except Jack and Drue Heinz (that's right: 57 Varieties) who came on a yacht for 2 days.

Hold Everything Dept.: Foxy's letter just arrived, containing answers to all the questions in paragraph One. Well, I'm glad your vacation is so near. Someday, and someday not too distant, you will come to stay with me in New York and we will have a smashing holiday!

There is a wild fox on the loose here, so we have to catch Sister and keep her in the house at night. So Sister is not very happy.

Any news of the Tates? You haven't mentioned them in the last month or two. I suppose they are in Colorado. What happened to Cap Burtis? Incidentally, what is his full name? I've never quite known. I want to send him a cheer-up missive.

I have taken a few weeks off from the book to write a piece for McCalls [*sic*]; but it does not go too well because 1) I am only doing it for the money, which is never a sufficient reason to write anything, and 2) I dislike working on anything other than the book.

So happy that my favorite detective was able to dispose of 2 of his 3 cases so swiftly.

How goes Marie's diet? I gave up on mine and will wait till Switzerland.

Love to the boys. Hugs for all—

T.

[Collection New York Public Library]

TO NEWTON ARVIN

[Palamós, Spain]
8 August 1962

Dearest Sige—

I have been wanting to write you for days, but have not been doing any writing of any kind, having had a severe attack of <u>rheumatism</u> in my right wrist. At least the doctor <u>says</u> it's rheumatism. Anyway it hurts; or hurt: some very unpleasant pills have chased it away for the moment.

Cannot believe that Marilyn M. [Monroe] is dead.[1] She was such a good-hearted girl, so pure really, so much on the side of the angels. Poor little baby. <u>God</u> <u>bless</u> <u>her.</u>

Did you read an article by John Aldrige [Aldridge] in The Times Book Review?[2] An attack on me, Norman Mailer etc.? It made me furious (needless to say) but also seemed to me a lot of shit. Just blanket statements backed up by no evidence whatever—"Capote is a classic example of precocity extended to a career"—what does <u>that</u> mean? Please tell me what you thought of this piece—if you saw it.

May I visit you next March or April for a few days? There is so much I want to talk about. Also I want you to see the mss. of my book while it is still, so to say, flexible.

About Duncan Aswell. He is teaching in the English Dept.—(at Columbia), a course called 'From Homer to Dostoievsky'—pretty comprehensive, eh? He has an apt.—but I don't know the address. You don't <u>need</u> a letter of Introduction. He remembers you <u>very</u> well. He has turned out a brilliant boy, and absolutely charming.

Hope you are finished with those worrisome chores and back with the work you want to do.

Much love, my sweet friend
T.

[Collection Smith College Library]

---

[1] Marilyn Monroe was found dead at her home in Los Angeles on August 5, 1962; she was thirty-six.
[2] In "What Became of Our Postwar Hopes?" in *The New York Times Book Review,* July 29, 1962, John W. Aldridge assessed what he perceived as the weaknesses of some of the younger American novelists, declaring that Capote's style is "indemnified by Faulkner and then powdered and perfumed by the ladies' fashion magazines."

TO ALVIN AND MARIE DEWEY

[Postcard]   [Palamós, Spain]
                                                        8 August 1962

Dear hearts—

Had a great adventure yesterday: a forest fire that burned the place next to ours and almost devoured us too. When the firefighters (over 400 of them) told us to leave the house the only thing I took was The Book and all the material pertaining to it. But the house escaped, thank God. Am _so_ unhappy about Marilyn Monroe: she was a sweet girl, and a close friend. I loved her.

Hugs— T.

[Collection New York Public Library]

TO ALVIN AND MARIE DEWEY

[Palamós, Spain]
16 August 1962

Darling Family—

Today you go to Cuchara—and I do hope it is cool and lovely and you have a very good time. Thanks for the clippings—that's a very good picture of Dewey. And how wonderful that Dale [Corley] got the nomination! I wish I could _vote_ for him.

As for Dale's theory about the execution date—yes, that sounds quite logical—though I did not realize a Governor could so dictate to a State Supreme Court. Also, I think it is disgusting to play politics in this fashion. Whatever the reason, it is really too depressing. November! My God! Will it never end!?!? Just when I thought things were moving along! Now I feel discouraged all over again. Please, will you ask Harrison what he thinks? He seems to hear all sorts of gossip in Topeka.

No visitors now, but Cecil Beaton (his photograph etc. is in "Observations") is coming on the 25th for a week. And after that (I hope) nobody: just want to get on with the book—though God knows why, since it looks like I'll never be able to publish it.

I wrote you about the forest fire that almost burned us up. It really was quite frightening—if the wind had slightly shifted we would have been caught. Though of course we could have escaped by boat.

No further news about Gloria V. and Nelson R. She has gone to California for a few weeks. As for Nelle—what a rascal! Actually, I know she is trying very hard to get a new book going. But she loves you dearly, so I'm sure you will be the first to hear from her when she <u>does</u> reappear.

I do hope Dale gets elected. Do you think it possible?

I love you all and miss you <u>so</u> much. Hugs and kisses—.

T.

[Collection New York Public Library]

TO ALVIN AND MARIE DEWEY AND FAMILY

[Palamós, Spain]
23 August 1962

Honey Hearts—

Are you back from Cuchara? Was it fun? I wish I could have gone, too.

Rcvd. today my notice for Renewal of Drivers License. Have filled out the form, sent the check, and gave my address as dear old Box 4.[1] So when it comes along you can forward it to me.

Also today rcvd. the jacket-design for the big 'Selected Writings' book Random House is publishing in March. It is very, <u>very</u> handsome—I'm sure you will like it. But how I wish it was Our Book coming out! My blood boils every time I think of that damned Anderson.[2] Although, the more I consider it, Dale's explanation doesn't seem <u>quite</u> logical. Because, after all, H & S would not have been executed before the elections (<u>no such luck</u>!). They simply would have filed an appeal with the Federal Courts. So it really doesn't make sense that Anderson would have wanted the setting of a date delayed. Does it? But then, nothing to do with the handling of this case ever makes too much sense. The Selznicks are in Europe and may visit here next month. Jennifer says she is going to retire from the screen: says

---

[1] The Deweys' post office box in Garden City, Kansas.
[2] John Anderson, Jr., governor of Kansas.

she is tired of keeping her figure. I have <u>completely</u> lost mine, but glad to hear darling Marie is holding the line! I love you all, and miss you all. Hugs
T.

[Collection New York Public Library]

TO MARIE DEWEY

[Palamós, Spain]
4 Sept 1962

Darling Marie—

Rcvd. today your sweet letter with all the clippings. It is awful of me to "panic" the way I do—but I am out on such a limb with this book that by now it really involves my entire future as an artist, and all this uncertainty, on top of the work itself, just <u>undoes</u> me. I must say you and Alvin are very patient with me, and deeply kind, and I appreciate it with all my heart.

Honey, this is just a note to enclose the enclosed: please buy Alvin a bottle of his favorite scotch—a birthday present from
Your loving
T.

P.S. Rather sad about the Mahars.[1] I'll bet there's a story there!

[Collection New York Public Library]

TO BENNETT CERF

[Palamós, Spain]
10 September 1962

Dear B.—

Yes, I think the jacket is <u>very</u> handsome: couldn't be more pleased; and thank you!

---

[1] Tom Mahar was the manager of the Warren Hotel in Garden City.

About "In Cold Blood." I am still working on Part Three (of the four parts): it is the longest, forty thousand words or so, and when I've finished (I expect in February) I am coming straight home; the book will then be more than three quarters written, and I will write the last part there. Of course, please bear in mind that I <u>cannot</u> really finish the book until the case has reached its legal termination, either with the execution of Perry and Dick, (the probable ending) or a commutation of sentence (highly <u>un-</u>likely). With the appeals still possible in the Federal courts the whole thing will certainly drag on at least until next summer.

However, I think you will be pleased with my work: if you thought the first half was exciting—<u>wait</u>! Nevertheless, it is the most difficult writing I've ever done (my God!) and an excruciating thing to live with day in and day out on and on—but it <u>will be</u> worth it: I <u>know</u>.

All my love to Phyllis, and <u>some</u> for you.

T.

[Collection Columbia University Library]

TO ALVIN DEWEY

[Palamós, Spain]
15 September 1962

Dear Alvin—

I was driving through town, and the man at the telegraph office came tearing into the street, waving his arms—as if he knew how anxious and pleased I would be to get the cable. As indeed I was. Bless you, dear Fox! You are my most favorite fellow. So: Oct. 25th.[1] At last we're getting some-where—I trust, and pray, and hope. But I wonder what will now transpire. Will Shyster Shultz continue?—or is he out of the picture? Will H & S live to a ripe and happy old age?—or will they swing, and make a lot of other folks very happy indeed? For the answer to these and other suspenseful questions tune in tomorrow to your favorite radio program, "Western Jus-tice," sponsored by the Slow Motion Molasses Company, a Kansas Product.

---

[1] The latest execution date for Smith and Hickock.

I'm glad my dear Deweys are settled down for another year of school and work and games.

I am leaving here October 1st—going back to: Poste Restante, VER-BIER, VALAIS, Switzerland. On the 15th of October I am going to Paris and London for a week or so. And I think I will telephone you from there. Just to hear all your nice, _real_ nice, voices.

However, before I leave here, I wish I could recieve [*sic*] the following information. Is your father buried in Valley View? If so, what are the dates of birth and death? How does the inscription read? This is quite important, so send a note by return mail if possible.[1]

Hugs and love to All

ME

[Collection New York Public Library]

TO ALVIN AND MARIE DEWEY

Verbier
8 October 1962

Precious ones—

I _loved_ my birthday card: bless and thank you all, especially Pete.

But I am worried about Alvin's stomach troubles. I am sure he has been to a good doctor—I hope it is better (though I know this is a long-time complaint).

Such a lot to tell. First off, we had (in Spain) the great storm and floods—1,000 dead or missing, thousands more homeless: an appalling catastrophe. We missed the worst of it but it was bad enough—no electricity, road washed out, sea-waves at the door. BUT, having survived that, we (Charlie, Sister and my friend Jack Dunphy), set forth for Switzerland—a two day drive. But at the Spanish-French frontier the most horrible thing happened. My Carte de Grise (a document that makes it possible to take a car from one country into another) proved to be outdated by five months. The French customs refused to let the car (which we filled with

---

[1] The inscription on Dewey's father's headstone is given on p. 196 of _In Cold Blood_ (Random House, 1966), and the book ends with a scene in which Dewey, having gone to the cemetery to weed his father's grave, has a chance encounter with Nancy Clutter's friend Sue Kidwell.

about 8 tons of luggage) into France, and the Spanish said if I brought it back into Spain they would confiscate it. What a dilemma! Finally we left the car at the border and took a taxi to Perpignan, the nearest French town of any size. I spent two hellish days going from office to office; they all said I would have either to abandon the car or pay a custom duty of around $1,000 and wait eight to ten days for new papers! At this juncture I blew my top. I decided to let them know with whom they were dealing. I called Paris and spoke to my friend the French Minister of Industry. And, after all that runaround, three hours later I drove the car into France with everybody bowing and scraping and apologizing like mad. I suppose the cynical moral of that little tale is: never bother with petty officials—go to the top (if you can).

Anyway, here we are back in Verbier, and very nice it is, too. Except for a brief visit sometime in November to Paris and London I expect to stay here working on Our Book until I go to New York (and Garden City) in the early months of 1963.

Dear God, do you realize it will soon be 3 years since all this started?! Yes, and I was a fairly young man when I began this book—but, before it's over, I shall be fat and bald and middleaged—heaven knows I'm well on the way.

I'm so glad the boys are doing well in school: I feel as though they were my nephews!

So Shyster Shultz is gone, and now we have this unknown Mr. Turner. Somehow I wish Shultz was still around. At least we <u>knew</u> he was a fool.

Write me! I love you all. Hugs & kisses

T.

[Collection New York Public Library]

TO NEWTON ARVIN

Verbier, Switzerland
15 October 1962

Dearest Sige—

There are certain people with whom one can be the closest and longest and most loving of friends—and yet they can quite quickly drop out of one's life forever simply because they belong to some odd psychological type. A type that only writes when he is written to, that only telephones when he is telephoned. That is—if one does not write him or phone one just will never hear from him again. I have known several people like that, and this peculiarity of theirs, this strange eye-for-an-eye mentality, has always fascinated me. Phoebe Pierce was like that: I have not heard from Phoebe in six years—merely because one day, in the nature of a test, I decided I'd wait and let her call <u>me</u>. And she never did. Never. After 16 years of the closest friendship! No quarrel. Nothing. It was just that all the mechanics of our friendship had been worked by me. But, of course, she would have behaved the same way with anybody: as I say, it's a type. Barbarra [Barbara] Lawrence is another good example. So is Jack Dunphy. And so, my dear, are you. Last winter, when I called you from New York, you said: "I was just thinking about you. I was wondering if I would ever hear from you again." But <u>why</u> shouldn't I have heard from <u>you</u>? Why, with people like you, must all initiative <u>always</u> come from the other side? I might be lonely, I might be ill, I might last month have drowned in the Spanish floods (and damn near nearly did); but you would never bother to inquire. These observations are not meant meanly; I just would like to know what makes people like you and Phoebe and Jack behave as you do. I'm sure you will write to tell me: you are always <u>meticulous</u> about <u>answering</u> letters.

Anyway, am back here bedded down with my never-ending book—now going into its fourth year. I hope you have been able to finish-up all your money-making projects and get started on the mysterious and exciting-sounding project.

Have you read the fantastic volume of Oscar Wilde's letters edited by Rupert Hart-Davis? I cannot tell you how fascinating I found them. Poor man, he was spared nothing. <u>Nothing</u>. I think it has been, or is being, published in America. If not, I will send it to you.

Give my love to Howard [Doughty] when you write him. I sent for his book, but it never came, though the bookshop claim they mailed it.

With much love, dear Sige. And hugs

T.

[Collection Smith College Library]

TO ALVIN AND MARIE DEWEY

[Verbier, Switzerland]
Sunday, 20 October 1962

Dearhearts—

What a week!—most of it spent phoning Mr. Shawn, who in turn phoned Cliff [Clifford R. Hope, Jr.], then Shawn would call me, then I'd call him again, then he'd call Cliff—on and on and hours and hours waiting by the damned phone. Finally I decided to fly over—had ticket, was packed and ready to leave yesterday when cables arrived (one from Shawn, one from B. Cerf, one from Cliff) announcing the non-necessity for such a journey.[1] So now we're right back where we started—yes? Except that I'm a nervous wreck.

Alvin, when the real time finally (pray God) comes, you <u>must</u> be there. I've always planned to use you as the point-of-view—so in a sense I'd rather you went than I did. I'm <u>shocked</u> there should be any question about it. You are the <u>one</u> person who has the most right and even <u>reason</u> to attend.

How was the football game in Lawrence? I'm sure the boys enjoyed it. You too, probably. I hope Alvin's stomach is better.

One pleasant thing last week—I spent a night at the Chaplins and saw their new 3 months old baby boy—their <u>8th</u> child! Really it's amazing: Oona doesn't look more than 22 (she's 38), and just think of Charlie!—73 years old and still turning them out!

I love you both, the boys too, and dear Pete.

T.

P.S. Thought the enclosed telegram would amuse you.[2] Rather impertinent, don't you think? Ha ha. I've found a new vet who seems to be helping Charlie J. Fatburger a good deal.

[Collection New York Public Library]

---

[1] He had been waiting for word that the execution date for Hickock and Smith had finally been set, without the possibility of further delays. But the date was once again postponed.

[2] Probably a telegram from a man at Yale who planned a party for Capote's thirty-eighth birthday on September 30.

TO NEWTON ARVIN

[Postcard]   Verbier—
                                                              25 Oct 1962

Sige—
    All is forgiven, as this pretty card should indicate. Yes, of course I shall come to see you in the spring—providing we survive Cuba, Berlin etc.[1] I shall soon write you a newsy long letter, too.
    Love—
    T.

[Collection Smith College Library]

TO CECIL BEATON

    30 October 1962
    Verbier, Switzerland

Dearheart—
    Does this find you back—though exhausted—from the mechanical excitements of Detroit? Well, I hope so; and I trust you've banked a fat check for your efforts.
    It has been snowing here for three days—very beautiful; though I worry about it on Charlie's account. However, a vet has given me a pill that does seem to keep the thing under some kind of control.
    Yes, I would love to come to lunch with La [Edith] Sitwell and the Queen Mother and June [Osborn]. Sounds tremendous! We plan to go to Paris 16 November, and I would like to come to London on the 25th. Would it be convenient for me to stay at Pelham those 4 or 5 days? It might easily not be—say frankly, as I could go to Slim or the Connaught.
    Had a letter—out of the blue—from Saint, who seems to have <u>bought</u> a very fancy house at 64th St. and Park Ave.!!! Is producing a movie; and in rehearsals with a Tony Perkins play.[2] Amazing, what?

---

[1] This card was written in the midst of the Cuban Missile Crisis.
[2] The play *Harold,* by Herman Raucher, lasted little more than two weeks. It opened on November 29 and closed on December 15.

Not sure where we will stay in Paris—if not the Continental, then the Vendome.

Am working with great Concentration—not even Cuba distracts me. Jack sends love. Love to Eileen. <u>Many</u> hugs—

[Collection St. John's College, Cambridge University]

TO DONALD WINDHAM

Verbier
2 November 1962

Dearheart—

It's 6 a.m.—I've already been up an hour: brushed, bathed, twisted for 30 minutes (my form of morning exercise), walked Charlie, and settled down with a cup of hot green mint. Oh yes, we mountaineers live early to bed, early to rise, very rugged sort of lives.

Please send me tear-sheets of the new 'New Yorker' story—I can't get the magazine here, and, though it is supposed to be sent to me each week it <u>never</u> is.

Also, months ago you told me Sandy was publishing a piece about [E. M.] Forster; I'd so like to see it.

I hope your story, the one you hope will finish the book, goes well, or is even done!

Yes, when we come home in Feb. or March we are returning to 70 Willow. At the moment am having it all repainted.

As a matter of fact, I think Sandy has the best job at the 'New Yorker.'[1] I <u>love</u> the checking dept. Mr. Perls [?] is helping me with my GREAT TASK.

Did you know J.R. Ackerley has won some terrific English literary prize?[2] Can't remember the name, but anyway it's lots of money. The prize was for "We Think the World of You." If you write him please convey my congratulations.

---

[1] Sandy Campbell, Windham's companion, had become a fact checker at *The New Yorker*.
[2] Ackerley won the 1962 WHSmith Award.

I almost went to Kansas last week—to visit my friends before the hang-man did. But at the last moment they got a stay of execution. To appeal the case in the Federal courts. All so incredible.

The English critics are treating K.A. Porter very roughly—and unfairly.[1] An especially bitchy review by Angus Wilson.

Oh, yes, Jerry [Jared French] is still in the wicked city. He writes Jack quite frequently. Jack won't tell what he says because he (Jack) says I'm a gossip (?!!!). But I think Jerry is supporting a family (or, rather, Margaret [French] is)—and sleeping with the father of it. One of those situations.

Did you see the Albee play?[2]

Miss you. Now write me. Much love—

T.

[Collection Beinecke Library, Yale University]

TO NEWTON ARVIN

Hotel Continental
Paris
27 Nov. 1962

Dearheart—

Am in Paris for a few days, but return end of the week to those impris-oning mountains. And my imprisoning book. Perhaps I will be glad to see them—by the end of the week. But oh dear, I do wish I was on my way home. Well, March is not so far away.

It is cold and rainy here, but very pretty all the same—and I am having a splendid lot of meals, and seeing a ludicrous variety of people, everyone from Janet Flanner to the Windsors.

Do you have proofs yet of your book? I want so much to read it—be sure and send me one of the first copies.

Did you read Jimmy Baldwin's long piece in the 'N'Yorker'?[3] He is a mysterious mixture of real talent and real fraud. I like him, though.

---

[1] Katherine Anne Porter's novel *Ship of Fools* was published in 1962.

[2] *Who's Afraid of Virginia Woolf?*, which had opened at Broadway's Billy Rose Theatre on Oc-tober 13.

[3] The November 17, 1962, issue of *The New Yorker* was almost entirely dedicated to James Baldwin's article "Letter from a Region in My Mind," about race relations, civil rights, Christian-ity and the Black Muslim separatist movement. The essay later appeared in Baldwin's book *The Fire Next Time* (1963) under the title "Down at the Cross."

Write me a sweet letter: that will be my Christmas present. Hugs and much love, dear Sige—

T.

TO ALVIN AND MARIE DEWEY

Verbier
5 Dec 1962

Dearhearts—

A joy to hear your dear voices the other night (or, in your case, afternoon). Such a good connection—I might have been at the Warren. But alas it makes me miss you all the more.

Have returned to work on the book with new energy and a fresh eye—I really was tired, but the little trip to Paris and London did me a lot of good. As for the Royal luncheon—there were six guests and I sat next to the Queen Mother, who is short and plump and pretty and very charming. Among other things, we talked about The Book and you and Garden City. The lunch lasted from one to three (the dessert was the best cake I've ever tasted—a sort of chocolate cream stuffed with fresh raspberries).[1] The ladies wore hats—the Queen wore an enormous red hat pinned with a huge ruby. We were served cocktails before, three kinds of wine during, and brandy afterwards. I went away with a somewhat floaty feeling. Needless to say there is a great deal more to tell but I will wait until I _can_ tell it to you (over cocktails of our own).

I see old Mac _did_ write a memo ré Lee Andrews. Not a very bright man—he contradicts himself every other sentence.

Dearhearts, please use the enclosed to buy a Christmas present _all_ the family will enjoy. Something for the house. Or whatever you want.

I love you all and send all kinds of hugs—

T.

---

[1] The English call such a concoction a "summer pudding."

TO DONALD CULLIVAN

>Verbier
>11 Dec. 1962

Dear Don—

Brazil! How fascinating for you. I was there ten years ago, and liked Rio, and really adored Bahia. Where you are going is far more primitive and, in the long run, I'm sure that much more interesting. I was there (Recife) very briefly—but it was tremendously <u>hot</u>; <u>and</u> they can certainly <u>use</u> a Sanitary Engineer!

As for Perry, whatever is going to happen will happen not too distantly. Lee Andrews, a boy who had been on death-row about the same time as P. & D., was executed last week. I just sent Perry a Christmas check and told him your news.

I don't know when my book will be published. Not for another year or so. It is quite long—it is perhaps 80 percent finished. I do hope you will like it, and I really think you will.

I can't tell you much about Nelle's new book. It's a novel, and quite short. But she is <u>so</u> secretive.

Don, do keep in touch as I want to let you know what happens. I wish you and your family the greatest good fortune in the Brazilian adventure.

Always—
Truman

[Collection Donald Cullivan]

TO MABEL PURCELL

>[Verbier, Switzerland]
>14 Dec. 1962

Dearest Grandmother—

As you see, I am here again; but will be returning to New York early March. I hope John and Frances are well, and that you all have a happy Christmas.[1]

---

[1] John Persons was one of Arch's two brothers; Frances was John's wife.

As for Arch, and all his complaining about my supposed neglect—well, I entered into a most friendly correspondence with him last spring. I wrote him a very affectionate and personal letter enclosing recent photographs of myself. In reply, with no mention of the personal aspects of my letter <u>or</u> the pictures, he wrote me a long <u>business</u> letter all about how I should lend Seabon Faulk $10,000 (so that Seabon, who has been having a difficult time, could set himself up in the scale business). I replied, in the pleasantest way, that I could not lend Seabon this amount. He <u>never</u> answered my letter at all!

Later, you wrote me that Arch himself was troubled about money. Perhaps, if he'd asked me directly to give him some, I might have done so. But that is not what he did.

In view of the above, I don't think I'm to blame for the fact that my relations with him are not what he calls "normal."

Anyway, I was very hurt by the whole thing, and when I said I had something to write you this was it. Much, much love

Truman

P.S. I was in London last week, and the Queen asked me to lunch. She was very bright and charming, and very pretty![1]

[Collection Gerald Clarke]

TO ALVIN AND MARIE DEWEY

[Verbier, Switzerland]
22 Dec. 1962

Dearest All—

Your box came this morning: I decided not to wait for Christmas, but opened it <u>right</u> away—<u>And</u> I <u>Love</u> my shirt!—A Beautiful edition [*sic*] to my collection of these jaunty numbers. It was so sweet of you, and many thanks to all four of you!

---

[1] He was, of course, exaggerating the facts to impress his grandmother. It was Cecil Beaton, not the Queen, who invited him to lunch, and the Queen was the Queen Mother, not the reigning monarch as he implied.

Guess who's here? David and Jennifer—both of whom send you their warmest greetings and wishes for the New Year. Jennifer is looking very beautiful—hard to believe she has a son [of] 22. But of course she takes such fantastic care of herself. They go back to California 5 Jan.

I had the wildest card from Myrt Clare—full of libelous accusations against the current Holcomb postmaster. Also had a card from Josie Meier, in which she said the Kansas authorities had told Wendle they would require his presence at the H. & S. executions.[1] Why on earth would Wendle be asked and not Alvin? Please let me know as soon as you hear about the Supreme Court. I've met Byron White—he's a close friend of the President's.[2] So if he doesn't get a move on—

Had a cable that our house on Willow Street is all repainted and ready for our return. I wish I were there now—it has been snowing here for five days and the drifts are so deep poor Charlie J. can't get out the door to (as I believe they say in polite society) take a leak. Or anything else.

So glad you didn't split up my Christmas present: what could you each have done with $12.50? So much better to splurge it all at the Broadmoor.

Happy New Year, and please write me some sweet loving letters. Hugs
T.

[Collection New York Public Library]

TO WILLIAM SHAWN

[Verbier, Switzerland]
December 26, 1962

Dear Mr. Shawn—
Toward the end of next month Random House is publishing a book of 'Selected Writings' from my work—both fiction and non-fiction (including, among other things, the Brando profile and the Russian pieces).[3] A great deal of work and care has gone into this book—which has an introduction by Mark Schorer. My reason for bringing the matter to your attention is to

---

[1] Wendle Meier, the undersheriff of Finney County, Kansas, had discovered the body of Kenyon Clutter in the basement of the Clutter home. His wife, Josephine, provided meals and magazines to Hickock and Smith while they were in the local jail.
[2] Nominated by President Kennedy, White was the newest member of the U.S. Supreme Court.
[3] "The Duke in His Domain" and *The Muses Are Heard.*

avoid the resentment I shall most certainly feel if the magazine treats me as it <u>always</u> has in the past: most insultingly. So if the magazine cannot review my book seriously and at some length (I said seriously, not favorably), then I ask you to see that it is not mentioned at all.

My Kansas work goes very well: I am really pleased—though exhausted. As for Kansas itself—from all recent reports I think the final outcome is not far off: ought to know by February.

I don't know whether to mail you Part Three or bring it myself. I'm not far from finishing it now. Oh God.

All good wishes for the New Year—

Yrs,

Truman C.

[Collection Unknown]

TO ALVIN AND MARIE DEWEY

[Verbier, Switzerland]
6 January 1963

Honey hearts

What a gay Christmas you had. Know what I did? Worked. Worked New Year's eve, too. Must. Otherwise I won't have got where I want to before leaving here. So I go to bed at ten and get up at four day in, day out.

Thanks for the clipping about the Clutter memorial. I contributed to the fund more than a year ago, and thought by now the thing would be completed. But it looks as if it will be quite nice.

Yes, we must talk to the Tates and McCoys[1] about Colorado. Do you know a place called Steamboat Springs?

I do wish we could hear soon from the Supreme Court. However, do you realize Perry has not yet filed an appeal? Just Hickock. I believe it's a trick to make the thing take twice as long. I've asked Cliff to investigate.

Am planning to come home by plane. <u>Provided</u> Swissair will let Charlie sit with me. He's <u>much</u> too delicate and nervous to be put with the luggage. God, what a trip—with Charlie and Sister and about a million dollars worth of overweight baggage.

---

[1] Lester McCoy was a well-known landowner and businessman in western Kansas.

Have you rcvd. the 'Selected Writings' book? Read 'A House on the Heights.' It's about 70 Willow. Mark Schorer, who wrote the Introduction, is head of the English Dept. at the University of California.

It's 7 P.M. I'm going to have a cold, cold martini. I need it.

Who loves you?

T does (for one).

[Collection New York Public Library]

TO NEWTON ARVIN

[Verbier, Switzerland]
11 January 1963

Poor dear Sige—

How awful! About your diabetes. Most of all, I would so hate not being able to have a drink. But of course I thought I'd never be able to stop smoking—but I did. And don't miss it anymore. Well, I <u>am</u> sorry honey, and I do hope you are feeling better and will take good care.

Am so looking forward to the arrival of the Longfellow. Will let you know soon as it comes. I hope the newspaper strike ends before publication day! I know it will get marvelous reviews.

My book will soon be three-quarters done (something over a 100,000 words), and I can't <u>wait</u> to leave here. I certainly intend to by the end of next month. I am weary beyond words of snow and mountains and isolation and the goddam Swiss, the ugliest race alive. The drabbest American alley would look like paradise to me.

I love you very much. All hugs

T.

[Collection Smith College Library]

TO BENNETT CERF

[Verbier, Switzerland]
14 January 1963

Dearest Bennett—

Hope this catches you before you leave for Barbados (gosh, how I wish I were going with you!). Anyway, when you get back I will have Part Three (over 40,000 words) of the book for you to read—and believe me truly you have an experience in store! But <u>before</u> I let you read it you must reread the first two parts. Part Four, in the works, is a book in itself—but at least I'm in the home stretch!

Thank you so much for sending the gift copies of my "Selected Writings."

For tax-reasons, I would now like to have a $12,000 advance on "In Cold Blood." I would like to have two separate checks, each for $6,000. sent to me here in Verbier. Mucho gracias!

Do hope you and dearest Phyllis and the Hornblows [Arthur and Leonora][1] (give them my love) have a marvelous holiday. All love—T.

[Collection Columbia University Library]

TO ALVIN AND MARIE DEWEY

[Verbier, Switzerland]
16 January 1963

Honey Hearts—

I just stopped working: I've been typing for seven hours, it's now six-thirty—my cocktail hour. Am writing you and sipping an icy-cold dry martini: lovely combination of activities.

Bless you for the Clippings and Marie's sweet letter. I guess I didn't make myself very clear. "A House on the Heights" is the title of a piece in the book I sent you, and which surely must have arrived by now—it was sent from New York, not here. The book will be published Feb. 18th—So I <u>do</u> hope the New York newspaper strike is over by then—because of the reviews and advertising.

---

[1] Arthur Hornblow was the producer of such movies as *The Asphalt Jungle* and *Witness for the Prosecution*.

For the last few days I've been haunted by the notion I would at any moment be getting a cable re H. & S. and the Supreme Court. I told Cliff to cable me, but he is so stingy about cabling. I don't know <u>why</u>—it's my money, not his. Yesterday, the 15th, he was supposed to have interviewed two men in Topeka that would have settled once and for all the question of my attending the H. & S. farewell. <u>Why</u> shouldn't he have cabled me the results?!

Alvin, I don't think you ought to go your diet <u>at all</u> if you have to pay for it to such a degree. It does worry me—thinking of you away from home and feeling ill.

Marie wrote: if they won't let me have Charlie on the plane, will they let him on the train. But darling, how does a <u>train</u> get across the ocean? Poor little Charlie, he really has a hard time with his bronchitis.

Love to the boys, and Mother Dewey, and our New Orleans kinfolk. Hugs and kisses

T.

[Collection New York Public Library]

TO NEWTON ARVIN

[Postcard][1]   [Verbier, Switzerland]
                                                        [ca. 19 January 1963]

CAPOTE'S INDEPENDENT DETERRENT[2]

Take heed, Sige, or my friend Charlie J. will get hold of you: he's trained to bite <u>all</u> literary critics! Especially ones named Kazin.

I hope you are feeling much better. As you can see, I'm a mite too plump.

Your book has not yet arrived.

All love

T.

[Collection Smith College Library]

---

[1] A real-photo postcard of Capote holding his bulldog, Charlie, in the snows of Verbier.

[2] Capote was playing on an item in the news. French president Charles de Gaulle was insisting that France have an independent deterrent—atomic bombs, in other words.

TO ALVIN DEWEY

[Verbier, Switzerland]
22 Jan. 1963

<u>Dear</u> Alvin—

Well, I finally heard from Cliff the results of his Topeka conferences re my attendance at the H. & S. farewells. The answer was No (Reason given: so many requests). I was merely the first to make a request! And hired a lawyer to do it! Jesus! However, it is not an answer I intend to accept. We shall see. But the important thing is—You. I think you best start maneuvering right now. Find out. Because if worse comes to worse I intend to bribe Hickock to designate me as a witness; I think he is allowed two, so maybe I could bribe him to designate both of us (money to go to his mother).

Alvin, I hope your ailments have quieted down. I want you in good health when next glimpsed—which, God willing, won't be too long now.

All love to All—

T.

[Collection New York Public Library]

TO CECIL BEATON

[Verbier, Switzerland]
4 Feb. 1963

Dearest Cecil—

I have been rising every morning at 3 or 4 to work—it is now 4. But <u>yesterday</u> I <u>finished</u> Part Three! I have never worked so hard in my life. But it is done, and I know you will be really thrilled by it. It is all I wanted it to be—which is saying a great deal. But I am exhausted; tense as nine newly tuned pianos—I don't know how I can recharge myself to write the fourth and final section—which will take at least another year. If only I could empty my soul and heart and head of it for awhile.

Am still waiting to hear from Kansas, but will in any event leave here the end of the month. As for when I shall see you—why not California?[1]

---

[1] Beaton was to do the designs for the Hollywood version of *My Fair Lady,* starring Rex Harrison and Audrey Hepburn.

Probably, by the time I go to Kansas, you will be in Hollywood, so I will just come on out and fly back to New York from there. Or perhaps we could also have a little <u>weekend</u> in San Francisco.

How awful it sounds—the cold and the discomfort! But apparently it is the same all over. It is <u>very</u> bitter here—I can't put my nose out the door once the sun goes down.

I don't understand about [Rudolf] Nureyev. What sort of sex life does he have? Is he in love with Erik Bruhn?[1] Myself, I think he (N.) is repulsive. But then we have never agreed on this subject (of what constitutes attractiveness).

I read in the papers about Mr. [Oliver] Messel's difficulties. So moronic.

Jack skis. Charlie barks. Diotima is sleeping away the winter. We're all so sorry you couldn't come—next year! Send a line—<u>all</u> <u>love</u>.

T.

[Collection St. John's College, Cambridge University]

TO NEWTON ARVIN

[Verbier, Switzerland]
10 February 1963

Dearest Sige—

Rcvd. notice from Little, Brown that they had sent me, almost three weeks ago: 'Longfellow, His Life and Works, by Newton Arvin.' So it should be along any minute now, and I can scarcely wait. I told Random House to send you my 'Selected Writings'—which has turned out to be a very handsome little book. What a shame our books are appearing during the newspaper strike—now we can't complain to the publisher about a lack of advertising.

This has been the coldest winter in Switzerland since 1875—twenty to forty below zero every night. The skiing resorts (including this one) are absolutely empty—it's just too cold to ski. But today I felt a certain thaw in the air—I suppose the sun will come out just as I leave. As of now, I plan

---

[1] A Dane, Bruhn was a star of the Royal Danish Ballet and the American Ballet Theatre.

to go 3 March—returning to 70 Willow Street, Brooklyn. And, of course, I will get in touch with you immediately.

I had a little note from Andrew the other day (on the whole I never hear from anyone: that's what happens when you evaporate for years on end) and he said he'd recently met a very bright young man (no name given) who told him he was reviewing your book for <u>The</u> <u>Reporter</u>, and who said it was "a really brilliant book, something of the first-order." Andrew is so fond of you. But he is just one of those <u>strange</u> types.

I notice (in this letter, and in my more formal writing as well) that I use the word 'just' constantly. I think it must be the <u>Kansas</u> influence. I have got my ear so adjusted to those prairie cadences!

Hope you got the picture of me and my dog-friend Charlie. He really is so funny. And <u>nice</u>.

So are you. Nice, I mean. I love you, Sige.

mille tendresse [*sic*]—

T.

[Collection Smith College Library]

TO BENNETT CERF

[Verbier, Switzerland]
14 February 1963

Dear Bennett—

Welcome back; I hope you and Phyllis had a wonderful holiday at Shady Lane.

I finished Part Three—and wept uncontrollably for two days afterwards: I'd been under such an appalling nervous strain. Anyway, Shawn has cabled me a lengthy string of superlatives and I long for your opinion. But I will not let you read it until you have re-read the first two parts. So do your homework. Because I will be back March 3rd. To stay. (Except for going to Kansas).

I've missed you and Phyllis so much. And love you both dearly—

So looking forward

T.

[Collection Columbia University Library]

TO ALVIN AND MARIE DEWEY

[Verbier, Switzerland]
15 Feb 1963

Dearhearts—

Hope you had a good time at the Broadmoor—though sorry it had to be so brief.

Well, I've heard from Dale and I've heard from Cliff; and, having talked it over, they've decided to do <u>nothing</u> until my Kansas visit.

Speaking of which—I wrote Cap Burtis the other day asking him to get a Chevrolet Corvette '63 for me and have it ready when I arrive in G.C. one reason being that I want a car with Kansas plates to go with my Kansas licence—otherwise I would have to have New York plates and take a N.Y. test (and you <u>know</u> I'd never pass it). Besides, I'd like to drive back across the country and pay a few visits. Have you seen these '63 Corvettes? I think they're sensational: more beautiful than any European sportscar—even a Ferrari. I asked Cap to write me whether he could have the car there by March 20th—but since then I've realized there isn't that much time before I leave here—would you please ask him to cable me? Because if he can't get the car—then I will have a friend buy one for me in California and drive it to G.C. (am going to California before G.C.). Oh dear, I'm always asking favors of you—but please tell Cap to cable me yes or no.

I think our friend Nelle will meet me in G.C. However, she is <u>so</u> involved in the publicity for her film (she owns a percentage, that's why; even so, I think it <u>very</u> <u>undignified</u> for any serious artist to allow themselves to be exploited in this fashion).

We leave here 3 March. Swissair has given Charlie Special Permission to ride with the Humans. Sister, too. Will write before departure.

Much, much love
T.

P.S. I just sent Part Three of the book to Mr. Shawn last week. He cabled me: "A masterpiece stop A work of art people will be reading two hundred years from today." So see—you're not only going to be famous, but immortal! And that's no joke.

[Collection New York Public Library]

TO NEWTON ARVIN

> [Verbier, Switzerland]
> as from:
> 70 Willow St.
> Brooklyn 1, N.Y.
> 18 Feb. 1963.

Dearest Sige—
  Your book came, and I read it all yesterday, and all of today, and finished it, and my great congratulations, Sige—it is very brilliant, and very beautiful, a fascinating book and a work of art, a real one.[1] I'm thrilled about it, and know it will make a tremendous impression everywhere. I like the <u>looks</u> of the book, too: the jacket is wonderfully striking, and the typography very handsome—I'm sure Van Wyck Brooks[2] must be proud of the dedication. And <u>I</u> am very proud of <u>you</u>, my friend.
  All love
  T.

[Collection Smith College Library]

TO MARIE DEWEY

> [Verbier, Switzerland]
> as from:
> 70 Willow Street
> Brooklyn 1, N.Y.
> 23 Feb. 1963

Dearest, Dearest Marie—
  I have been so worried about Alvin, and praying for him: I admire him so, I'm devoted to him—I do hope with all my heart that by now he is more comfortable and on the way to total recovery.[3] I marvel at your wonderful good spirits, and am so grateful (and <u>very</u> touched) that you have taken the

---

[1] The book was Arvin's biography of Longfellow.
[2] Van Wyck Brooks was Arvin's friend and mentor, a critic and scholar who specialized in nineteenth-century American literature.
[3] Dewey had suffered two massive heart attacks.

time to keep me informed. I've longed to telephone you—but that is very difficult to do from this little town. However, I will call you the instant I arrive in New York (or will <u>if</u> the phone is connected—I rather expect to find the place in a shambles).

Anyway, don't be surprised if you receive this letter one day and hear from me the next.

My best love to Alvin and the boys. Many hugs, precious Marie

T

[Collection New York Public Library]

TO NEWTON ARVIN

[Verbier, Switzerland]
as from:
70 Willow Street
Brooklyn 1, N.Y.
27 Feb. 1963

Dearest Sige—

How very, very sorry I am to hear you've been so ill, and so long in the hospital. It was kind of your sister to write me, and I know it must be a comfort having her there.

I am coming home next week, and will call your sister—and hope you will be out of the hospital by then. I was supposed to go on out to Kansas; but will postpone that to come and see you; or, if you're not feeling up to a visitor just yet, will come later (after Kansas).[1]

God bless you. My love always

T.

[Collection Smith College Library]

---

[1] Arvin died of pancreatic cancer a month after this letter was written. Capote spoke with him by telephone shortly before his death.

TO CECIL BEATON

as from:
70 Willow Street
Brooklyn 1, N.Y.
28 Feb 1963

Dear heart—

We leave tomorrow—though God knows how: Jack's passport is out of date (one year!) and the papers for the animals, despite endless calls to the vet, have still not arrived—and oh <u>endless</u> chaos of all kinds! Still, I am hoping we will reach the above address in good shape (worry time to indicate <u>nervousness</u>).

Look!—I'm spilling ink everywhere.[1]

I saw that 'Turandot' opens tonight.[2] Bon fortune—though I'm sure there will be nothing but ovations for you and your work. What a shame you should miss it.

Are you miserable in H'wood? Or just too busy to notice. Well, I am coming to see you. I've done a wild extravagant thing: bought myself a very jazzy sport's [*sic*] car—a Corvette Stingray (makes a Jaguar or even a Ferrari, look like a child's toy). I can't afford it, to say the least. But after all these years of keeping my nose to the grindstone something in me suddenly exploded—and I bought this car. It's being delivered to me in Kansas. So I <u>could</u> drive it out to California. We could meet for a <u>weekend</u> in Las Vegas. Then I could take you back in my divine voiture. Then we could go up to San Francisco the next weekend. Well, it's something to think About. Anyway, <u>I</u> <u>need</u> <u>a</u> <u>rest</u> <u>from</u> <u>my</u> <u>book</u>.

My dear detective (Al Dewey) is in the hospital, having suffered <u>two</u> massive coronaries. And my sweet old friend Newton Arvin has only a few weeks to live (cancer).[3] So it's one thing, and then another. Except that one cares.

Much love, dearheart. Drop a note and let me know if you are still at the hotel. Or where I can call you.

Jack says Hello. Charlie, too—who has somehow survived the winter. Diotima looks wonderful: <u>even</u> a little fat.

Hugs

T.

[Collection St. John's College, Cambridge University]

---

[1] There are ink blots on the page.
[2] Beaton had designed both sets and costumes for a Metropolitan Opera production of Puccini's opera.
[3] Arvin died on March 21, 1963.

TO ALVIN AND MARIE DEWEY

[Bridgehampton, N.Y.]
[20 July 1963]

Dearhearts
Will call before you leave for Cuchara; but meantimes—this.
Poor Dewey. But I'm sure all this construction work will do marvels for his figure: maybe I should get that sort of job. Anyway, hope his hands have hardened now; and trust, too, that Alvin is less 'down in the back.'
Guess what? Perry Smith's lawyer, Robert Bingham, called to ask if I would come to their Habeas Corpus hearing and testify as to what an unfair trial the boys had in G.C. Well, you can imagine what I told him. But apparently they are not even having the Hearing until <u>September</u>. My God.
Have you seen page 61 of the current (July 22) 'Newsweek'. Did it make you laugh?
I am definitely going to California around the 20th of October, and will come back via G.C. for a little visit.
I spoke with Miss Lee yesterday, and she said she was going to call you, so perhaps she has—anyway, she is in the city, where they are having a Heat Wave and High Humidity.
Alvin, while you are safe-proofing those banks, why not figure a foolproof way to rob one: I'll help you.
Miss you and love you all
T.

P.S. The enclosed is a Reward for Paul's gardening blisters. He must spend every penny in Cuchara.

[Collection New York Public Library]

TO PERRY SMITH

[Bridgehampton, N.Y.]
7 August 1963

Dear Perry—
Here once more are the photographs—or at least those (of the Curtis group) that could be whittled down to size. All the smaller ones are by Avedon. I have measured them carefully, so I hope they reach you this time.

I spoke to Nelle on the phone; she said she was writing you today.

I have found the first stanza of the poem you wanted—I'm certain it has two long stanzas, but for some reason I copied the first in a notebook (three years ago!) and either did not do the second or lost it. Sorry.

> *There's a race of men that don't fit in*
> *A race that can't stay still;*
> *So they break the hearts of kith and kin;*
> *And they roam the world at will.*
> *They range the field and they rove the flood,*
> *And they climb the mountain's crest;*
> *Their's [sic] is the curse of the gypsy blood,*
> *And they don't know how to rest.*
> *If they just went straight they might go far*
> *They are strong and brave and true;*
> *But they're ever tired of the things that are,*
> *And they want the strange and new.*[1]

Always—
Truman

Truman CAPOTE

Box 501
Bridgehampton, N.Y.

[Collection Gerald Clarke]

TO MARIE DEWEY

[Bridgehampton, N.Y.]
[8 September 1963]

Dearheart—

Rcvd. your (as always) sweet letter this morning. The enclosed is for Alvin's impending birthday—please get him his favorite scotch and a good-sized steak.

---

[1] From "The Men That Don't Fit In" by Robert W. Service, in his book *The Spell of the Yukon and Other Verses* (1907).

Have just come back from a few days in the city—got myself measured for some new winter suits (something suitable for the Brown Palace[1]). It does sound like fun—and I'm greatly looking forward. I had lunch with Anne Ford last Saturday—who says she has decided she <u>will</u> divorce Henry: no great loss—he is a terrible bore, whereas she is just the opposite: she is getting a settlement in excess of 10,000,000—and I don't mean sardines.

Am going to L.A. the 5th of November. Will stay with Audrey Hepburn—until the 15th, then take plane to meet you.

Much love, my darling friend

T.

[Collection New York Public Library]

TO ALVIN AND MARIE DEWEY

[Bridgehampton, N.Y.]
[11 September 1963]

Dearhearts—

Enclosed is the clipping I mentioned. Also a letter which I know you will find very touching—a response to the letter I wrote them about Patrick's death (know I need not say that I send you this in confidence).[2]

Am planning to call you tomorrow, so will just add that—

I am your devoted and always loving

Truman

P.S. Would appreciate it if you returned the clipping and J's letter.

[Collection New York Public Library]

---

[1] A hotel in Denver.

[2] Capote had sent flowers and a letter of condolence to the Kennedys upon the death of their newborn son. Jacqueline Kennedy responded on August 26, 1963: "I keep thinking what power a great writer has. All the things you write move people. It is a selfish thought—but if all you have written all your life was just training to write those seven lines which were only seen by me—and Jack—I am glad you became a writer."

TO BENNETT AND PHYLLIS CERF

[Telegram]   Southampton, N.Y.
                                                  Sept. 17, 1963

ON YOUR TWENTY FIFTH ANNIVERSARY I PLAN TO GIVE YOU SAM
SPIEGEL'S YACHT[1] MEANWHILE ACCEPT HUGS AND LOVE AND LOTS
OF DELICIOUS KISSES FROM THE ONE AND ONLY TRUMAN CAPOTE

[Collection Columbia University Library]

TO CECIL BEATON

17 Sept 1963
Bridgehampton, N.Y.

Dearest One—

Had your sweet letter today: loved the bit about camping in the Big Sur
and Kin fishing off silver rocks.[2] I should think that would make up for
quite a lot.

Am still by the sea, which now is rather grey and wintry: We seem always to come too early and stay too late; but I hope to linger until the middle of next month. I am coming to you November 10th. I realize I will have
missed both the Ascot and the Ball scenes—but I have some serious complications regarding my book and I cannot leave before then. Actually, I
don't care whether I do the 'Fair Lady' piece. That's the least of my worries.
I'd just like to spend a little time with you <u>period</u>.

I am in a really appalling state w/ tension and anxiety. Perry and Dick
have an appeal for a <u>New Trial</u> pending in Federal Court: if they should get
it (a new trial) I will have a complete breakdown of some sort. The Hearing is Oct 9th and the decision should be handed down by the 15th. Actually I don't think they <u>will</u> get the trial. But you can't tell. Anyway, if all goes
well, I should be able to finish the book by Spring. <u>If</u> I can <u>stand</u> it that
much longer.

---

[1] Spiegel was the producer of such films as *The African Queen* and *Lawrence of Arabia*.
[2] Kin was Beaton's new, young American lover.

I never see anybody—except for one weekend at the Paleys—where saw C.Z. [Guest]—so pregnant that really she is grotesque and ought not to be allowed in public.[1] Jack is fine—he has been painting pictures of Diotima and they are <u>very</u> charming. Give my love to Chris [Isherwood] and Don [Bachardy].

All hugs, dear heart
T.

[Collection St. John's College, Cambridge University]

TO PERRY SMITH

70 Willow Street
Brooklyn, New York
15 December 1963

Dear Perry—

Last night I woke up and suddenly thought: Perry says he doesn't know anything about me, not <u>really</u>. I lay awake thinking about it and realized that, to a certain extent, it was true. You don't know even the surface facts of my life—which has a few certain similarities to yours.[2] I was an only child, and very small for my age—and always the smallest boy in school. When I was three, my mother and father were divorced. My father (who has been married five times since) was a traveling salesman, and I spent much of my childhood wandering around the South with him. He was not unkind to me, but I disliked him and still do. (I never see him; he lives in New Orleans). My mother, who was only 16 when I was born, was <u>very</u> beautiful. She married a fairly rich man, a Cuban, and after I was 10 I lived with them (mostly in New York). Unfortunately, my mother, who had several miscarriages and as a result developed mental problems, became an alcoholic and made my life miserable. Subsequently she killed herself (sleeping pills). I quit school when I was 16 and have been on my own ever

---

[1] Guest's daughter, Cornelia, was born in November.
[2] This capsule biography gives an accurate account of Capote's emotional history, but the facts are only approximate. His parents divorced when he was seven, not three, for example, and, as best as can be determined, his father only remarried twice.

since—getting a job on a magazine (having started to write at a very early age). I was always intellectually and artistically precocious—but emotionally immature. And, of course, I always had emotional problems—largely because of a "question" you yourself asked me on our last visit and which I answered truthfully (<u>not</u> that the answer isn't obvious)![1]

This is a <u>very</u> sketchy resumé. But I am not in the habit of making such confidences. However, I do not mind telling you anything.

Always,
Truman

[Collection Unknown]

TO ALVIN AND MARIE DEWEY

12 Indian Creek Island[2]
[Miami Beach, Fla.]
18 January 1964

Dearhearts—

Just rcvd. Pappy's 'cheerful' communiqué—and it was wonderfully sweet of him to be so thoughtful. I really have been feeling very low—almost bitter. It's all absolutely beyond belief. My God! Why don't they just turn them loose and be done with it. Nothing would surprise me any more. How idiotic not to have made a transcript in the first place! No, I haven't told either The New Yorker <u>or</u> Random House. I just can't face it. Of course it's not my fault, but they are going to be <u>very</u> annoyed with me—perhaps rightly, because I had given them every assurance. Well, there's nothing to be done—except try to get through another year of this totally absurd and unnecessary torture.

The weather here is certainly very variable—hot one day, freezing the next. But it's a beautiful house, and Charlie likes it—he's got a girl-friend: a great big boxer.

---

[1] Smith had asked Capote if he were homosexual. Capote told him he was.
[2] Capote was visiting his friends Gardner and Jan Cowles. Cowles owned *Look* magazine, among other things.

I am going to send you a crate of fruit one day next week when I get into town—there's nothing on this island except a golf club. I mean, no shops.

All love to the boys and Pete, too.

Hugs and kisses

T

P.S. As you can see from the enclosed clip, our plight is no secret on either side of the Atlantic—[1]

[Collection New York Public Library]

TO ALVIN AND MARIE DEWEY

Gemini
Boynton Beach, Florida
[4 February 1964]

Dearhearts—

Enclosed is a picture of this place—or one _small_ area of it. There are 22 servants, and a private golf-course. Charlie and I have our own little beach house with our _own_ butler. Pretty snazzy. Mr. G. has his own turbo-jet (complete with hostess) and we are flying to Nassau tomorrow—just for _lunch_.[2] So if I've got to suffer, I'm better off suffering _here_. Eh what?

Sent a crate of grape-fruit, but no avocados as they didn't have them.

Will ring you later on next week. I miss you and love you

T.

[Collection New York Public Library]

---

[1] Enclosed was an article entitled "Writers at Work: A Progress Report for the New Year" from _The Sunday Times_ (London), January 5, 1964, in which Capote marked the passage "Truman Capote must play an unhappy waiting game before he can finish what promises to be a most remarkable exercise in what may be called enriched documentary: 'In Cold Blood,' a picture of the impact of a murder in Kansas which still awaits its actual dénouement." Capote underlined "unhappy."

[2] Capote was visiting his friends Loel and Gloria Guinness.

TO ALVIN AND MARIE DEWEY

Gemini
Boynton Beach, Florida
14 February 1964

Dearhearts—

To follow up on our conversation last night—I really meant it: I'd love to have you as my guests for a spring holiday in San Francisco. I have lots of <u>very</u> attractive friends there, and I know we would enjoy it. We could stay at the St. Francis (or the Mark Hopkins) for a week—and maybe go down to Hollywood and let the Selznicks give a big party for us. Maybe, instead of going to New York, Vi [Tate] would like to come with us.[1] The middle of April would be the best time. Think it over and let me know as soon as you can.

Charlie and I are alone here now—except for 22 servants (<u>not</u> counting 2 French chefs and a small army of gardners [*sic*]), <u>so</u> <u>come</u> <u>on</u>!

Incidentally, Marie, don't be upset about Nelle. That's just the way she is. And always will be. It doesn't mean a thing. She <u>adores</u> you both.

I forgot to thank you for the dear valentine. I loved it!

Hugs & kisses

T.

[Collection New York Public Library]

TO ALVIN AND MARIE DEWEY

Gemini
Boynton Beach, Florida
28 Feb 1964

Darling Folks—

Had Marie's sweet letter today. The G's came back from Mexico, and we've been flying around. Went to the Liston-Clay fight—which was fun (<u>if</u>

---

[1] Tate's husband, the judge who had presided over the Smith-Hickock trial, had died the previous November.

rather phony).[1] Jackie and Mrs. Rose Kennedy here for a quiet dinner last night—Jackie <u>very</u> thin and sad but able to smile a bit. Charlie and I [are] leaving Tuesday for New York and I will call you then (when we get there).

About S.F. Actually, the invitation <u>included</u> the plane tickets (what kind of host do you think I am, eh?). You could fly from Denver. Come on. Let's go. It won't cost you nothin'. Think it over. Incidentally, don't mention it to Vi if you're <u>not</u> going. I'm very fond of her, and would like to cheer her up, but I wouldn't want to be solely responsible for her on such a junket.

Love and hugs

T.

[Collection New York Public Library]

TO ALVIN AND MARIE DEWEY

[Brooklyn, N.Y.]
28 March 1964

Dearhearts—

I think you had better write to Vi, and advice [*sic*] her of our program, and get our schedules co-ordinated. Here is a <u>partial</u> list of engagements—

April <u>18th</u>: Reservations St. Francis Hotel, S.F. Arrive no later than 6 P.M.

<u>Saturday, April 18th</u>: dinner-party at Whitney Warren's. 8 P.M. Whitney is a bachelor (highly eligible). He is certainly the most elegant, and <u>probably</u> the richest, man in California.

Sunday, April 19th: <u>Lunch</u>: Fisherman's Wharf.

Evening: dinner-party given for us by Mr & Mrs. Herbert Caen. They are young and very amusing. He is leading writer on San Francisco Chronicle. She is a famous Mexican beauty.

Monday. April 20th. Lunch: not settled.

Evening: Dinner in Chinatown with Kenneth Hoitsma.

<u>Tuesday. April 21st</u>. Lunch: with Mr. & Mrs. Barnaby Conrad— Very High Society.

---

[1] On February 25, 1964, boxer Cassius Clay (later known as Muhammad Ali) defeated Sonny Liston at the Miami Beach Auditorium to win the world heavyweight title for the first time.

Evening: dinner with Mr. and Mrs. William Wallace. Also High Society. He leading S.F. lawyer. She former Ina Claire.

<u>Wednesday, April 22</u>. Depart for L.A. Reservations Hotel Bel-Air, Beverly Hills.

Evening: dinner-party given by Selznicks. Lots of movie people.

April 22nd. Dinner party given by Mr & Mrs. Irving Lazar.[1]

And so on!—Enclosed check is for Tickets Denver to S.F.—Will call soon. Love

T.

[Collection New York Public Library]

TO MARIE DEWEY

[Brooklyn, N.Y.]
as from: Box 501
Bridgehampton, N.Y.
8 May 1964

Dearest Marie—

Forgive me for disregarding your request, but I feel I must comment on your letter which arrived this morning. First of all, I knew you were not feeling too well at times, but I had no <u>idea</u> of the real strain you were under. You seemed, as always, so sweet and charming and warm and easy-to-be-with—indeed, you could not have "pleased" me more: I thought you were <u>wonderful</u>, and so did all my friends—and it deeply distresses me that you could have thought otherwise. You have such a kind of natural gaiety and self-assurance that it just never occurred to me that you needed the little boosts that Vi, being alone and not an intimate friend of mine (as you and Alvin are), needed. I'm sorry: I should have been more sensitive. Believe me, it would be impossible for me to be fonder of anyone than I am of you. Or prouder of you than I was. That is the truth, and anything else is a misconception.

---

[1] Lazar, usually referred to as Swifty, was one of Hollywood's most prominent agents.

I hope the foregoing is clear, but it may not be as I have just come from the doctor where I got quite a shock. It seems that the trouble I've been having with my upper lip is caused by a cancer. They won't know until next Friday what sort of treatment I must undergo—whether surgery (which will leave me very disfigured) or X-ray. They don't think it is anything very critical, but of course I can't help being upset. I will call you when I know what will happen. Incidentally, don't mention this to anyone.

My love to you and dearest Alvin.

always your loving friend

T.

[Collection New York Public Library]

TO ALVIN AND MARIE DEWEY

[New York]
Monday
[18 May 1964]

Dearhearts—

This a hurried note to tell you everything is Okay! Dr. March was <u>wrong</u>—I could kill him for putting me through such an ordeal. The Biopsy came out negative—and though there is something wrong it ain't cancer. Boy, these so-called Specialists!

So I was in a good mood for the weekend with Jackie, and she was in better spirits than usual. So it was very pleasant in a quiet way.

Am going back to the beach on Friday.

Hope all is well.

Much love

T.

P.S. I saw Nicky Dunne on the street, and he said he and Lynne had had <u>such</u> a sweet letter from you.[1]

[Collection New York Public Library]

---

[1] Dominick Dunne was at this time a television producer. He and his wife, Ellen, nicknamed "Lenny," lived in Beverly Hills. During their visit to California, Capote, the Deweys and Violet Tate had attended a party the Dunnes gave for their tenth wedding anniversary.

TO ALVIN AND MARIE DEWEY

Bridgehampton, N.Y.
Box 501
23 May 1964

Dearhearts—

I was going to call you tonight, but there is something wrong with the phone—they have put in some new kind of dialing system, and the lines seemed to have got all mixed up. Incidentally, the number has been changed to: 516 5370507. So will wait now till next weekend, when maybe we will have heard something about the hearing. Although the court probably won't hand down any decision until the following week. I don't know if I can endure the suspense!

I spent all of last week in the city—where [I] was caught by Mr Duane West. Nelle and I (for our sins) took them to see "Hello, Dolly"—ugh. I thought he was bad, but <u>the wife is worse</u>! The End! What a pair! Never again.—Saw Pat Lawford, who sends you her best, and said to tell you she has at last found an apartment (in N.Y.) and when you come will give you a party.[1] The ceremony at the Institute (see clippings) was quite impressive.[2] I wish you could have seen me sitting on the Dais trying to look Distinguished. Ha Ha. I love you and miss you!

Hugs
Coach

[Collection New York Public Library]

---

[1] Pat Lawford, sister of President Kennedy, was married to actor Peter Lawford.

[2] Enclosed was a *New York Times* article from May 21, 1964, about the induction of Capote and others into the National Institute of Arts and Letters the previous day. Among the other new members were James Baldwin, Leon Edel, Ralph Ellison, Bernard Malamud and John Updike.

TO ALVIN DEWEY III

[Bridgehampton, N.Y.]
25 May 1964

Dear Dewey—
You have a very real talent—one worth training and developing: I don't say that very often to anyone—the world is too full of frustrated (and misguided) artists.

"True Blue" is interesting, and shows a distinct flickering of a real litererary [*sic*] gift—faint but definitely <u>there</u>. But it is not a play, not even a one-act play. Technically, it is a sketch—and even so it is not entirely realized. The method of the Absurd (which is really only a momentary literary fashion) is a beguiling trap for young would-be writers—because the contents are so arbitrary, so undisciplined, so easy to come by. And because it is so easy to <u>seem</u> meaningful and profound when one is being merely enigmatic and pretentious (and full of hot air). This is not true of All the Absurd school (Beckett is gifted, and so, to a lesser degree, is Ionesco); but it is neither a healthy or helpful form for young writers to imitate.

One cannot be taught to write. One can only learn to write by writing—and <u>reading</u>. Reading good books written by real artists—until you understand <u>why</u> they are good. I'm quite sure you have never done this; and you must. Here are a few books which I want you to get from the library; I choose them because I think you will enjoy them and because they are what real writing is all about. 1) "The Red Badge of Courage", by Stephen Crane. 2) "My Antonia" by Willa Cather 3) "A Lost Lady" by Willa Cather 4) "The Collected Short Stories of Katherine Mansfield" 5) "The Heart is A Lonely Hunter" by Carson McCullers.

This might seem to some people a curious list; but I have my reasons. Moreover, it is only a beginning; and when you have read these books I will send you another list. If the books are not available at the library tell me and I will obtain them for you.

Meanwhile, forget about publishing. You have lots of time and a long way to go. And a hard one. But with your sensitivity, and your imagination, I think you just might make it. And I will help you all I can.

Love to Paul and Pete and Pappy and Marie and <u>you</u>
Truman

[Collection New York Public Library]

TO CECIL BEATON

Box 501
Bridgehampton, N.Y.
11 June 1964

Dearest Cecil—
Forgive this invalid scrawl, but I'm just up from my days in bed with the most paralyzing, agonizing attack of shoulder bursitis. Ugh. Prior to <u>that</u>, I went through two hellish weeks because a doctor believed I had lip-cancer. They cut a chunk out of my lip, (leaving quite a scar), and sent it for biopsy—which turned out <u>negative</u>. These damn doctors! Anyway, very little has been coming up roses since last I wrote you.

But I hope the story with you is very different. I hope Kin has arrived, and you are doing marvelous things together. Probably at this very moment you are somewhere bathing in the twilight of Gothic things.

Obviously Jack and I are here at the beach. We have a very cozy, charming little hut. A good place to work, and I hope to get cracking now.

Don't know any gossip. Quite some time ago I went to dinner with Jackie K. at the [James and Minnie] Fosburghs, and the Fosburghs got mad at me because Jackie et moi spent the whole evening talking about sex. They thought it was <u>my</u> fault. Ha Ha. Love to Kin. Hugs & kisses
  T

P.S. nothing new from Kansas.

[Collection St. John's College, Cambridge University]

TO CHRISTOPHER ISHERWOOD

> 18 June 1964
> Box 501
> Bridgehampton, N.Y.

Dear Christopher—

Yesterday I read "A Single Man" straight through.[1] Today, unable to get it out of my mind, I read large portions of it over again. This is your most beautiful and powerful writing. A stylistic tour-de-force of the greatest distinction; but ah!—so much more than that. How often the accuracy and honesty of your insight, make one laugh and shudder simultaneously. It is harrowing stuff, and yet very funny, and always, <u>always</u>, deeply moving. What shines through is the real nobility of your mind and art. I am very proud of you, and envious as well.

I lost my address book, and so am sending this in care of your publishers. I hope it finds you well, and working. At least I'm working—though I wonder to what purpose, for the prospect of either finishing or publishing seems to get ever remoter. My love to Don. To you: an embrace and a salute!

Truman

[Collection Henry E. Huntington Library]

TO ALVIN DEWEY III

> [Bridgehampton, N.Y.]
> 1st July 1964

Dear Dewey,

Forgive the long delay in answering your letter, but I have been immobilized by these court activities—or should I say <u>lack</u> of activity?

Anyway, what interested me most was your reaction to "My Antonia". You say you were too absorbed by it to "learn" anything from it. But one can't learn anything from a book, at least artistically, unless one <u>is</u> ab-

---

[1] Isherwood's *A Single Man* was published in 1964.

sorbed. It is not a <u>conscious</u> process—or only very rarely. One only really learns from what one enjoys. If a book or story bores you, then you might as well put it down. At this point, all I want you to do is try to develop an <u>instinctive</u> knowledge between good writing and bad writing. It will happen of itself—you'll see. Incidentally, what did you think of "The Heart Is a Lonely Hunter"?

Here are some more books I would like you to try.

"A Farewell to Arms" by Hemingway.
"Out of Africa" by Isak Dinesen.
"Winesburg, Ohio" by Sherwood Anderson
Collected Poems of Robert Frost

Love
Truman

If "Out of Africa" (marvelous book!) is unavailable I will send it.

[Collection New York Public Library]

TO ALVIN DEWEY III

[Bridgehampton, N.Y.]
4 July 1964

Dear Dewey,

I enjoyed your letter very much. To answer a few of your questions: yes, Holly [Golightly][1] was a real girl—but the incidents described in the story, or at least most of them, are fictional. I often use 'real' people in my work, and then create a story around them. Most of the people in Nelle's book are drawn from life. My story, "A Christmas Memory" is entirely autobiographical.

As for "Other Voices—" —this <u>is</u> a very difficult book. First of all, it isn't really a novel—but a long prose-poem. The "secret" of the book, the meaning (and it has one) lies in the last few pages. I don't intend to tell you

---

[1] The heroine of *Breakfast at Tiffany's*.

what it is, for someday you will see it for yourself. You do not yet know quite enough about life—

You mention the short stories of Evan Hunter. He is an extremely mediocre writer. Now, it is quite all right to be entertained by bad writing (I'm quite fond of a number of really terrible writers—Agatha Christie, Ian Fleming etc.), but it is important to be <u>aware</u> of the fact that they <u>are</u> bad. But this is something you will only discover as your reading progresses and your taste instinctively develops.

You must get into the habit of writing, even if it is only a paragraph a day. Try keeping a journal. One good exercise is to describe, in a page or two, some scene or person exactly as you see them: when I was your age I used to do this exercise religiously—it strengthens you, like piano practice. At this point, it is not necessary for you to attempt a whole short story. In any event, <u>write</u> <u>about</u> <u>what</u> <u>you</u> <u>know</u> <u>about</u>.

I am going to send you a book "Writers At Work" which I think you will find helpful.[1]

No, Joe Bell[2] was not inspired by Carson McCuller's [sic] bartender.

Have you read "Look Homeward, Angel" by Thomas Wolfe? I have many reservations about it, but definitely think you should read it. And of course you must read "The Catcher in the Rye"—though perhaps you have.

Show the enclosed clipping to your Mom and Pa.

All love to all

T.

[Collection New York Public Library]

TO ALVIN DEWEY III

[Bridgehampton, N.Y.]
16 July 1964

Dear Dewey—

The 'sketch' is interesting, but too disorganized. As I've said before, you should limit yourself for the time being to 'exercises'— Describe Pete in one

---

[1] *Writers at Work* (1958) is a collection of author interviews from *The Paris Review,* including Pati Hill's 1957 interview with Capote, in which he describes such things as his reading habits and methods of composition.

[2] A character in *Breakfast at Tiffany's.*

or two paragraphs of simple, declarative sentences. Describe the men you are working with. What they look like, the sort of men you think they are, what they eat and talk about, quote their conversations. Describe your farm. Stick with simple things you know about. Perhaps this sort of material will not seem to you inspiring—not <u>at</u> <u>first</u>. But it will teach you a great deal about writing. Please send me all the exercises you do, and I will criticize them in detail. It really isn't possible to criticize this last sketch, because it really isn't <u>about</u> anything specific or real. As you see, I'm going to be truthful and tough.

I've ordered some books for you, but they haven't arrived yet.

My love to you and Pauly and your adorable mother and <u>The</u> Detective (one and only).

Hugs—

T.

[Collection New York Public Library]

TO ALVIN AND MARIE DEWEY

[Bridgehampton, N.Y.]
Tuesday
[28 July 1964]

Dearhearts—

I've just finished talking with Clifford H. about this Bobby Rupp business.[1] Billy Wilder[2] is <u>very</u> anxious to have him sign the release, and has been putting a great deal of pressure on me about it. If Alvin were to speak to Bobby, and tell him that he has read the manuscript, and that it is very nice about Bobby (which God knows it is), and contains nothing that could possibly embarass [*sic*] him, perhaps Bobby could be persuaded to stop being adolescent. However, there may be reasons why Alvin would not care to do this. However, if Alvin is willing—please call Cliff. He will give you <u>two</u> releases—one is the original release, and the other is something special. Bobby told Cliff that he had no objection to his character and personality being used in a film, as long as he wasn't identified by name. The second release is a compromise on that basis, and could be offered <u>if</u> he

---

[1] Bobby Rupp was Nancy Clutter's boyfriend.
[2] Billy Wilder was the director of such films as *Sunset Blvd., Sabrina* and *Some Like It Hot.*

balked at signing the first and original release. I hate to ask such a trouble-some favor, but alas it has become important. I will call you Saturday from New Hampshire—where am going to stay with the Paleys for a few days at their lake house.

I hope Alvin's cold improved sufficiently to trounce poor Harrison and his bride.

Tell Dewey that I rcvd. his exercises, and that they show great im-provement. He is on the right track, and must keep on it. However, I will write to him directly soon—

I miss you, dearest Marie. I miss you both. Hugs and love
T.

[Collection New York Public Library]

TO ALVIN DEWEY III

[Bridgehampton, N.Y.]
30 July 1964

Dear Dewey—

The 'exercises' show much improvement. The quality of observation is good, visually. But you should include facts—one wonders: is that man married, what is his age, his probable income, does he have children. I don't mean such matters are <u>always</u> pertinent—that is something you will have to come to judge for yourself.

However, you go out of your way to find an odd or long word, where a simpler one would do. Most beginning writers do this—apparently under the impression that good writing is fancy writing. It isn't. Strive for <u>sim-plicity</u>—the plain, everyday word is usually the best. It is how you arrange them that counts. Try this exercise—write a portrait of someone you like very much, then one of someone you really dislike.

I sent you a little novel called "The Collector"—it's no masterpiece, but it is fairly well-written, and I think you will find it entertaining.[1]

---

[1] *The Collector* (1963) was the first book by British novelist John Fowles.

Well, you are making progress! As for Simenon—I know him a little, and I wouldn't say he was unhappy: he's the richest writer in the world![1] Ha ha.

Love

T.

[Collection New York Public Library]

TO BENNETT CERF

22 August 1964
Bridgehampton, N.Y.

Dear Bennett—

Why has my "Selected Writings" book not been put into the Modern Library? I was promised it would be—indeed, that was the main reason for doing the book; and it seems to me the matter has been delayed long enough. Can you imagine how very galling it is for me to see so many of my contemporaries (Mailer, Salinger, Bernard Malamud etc.—none of them Random House authors) included in this series, while the publisher of same ignores its own writer? It's unjust—both humanly, and in terms of literary achievement. By reason of the latter, not only should the "Selected Writings" be issued in the Modern Library, but also "Other Voices, Other Rooms" (which Penguin is including in their "American Classics" series this autumn). As you well know, I have always been loyal to Random House, happy with everything and everyone there; and I plan to continue to be. But loyalty is a reciprocal matter—and it is most unfair, and really not understandable policy, for Random House to disregard my work, but promote that of Mailer, Malamud etc. This is a serious matter to me, a serious complaint—and I know you will treat it as such, for I'm sure you will see the legitimacy of it.

"In Cold Blood" is nearly completed; I'm taking a few weeks away from it to write an outline of the novel I intend to write this winter. I will let you read the outline.

My love to you

[Collection Columbia University Library]

---

[1] Belgian novelist Georges Simenon, one of the writers interviewed in *Writers at Work*.

TO ALVIN DEWEY III

[Bridgehampton, N.Y.]
25 Aug 1964

Dear Dewey—
"The Bet" and "The Shack" are very good. So is "John Howard"—but
they all show you are making progress. When I come to G.C. in October
we will go over these pieces in detail—that is the only way to explain why
I think something is right or wrong.[1]
I'm <u>glad</u> you spend so much time worrying what to write about. That's
a good habit to get into. You must write something every day—regardless.
And you must learn to <u>rewrite</u> things. Polish them. I wish you would take a
typing course this winter. <u>It would be invaluable to you</u>!
Love to all
T.

Do not use dots (. . .); use dashes (—)

I am going to [send] a small, but <u>marvelous</u>, book on punctuation and
general English usage. I want you to <u>memorize</u> it.

[Collection New York Public Library]

TO ALVIN AND MARIE DEWEY

[Bridgehampton, N.Y.]
1 September 1964

Dearhearts—
How about Friday, Oct. 23rd? We could meet in Denver, and go to G.C.
on Sunday. I am going to California Oct. 8, and will have to be there two
weeks. Anyway, if this sounds okay, <u>darling</u> Marie can make the reserva-

---

[1] Capote edited the manuscripts of Dewey's sketches, writing at the head of one of them:
"Dear Dewey— I have made corrections on all of these. You are doing well. I'm pleased with the
progress. Love to all— T."

tions at the Brown Palace for the four of us (am including Vi, as I know she wants to go).

I am going to spend the labor-day week-end with the Cerfs in Mt. Kisco; otherwise would call you, but don't like to use the phone in other folk's houses. However, will call you later on next week.

Under separate cover I am sending you a copy of a long (88 pages) and amazing letter Hickock has written to the Supreme Court. He sent it to me for criticism (!!!)—and, after having it copied, I sent it back. Alvin, please don't show it to anyone. Just keep it, and you can give it back when I come to G.C.

Love and hugs. I _miss_ you!

T.

[Collection New York Public Library]

TO MARY LOUISE ASWELL

[Bridgehampton, N.Y.]
22 Nov. 1964

Darling Marylou—

Bless you for your sweet letter, precious one. I _adored_ our little jaunt, and you were an angel—all those 'prairie billys' (as Perry Smith calls them) were _mad_ about you: you should see the letters they've written me.[1] You were a darling to send Marie the gifts: you can imagine how happy they made her.

Have been staying at the beach off and on all November, but am returning to town tomorrow, mainly to see a lot of Jackie this upcoming week: she is very tense and tired and blue, what with all the memorial goings-on. To think it was only a year ago today—it seems so much longer.

That you really liked my book was so touching, and such a _reward_.[2] I sort of dreaded your reading it—because I knew that if I was fooling my-

---

[1] In October, Capote had gone to Garden City with Sandy Campbell, his fact checker at _The New Yorker_. They flew first to Denver, where Capote entertained the Deweys and some other Garden City friends, as well as Aswell, who lived in Santa Fe, New Mexico.
[2] He had asked Aswell, whose judgment he respected above almost all others', to read _In Cold Blood_.

self, and had made a real mistake (about the artistic possibilities of re-portage) you wouldn't have [been] able to lie (successfully).

Am supposed to go to Switzerland around Dec. 20th. I don't want to go. Maybe I won't. But I have to go some place to work—finish those 30-40 pages. I really wouldn't mind staying here on Long Island. But I couldn't do it alone. And it would be too mean to make Jack forego [sic] the mountains. Anyway, I'm definitely coming to see you and Aggie in April or thereabouts.

I love you. More than ever (and that's saying mucho). Love to Aggie. Love from Jack.

Always your friend
(Little) T.

Write me!

[Collection Aswell Family]

TO PETER OWEN

[Brooklyn, N.Y.]
[23 November 1964]

Dear Mr. Owen

This is in response to a request for a comment on Jane Bowles' novel: "Two Serious Ladies."[1]

"My only complaint against Mrs. Bowles is that she publishes so infre-quently. One would prefer larger quantities of her strange wit, thorny in-sights. Certainly she is one of the really original prose-stylists, as anyone who has ever read 'Two Serious Ladies' can testify."

Sincerely
Truman Capote
23 Nov 1964

[Collection the University of Texas at Austin]

---

[1] Bowles's only novel, *Two Serious Ladies,* was originally published in 1943. Peter Owen pub-lished an English edition in 1965.

TO SANDY CAMPBELL AND DONALD WINDHAM

[Postcard]   [Verbier, Switzerland]
                                                             [23 December 1964]

Dear ones—
  Arrived okay, and am ensconced in my icy eyrie. But still haven't quite
caught my breath: will write you when I do. Keep an eye on the Times
every Tuesday.[1] Miss you. Love
  Truman

[Collection Beinecke Library, Yale University]

TO ALVIN AND MARIE DEWEY

  [Verbier, Switzerland]
  28 Dec. 1964

Dearhearts—
  Had a <u>very</u> quiet Christmas—spent it working, and expect to do the
same New Year's Day (<u>and</u> New Year's eve). I'm so glad and grateful to be
quiet and away from all the chaos. Now if only Charlie would calm
down!—but the mountain air seems to have pepped him up—he's very
rambunctious and pesters me all day long.
  Jackie went to Aspen with Pat and Bobby and Jean and All Those
Brats.[2] Told Pat Aspen was not too far from you, and she said she might
give you a ring— All I can say is, I'm <u>So</u> glad <u>I'm</u> not in Aspen.
  Haven't heard from H & S since arriving here; and if they saw that article in 'Newsweek', maybe I never will again (I don't think Dick will take
kindly to being called a "pragmatic monster"—Ho! Ho!).[3]

---

  [1] Capote had asked Campbell to report to him on the Supreme Court's Monday decisions as
summarized in *The New York Times* each Tuesday. The justices were due to consider Hickock and
Smith's request for a review of their conviction.
  [2] Jacqueline Kennedy and three of the late president's siblings—Patricia Kennedy Lawford,
Bobby Kennedy and Jean Kennedy Smith—and their children.
  [3] An article entitled "The Fabulist" appeared in *Newsweek,* December 28, 1964, reporting on
Capote's reading from *In Cold Blood* at the 92nd Street Y Poetry Center in New York just before
Christmas.

I really am living a very spartan life: get up at 5 A.M, work on and off all day, have drinks at 6:30, eat at 8, go to bed at 9.

I hope dearest Pappy isn't having to run around too much. I miss you-all very much, and wish it wasn't <u>so</u> expensive to telephone (not to mention the inconvenience of the time difference).

Am interrupting my schedule tomorrow to visit the Chaplins for a few days. As you know, I adore Oona and am greatly looking forward to seeing her after so long.

I love you, too. All of you—Pete included. Write me. Hugs & kisses
T.

[Collection New York Public Library]

TO ALVIN AND MARIE DEWEY

[Verbier, Switzerland]
9 Jan. 1965

Honeylambs—

My, your Christmas festivities sounded merrily exhausting! However, one paragraph in Marie's otherwise delightful letter, rcvd. today, sent a slight chill along my spine. I know, when I've had a scotch of two (or fifty: ha ha), I'm liable to invite people to take a world cruise—<u>but</u>: did I <u>really</u> invite the Maxfields to come to New York, and if so <u>when</u>? Also, I don't remember a darn thing about Kay Wells and Los Angeles?!!? But, what <u>is</u> true (and between us strictly) Vi expects me to be in New York when she arrives there in March—though I never said I would be, and don't see how I can be. However, maybe that will be all right because I have to go to Rome the end of next month, and I gather this somehow coincides with her cruise—I have lots of marvelous friends in Rome, so I guess she would enjoy that and not feel disappointed if I fail to do the New York bit. Oh well—one can do just so much. Anyway, the New York bit (<u>full</u>-treatment) is what I'm saving for you—

Sandy [Campbell] sent me the pictures, and enclosed is the one Marie took of us that he didn't send you (the rat). Did he send the one of us all gathered round the hobby-horse? I liked that best.

Had long letters from H & S, all very friendly, so I guess they hadn't seen the article. As usual, they are full of legal plottings, and were very excited about the Caril Fugate ruling (which clipping you sent me).[1] I have a hunch that by the time you receive this letter the Supreme Court will have made a decision on their writ.

Was amused by the clipping about 'Squares.'[2] But there are good squares and Bad Squares. Bad Squares are know-it-All know-nothings like Duane West and his Beautiful Bride, Jehosophat.

That's bad luck about the job. But who knows, maybe by then you won't need a job. I mean, miracles _have_ happened. And isn't it just about our turn? Love to the boys and hugs and kisses—

        T

[Collection New York Public Library]

TO SANDY CAMPBELL

[Verbier, Switzerland]
[13 January 1965]

Dear Sandy—

I thought the pictures were <u>very</u> good; many graçias, Señor. The Deweys were pleased, too. Vi Tate has gone off on a world-cruise. Nothing new with Perry and Dick—they are just waiting expectantly on the Supreme Court.

<u>So am I</u>. Listen. The court is going to recess the entire month of February. Resuming in March. Which means there are only 2 Mondays left in Jan. when they might hand down a decision—the 18th and 25th. Please watch the Times, and cable on each of those days as follows—"Writs de-

---

[1] Charlie Starkweather, accompanied by his fourteen-year-old girlfriend, Caril Ann Fugate, killed eleven people in a 1958 murder spree across the farmlands of Nebraska and Wyoming. Starkweather was executed in 1959, while Fugate was sentenced to life in prison. Following the Supreme Court's 1964 *Escobedo* decision (that testimony by a defendant not informed of his or her right to counsel is inadmissible in court), Fugate's attorneys filed a petition for habeas corpus, and a judge ruled that the manner in which her original statement had been taken was a violation of the principle of law established by *Escobedo*. This did not, however, result in a new trial, as the Supreme Court subsequently decided in 1966 that *Escobedo* should not be applied retroactively. Fugate was eventually paroled in 1976.

[2] A clipping in which Senator Margaret Chase Smith of Maine defined the changing meanings of the word "square."

nied" or "Writs Granted" or, if there is nothing, just "Nothing." Please do this as I can't bear the suspense of not knowing one way or the other.

Hope all goes well. Miss you. Love to Don et vous
T.

[Collection Beinecke Library, Yale University]

TO SANDY CAMPBELL

[Postcard]   [Verbier, Switzerland]
                                               19 Jan 1965

Sandy—

Just got the cable.[1] Bless you! Now let's keep <u>everything</u> crossed—knees, eyes, hands, fingers! Much love to Donny et vous
T.

[Collection Beinecke Library, Yale University]

TO PERRY SMITH

[Verbier, Switzerland]
January 24, 1965

Dear Perry—

I've only just heard about the court's denial. I'm very sorry about it. But remember, this isn't the first set-back. Please send me [Robert] Bingham's address, which I haven't got here, and also his telephone number.[2]

Nelle is in the hospital, the result of a serious kitchen accident. She burned herself very badly, especially her right hand. It seems some sort of pan caught fire and exploded—all that at her home in Alabama.

You ask about my religious beliefs. As a matter of fact, we <u>did</u> discuss

---

[1] On January 18, 1965, the United States Supreme Court refused to hear Hickock and Smith's latest appeal.

[2] Robert Bingham was Smith's lawyer.

this once but I guess you've forgotten. Anyway, I belong to no church and am not a "Believer" in any formal sense. At one time I was very interested in Oriental religions, and felt, and still somewhat feel, that it might be possible for me to accept Buddhism,[1] perhaps because it is really more a [unclear] than a religion.

Only Catholicism can be taken seriously, with the sense that it gives adherents a personal sense of identity with [unclear] GOD, and offers genuine consolation when they fail to achieve it (by way of confessional).[2] But as for me, I just go my way by myself.

Affectionately,
Truman

[Collection Unknown]

TO CECIL BEATON

[Verbier, Switzerland]
27 Jan 1965

Dearheart—

As usual, I'm abed with a cold: I seem to have had one almost uninterruptedly since last September. Anyway, your letter was a joy in my not overly joyous existence. I've been working 8–9 hours a day—not needless to say, on the film-script. No, I'm finishing the last pages of my book—I must be rid of it regardless of what happens. I hardly give a fuck anymore what happens. My sanity is at stake—and that is no mere idle phrase. Oh the hell with it. I shouldn't write such gloomy crap—even to someone as close to me as you.

Occasionally read the English papers, and am delighted by the triumph, and your triumph, avec 'Lady'. I very especially liked Isabel Quigly's comments in "The Spectator".

---

[1] After Capote's endorsement of Buddhism, Smith wrote "ditto" in the margin.

[2] In the margin Smith wrote, "Please read Philip Wylie's 'Night Unto Night'—the special chapter is Rebus Incognitis. It influenced me greatly in deciding spiritual matters. Please read it." Wylie wrote science fiction and mystery novels, as well as such nonfiction books as *A Generation of Vipers*. *Night Unto Night* (1944) is a ghost story, with afterlife adventures. The author's preface begins: "Here is a novel about death—a novel that is about the living & their thoughts of death."

Yes, I did discuss "The Gainsborough Girls" with someone who seems to be quite interested: Fred Kohlman, a <u>very</u> pleasant producer at 20th Century. He thought it might be a good project for S.M. Behrman, who is one of his pets. Kohlman is the guy I'm supposed to write the script for—if ever I really do. I did a Treatment which he didn't like—no doubt rightly. I couldn't grasp what you were saying about Lazar—I mean, it wasn't clear. And I wish it had been: because I just received a check from him that was some $12,000 short of the amount expected.

Jack is fine, ditto Diotima and my Harrod's pup.[1] All love to Kin.

Mille Tendresse [*sic*]

T.

Please write.

[Collection St. John's College, Cambridge University]

TO SANDY CAMPBELL

Le Beau Rivage[2]
Lausanne-Ouchy
2 February 1965

Dear Sandy—

A new date has been set for H&S: Feb 18th. There seems to be every indication this date will hold. Without going into all the reasons, I've decided not to attend the executions—suffice [it] to say, it has become unnecessary from the literary standpoint.

However, Alvin is going in my place—so to say. Now on Thursday morning, the 18th, Alvin will call you at your office. He will read you the Text of the execution story in Kansas City Star. You, please, will write this down, and <u>cable</u> it to me <u>word</u> for <u>word</u> (at the magazine's expense, naturally). Prior to this, I will have talked to Alvin myself.

---

[1] He bought Charlie at Harrods in London.
[2] Le Beau Rivage is a luxury hotel overlooking Lake Geneva in Switzerland.

Hope this doesn't sound insane. But, the way I've constructed things, I will be able to complete the entire mss. within hours after receiving cable. Keep <u>everything</u> crossed.

All love

T.

[Collection Beinecke Library, Yale University]

TO SANDY CAMPBELL

[Postcard]   [Verbier, Switzerland]
                                              7 Feb 1965

Dear Sandy—

Guess what? The Supreme Court granted another stay pending appeal! What a country! What a law system! We won't hear anything further before March or April. Love to Don. et vous.

T.

[Collection Beinecke Library, Yale University]

TO ALVIN AND MARIE DEWEY

[Verbier, Switzerland]
9 Feb. 1965

Dearhearts—

I guess I didn't sound too jolly on the phone, but the news was rather lowering to the spirit. Anyway, it was good to hear your dear sweet voices!

Yesterday, I decided to find out what "Fang" Jenkins[1] is really up to. So I had a long conversation with him (about $200. worth!). He said he'd sent

---

[1] Joseph P. Jenkins was a Kansas City attorney who, along with Robert Bingham, represented Hickock and Smith after Russell Shultz resigned from the case.

the Supreme Court a list of new allegations (didn't specify), and also an in-
vidual [*sic*] copy of his brief for each justice ("I wish to be sure they <u>all</u> see
it—not just Byron White and a couple of clerks. Because that nightmare
trial must not be allowed to stand"). He told me the Kansas Bar Association
is "backing us to the hilt." Which rather amazed me: I thought they had retreated. <u>Then</u> Jenkins said: "I still think we may get a new trial. And if we
do, this time they won't be able to convict those boys. They'll go free." And
I thought: yes, and I hope you're the first one they bump off, you sonofa-
bitch. But what I actually said was: "Is that really your idea of justice?—
that after killing four people, they ought to be let out on the streets?
Doesn't that notion rather disturb you?" He had the grace to admit it did.
Lawyers! What hypocrites! Well, enough of that. Nothing now will happen
until March. <u>If</u> then.

I gather Nelle is much improved. You were angelic to call her. I don't
know why I never got Dewey's exercises—I was just about to scold him.
That's a shame about the debate prize. <u>Doesn't</u> <u>he</u> <u>graduate</u> <u>this</u> <u>spring</u>?
The Feb. 18th matter changed all my plans—but now I may as well go to
Rome for a week the end of the month (had a note from Vi, written from
Hong Kong, and she wants to meet me in Rome for 4 days). More later, but
all love <u>now</u>. Hugs and kisses

    T.

[Collection New York Public Library]

TO DONALD WINDHAM AND SANDY CAMPBELL

[Postcard]   [Verbier, Switzerland]
                                              [18 February 1965]

Dearhearts—

Except for a vital page or two, finished the book today—on, ironically,
the 18th. Exhausted. Home in about 3 weeks. Love you both, and miss you
mucho.

    xxxooo
    T.

[Collection Beinecke Library, Yale University]

TO BENNETT CERF

[Verbier, Switzerland]
20 Feb. 1965

Dearest B.—

Yesterday I finished "In Cold Blood"—except for a few paragraphs, and I <u>do</u> mean paragraphs. I'm mailing the mss. to Joe Fox, but I'd just as soon you did not read it until I've added that final note.[1]

The Supreme Court denied the appeals for the <u>second</u> time, and the execution was set for Feb 18th. <u>But</u> they got still <u>another</u> stay. However, I do not think the day of reckoning is now too distant.

Thank you for the Modern Library edition of my book. I think it is very handsome, and am <u>very</u> pleased.

I will be home in about three weeks, and longing to see you. All my love to my precious Phyllis! Love
Truman

[Collection Columbia University Library]

TO SANDY CAMPBELL

[Verbier, Switzerland]
20 Feb. 1965

Dearest Sandy—

Alvin has written, greatly distressed over the 52 questions you sent him.[2] As you know, he is not really well and very much overworked by the K.B.I [Kansas Bureau of Investigation]—and he just has not the time to answer all those queries beyond those he immediately knows the answer to. He <u>can't</u> go around conducting a new investigation—for one thing, Logan Sanford, the K.B.I director, would be furious. He already almost lost his job twice because of me. So would you please relieve his mind by call-

---

[1] Joseph Fox had replaced Robert Linscott as Capote's editor. Linscott had retired from Random House in 1958 and died in September 1964, at the age of seventy-eight.

[2] In his capacity as a *New Yorker* fact-checker, Campbell had sent Dewey a long list of factual questions. The purpose was to verify the accuracy of Capote's story.

ing him (BRidge 6-3563) and tell him to just do what he easily can and no more? I appreciate what you are doing with all my heart. But I just can't bear to get Alvin into any more trouble. All my love to you and Don—

T.

[Collection Beinecke Library, Yale University]

TO ALVIN AND MARIE DEWEY

[Verbier, Switzerland]
[20 February 1965]

Dearhearts—

I was <u>very</u> happy to have Pappy's good letter today. I loved the picture of him in previous letter—have it on my desk here.

Unfortunately, in the same mail there was a letter from Charles McAtee[1] (enclosed) with a monumentally depressing piece of news (which I've very unneccesarily [sic] underlined). If this is valid, and they <u>do</u> get back in the state courts—well, it means they can appeal all the way back to the U.S. Supreme Court. But I'm not sure that it <u>is</u> valid. Because such a writ is a <u>civil</u> action, and the state district judge is not compelled to grant the writ (I <u>believe</u>). Anyway, I can't imagine any Finney County judge would do it if he didn't have to. Oh God, I'm so weary and sick of it all. And Lord knows I know you are, too.

Pappy, <u>please</u> don't bother about Sandy's questions. <u>Please</u>. I can't bear to have you waste your time. You've been overly kind and patient and generous already. I will write and explain that you can't do more than you have. Someday I will make it up to you. Of that you can be sure.

It's true that I've finished the book—minus a few <u>vital</u> paragraphs. Part Four runs 140 pages. Shawn cabled me: 'Incomparable. An authentic masterpiece.' Well, at least it now <u>exists</u>—though hidden under a barrel.

I loved my valentine, precious Marie. Did you get one from a 'Dark Handsome Stranger'? Did those chocolates ever arrive?

Am trying to work up some spirit to go to Rome. I'm afraid Vi will be disappointed, as I haven't been in the mood to make many social arrange-

---

[1] Director of the Kansas State Penal Institutions.

ments. But I will be glad to get away from here for a week! Will return here on March 5th and depart for the U.S. around March 20th. All my love—

T.

[Collection New York Public Library]

TO CECIL BEATON

[Verbier, Switzerland]
20 March 1965

Dearest Cecil—

Finished book. Was bored and badly depressed, so went to Rome for 2 weeks, where promptly succumbed to Asian Flu. When somewhat recovered went to St. Moritz with the Agnellis[1]—seemed like every potentate in the world was there: all the Communists needed to do was bomb the Corviglia Club. Saw Figi there (she staying with Niarchos).[2] Also Brandolinis[3]—who gave me recent news of you.

It was kinda fun. But what a silly lot they are really. Anyway, I'm off to New York tomorrow—Jack is going only as far as Paris, where he plans to stop 10 days.

Thought the enclosed clip from the current <u>Time</u> might amuse you. Saint has another big hit: "The Odd Couple."[4] I have to go to Calif. late this spring about the <u>stupid</u> movie; and will tackle Kahlman [Kohlman] again about "Gainsborough Girls."

All your friends that I saw in both Rome and St. Moritz mentioned Kin, and how much they liked him. One of them being Lady Diana [Cooper].[5] Her face scarcely changes, but the rest is beginning to be rather aged. Poor Judy M. [Montagu] looked <u>ghastly</u>. A death's head!

---

[1] Gianni Agnelli was head of Fiat, the Italian car company, and was one of Italy's leading industrialists. He and his wife, Marella, were Capote's close friends.

[2] Stavros Niarchos was a rich Greek shipowner.

[3] Count Brando Brandolini d'Adda, a rich Venetian nobleman, was Gianni Agnelli's brother-in-law.

[4] Neil Simon's *The Odd Couple* opened on Broadway on March 10, 1965, and ran for nearly a year and a half, closing on July 2, 1967.

[5] The third daughter of the eighth duke of Rutland, Lady Diana Cooper had long been a brilliant social figure. She was the widow of Duff Cooper, a British politician who had held several high-ranking jobs before and during World War II and was later British ambassador to France.

How nice that you are able to spend so much time at Broadchalke. As soon as I get home, I'm going out to my Long Island house. Unfortunately, it isn't at all furnished—and I can't afford to buy anything. If only I knew when I will be able to publish my book!

Charlie and Diotima seemed to have survived the winter; I'm taking them both with me on the plane. Jack sends love. Love and all fine wishes to Kin. And dear Eileen.

mille Tendresse [*sic*]

T.

[Collection St. John's College, Cambridge University]

TO ALVIN DEWEY III

[Verbier, Switzerland]
[Probably 22 March 1965]

Dear Dewey—

Again, I think the writing is good in a sentence by sentence way, and the characters are more roundly developed this time, and the narrative line is more complete. But the whole concept is overly familiar and the ending is very weak. Perhaps he was drafted after all and was one of the people sending you rude postcards? Keep at [it]; it may take 50 to 100 stories before style and subject and technique will suddenly come together. It's like learning to swim.

Excuse the haste, but am leaving for New York—

Love

T.

[Collection New York Public Library]

TO CECIL BEATON

[Brooklyn, N.Y.]
19 April 1965

Dearest Cecil—

This just an exhausted scrawl (you owe me a letter <u>any</u>way), but I wanted you and Kin to know the case is over and my book is coming out next January. Perry and Dick were executed last Tuesday. I was there because they wanted me to be. It was a terrible experience. Something I will never really get over. One day I will tell you about it—if you can bear it.

It is still wintry here. But I read where you are having a lovely spring. My love to you and Kin and Eileen.

Hugs—
T.

P.S. Jack is well. So is Diotima. Charlie, as always, is a semi-invalid. Our house at the beach is going to be very pretty—in a simple way.

P.P.S. Have seen no theatre except "The Odd Couple"—which I thought <u>very</u> funny. It's making Saint intolerably rich.

[Collection St. John's College, Cambridge University]

TO CECIL BEATON

Box 501
Bridgehampton, n.y.
16 June 1965

Dearest Cecil—

Finished the final Pages of my book three days ago. Bless Jesus. But incredible to suddenly be free (comparatively) of all those years and years of tension and aging. At the moment, only feel bereft. But grateful. Never again!

How wonderful about your new studio. And I'm so happy that you are able to devote so much time to your painting. It must be difficult, to say the least; but exhilirating [*sic*].

I will be in London June 12 & 13, leaving 14th for Athens and a long cruise to Istanbul [*sic*], the Turkish coast, then Rhodes, Crete etc.

It will be the first real holiday I've had in almost 6 years—free from my monumental obsession. Will you be in London then? I don't suppose you will. Drop a line. Don't know yet where I will stay, but will let you know. Will return here August 12th.

Jack is fine. Diotima is catching her quota of birds. Charlie is holding his own. My love to Kin. And Eileen.

mille Tendresse [*sic*]

T

[Collection St. John's College, Cambridge University]

TO JACK DUNPHY

[Spetsopoula, Greece]
22 July 1965

Precious Jack—

Rcvd. Your sweet, very <u>amusing</u> note just as I was leaving the Athens hotel. That Tillotson![1]

Marella Agnelli's father died suddenly and she had to fly back to Italy. So I sailed alone on the yacht with Kay Graham.[2] Imagine that!—having a whole huge yacht to yourself.

However, the Agnellis, plus other guests, are rejoining the boat at Rhodes on the 26th. We are going to bypass Istanbul [*sic*] and go directly along the coast to Smyrna.

<u>Spetsopoula</u> is the private island of Niarchos. Fantastic! Beautiful! Have been here 2 days, but leave this morning.

Hope all is well with Charlie and sister. I love you and miss my darling one

T.

[Collection Gerald Clarke]

---

[1] Tillotson was a man who did yard work for Capote and Dunphy on Long Island.
[2] Katharine Graham was the publisher of *The Washington Post*.

TO CECIL BEATON

[Brooklyn or Bridgehampton, N.Y.]
20 Sept. 1965

Dearest Cecil—

These have been frantic days. My book starts in The New Yorker this week.[1] Hard to believe—after all these years. Feel too restless and tense to just sit here, so am going to New Mexico for two weeks—alone.

I had to go to Boston last week, and while there saw the Lerner show, which got very bad reviews.[2] The first act has some charm, and two good songs, and Barbara Harris is <u>fine</u>. But the second act is a total let-down, really pointless and dreary. Oliver's work is simply ugly. The show may have a certain success, but I'm sure you are well out of it. Also saw Leland's musical, "Hot September" (adaptation of "Picnic"), which also got bad reviews, but which I kind of liked.[3]

Rcvd. your card from Venice, and noted, with pleasure, its cheerful tone. I hope you are able to be in the country and work on your new painting. I was <u>deeply</u> impressed with the ones I saw—they were so original, vital, forceful: truly <u>painted</u>. A wonderful departure and growth.

Jack is fine; Charlie is holding his own, and Diotima is the same as ever. I miss you. I love you.

T.

P.S. How I could make you <u>laugh</u> with stories about the Social Preparations for the impending visit of the Armstrong-Jones [*sic*]!![4] Unbelievable!

[Collection St. John's College, Cambridge University]

---

[1] *The New Yorker* published *In Cold Blood* in four consecutive issues.
[2] *On a Clear Day You Can See Forever*, book and lyrics by Alan Jay Lerner and music by Burton Lane, opened at Broadway's Mark Hellinger Theatre on October 17, 1965. Oliver Smith, another of Beaton's rivals, designed the scenery.
[3] He was one of the few who did like it. Leland Hayward, the show's producer, closed it in Boston.
[4] He was speaking of Antony Armstrong-Jones, the earl of Snowdon, and his wife, Princess Margaret. Snowdon was yet another of Beaton's rivals, although as a photographer, not as a set designer.

TO KATHARINE GRAHAM

[New York]
[23 November 1965]

Precious KayKay—
Bless you for the beautiful visit. Our Kansas friends were bedazzled and thrilled—and <u>so</u> was I.[1] You were an angel to do that, really kind and thoughtful and generous, and I shall always remember it with great happiness and gratitude—
Love, et mille tendresse [*sic*]
Trubaby

[Collection Katharine Graham Estate]

TO ALVIN AND MARIE DEWEY

[Verbier, Switzerland]
15 Feb. 1966

Dearhearts—
I spent my first week here in a hospital room battling some kind of virus. But at last I have strength to hold a pen. Otherwise, found everything here okay—Sister in fine fettle, and Charlie's asthma no worse than usual.
Hope you got my Valentine-day cable. I loved Marie's sweet card. I had a very nice note today from Theda[3]—Dean sure gets around! Also had a note from Vi, who seems to be enjoying her boat-ride.
My hand-writing seems a little wobbly?—never mind.
It was nice of you to be kind to the 'London Mirror' reporter. But I really don't know why you should be. <u>The hell with them</u>. Let these people shift for themselves. As time goes on, all kinds of people will be after you. Of course a lot of it will be fun and interesting. But watch out for the phonies!

---

[1] Graham had entertained Capote, together with Alvin and Marie Dewey and Violet Tate, in Washington, D.C.
[2] Theda was Marie Dewey's sister.

The book is being published in England March 14. I will see that you get the reviews—which, am told in advance, are <u>great</u>: even better than U.S.

I will be home around March 20th. Maybe before. The weekend after my U. of K. appearance,[1] why don't we go to the Broadmoor? Sat. & Sunday. You decide.

I love you both. I love Paul and Dewey. And I miss you mucho.

Hugs & kisses

T.

[Collection New York Public Library]

TO DON CARPENTER[2]

[New York]
[11 May 1966]

Dear D.C.

I read your review in <u>Ramparts</u>. That's a <u>passionate</u> embrace compared with some of the blows I've rolled with over the years. As for your own re-action to criticism, you'll just have to learn to ignore it. Of course, with a first book that's very tough to do. But it's a <u>good</u> book, and it will find its own appreciative admirers.

I have reccomended [*sic*] you for a grant in creative writing from the National Institute of Arts and Letters. The decisions are many months away, and I don't know whether you will get it—but we'll see.

I hope you are at work on a new book.

With all good wishes

T. Capote

[Collection Edmond Miller]

---

[1] In April 1966, Capote read to an estimated 3,500 students at the University of Kansas in Lawrence, where the student newspaper proclaimed him the "Lion of American Literature."

[2] Don Carpenter was a California novelist and screenwriter. He published a mixed review of *In Cold Blood* in the April 1966 issue of *Ramparts,* the literary magazine of the New Left and the counterculture. When his own first novel, *Hard Rain Falling,* which appeared in the same season, began to attract mixed notices, he wrote to Capote to soften the blow of his critical remarks on *In Cold Blood,* and Capote graciously replied with this letter.

TO JACK DUNPHY

> [Hotel Ritz]
> [15, Place Vendôme, Paris]
> [27 July 1966]

Darling Jack—

Everything here incredibly hectic, but I guess it's worth it.[1] Reception at airport was like Lindbergh: even television crews. However, am going to Portugal on Sunday.

> c/o Radziwill
> —the address is: Quinta da Commenda
> Setubal
> Portugal
> (until August 8)

I wish you had called me from Beach Haven; I wanted to talk to you before I left.[2] Everything in Washington went okay.

I miss you, dearest one, and love you so much. Hope all is fine, and hugs for Charlie and sister.

Mille Tendresse [*sic*]

T.

[Collection Gerald Clarke]

---

[1] He was promoting *In Cold Blood*.
[2] Dunphy was visiting relatives in Beach Haven, New Jersey, an ocean resort.

Prayers:
Answered and Unanswered

"YOU MIGHT SAY TRUMAN CAPOTE has become omnipotent," proclaimed one paper at the end of the sixties. International society, with which he had been flirting since the early fifties, competed for his presence on their yachts and in their grand houses and palazzos. In New York, no party seemed complete without his sly wit and infectious laugh. With the money that was coming his way, he and Dunphy moved from a small apartment in Brooklyn Heights to a fancier one in Manhattan, overlooking the East River and the neighboring United Nations Building. In the heat of the summer they also had a cool retreat in eastern Long Island, and in the winter they had their condominium in the Swiss Alps. Just forty-two when he emerged from the triumphs of 1966, Capote seemed to have everything a writer, or anyone else, could want.

He often said that the harrowing years he spent researching and writing *In Cold Blood* had changed him inalterably. "No one will ever know what *In Cold Blood* took out of me," he said. "It scraped me right down to the marrow of my bones." And he seemed to be right. Despite his often playful demeanor, Capote had, in fact, been a writer of stern and unsmiling discipline. Novels, short stories, travel articles, profiles, plays and screenplays—he was adept at all of them. Even those that were unsuccessful, like his two plays, showed the talent and craftsmanship of the true writer.

As the sixties merged into the seventies, however, it became clear, even to him, that he had lost his way. He worked on television shows that were never produced, he wrote a movie script that was rejected, and he spent weary months trying, against all logic, to turn Jacqueline Kennedy's pretty but untalented sister, Lee Radziwill, into a television and movie star. All the while he was drinking too much and experimenting with the fashionable drugs of the era. Soon, by his own description, he was an alcoholic, making frequent trips to rehabilitation clinics that failed to rehabilitate him.

Though Jack Dunphy remained his one true companion—the only person in the world he trusted completely, Capote said—they spent less and less time together. Too restless to stay very long in one place, Capote often seemed to be in transit. Dunphy, by contrast, maintained an invariable routine: summer on Long Island, fall in Manhattan and winter in Verbier. To Capote, who had written most of *In Cold Blood* there, that Alpine retreat now seemed like a prison. Capote persuaded Dunphy to try his new house in Palm Springs, but Dunphy recoiled. "Thirst's End" he labeled that desert oasis, and he quickly retreated to Verbier.

Ever lonelier, despite a list of friends that could fill a telephone book, Capote engaged in a series of affairs with married or divorced men, the last and most prominent of whom was John O'Shea, a father of four from the middle-class suburb of Wantagh, New York. The breakups that inevitably followed such affairs left Capote hurt and shaken, vowing and sometimes obtaining revenge.

Despite so many problems, Capote continued to write, and write well. Drunk or sober, he always knew the difference between bad writing, good writing and superb writing, and he never let anyone see a sentence that fell short of his own skyscraper-high standards. For years he had spoken of the book that would be his masterpiece, *Answered Prayers,* which he compared to Proust's *Remembrance of Things Past.* Finally, in the fall of 1975, he let *Esquire* publish a chapter, "La Côte Basque, 1965"—La Côte Basque was a famous Manhattan restaurant in which much of the action took place. Capote had modeled some of his unsavory characters on his rich friends, and their reaction was instantaneous. They had entrusted him with their secrets, and when he revealed them, they turned on him as if he were nothing but a gate-crasher. He was omnipotent no more.

More chapters from *Answered Prayers* were published, and Capote managed to produce another book of collected stories and articles, *Music for Chameleons.* His correspondence dwindled to postcards and telegrams—when he wanted to say something, he picked up the telephone—that lack the brio and zest of earlier correspondence. "Better Death in Venice than life in Hollywood," he had written on his first trip to California in 1947. But, in an irony he might have appreciated, it was there that Truman Capote died, probably of a drug overdose, on August 25, 1984.

TO ALVIN AND MARIE DEWEY

[Postcard]   [Verbier, Switzerland]
                                                    [31 January 1967]

Dearhearts—
    Back today from Morocco[1] and found your sweet letter. Will write end
of week. Or maybe will telephone. All hugs and Love—
    T.

[Collection New York Public Library]

TO ALVIN AND MARIE DEWEY

[Postcard]   [Capri, Italy]
                                                    [Early February 1967]

Am here with the Paleys, who send all regards. Lovely house. Rcvd. Alvin's
letter with storm-clippings. My god! Certainly not a _safe_ place to live—
from _any_ point of view. Miss you mucho. Home end of month. Hugs and
Love—
    T.

[Collection New York Public Library]

---

[1] Capote had visited Morocco with Lee Radziwill.

TO DONALD WINDHAM AND SANDY CAMPBELL

[Postcard]   [Verbier, Switzerland]
                                                   [23 February 1967]

Dearhearts—
    Have missed you very much. Had a fascinating trip in the Sahara, but
otherwise have been flu-ridden here. Home early March. Much love to
both—
    T.

[Collection Beinecke Library, Yale University]

TO KATHARINE GRAHAM

    La Cerrada
    [Palm Springs, Ca.]
    [Early January 1968]

Darling Kay—
    That caviar!— I ate the whole pound Christmas day, which I spent
alone in the country. Ate it with 3 baked potatoes. It <u>almost</u> made up for my
robbery.[1] Bless you and thank you.
    I love my house here. <u>Very</u> pretty. <u>This</u> is where you ought to spend your
winter holiday. What a climate!
    I miss you. Much love
    Truman

    P.S. I drove all the way across the country by myself.[2] Hard—but sort
of fun. Took 6 days.

[Collection Katharine Graham Estate]

---

[1] Capote's house on Long Island had been burglarized shortly before Christmas 1967. Three
men were later arrested and accused of the crime.
[2] Actually, Donald Windham accompanied Capote to California.

TO JACK DUNPHY

[Telegram]   [Palm Springs, Ca.]
                                                        [17 January 1968]

        JACK DUNPHY VERBIER
HAPPY PUBLICATIONS DAY DEAREST JACK AND ALL LOVE FROM—
TRUMAN AND CHARLIE AND HAPPY[1]

[Collection Gerald Clarke]

TO CECIL BEATON

        TRUMAN CAPOTE
        [New York]
        [Spring 1968]

Dearest Cecil—
        I saw the photographic proofs of the book today—and it <u>is</u> The Best of
Beaton. A marvellous selection—truly impressive and original. Everything
about it, selection and design, is first-rate. As I cabled you, anything you
want to do about magazine publication is fine by me.
        I have been working hard, doing nothing else, but it all has been so frag-
mented—writing my book, and doing (all by myself) a very complicated
documentary film. That, and all the Tragedy in our American lives, has kept
one feeling like an insolvable jigsaw puzzle.[2] Jack is fine; Diotima is sitting
in the chair beside me; poor Charlie holds up! I miss you; I love you—
        T.

[Collection St. John's College, Cambridge University]

---

[1] Dunphy's novel *The Nightmovers* had just been published.
[2] He was doubtless referring to the war in Vietnam, the violence on college campuses and,
most probably, the assassination of Martin Luther King, Jr., which occurred on April 4, 1968.

TO CECIL BEATON

[Bridgehampton, N.Y.]
[Autumn 1968]

Cecil my love—

Yesterday (in a flower shop) I caught a whiff of tuberose—and dreamed of you that night. I think of you so often with such love and affection—two very different things, the second requiring respect. Am always thinking: I must write Cecil. But have been so wearied of writing <u>anything</u> because of the labours on my book.[1] Anyway, nothing very interesting in my life. I bought that house in Palm Springs—gutted it, and changed it completely. I know you don't like the place, but the house is quite attractive now.

Charlie is still alive, and very <u>lively</u>, and so is Diotima—more elegant than ever. Jack, too. We are all here at the Beach on Long Island. Jack refuses to go to California under any circumstances—same old Jack!

I'm going to see your exhibit next week. It has had great 'coverage' here and much acclaim.

As of now, I have no plans to come to London and/or Europe this year, as am really concentrated on my book.

Forgive this idiot note; I just wanted to say I miss you and love you. Big hug! Et mille Tendresse [*sic*]

T.

[Collection St. John's College, Cambridge University]

TO JACK DUNPHY

[Palm Springs, Ca.]
12 Jan. 1969

Precious Beloved Jack—

Your letters, sent to New York and now returned, finally arrived; and I've read them and read them—because I miss you so much. I think about you all through the day.

---

[1] *Answered Prayers.*

It is so quiet here, and I do love the garden and the pool and the sun; and I am working pretty good. I go to bed by nine-thirty and get up about seven-thirty. Charlie sleeps in the big bed with me. He hasn't been throwing up too much.

No, I'm not eating any of Myrtle's 'night-club' (very funny) lunches.[1] She comes every other day and makes me a meat-loaf I can have for supper. Annie comes only <u>once</u> a week to clean.

I'm so glad you got a good phonograph. I brought out here the Columbia phono that was stolen from you—it works perfectly.

<u>Please</u> have a phone installed. Please.[2] I have a new number here—714 (area code) 325 6682. Call me—Charlie would love it, and so would I. All my love, darling

T.

[Collection Gerald Clarke]

TO JOHN MALCOLM BRINNIN

[New York]
[November 1969]

Dearest M.

Yes indeed I came very close to being killed and am just now out of the hospital; now just waiting to have the stitches removed.[3] Did you ever get the letter I wrote you to Yucatan?—or <u>wherever</u> it was. I have a house in Palm Springs (of all places!) and wanted you to stop there. It's a lovely house—<u>if</u> you like the desert. I will be here until 1st December and would like to see you. Love to Bill [Read]. You, too.

T.

[Collection University of Delaware Library]

---

[1] Myrtle Bennett was his housekeeper in Palm Springs.

[2] Despite his pleading, Dunphy refused to have a telephone installed in their Verbier condominium.

[3] In October he was nearly killed when a new bulldog, Maggie, tried to jump out of his Jaguar convertible on a Long Island road. In his confusion, he stepped on the accelerator instead of the brake, crashed the car into a tree, and was propelled through the windshield. Knocked unconscious, he spent two days in Southampton Hospital. Maggie was unhurt; the car was demolished.

TO JACK DUNPHY

[New York]
[Early 1970]

Precious Beloved Baby,

I'd just sat down to write you when the mail came with your little note. . . . about how bad the weather has been, and that you are feeling bored and nervous; you always stick to things too steadily, why don't you break it up, go to the Ritz in Paris for a spell . . . it's stupid not [to] take more advantage of <u>having</u> an apartment in Europe and get around on little trips once in a while.[1] Even Diotima likes the Ritz! Anyway, I'm glad you are feeling more deeply drawn into your book; as for your not being sure now what it is about, does anyone <u>ever</u> know completely what they are writing about—if they are any good?

No, we're not going to have a Bull Dog Farm. Maggie came through fine. She and Charlie really get along famously. He loves to play with her, and now even instigates the games once in a while.

My hemmorhoids [*sic*] are really bothering me again; the only cure is an operation (painful, but not serious) and I suppose I ought to face up to it, but ugh . . . what thinkest thou?

Gosh, I wish you would get a phone installed there so we could talk.

I notice that some of these bills (Animal Shelter, for instance) have been appearing month after month. Haven't you paid them?

Hugs and a kiss and all the love in the world . . .

T.

[Collection Gerald Clarke]

---

[1] Dunphy was in Verbier.

TO JACK DUNPHY

Cela Fe La Horta
Mallorca
Spain
July 1970

Dearest Jacksie—

This is the most beautiful finca—right in the sea with lovely caves. It is very remote—the nearest village (and it's just a cluster of houses) is 8 miles away—and Palma, which is rather like a small Barcelona, is a three hour drive. So one leads a very quiet, healthy life. I feel so much better. It is so wonderful to be free for a while of all my worries—the IRS., the California courts, all the pending trouble with 20th Century Fox, etc. etc. etc.[1] I'm just not going to think about any of it. I wish I could go on a trip around the world for a whole year. Alas! Am going to Verbier next Tuesday (and if it is nice will stay there a week and afterwards either come back or go to visit the Brandolini's [*sic*] (Gianni Agnelli's sister) in Venice. Anyway will let you know so you can have guests if you want.

Hope Abbe has stopped sneezing and Dio is staying home and Maggie being not too rambunctious.

I miss you, precious love. All my love

T.

[Collection Gerald Clarke]

---

[1] He had interviewed a convicted California killer for a television documentary. When the conviction was overturned on a technicality, Capote was subpoenaed to testify in a new trial. Believing that the interview had been confidential, he ignored the subpoena and fled the state. Cited for contempt of court, he surrendered in October 1970 and was fined five hundred dollars and sentenced to three days in jail, of which he was forced to serve only eighteen hours. In the fall of 1967, Twentieth Century–Fox bought movie rights to his projected novel, *Answered Prayers*, for $350,000. As the deadline, January 1, 1971, approached, Capote had still not written the novel, however, and Fox was demanding return of its first installment of $200,000, a sum he was, in fact, forced to pay.

TO JACK DUNPHY

5 August 1970
Verbier

Dearest Jack—

Rented a car and drove up here and really it's lovely—snow on the mountains, flowers in the fields. Alas, they are building still another apartment chalet across from us. But at least it will be the <u>last</u> because there is no more room.

I've seen <u>everyone</u>. Mme. Guinnard says she has some laundry for you, and I said I'd pick it up. Mme. [unclear], who looks <u>wonderful</u>, <u>very</u> trim, was happy to see me, and I had lunch today with the Cortleys. I expect I will stay here until [the] weekend, then go to Turin (Agnelli) and Venice (c/o Count Brandolini, Palazzo Brandolini, Venice) and then come back here for a bit before taking the plane.

Saw Mme. Michieli, and she was fine and the apartment [is] in <u>perfect</u> shape. Really, it is such a cozy, pretty place. The rugs look great. Don't worry. I will leave everything spic & span.

Saw in the paper about the New York heat-wave. Hope it didn't affect you & Maggie too badly. I love you.

A Biêntôt—[*sic*]

T

[Collection Gerald Clarke]

TO JACK DUNPHY

[Palazzo Brandolini]
[Venice]
15 Aug. 1970

Happy Birthday, Angel Jack![1]

Arrived here yesterday after a really pleasant cool quite [*sic*] week in Verbier. I really love that little apartment.

---

[1] Dunphy's birthday was August 22. He was born in 1914.

Am living here in a vast apartment in this most beautiful palace. I plan to stay here until the end of next week and then drive back to Verbier for a few days and then take a plane to London for a few days with the Radziwills—so will be home in about 2½ weeks.[1] I've really enjoyed this holiday because it is the first time I've just wandered around feeling carefree and uncommited [sic]. Still, I'll be glad to get home to all my loved ones.

I went to the bank in Lausanne (Credit Suisse) and we have $18,000 there. I didn't take any one.

I am having 2 suits made here at Cecconi. My weight is good. <u>Walked</u> miles in Verbier.

I love you.

XXX

T.

[Collection Gerald Clarke]

TO MARIE RUDISILL

[Bridgehampton, N.Y.]
[25 September 1970]

Dearest Tiny—

I am so sorry to hear of your illness—I have been away all summer, and only just returned.

As for the advance you asked me to make, I won't beat around the bush either: I can't do it just now. I've had a terrible year on the stock exchange and I have a lot of money tied up in a new business opening in California. You know I've always helped you when you needed it, and maybe, after the first of the year, when I know what my income will be, I can manage this.

I will be here for the next few months. I know you are disappointed, and I'm sorry; but really I <u>do</u> love you and hope so much that you are feeling better—

T.

[Collection Edmond Miller]

---

[1] The Radziwills lived in London.

TO JACK DUNPHY

Hotel Ritz
15, Place Vendôme
Paris
[22 July 1971]

Darling Jack—
    Nice flight, but it is lonely here in our old nest without you to wake up and pester and have grapefruit avec honey. I will probably be back before you get this. Hope you had a good visit with Gloria.[1] A kiss for Mags and Dio and AP. I love you.
    T.

[Collection Gerald Clarke]

TO KATHARINE GRAHAM

[Postcard]   VERBIER, Suisse
                                              [10 February 1972]

Kay—
    Here, all ice and silence. But gradually I am feeling a recession of all those bad vibrations that have been so incessantly vibrating the last three years. Miss you, all love—
    T.

    P.S. Expect to be here until April

[Collection Katharine Graham Estate]

---

[1] Gloria Dunphy was Dunphy's favorite sister.

TO JACK DUNPHY

[New York or Bridgehampton, N.Y.]
5 July '72

Darling Jack—

I finished the Hazlitt book, and fell asleep, and woke up with such a feeling of warmth and gratitude and love for you.[1] You are the only good thing that ever happened to me. I admire and respect you so. I think that is more important perhaps than loving you. You can love for such shallow and wrong reasons. I love you for the right ones.

T.

P.S. This isn't your birthday present. I just want you to have it now.

[Collection Gerald Clarke]

TO LOUIS NIZER

Bridgehampton
New York
16 May 1973

How pleasant to have a letter from the admirable Mr. Nizer—<u>even</u> a scolding one.[2] It was so well written; if only your client, Miss Susann (sp?) had

---

[1] He was presumably referring to a work by William Hazlitt (1778–1830), the English essayist and critic.

[2] Capote was involved in several literary feuds. The most amusing was the one with Jacqueline Susann, the author of such bestselling potboilers as *Valley of the Dolls.* Capote began the fight in 1969 by slighting her literary abilities in an appearance on Johnny Carson's *The Tonight Show.* She later retaliated on the same show, ridiculing his effeminate mannerisms, imitating his high-pitched, baby-like voice and all but pronouncing him a homosexual. His turn came again when he next appeared on Carson's show. Susann, he told Carson and his millions of viewers, looked "like a truck driver in drag." That wounded her—she did indeed have heavy, somewhat mannish features—and she and her husband marched into the office of her lawyer, the eminent Louis Nizer, and demanded that Nizer draw up a suit for libel. "Words are like chemicals," Nizer later wrote. "Some combinations fizzle. Others explode. The laughter which burst across the nation drove her and Irving Mansfield, her husband and gifted partner in the dissemination of her works, right into my office." Though Nizer believed that Capote had in fact committed a libel, he advised Susann against a suit. He changed his mind, however, when, a few years later, Capote bragged to an interviewer that the reason Susann failed to sue him was that Nizer had informed her that she would lose any such lawsuit. All Capote's lawyer had to do, Nizer had supposedly told his client, was to dress a dozen real truck drivers in women's clothes and to parade them in front of a jury, which would thereupon conclude that Capote was right: she did look like a truck driver in drag. Nizer never told Susann any such thing, of course—Capote had invented his exchange with his client—and he wrote Capote a letter in which he demanded an apology. Capote's reply—this letter—appeased both him and Susann, and the matter was dropped.

your sense of style! As for my "offense"—well, I was told, lo these years ago, that Miss S. and her husband had requested a screening of the Carson program, and that they were attended by their attorney (presumably you, since I read in some paper that you were the lady's legal counsel.) Perhaps it was someone from your office? Or never happened? In any event, I do see your point, and I do apologize.

Still, I don't understand why you think what I said about your client was "libelous." All I said was that, in certain of her publicity photographs, she "looks like a truck driver in drag." That seems to me merely an aesthetic opinion—a spontaneous observation. Bitchy, yes; malicious, no.

I feel no malice for your client; on the contrary, I respect her as a very professional person who knows exactly what she's doing and how to do it.

On the other hand, I suggest you examine a few of the remarks Miss S. made about me—as recently as an interview 3 weeks ago in the Los Angeles Times. Over and again she has implied that I am a homosexual (big news!) and a lazy bones jealous of her productivity.

As far as I'm concerned, I couldn't care less if she won the Nobel Prize—so did Pearl Buck, alors.

Anyway, thank you for calling my attention to the magazine After Hours (Dark?).[1] I'd never heard of it. The interview in question was given last fall in New Orleans and printed in the N.O. Times Picayune.

I've never written, much less answered, more than ten or so letters. So save this. Maybe someday I'll be famous and your grandchildren can sell this at Sotheby's. But who could fail to answer someone who so charmingly suggests he might sue you?

Truman C.

TO KATHARINE GRAHAM

The Broadmoor
Colorado Springs, Colorado
[Early March 1974]

Darling Kaysie—
Am here for a week recovering from my hospital experience.[2] Feel much better, and bless you so much for the flowers.

---

[1] *After Dark* was the magazine in which Capote's interview appeared, detailing his fictitious account of Nizer's advice to Susann.

[2] Capote had been hospitalized at the Eisenhower Medical Center in Rancho Mirage, California.

Funny how everything evolved—how I got bronchial pneumonia, then the trial was delayed for 6 months after all! Not that I ever want to get back into that fray.[1]

I know that you are concerned about me on several levels. Don't.

I expect to be back in New York very soon, and hope we can have a really good talk. I know you are one of the only friends I can rely on—but I think you will find my head on your shoulder less heavy.

I love you

T.

[Collection Katharine Graham Estate]

TO JACK DUNPHY

[Denver]
March 1974

What a winter! Diotima was the worst of it, and I think of it every day, and know how much you must miss her.[2] Me, too. And you. And Maggie. But it will not be too long now.

I am still at Mt. [unclear] hospital in Denver—but will be discharged in about five days—totally disintoxicated from both booze and pills. It hasn't been easy, and I don't think I could have done it without all this good and kindly professional help. I have met the most exceptional variety of people here, and, except for a few helpless zombies, liked them all.

I sold the P. Springs house! Didn't get a very good price, but it is a great step forward toward simplifying this all too-entangled life.

I have put everything aside to write a short novel—maybe 60,000 words. I feel optimistic but the important thing is to work and finish something. Yes it has been difficult, the bronchial pneumonia, the operation and, most of all, this withdrawal from all chemical associations. But feel I'm headed somewhere.

---

[1] Capote's illness allowed him to get out of his contract with *The Washington Post* to report on a sensational Houston murder trial involving sex and torture.

[2] When Capote and Dunphy were on the Greek island of Páros in 1958, Dunphy rescued a kitten a boy had thrown into the sea. "I have called her Diotima after the woman who taught Socrates all about love," he wrote his sister Gloria. Diotima died in February.

When I've finished my business in P. Springs, will head for New York—though don't know how I'll get there with all the gas shortages et al. Anyway, will get there early on in April.

Am so looking forward to a nice fire in the fireplace of your pretty cottage. Again, darling, Jack, I miss [you] and send so much love.

T.

P.S. Is the deed to the Springs house in your safe-deposit box? If so, where is the key? Send the reply to 853 Paseo El Mirador; P. Springs.

Hugs
T

[Collection New York Public Library]

TO LEO LERMAN[1]

Bayouboys Limited
3445 Stephen Lane
Wantagh, L.I., N.Y.
April 17, 1974

Dear Leo

May I ask a favor? The myriad details of business have, more and more, made it very difficult for me to find the time to "do my thing."

As many of you are aware, communications with me are often difficult, sometimes impossible, to establish or maintain because of the vast amount of travel I enjoy. To facilitate communications I have asked my associate, John O'Shea to function as my business manager, agent, secretary and advisor.

---

[1] This was a form letter, sent to several of Capote's friends, formally announcing John O'Shea's entrance into his life as business manager—and just about everything else. The address is O'Shea's small suburban house in Wantagh, Long Island, not far from New York City. Capote's friends were appalled by the letter, which they viewed as his surrender to O'Shea's demands for control over his affairs. The letter was almost certainly written by O'Shea, and parts of it make no sense. This one is addressed to Lerman, for instance, but the second paragraph, which begins "as many of you are aware," addresses several people.

Mr. O'Shea is completely and constantly attuned to my interest in, and availability for, new projects; and knows the current status of present undertakings. He can and will speak with authority in the functional areas described above.

Please communicate with us through the phone and address on this letterhead only for prompt response.

Our whereabouts will always be available there.

Please circulate this as you see fit.

And thanks a lot.

Cordially,

Truman Capote [signature]

Truman Capote [typed]

[Collection Columbia University Library]

TO DORIS ROBERTS GOYEN[1]

[After 9 January 1975]

Dear Mrs. Goyen—

Kindly ask your "husband" to recall the review he wrote of my book "Breakfast At Tiffany's" and you will realize how really ludicrous your note is.[2] I was helpful and kind to your friend at the beginning of his career—his response was (as it was to K. A. Porter and his former lover Stephen Spender) one of total treachery.

By the way, I think you are a _very_ fine actress.[3]

Sincerely

T. Capote

[Collection Unknown]

---

[1] Doris Roberts, William Goyen's wife, had written Capote asking for comments to commemorate the twenty-fifth anniversary edition of her husband's novel _The House of Breath._

[2] Goyen had written an unfavorable review of _Breakfast at Tiffany's_ ("That Old Valentine Maker," _The New York Times Book Review,_ November 2, 1958), deriding what he regarded as Capote's whimsy, excess, want of seriousness, and lack of "full imaginative control."

[3] Roberts was highly regarded as an actress.

TO JACK DUNPHY

[Key West, Florida]
2 March 1975

Dearest Jack—
I don't know if you got my letter from Cozumel (Mexico)—what an awful place! Gloria and Loel [Guinness] rescued me from there and sent me to Nassau in their plane, where I stayed two days with the Paleys. Then came here to Key West, where have been lent a charming little house by David Wolkolsky in exchange for a week's stay at 870.[1] It is very quiet and nice, and I have finished my story <u>Mojave</u>, which Esquire has bought for $10,000 and which will be in their June issue. In some ways I think it is one of my best stories. Am going to do some lectures at various colleges starting March 18 and ending April 18th. Have been doing a lot of exercising and swimming and am in pretty good shape. My address here is <u>Pier House</u>, Key West, Florida. It is sort of breezy and not as humid as the rest of this unattractive state. If you did not get to Paris, I suppose you will.[2] I seem to have recovered my creative energy and have been putting in a good many hours of solid work every day. From all I hear, it has been a mild winter in Wainscott, so maybe (crossed fingers) there won't be any floods.[3] Hope Maggie is okay, and that you have been having a productive season in your aerie. Much love, and many hugs. I miss you—
T.

[Collection Gerald Clarke]

---

[1] In 1965, following the success of *In Cold Blood,* Capote had moved from Brooklyn Heights to an apartment overlooking the East River at 870 United Nations Plaza in Manhattan.

[2] Dunphy, who spent winters in Verbier, usually stopped off in Paris on his way home to New York.

[3] Capote and Dunphy had small, neighboring houses on Long Island. Both homes were prone to leaks after a severe, snowy winter.

TO WILLIAM STYRON

[Beverly Hills, Ca.][1]
9 January 1976

Dear Bill—

I greatly appreciated your note about the chapter from my book.[2] The reaction in many quarters has ranged from the insane to the homicidal. Still, with the support of a few well-wishers like you (not that there seem to be many of those) I guess I'll stay the course. The next installment (really long, over 40,000 words) is scheduled for the May issue of Esquire. It's called <u>Unspoiled</u> <u>Monsters</u>. Ha ha. Much love to Rose. You, too!

Truman

[Collection Perkins Library, Duke University]

TO JACK DUNPHY

[Beverly Hills, Ca.]
11 Jan 1976

Dear Jack and Mags

I hope you had a good flight and found everything snowy and snug in good old Verb.

I spent about four days out at the beach—most of it cleaning my studio.[3] It sure needed it. The weather was a bit cold, but blue and clear, very beautiful really. I drove back to town and left the car at the Carlton garage for Mr. Bailey to collect.

I came back here yesterday and will be at this address until Feb 15th when I start my college tour (at the University of Oklahoma); I tried to get out of it altogether, but couldn't without a real legal hassle. However, I did manage to curtail it somewhat.

---

[1] Capote had rented a house at 9421 Lloyd Crest Drive in Beverly Hills, and he was living there with John O'Shea.

[2] "La Côte Basque, 1965," a chapter from Capote's novel in progress, Answered Prayers, had appeared in the November 1975 issue of Esquire.

[3] He is referring to his house on Long Island.

I hope you have got a good dark pair of goggles. I'm sure it's the sun that causes the eye trouble.

Am working on Answered Prayers. The next installment is now scheduled for May.

Please write me here. You too, Mags. Hugs and love galore

T.

[Collection Gerald Clarke]

TO JACK DUNPHY

[Beverly Hills, Ca.]
[2 February 1976]

Darling Jack—

Finally got both your letters out here in Dizzyland and was so happy you and Mags arrived okay, especially to catch the <u>bus</u> to V [Verbier]. Every centime counts these days. Speaking of which, here enclosed are some checks to pay the Verbier expenses etcetera.

The next chapter of my book (42,000 words long) is scheduled for the May Esquire and there is going to be a great photo of me (in a black Borsalino) on the cover.[1]

I can't send you the address of the publisher you want until I go back to N.Y.—on Feb 20th.[2] Why don't you get it from the Donadio office?[3]

I have been turning down movie roles right and left—though <u>one</u> I am <u>very</u> intrigued by: Ken Russell is doing a film about Nijinsky, with Nureyev, and he wants me to play Diaghilev.[4] Wouldn't that <u>infuriate</u> Lincoln Kirstein!!!

I will send Maggie a bone from here.

I'm really sorry about poor Moret. The whole thing is like a Simenon novel.

---

[1] The chapter, titled "Unspoiled Monsters," was actually about 24,000 words. Capitalizing on the furor caused by his previous chapter, "La Côte Basque," which it had published the previous fall, *Esquire* put Capote on its cover, dressed in black and with an ivory-handled stiletto in his hands, as if he were an assassin. "Capote Strikes Again!" read its headline. "More from *Answered Prayers*: the most talked-about book of the year."

[2] *John Fury*, Dunphy's first novel, was being reissued by another publisher.

[3] Candida Donadio was Dunphy's literary agent.

[4] Capote never made such a movie.

Hope you are working, and getting some use out of the new ski boots.
A big kiss for Mags. All love
    T.

Just recvd. your letter. Here is a check for $1,500. I don't understand
why you had to borrow from Gloria [Dunphy]. Whenever you need anything for your checking account just say so.

Hugs—
T.

[Collection Gerald Clarke]

TO JACK DUNPHY

    [Beverly Hills, Ca.]
    3 Feb 1976

Dearest Jack—
    Myrtle [Bennett] died, and I am just back from P. Springs. She was
buried in a lovely quiet place in an oasis in the desert between the mountains. Now I doubt that I will ever go there again.
    I found exactly the kind of bone Maggie likes, and it was sent off today.
The weather has been very good—I hope your snow conditions have improved.
    I will be in New York around Feb 20th for a few days and for a week or
so around 1st March. The tour ends mid-April, and I certainly shall never
do another.
    It is now definitely settled that Esquire is devoting their entire May
issue to the 42,000 word chapter from my book. So we shall see.
    I hope you got the address of the 'John Fury' publisher. I hope you recd.
my letter with the check. If you need anything suddenly while I am on tour
cable me c/o Joe Fox, Random House, 201 East 50th St.
    I saw the most lovely French film "The Story of Adele H."[1] You would
love it. Be <u>sure</u> and see it.

---

[1] François Truffaut's *The Story of Adèle H,* starring Isabelle Adjani, told of the romantic obsession Victor Hugo's daughter had with a French army officer.

Why don't you call Oona [Chaplin]? I think she is very lonely and would love to see you.[1] The number is Vevey 51-03-51. Also, I wish you would write Cecil [Beaton] (8 Pelham Place, London) as it would be a great kindness. I've had 2 letters from him—handwriting very wobbly but mind alert.[2]

I had to have the hedges trimmed a bit at Wainscott because Mr. Pulver refused to deliver any more gas to your tank—which meant frozen pipes etc. I arranged this through Dayton (via phone from here) and so don't worry, all has been taken care of.

Give my love to Mme. Micheli.

Mucho mooches for Mags and love to you both—

Namurt Etopac

[Collection Gerald Clarke]

TO WILLIAM STYRON

[Hotel Fontainebleau]
[Miami, Fla.]
as from: 870 U.N. Plaza
New York, N.Y.
6 Sept. 1976

Dear Bill

The chapter (in current Esquire) from "The Promise" is a promise indeed; a pleasure to the ear and the heart—and hilarious, to boot.[3] The intelligence of your work, the sensitive strength of it, always refreshes me.

You may wonder <u>what</u> I am doing in this empty, heat-heavy, atrocity: Miami. Well, I wanted to go some place where I could be alone, really alone, and spruce up the remaining chapters of my book. So I thought of this hideous hotel. And in a way it has worked out very well. I've lost 35

---

[1] The Chaplins lived in Switzerland, not far from Verbier.

[2] Beaton had suffered a serious stroke in July 1974.

[3] "The Seduction of Leslie," an excerpt from Styron's novel *Sophie's Choice* (1979) in which the narrator, Stingo, pursues the coy Jewish American princess Leslie Lapidus, appeared in the September 1976 issue of *Esquire*.

pounds since your birthday and am the picture of health.[1] Have become a lifetime teetolar [*sic*], and really enjoy it. My love to Rose!
  Affectionately
  Truman

[Collection Perkins Library, Duke University]

TO JOHN MALCOLM BRINNIN

  [Bridgehampton, N.Y.]
  [21 September 1976]

Dear Heart—
  G. Clarke is a very good writer and v. nice.[2] You and Bill will like him. Tell him whatever you want—God knows everyone else has. I've lost 35 pounds, had a million dollars worth of dental work and look 16.
  Love—T.

[Collection University of Delaware Library]

TO JACK DUNPHY

[Postcard]   [New York]
                                                   [28 January 1978]

Dear Jack and Mags—
  I [unclear] you a postcard but forgot to put <u>stamps</u> on it. So am sending another. I feel <u>good</u> and am behaving myself perfectly. Off to Martinique tomorrow taking as my only reading a one-volume complete Simone Weil. She better be as good as you say! Hugs to both, I love you—T.

[Collection Gerald Clarke]

---

  [1] Styron turned fifty-one on June 11, 1976.
  [2] Gerald Clarke, Capote's biographer, had asked Brinnin for an interview. Clarke's biography, *Capote*, was published in 1988.

TO JACK DUNPHY

[In flight] to Martinique
Jan 29 1978
Up in the air

Dearheart—

Couldn't sleep last night, so reread some of your letters. So sad about Moret. What a story. It's like Simenon.

Don't worry: I am taking antabuse[1] faithfully, going to Gym, seeing Dr. Potter (I am going to have to either see less of him or get him to reduce his <u>fees</u>: <u>very</u> expensive.) I feel so clear and optimistic. Just keep those candles burning for me.

I had dinner with Gerald Clarke; why don't you drop him a line—when I asked if he had heard from you, he said, rather wistfully, no.

The new work on the apt. goes slowly—they are taking up all the carpets Feb 15. Once the floors are polished, I will see more clearly how to go.

No news from the coast, except O'Shea <u>now</u> says he has spent all the money and cannot repay any of the money. He is back drinking, and calls friends of mine at four or five in the morning and [unclear] them, saying if only I would suddenly drop dead all his problems would be solved! Oh well, the hell with all that.

P.S. I hope I can get a real rest in Martinique; this has been a high pressure winter. I miss you. Kiss Mags. Darling Jack, you are the great love of my life. You <u>are</u> my life.

[Collection Gerald Clarke]

---

[1] Antabuse is an abstinence-maintaining drug for alcoholics. If a person taking it drinks even a small amount of alcohol, the results, including vomiting, are extremely unpleasant.

TO LEO LERMAN

[Postcard]   [Schoelcher, Martinique]
                                                        3 Feb 1978

Dearest Myrt—

The piece I am doing is going to be very good. It's called <u>Music</u> <u>For</u> <u>Chameleons</u>: <u>A</u> <u>Winter</u> <u>Visit</u> <u>to</u> <u>Martinique</u>.[1] Am fine and thin and brown and healthy. Love to Gray. You, too

Marge

[Collection Columbia University Library]

TO JACK DUNPHY

[Postcard]   [Martinique, West Indies]
                                                        3 Feb 1978

Are you interested in a Capote original? This is me writing under a palm tree.[2] There is a fabulous non-alcoholic drink here called UN CARESSE. Some people put rum in it. But not me. Love to Mags. A big hug

T

[Collection Gerald Clarke]

---

[1] *Music for Chameleons: New Writing by Truman Capote* was published by Random House in 1980. It included the title story and five others, a nonfiction piece called "Handcarved Coffins," and seven "conversational portraits"—Capote's description.

[2] See frontispiece.

TO MAGGIE

[Postcard]   [Martinique, West Indies]
                                              [9 February 1978]

Darling Mags
    There are lots of dogs here but you wouldn't like them—they are poor,
scruffy things. Miss you—Love—
    T.

[Collection Gerald Clarke]

TO JACK DUNPHY

[Postcard]   [Center City, Minn.]
                                              2 Aug. 1978

Dearest Jack
    Having wonderful time. Wish <u>you</u> were here. No. I wouldn't wish that
on my best friend, which you are.[1] Love to Mags. Hugs—
    T.

[Collection Gerald Clarke]

---

[1] Capote was being treated at Hazelden, an addiction-rehabilitation clinic fifty miles north of
Minneapolis.

TO JACK DUNPHY

> [The Sea View]
> [9909 Collins Avenue]
> [Bal Harbour, Miami Beach, Fla. 33154]
> 20 January 1979

Darling Jack—

Have been here for five days, hoping for a little sun; alas, it has been mostly clouds and rain, and I am returning demain.

Notice the envelope: 'the Ability to write—a Root of Democracy.'[1] I got these stamps just for you. Show them to Camille: Americans are civilized.[2]

Rain or no, I have done a lot of swimming, am soberer than ever (you will be pleased to hear) and have got some writing done.

Hope you got my cable saying your Rose des Vents check had been covered. I don't see how we could owe them that much money. What is the maintenance there per month?[3] Get to the bottom of this.

I went to the bank and talked to your banker. I liked him—sort of a tough Mr. Milquetoast. And he adores you. Showed me the letter you had written him, chuckling—as though to say: "That Jack what a character!"

Well, I see Social Security is going to give you $199 a month spending money. At least that will keep you in cigarette money, especially since you don't smoke.

I hope you are okay, and Maggie too. My new dentist broke his leg skiing. I love you and miss you, darling one. Forever.

T.

P.S. The picture is of me jumping on a trampoline here; so you can see I'm in good shape.

[Collection Gerald Clarke]

---

[1] The envelope was surrounded with one-cent stamps containing a drawing of an inkwell and a quill pen, above which were the words THE ABILITY TO WRITE. A ROOT OF DEMOCRACY.

[2] Dunphy was in Verbier. Camille was presumably a Swiss or French friend.

[3] He is referring to the maintenance on their Verbier condominium.

TO ALAN ROSS[1]

[Palace Hotel]
[Madrid, Spain]
as from—
870 U.N. Plaza
New York, N.Y.
29 March 1979

Alan Ross, Esq.
Editor
The London Magazine

Dear Mr. Ross—

Apparrently [*sic*] a letter I wrote you in late August, 1978, never reached you. It concerned the article by Dotson Rader about the book "Tennessee Williams' Letters To Donald Windham." It concerned certain remarks attributed to me by Mr. Rader; remarks I never made, specifically an allegation that Mr. Williams was "furious" because Mr. Windham had published his letters without his consent or knowledge.

The rest of the letter concerned Mr. Rader's general estimate of Mr. Windham's rating, both as a writer and as a man, which he set at a low level—when, in fact, the opposite is true.[2] Mr. Windham is exceedingly well regarded as a writer and, generally speaking, is well known as a man of integrity.

Sincerely
Truman Capote

[Collection Beinecke Library, Yale University]

---

[1] Alan Ross was the editor of *The London Magazine*.

[2] Rader's article "The Private Letters of Tennessee Williams" had appeared in the July 1978 *London Magazine*. Rader wrote: "Professionally, Donald Windham is known, if known at all, as a writer of effetely precious prose. He is a person of . . . petty resentments and embittered false pride rubbed sore by too little achievement in too long a career." On August 26, 1978, Capote told Windham he'd written a "strong" letter to *London Magazine* in Windham's defense. That letter apparently went astray, so Windham urged him to send another, which Capote finally did after an angry phone call from Sandy Campbell on March 21, 1979. The long friendship ended at this point, and Capote never again saw either Windham or Campbell. Subsequent to these unhappy events, Capote and Tennessee Williams had a belated reconciliation, and Capote dedicated *Music for Chameleons* to him.

TO SANDY CAMPBELL

29 March 1979
Palace Hotel
Madrid, Spain

Dear Sandy—

You say that I have "lost two 'more' friends," namely you and Don. If true, I am more sad than I can say. However, in Don's case, I think Don's [*sic*] should speak for himself. If he chooses to relinquish a friendship of thirty years, one which I have cherished (as, indeed, I have <u>yours</u>), then I think I at least deserve to be told so directly.

After recovering from the initial astonishment, and subsequent anger, inspired by your telephone call (the injustice of it, at any rate what I felt, rightly or otherwise, to be the unjustness of it), I have recovered enough to try and understand it from your point of view. Lawsuits are an expensive and claustrophobic experience (as I well know, having gone through four of them, two still pending); one does lose perspective, become myopic. Still, I am puzzled; I cannot imagine what I have done to disturb you. I did write a letter to The London Magazine—whether you accept that or not (and did so when I was in treatment at Hazleden [Hazelden], and not in a condition to write a dying grandmother). As for Alan Schwartz,[1] neither you or Alan have asked me to write any kind of letter or provide any sort of affadavit [*sic*].

During our conversation, you threatened, among several threats, to "brand" me as "a liar". At the time, my first thought was: "Well, you've already done that, and in the most public manner possible, in the comments attributed to you in <u>The</u> <u>New</u> <u>York</u> <u>Times</u> <u>Magazine</u> articles last July." I did not comment to you about this, nor did I do so to anyone else (though God knows everyone else mentioned it—I'm referring to the story about Oliver Smith's house etc.).[2] Indeed, I should refrain from mentioning it now; still, some human need provokes me to do so.

The same sort of need, I suspect, that provoked you to call and reprimand me. Gerald Clarke casually remarked to me that Don was under the impression that I was talking to and seeing a great deal of [Dotson] Rader and T.

---

[1] Capote and Windham's attorney.
[2] Anne Taylor Fleming had quoted Windham and Campbell's story of Capote's once giving a journalist the impression, in their presence, that the Willow Street house in Brooklyn was entirely his, when in fact he only rented the basement apartment.

Williams. It is true that I have spoken four or five times with Rader on the phone, but the lawsuit was mentioned on only one of those occasions, and then only in the most peripheral manner. Williams I have seen just once—at a small dinner party where we spoke very briefly, and not at all about you.

Sandy, I very much hope that we will again be the friends we were; if not, I want to thank you for your past generosity—I will never forget the great kindness of you and Don, especially during my long illness.

And this is sent to you both with love, an affection enduringly real and true, from

Truman

P.S. I do not have a typewriter with me, or the address of The London Magazine—so will you please see that the enclosed reaches Mr. Ross?

[Collection Beinecke Library, Yale University]

TO JACK DUNPHY

[New York]
15 Feb 1980

Dearest Jack
I will not bore you with the agonies of the voyage. No matter—it was pure joy to see you and Maggie. You are both so beautiful!
I love you, Jack. Hurry home, and bring me a big hug—
T

[Collection Gerald Clarke]

TO READERS OF INTERVIEW MAGAZINE[1]

[April 1980]

Dear Friends,
I hope you enjoyed my December contribution ("Handcarved Coffins"), and will be pleased to hear that it was bought by the movies for

---

[1] Published as "A Letter from Capote" in the April 1980 issue of *Interview*.

a lot of money. Otherwise, all has been a disaster. I went to Switzerland and was run over by a drunken skier weighing more than 250 pounds. It's a wonder that I escaped with only a sprained wrist, sprained back, and a head concussion. So off I flew to California to recuperate, only to arrive during the infamous storms and floods of February. The house of my hostess was in danger of sliding off a cliff.[1] Several rooms were filled with mud. Still, the house survived—and so did I, more or less.

Actually, what I wanted to say is that my appearances in *Interview* will be irregular for a while because I am at long last finishing "Answered Prayers." However, I am preparing a surprise for the September issue: a very long piece, very: a sort of homemade bomb.[2] Meanwhile, all the best, T.C.

P.S. In September I am publishing a book that contains many of my *Interview* pieces. The book is called "Music for Chameleons."

P.P.S. One thing more. Do any of you remember "A Day's Work"?—It was about Mary Sanchez, my cleaning lady, and the day I spent accompanying her while she cleaned various apartments.[3] Anyway, that too is going to be a movie.[4] But we are having a hard time finding the right person to play Mary. Ethel Waters, when she was fifty, would have been very good. It must be a very fine black actress (50 to 60) who has real range, and a sensitive understanding of the comic, the absurd. If any of you can suggest a suitable actress, please write me. I would be very grateful.

---

[1] He stayed with Joanne Carson, ex-wife of television talk-show host Johnny Carson. Her house was in the Bel Air section of Los Angeles, on a hill just above Sunset Boulevard.

[2] This piece did not appear; Capote's letter in the May 1980 issue was his last contribution to *Interview* that year.

[3] "A Day's Work" appeared in the June 1979 issue of *Interview*.

[4] Neither "Handcarved Coffins" nor "A Day's Work" was ever made into a movie.

TO READERS OF INTERVIEW MAGAZINE[1]

[New York]
[May 1980]

Dear Friends—

Cecil Beaton died—not unexpectedly, as he had suffered a stroke some four years ago.[2]

We had travelled many places together. All over Europe, Africa, the Orient: He was the perfect travelling companion: I loathe sightseeing, which was his passion; so, while I lounged about, he diligently sought the sights, recording them on his camera for the both of us.

Over the years, he gave me hundreds of pictures; but the only one I have on view was taken one summer on the rocky shores of Tangiers.

Jane Bowles is in the picture, and that is why I especially like it. I have never understood why Jane, one of the most original and mysterious phenomenons ever to come from out of nowhere (actually, she was a Jewish girl from Ohio) never received the honors and audience her very unique writings deserved. She wrote only three works, *Two Serious Ladies* (a novel), *In the Summer House* (a play), and *A Stick of Green Candy* (short stories), but they were all brilliant, and utterly unlike the work of anyone else. She died ten years ago in a Spanish nunnery. A book of her Selected Writings has been published.[3] Read it.

I want to thank all of you who suggested actresses to play Mary Sanchez, the cleaning woman who appeared in my *Interview* piece *A Day's Work*. We are following all the leads. Many people suggested Esther Rolle. And she *is* good; but rather *too* professional. Remember: Mary is black, between fifty and sixty, maybe sixty-five. I have a hunch that when we find her she will be someone in the entertaining field, but not necessarily an actress. Perhaps a singer, a forgotten vaudeville personality, an actress with a regional group. Really, it is extraordinary the amount of talent, even genius, unused, undiscovered. Look at Jane Bowles! I'm sure there are many people who are not only greatly gifted but do not suspect the nature of their gift. I had an elderly cousin, the woman in my story *A Christmas Memory*, who was a genius; she certainly didn't know it, nor did anyone else: most

---

[1] Published as "A Letter from Capote" in the May 1980 issue of *Interview*.
[2] Beaton died on January 18, 1980, at the age of seventy-six.
[3] Jane Bowles died in 1973. "A Stick of Green Candy" is a story in her collection *Plain Pleasures* (1966). *The Collected Works of Jane Bowles* (1966) brings together the novel, the play and the stories in a single volume, with an introduction by Capote.

people thought she was an eccentric, simple-minded lady with an unusual talent for making scrapquilts.

I went to California again (how can anyone live there; it's unendurable) to discuss the casting of *Handcarved Coffins*. The producers, Lester Persky and United Artists, have several rows of names. Row A reads: Jake Pepper—Robert Duvall; Mr. Quinn—Steve McQueen; Addie Mason—Ellen Burstyn. I admire all three of these performers. But personally I would prefer an all non-star cast.

Otherwise, I've been working on my book *Answered Prayers*.

The other day, a man stopped me on the street and asked if I knew how to get to Chinatown. I said: "It's downtown. Just keep walking downtown."

Then I remembered a childhood neighbor, a husky boy who spent one whole summer digging a huge deep hole in his backyard. At last I asked him what was the purpose of his labor.

"To get to China. See, the other side of this hole, that's China."

Well, he never got to China; and maybe I'll never finish *Answered Prayers*; but I keep on digging!

All the best,
T.C.

TO JACK DUNPHY

[Telegram]   [New York]
                                                             [25 February 1982]

jack dunphy
(1936) verbier
miss you need you cable when can i expect you Love Truman

[Collection Gerald Clarke]

A Capote Chronology

1924   Born in New Orleans (Sept. 30) to Arch Persons and Lillie Mae Faulk Persons; he is christened Truman Streckfus Persons.

1930   Is left with elderly Faulk cousins in Monroeville, Alabama.

1931   Mother goes to New York for the first time; changes her first name from Lillie Mae to Nina and divorces Arch (Nov. 9).

1932   Mother marries Joseph Capote (March 24). Several months later she brings Truman to her new home in New York City.

1933–36   Attends the Trinity School, a private Episcopal boys' school on the West Side of Manhattan, for the fourth, fifth and sixth grades.

1935   Adopted by Joe Capote (Feb. 14), and his last name is changed from Persons to Capote.

1936   Is enrolled in St. John's Military Academy, an Episcopal school in Ossining, New York, thirty miles from Manhattan.

1937   Returns to the Trinity School.

1939   The Capotes move to Greenwich, Connecticut, a wealthy suburb of New York City, and Truman enters Greenwich High School.

1942 The Capotes return to New York, to an apartment at 1060 Park Avenue. Truman, who failed to graduate with the Greenwich High School class of 1942, enters the Franklin School, a private school on the West Side, from which he finally graduates in 1943. While attending Franklin, he takes a job as a copyboy at *The New Yorker.*

1943 Publication of his first short story, "The Walls Are Cold," in *Decade of Short Stories.*

1944 Two more short stories, "A Mink of One's Own" and "The Shape of Things," are published in *Decade of Short Stories.*

1945 "Miriam" is published in the June issue of *Mademoiselle.* This is his first appearance in a magazine of large circulation, and it immediately catches the attention of literary New York. Other stories soon follow in *Mademoiselle* and its rival *Harper's Bazaar.* On the strength of "Miriam," Random House signs him to a contract for his first novel, *Other Voices, Other Rooms.*

1946 Spends eleven spring and summer weeks at Yaddo, a retreat for artists, writers and musicians in upstate New York. It is here that he meets and begins a long relationship with Newton Arvin, a professor of literature at Smith College in Northampton, Massachusetts. In the fall, his mother's alcoholic rages prompt him to move from their apartment on Park Avenue to rooms in Brooklyn, an arrangement that lasts only a few months.

1947 Spends the summer on Nantucket. Finishes *Other Voices, Other Rooms.*

1948 *Other Voices, Other Rooms* published (Jan. 19).

   Goes to Haiti for *Harper's Bazaar.* Later writes a short story, "House of Flowers," set in Port-au-Prince.

   Sails to Europe (May 14). Returns in early August.

Meets Jack Dunphy (October).

1949   Sails to Europe with Dunphy (Feb. 26). Returns to New York in December.

1950   Sails for Europe again (April 7), and he and Dunphy settle in Taormina, Sicily. Begins work on *The Grass Harp*.

1951   He and Dunphy return to New York (August). *The Grass Harp* is published in September; he begins work on a play version.

1952   *The Grass Harp* opens on Broadway (March 27) but runs only a month.

He and Dunphy return to Taormina. In September they move to Rome, where David O. Selznick recruits him to help with the script of *Stazione Termini*, which stars Selznick's wife, Jennifer Jones, and Montgomery Clift.

1953   In Ravello to write the script, together with director John Huston, of *Beat the Devil*, an offbeat comedy that stars Jennifer Jones, Humphrey Bogart, Gina Lollobrigida, and Robert Morley.

In June he and Dunphy go to Portofino, where Capote adapts his short story "House of Flowers" as a Broadway musical.

1954   Capote's mother, Nina, dies after swallowing a bottle of sleeping pills (Jan. 4). Capote rushes home from Paris.

House of Flowers opens on Broadway (Dec. 30).

1955   *House of Flowers* closes (May 22) after 165 performances.

Travels to the Soviet Union (late December) with a *Porgy and Bess* troupe.

1956   He and Dunphy rent an apartment in Brooklyn Heights, which is their New York home for nearly a decade.

The Muses Are Heard, his account of his trip to the Soviet Union, is published in *The New Yorker* (Oct. 20 and 27), and in book form by Random House (November).

Leaves for Asia with Cecil Beaton (Dec. 27) to write a story on the making of the movie *Sayonara,* starring Marlon Brando.

1957   Returns from Asia (mid-February).

His profile of Brando, "The Duke in His Domain," appears in *The New Yorker* (Nov. 9).

1958   Visits Moscow again for a story that he later abandons.

He and Dunphy sail for Europe (May 29); they spend the summer on the Greek island of Páros and return to New York in October.

Breakfast at Tiffany's is published in *Esquire.*

1959   Reads story about the Clutter murders in *The New York Times* (Nov. 16); later leaves for Kansas with Harper Lee.

Dick Hickock and Perry Smith arrested in Las Vegas (Dec. 30) and returned to Kansas to face charges for the Clutter murders.

1960   A jury finds Hickock and Smith guilty of the Clutter murders (March 29).

Rents a house for the spring and summer in Palamós, Spain, where he plans to write the book he will title *In Cold Blood.* In the fall he and Dunphy move to Verbier, a small village in the Swiss Alps.

1961   Again spends spring and summer in Spain, winter in Switzerland. Adapts Henry James's *The Turn of the Screw* for the movies under the title *The Innocents.*

1962   Returns to the United States to interview Perry Smith's sister

(January). Once again in Spain for the summer and in Verbier for the winter.

1963 Newton Arvin dies of cancer (March).

Capote and Dunphy return to the United States and their apartment in Brooklyn Heights. They spend the summer and fall in Bridgehampton, Long Island.

1964 Finishes all but the last chapter of *In Cold Blood,* which he cannot write until he knows what will happen to Hickock and Smith.

1965 Attends execution of Hickock and Smith (April 14).

The New Yorker runs *In Cold Blood* in four installments, beginning Sept. 25.

Moves from Brooklyn to the United Nations Plaza in Manhattan.

1966 *In Cold Blood* is published by Random House and immediately becomes a publishing phenomenon (January).

Capote gives the party of the decade at Manhattan's Plaza Hotel (Nov. 28).

1967 Movie of *In Cold Blood* released (December).

1970 In Palm Springs (winter and spring); says his new novel, *Answered Prayers,* is half finished.

1975 First chapter of *Answered Prayers,* "La Côte Basque, 1965," published in *Esquire* (October). Furious to see themselves as thinly disguised characters, his rich friends turn against him.

In Los Angeles to appear in the film version of the Neil Simon comedy *Murder by Death* (November).

1976 *Murder by Death* is released (June).

1980   *Music for Chameleons,* a collection of fiction and nonfiction pieces, is published. It is his last book.

1981   Capote's father, Arch Persons, dies (June 7).

1984   Suffers two bad falls and is treated for phlebitis, a potentially fatal illness (winter).

         Dies in Los Angeles (Aug. 25), just a month shy of his sixtieth birthday.

Acknowledgments

Truman Capote's letters can be found in libraries and personal collections throughout the United States and Britain. The largest collection is housed in the New York Public Library, which has Capote's letters to Alvin and Marie Dewey; to Andrew Lyndon, one of Capote's best friends; to Catherine Wood, his high school teacher; and to William Shawn, his editor at *The New Yorker*. It also has some letters to Capote's father, Arch Persons; to his longtime companion, Jack Dunphy; and to Elizabeth Ames, the director of Yaddo, the artists' and writers' retreat in upstate New York. I thank the librarians at the Fifth Avenue library who so kindly provided copies of those many letters.

Another large Capote collection can also be found in New York City, and I want to thank the helpful librarians at the Columbia University Library, which has the Random House collection. In that collection are Capote's letters to his longtime editor, Robert Linscott, and to Bennett Cerf, co-founder of Random House. Capote's letters to Leo Lerman will eventually go to Columbia. I thank Stephen Pascal, who is cataloging Lerman's papers, for allowing me an early look at them. The Beinecke Library at Yale has Capote's dozens of letters to Donald Windham, and the University of Delaware Library has his correspondence with John Malcolm Brinnin. Both Windham and Brinnin were close to Capote for many years, and I appreciate the attention both libraries gave to my requests. Another important Capote collection—his letters to Cecil Beaton—is in the library of St. John's College, Cambridge University; I appreciate the help of Jonathan Harrison, that college's librarian. Smaller collections can be found at the University of Texas at Austin, Smith College (Capote's letters to Newton Arvin), Duke University, Radcliffe College, Washington University in St. Louis, and the Henry E. Huntington Library in California. I wrote or called librarians at many other institutions to determine if they had letters I could include. There were several dozen, and I hope they will excuse me if I do not list each one. All were helpful, and I stand in debt to several score librarians, all members of a much underappreciated profession.

Letters can also be found in private collections. The family of Mary Louise Aswell let me see Capote's many letters to her. The late Katharine Graham gave me copies of her letters, and so did Richard Avedon, Pearl Kazin Bell, Donald Cullivan, Peter Geyer, Waldemar Hansen and Kenneth Silverman. Others pointed out possible sources or helped in one way or another: Spyros Andreopoulos, Steven M. L. Aronson, Caroline Brass, Jane Brien, Joy and Michael Brown, William Buckley, Karen Cook, Anthony Crawford, David Farneth, William Grace, Kate Guyonvarch, Greg Johnson, William Miglore, Norman Mailer, Matt Rhodes, Jeffrey Smalldon, Annette Tapert and Hugo Vickers.

I have edited this book in collaboration with the Truman Capote estate, which is overseen by Capote's executor, Alan U. Schwartz, and I extend my thanks to him as well. He gave support without interference, and no editor could ask for more. Though I have benefited from the always wise counsel of my own Random House editor, Robert Loomis, the responsibility for deciding which letters to include, and which to leave out, is mine. I am also grateful for the behind-the-scene support of many members of the Random House team, including Dana Isaacson, Casey Reivich, Laura Goldin and Vincent La Scala. As always, thanks go to Helen Brann, my agent, who put together my part in this complicated project.

My final thanks must go to three who labored mightily to present this book. Steven Varni helped in the initial stages, contacting libraries and helping to trace collections of letters. Barbara Shalvey typed hundreds of letters, picking through Capote's sometimes difficult handwriting; she also did the research for many footnotes. Edmond Miller also typed hundreds of letters and performed many other vital tasks; like a good detective, he had an uncanny ability to find out information about even the most obscure people mentioned in the letters. My thanks go to all three.

Index

ANSWERED PRAYERS

This last novel, unfinished at the time of Capote's death, offers a devastating group portrait of the high and low society of his time. As it follows the career of a writer of uncertain parentage and omnivorous erotic tastes, *Answered Prayers* careens from a louche bar in Tangiers to a banquette at La Côte Basque, from literary salons to high priced whorehouses. This malevolently funny book displays Capote at his most relentlessly observant and murderously witty.

Fiction/Literature/0-679-75182-3

BREAKFAST AT TIFFANY'S

In this seductive, wistful masterpiece, Capote created a woman whose name entered American idiom and whose style is part of the literary landscape. Holly Golightly knows that nothing bad can ever happen at Tiffany's; her poignancy, wit, and naïveté continue to charm. This volume also contains three of Capote's best-known stories, "House of Flowers," "A Diamond Guitar," and "A Christmas Memory."

Fiction/Literature/0-679-74565-3

THE COMPLETE STORIES OF TRUMAN CAPOTE

The Complete Stories brings together Capote's life's work in the form he called his "great love," and confirms his status as a master of the the short story. This first-ever compendium features a never-before-published 1950 story, "The Bargain," as well as an introduction by Reynolds Price. Ranging from the gothic South to the chic East Coast, from rural children to aging urban sophisticates, all the unforgettable places and people of Capote's oeuvre are here, in stories as elegant as they are heartfelt, as haunting as they are compassionate.

Fiction/Literature/Short Stories/1-4000-9691-X

THE GRASS HARP

Set on the outskirts of a small Southern town, this is the story of three endearing misfits—an orphaned boy and two whimsical old ladies—who take up residence in a tree house. As they pass sweet yet hazardous hours, *The Grass Harp* conveys all the pleasures and responsibilities of freedom, as well as the sacredness of love.

Fiction/Literature/0-679-74557-2

IN COLD BLOOD

On November 15, 1959, in the small town of Holcomb, Kansas, four members of the Clutter family were savagely murdered by blasts from a shotgun held at close range. There was no apparent motive for the crime, and there were almost no clues. As Truman Capote reconstructs the murder and the investigation that led to the capture, trial, and execution of the killers, he generates both mesmerizing suspense and astonishing empathy.

Nonfiction/Literature/0-679-74558-0

MUSIC FOR CHAMELEONS

In these gems of reportage, Truman Capote takes true stories and real people and renders them with the stylistic brio we expect from great fiction. Here we encounter an exquisitely preserved Creole aristocrat sipping absinthe in her Martinique salon; an enigmatic killer who sends his victims announcements of their forthcoming demise; and a proper Connecticut householder with a ruinous obsession for a twelve-year-old-girl he has never met.

Nonfiction/Literature/0-679-74566-1

OTHER VOICES, OTHER ROOMS

Capote's first novel is a foray into the mind of a sensitive boy as he seeks out the grown-up enigmas of love and death in the ghostly landscape of the deep South. Joel Knox is summoned to meet the father who abandoned him at birth. But when he arrives, what he finds is a sullen stepmother, an uncle with the face and heart of a debauched child, and a fearsome little girl named Idabel who may offer him the closest thing he has ever known to love.

Fiction/Literature/0-679-74564-5